PENGUIN  C

THE GREEK SO

JOHN DILLON was born in 1939 and educated at Downside School and Oriel College, Oxford, gaining a PhD from the University of California, Berkeley. He taught Classics at Berkeley from 1966 to 1980, returning from there to become Regius Professor of Greek at Trinity College, Dublin. His publications include *The Middle Platonists* (1977, 2nd edn 1996), *Two Treatises of Philo of Alexandria* (with David Winston, 1983), *Alcinous: The Handbook of Platonism* (1993), and *The Heirs of Plato* (2003).

TANIA LOUISE GERGEL was born in 1972 and educated at Bristol University, University College London, and King's College, London, where she did a doctorate on Plato. She is currently lecturing in Greek language and literature at King's College, London, and her main research interests are ancient Greek philosophy and stylistics. As well as various articles, she is now working on a book entitled *Style and Argument: An Investigation of Plato's 'Phaedo'*, and has also just finished editing a volume on Alexander the Great, to be published in Penguin Classics in 2003.

The Greek Sophists

Translated and with an Introduction and Notes by
JOHN DILLON *and* TANIA GERGEL

PENGUIN BOOKS

PENGUIN BOOKS

Published by the Penguin Group
Penguin Books Ltd, 80 Strand, London WC2R ORL, England
Penguin Putnam Inc., 375 Hudson Street, New York, New York 10014, USA
Penguin Books Australia Ltd, 250 Camberwell Road, Camberwell, Victoria 3124, Australia
Penguin Books Canada Ltd, 10 Alcorn Avenue, Toronto, Ontario, Canada M4V 3B2
Penguin Books India (P) Ltd, 11 Community Centre, Panchsheel Park, New Delhi – 110 017, India
Penguin Books (NZ) Ltd, Cnr Rosedale and Airborne Roads, Albany, Auckland, New Zealand
Penguin Books (South Africa) (Pty) Ltd, 24 Sturdee Avenue, Rosebank 2196, South Africa

Penguin Books Ltd, Registered Offices: 80 Strand, London WC2R ORL, England

www.penguin.com

First published 2003
025

Translation, Introduction and Notes copyright © John Dillon and Tania Gergel, 2003
All rights reserved

The moral right of the translators has been asserted

Set in 10.25/12.25 pt PostScript Adobe Sabon
Typeset by Rowland Phototypesetting Ltd, Bury St Edmunds, Suffolk
Printed and bound in Great Britain by Clays Ltd, Elcograf S.p.A.

www.greenpenguin.co.uk

Penguin Books is committed to a sustainable
future for our business, our readers and our planet.
This book is made from Forest Stewardship
Council™ certified paper.

Contents

Chronology		vii
Introduction		ix
Further Reading		xxiv
A Note on the Text		xxx
1	PROTAGORAS OF ABDERA	1
2	GORGIAS OF LEONTINI	43
3	PRODICUS OF CEOS	98
4	HIPPIAS OF ELIS	118
5	ANTIPHON	133
6	THRASYMACHUS OF CHALCEDON	203
7	CRITIAS OF ATHENS	217
8	EUTHYDEMUS AND DIONYSODORUS OF CHIOS	266
9	ALCIDAMAS OF ELAEA	283
10	THE *ANONYMUS IAMBLICHI* AND THE *DOUBLE ARGUMENTS*	310
	Appendix: A Conspectus of Sources	335
	Notes	339
	Index of Rhetorical Terms	413
	Index	415

Chronology

All dates are BC.

*c.*485 Birth of Protagoras, in Abdera.

*c.*483 Birth of Gorgias, in Leontini.

480–79 Invasion of Greece by Persian king Xerxes, and his defeat, at Salamis and at Plataea.

477 Foundation of the Delian League under the leadership of Athens; beginnings of an Athenian maritime empire.

*c.*475 Birth of Antiphon, in Athens.

470–69 Birth of Socrates, in Athens.

*c.*470 Birth of Prodicus, in Ceos.

*c.*460 Birth of Critias, in Athens.

460–429 Political domination of Pericles at Athens; flourishing of Athenian economy, and of extreme democracy.

*c.*455 Birth of Thrasymachus, in Chalcedon.

444 Protagoras invited by Pericles to draft a law-code for the 'pan-Hellenic' colony of Thurii in southern Italy.

*c.*433 Dramatic date of Plato's *Protagoras*, presenting Protagoras, Hippias and Prodicus as visiting Athens.

431 Outbreak of the Peloponnesian War.

429 Death of Pericles.

427 Gorgias comes to Athens, on embassy for Leontini, and gives displays of the 'new rhetoric'. Birth of Plato.

421 'Peace of Nicias': interlude in war. Euthydemus and Dionysodorus active.

*c.*420 Birth of Alcidamas, in Elaea.

*c.*418 Death of Protagoras (possibly by drowning, on his way to Sicily).

416 Athenian capture of the island of Melos, providing the occasion for the 'Melian Dialogue', as presented by Thucydides (*History* V 84–114).

414–404 Second phase of the Peloponnesian War, culminating in the complete defeat of Athens.

*c.*412 Dramatic date of Plato's *Republic*, featuring Thrasymachus (in Book I).

411 Short-lived oligarchic coup of the 'Four Hundred', in which Antiphon was involved, and which led to his death.

404–3 Regime of 'Thirty Tyrants', dominated by Critias, which leads to his death in 403.

*c.*400 Death of Prodicus.

399 Trial and execution of Socrates.

*c.*395 Death of Hippias.

*c.*375 Death of Gorgias.

Introduction

HISTORICAL BACKGROUND

Athens, in the middle of the fifth century BC, was one of the most intellectually lively societies the world has ever seen. Having been instrumental in the spectacular and quite unanticipated triumph over a (numerically) vastly superior invading Persian expeditionary force in 480/79, the city-state of Athens, over the next half-century, built itself up into the political, economic and cultural powerhouse of Greece. It employed fairly ruthless tactics to transform, by easy stages, an original anti-Persian defensive alliance (the so-called Delian League) into a straightforward maritime empire, largely by the device of commuting contributions of men and ships to the 'allied' forces into a system of money payments, which became an imperial tribute. Ultimately (454–3 BC), the treasury of the League was moved from the island of Delos to Athens, and Pericles, the great leader of Athens in the mid-century, authorized the use of a proportion of the moneys accruing to the treasury for the beautification of the city, particularly in respect of the reconstruction of the buildings on the Acropolis, most spectacular of which was the Parthenon, the temple of the goddess Athena, patron deity of the city.

In the same period, domestically, Athens became by stages (culminating in the reforms of Pericles and Ephialtes in around 458 BC) an extreme participatory democracy, ruled by a sovereign assembly (with a quorum of 6,000 male citizens), and by those popular orators who were able to command the attention and allegiance of the common people. A situation thus arose in which, while the people were officially all-powerful, and office-holders weak and transitory – frequently selected by lot, and never for longer than a year, with public scrutinies before and after leaving office – in fact a prosperous, and sometimes extremely rich, elite also flourished, and managed to extend its influence from the social and economic into the political sphere, while at the same time remaining vulnerable to vexatious lawsuits directed at its members through the popular courts. A premium was thus placed, if one were well-off and aspired to a public career (or even to hold one's own in a private law-suit), on acquiring a facility in public speaking.

Athens, we must remember, never developed any system of 'higher' education – indeed, little more than what we would regard as 'primary' education (ending at about the age of fourteen) was ever the norm, and even that was privately funded – so that, as a demand arose for further training in the arts of thinking and speaking, a gap in the market manifested itself that cried out to be filled. And filled it duly was, by a remarkable series of individuals, coming from various parts of the Greek world but converging on Athens like flies to a honey-pot – those individuals whom we term collectively 'the sophists'.

The word *sophistês*, which seems first to gain currency early in the fifth century, means originally, with a favourable or at least neutral connotation, something like 'expert' or 'pundit', one who is skilled or 'wise' (*sophos*) in a particular art or craft. The natural suspicion of the man in the street for experts in any particular arcane discipline, or for intellectuals in general, helped to give the word also a derogatory sense, but it was not until the latter part of the century, when Athens became the venue for this kind of travelling 'expert' in the arts of discourse and persuasion, that it acquired the particular hostile overtones that are manifest in Plato's dialogues. Already in 423 BC, however, the comic poet Aristophanes, in his play *The Clouds*, can assume this sense of the word to be perfectly familiar to his audience when he uses it of Plato's own hero Socrates (whom he employs, rather unscrupulously, as a representative sophist). By this time, in fact, all the major figures in the movement had made their appearance in Athens.

It would be misleading to suggest that Athens was the only arena in which these sophists plied their trade – the great cities of Sicily and southern Italy, in particular, were also avid customers, and the chief sophists, so far as we can observe, were continually on tour – but it is certainly the case that Athens was the venue of choice in the second half of the fifth century. Such men as Protagoras, from Abdera on the coast of Thrace, Prodicus, from the small Aegean island of Ceos, Gorgias, from the city of Leontini in Sicily, and Hippias, from Elis in the western Peloponnese (an area not otherwise noted for its intellectual interests or achievements), converged on Athens, in approximately that chronological order, from the early 450s on, to give public lectures and, more importantly, private instruction to those who were willing and able to pay the price – which, by all accounts, was considerable. This was definitely luxury education for the chosen few, and in consequence it attracted consistently unfavourable attention from the common people and their champions – though the great statesman Pericles, it must be said, popular leader though he was, was on friendly terms with Protagoras, at least (as he was also with the philosopher Anaxagoras). The sophists also, as we learn from the writings of Plato in the next generation, provoked the opposition of that remarkable figure Socrates (460–399 BC), a native of Athens, who, while himself appearing to the vulgar eye as part of the movement (which is why Aristophanes could feature him in the play mentioned above), challenged the basic suppositions of Protagoras in particular, in ways that were to have (through the medium of Plato) momentous consequences for the subsequent reputation of the sophists, and for the course of European philosophy as a whole.

We learn from the pages of Plato a certain amount about the conditions under which the great sophists operated when they came on a visit to Athens. It would be normal for them to stay with one or other prominent member of society who was a patron of the 'new learning', such as the millionaire Callias, son of Hipponicus, at whose house Protagoras is staying when Socrates goes to visit him (at the urgent request of a young protégé of his, Hippocrates, who wants to be introduced to the great man) in Plato's dialogue *Protagoras*. At this gathering we also find the other prominent sophists Hippias and Prodicus, who will have been in town at the same time, and quite a scattering of prominent Athenians (including the two sons of Pericles, and the notorious young playboy Alcibiades). Protagoras has with him one of his chief pupils, Antimoerus of Mende (a small town on the Chalcidian peninsula), who plainly travelled round with him. Again, in the *Gorgias*, we find Gorgias, accompanied by his chief pupil Polus, established in the house of the prominent aristocrat Callicles (who himself has strong views of a sophistic nature, which he does not mind expressing). Socrates meets Hippias, in the *Lesser Hippias*, in the house of Eudicus, son of Apemantus, where he has been giving a display-speech, and from the *Greater Hippias* (286A) we learn that he is about to give a public lecture, at Eudicus' request, in 'the school of Pheidostratus'. Thrasymachus of Chalcedon, too, one of the second rank of sophists, we find similarly ensconced in the house of the prosperous resident alien Cephalus, in the Piraeus, when Socrates comes to visit in the *Republic*. As for the preposterous sophistical brothers, Euthydemus and Dionysodorus, who hail originally from Chios, Socrates comes upon them, in the *Euthydemus*, in the Lyceum gymnasium, surrounded by a crowd of followers, but they were doubtless staying with some patron also.

All this is fiction, of course, but we have no reason to doubt the essential accuracy of the background situations. From such comfortable bases, the great sophists could move out to give public courses in schools or gymnasia around the city, or, if they were in town on public business – as ambassadors for their respective cities, for example (as was Gorgias, on behalf of Leontini, on the occasion of his first appearance in Athens in 427 BC) – to address the Assembly or the Council. The fees quoted for a full course from Protagoras or Gorgias, 100 minae (upwards of £100,000 or $160,000 in today's prices), seem almost unbelievable, but we have various testimonies to such sums, as we shall see. Socrates himself testifies, ironically, to having taken the one-drachma (about £10 or $16)[1] course in etymology from Prodicus, rather than his fifty-drachma one (*Cratylus*, 384 BC), which means that he is not really competent in the subject. The one-drachma course can only have been a sort of 'trailer' for the real thing.

So the main sophists made an excellent living, not only in Athens, but in many parts of the Greek world.[2] Socrates, in the *Greater Hippias* (282A), speaks of Prodicus, while in Athens on an embassy from his native Ceos, as 'earning an incredible amount of money from giving lectures as a private individual, and meeting with our young men' – far more than would a practitioner of any other craft. To this the boastful Hippias responds (see ch. 4, §7, below):

> Socrates, you don't know anything about just how good this is. For if you knew how much money I have made, you'd be amazed. Forget about the other instances; but once, when I came to Sicily, even though the old and distinguished Protagoras was staying there, I, a much younger man, earned more than 150 minae in a short space of time; and also, from one very small place, Inycum, more than 20 minae. And when I came home with this I gave it to my father, so that he and my other fellow citizens were utterly amazed. Now I really think that I have earned more money than whichever two of the sophists you choose.

So the pickings were rich, if you had the right stuff to impart. Let us now consider what were the chief elements of the sophists' teachings.

CHARACTERS, DOCTRINES AND ISSUES

Biographical details of the chief characters involved are given at the head of the chapters devoted to them, so will not be presented here. It is worth noting, however, that, besides the distinguished visiting figures mentioned above, this collection includes two interesting figures indigenous to Athens, Antiphon and Critias, to each of whom problems are attached. In the case of Antiphon, the problem is that of deciding how many Antiphons are involved. We will not go into the details here, except to say that, despite misgivings, we have taken a generous view of the unity

of the author of the various documents that we have, since
the result is a pleasingly complex figure, who would seem to
constitute a native Athenian reaction to the sophistic phenomenon (Socrates, of course, being another conspicuous one!).
As for Critias, the problem concerns his authorship of certain
disputed tragedies, of which fragments remain (the alternative
being that they are simply by Euripides, as a number of the
sources assume). We feel, however, that the question of Critias'
authorship would never have been raised had there not been
some warrant for it. It is much easier to see how these plays
would in later times have been subsumed under the far more
famous name of Euripides than how the notion of Critias'
authorship could have arisen in some quarters, if there were no
basis for it. Once again, attribution to Critias makes for an
interesting, if far from likeable, character. Readers, however,
must make up their own minds.

Another figure for whose inclusion some explanation is
required is Alcidamas, the pupil of Gorgias, who is the subject
of chapter 9. He is only one of a group of 'second-generation'
sophists, who flourished in the fourth, rather than in the fifth,
century, of whom the most famous is Isocrates, another pupil
of Gorgias. Isocrates' works, however, survive extensively, and
could not be included in a volume of these dimensions, while
other known sophists, such as Lycophron, Anaximenes and
Theodorus of Byzantium, have very little remaining that could
be included. Alcidamas, on the other hand, is the author of two
surviving documents of some interest, and so there seemed to
be a case for including him as a representative of the younger
generation.

As well as Alcidamas, we have included (in chapter 10) two
interesting anonymous documents, both probably dating from
the early fourth century, the so-called *Double Arguments* (*Dissoi Logoi*) and a discourse of an unidentifiable sophist made use
of by the Neoplatonist Iamblichus in his late third-century AD
Exhortation to Philosophy, and therefore christened the
Anonymus Iamblichi. Both of these, despite their shortcomings,
are interesting as airing a number of basic sophistic themes.

Apart from all the figures, named or anonymous, included

here, there are numerous documents or fragments of the fifth and fourth centuries which betray sophistic influence, such as a number of the medical treatises included in the *Hippocratic Corpus* (e.g. *On Ancient Medicine, On the Nature of Man*), various speeches and other passages from Thucydides' *History* (notably the Melian Dialogue, in Book V),[3] many passages from both surviving and lost plays of Euripides, and some unattributed passages from Plato and even the Demosthenic corpus (e.g. various passages in the speech *Against Aristogeiton* – not by Demosthenes himself). But to include all of these would have made the task unmanageable, so we must rest content with the reflection that the influence of 'sophistic' ideas spread out widely into the community – a miasma or a leaven, depending on one's outlook.

What, then, were these ideas? They will be dealt with as they arise in connection with the various personalities, but it will be helpful to outline the salient ones at the outset.

The most notable and pervasive, perhaps, is the strong contrast that is set up between Nature and Convention, *physis* and *nomos*. Such a contrast is not, indeed, first set up by the sophists. We can find instances of it – or at least of the concept of a law (of God, or of Nature) which is antecedent, and on occasion antithetical, to man-made laws in such authors as Pindar (Fr. 152 Bowra)[4] and Sophocles, in the *Antigone* (composed around 440 BC), but the *nomos–physis* antithesis in its developed form is certainly characteristic of the sophistic movement. Once one has set up such a contrast, however, one can take up one of two attitudes to it. The first, represented most notably by Protagoras, but also, in our view, by Antiphon in his treatise *Truth*, is that Nature may well be more fundamental, but Law or Custom is a modification of it necessary to the development and preservation of civilized society, and so to be preferred.[5] The alternative position, later to be adopted by the German philosopher Nietzsche, that Nature must be preferred to Law or Convention, and that it dictates unlimited self-aggrandizement and domination on the part of the stronger over the weaker, is represented most starkly, in Plato's works, by the Athenian aristocrat Callicles (who may or may not be a real person) in the *Gorgias* and by the character of Thrasymachus (who may or may not be a fair representation of the real Thrasymachus) in Book I of the *Republic*, as well as by the Athenian negotiating team in Thucydides' 'Melian Dialogue' (*History* V 84–114). Probably no responsible sophist maintained such a position, at least in public, but it is certainly a conclusion that could be, and doubtless was, drawn by their more unscrupulous followers.

A peculiarity of this position is that the *natural* state of man is conceived, for the purpose of the argument, to be one of absolute individualism, a war of all against all, whereas it is just as plausible to argue that man is a naturally gregarious animal, and that thus a considerable degree of social cooperation and compromise is intrinsic to human nature. Such, indeed, is the message to be derived, when the mythical superstructure is deconstructed, from the so-called 'Great Speech' of Protagoras in Plato's *Protagoras* (below, ch. 1, §18), which we feel may reasonably be taken as representing his views. However, the contrast set up between Nature and Convention is certainly a fruitful and thought-provoking one, and can be seen as constituting the beginning of sociological theorizing in Greek, and therefore European, culture.

This major antithesis can also be seen as being at the root of most of the other doctrines associated with the sophistic movement, but they must nevertheless be set out separately. First, we may note the doctrine associated particularly with the name of Protagoras, 'Man is the measure of all things' (cf. below, ch. 1, §§7–11), which advances the concept of the relativity of values. It has, certainly, epistemological implications as well (e.g. the wind is cold for you, not cold for me; this wine is sweet for me, not sweet for you), but Protagoras, and (disapprovingly) Plato, were primarily concerned with its ethical implications. Protagoras seems to have maintained that there was no such thing as objectively right or wrong conduct, simply conduct that was 'profitable' or 'useful' (*khrêsimos*) and that which was not – and he was there (for a fee!) to teach people conduct, and attitudes, which were more *useful*. This certainly did not preclude their being also more socially beneficial, and indeed it would seem to have been Protagoras' position that they necessarily were so; he is far from being the immoralist that Plato would like to portray him as being. All he would dispute is that there is any such thing as a Platonic Form of Justice, or Self-Control, or Beauty; all such concepts are based upon convention and compromise.

Arising from the acceptance of this general principle, one might raise questions about the naturalness of the family, private property,[6] the status of women,[7] slavery,[8] or the distinction between Greeks and 'barbarians' (*barbaroi*, the rather dismissive Greek term for all types of foreigner),[9] and about the very existence of the gods, or of their providential care for mankind. We have some evidence of the raising of all of these questions by the major sophists, or their followers, during the latter part of the fifth century and the first half of the fourth.

On the sensitive question of the existence of the gods and the origins of religion, Protagoras once again set the agenda, with the provocative opening of his treatise *On the Gods*: 'Concerning the gods, I am not in a position to know either that they exist, or that they do not exist; for there are many obstacles in the way of such knowledge, notably the intrinsic obscurity of the subject and the shortness of human life' (ch. 1, §17). Prodicus, in his turn, is credited with the theory that men originally 'accounted as gods the sun and moon and rivers and springs and in general all things that are of benefit for our life, because of the benefit derived from them' (cf. ch. 3, §§ 20–21); while Critias, in a famous speech from his play *Sisyphus*, makes Sisyphus set forth a thoroughly cynical explanation of the origins of religion from the concern of some clever man to provide a source of terror for evil-doers in the notion that their actions were being observed by God, even if they escaped the notice of men (ch. 7, §47).

The raising of such questions naturally aroused the ire of orthodox-minded politicians, such as the late fifth-century democratic leader Anytus (cf. Plato, *Meno* 91C), who was himself instrumental in bringing Socrates to trial; but they also provoked the indignation of Socrates himself, as well as of his follower Plato, who portrays the jousts of his master with all of the major sophists in a series of brilliantly composed dramatic dialogues, the *Protagoras*, the *Gorgias*, the *Hippias Major* and

Minor, the *Euthydemus* and Book I of the *Republic*, from all of which we shall have repeated occasion to quote during the course of this volume.

A further major question, going to the root of the whole sophistic enterprise, is whether virtue, or excellence (*aretê*), can be taught: that is, whether one can be trained to be a superbly functioning political animal. The urgency of this, in the context of Athenian society, is explained by the circumstances outlined in the first paragraphs of this introduction: the necessity of prominent (or would-be prominent) citizens to sway the crowds in the assembly, or to defend themselves in the law-courts. And this brings us back to the main thrust of the instruction offered by the sophists, whether it appeared to involve epistemology, etymology, physics, history, geography or mathematics; it was in reality all about rhetoric: effective reasoning, and the effective public speaking that would follow from that. That is why the distinction set up by some authorities[10] between sophistry and rhetoric, according to which a man like Gorgias, for example, is a teacher of rhetoric, but not a sophist, seems an unreal one. All these men were in the business of creating effective public speakers. That is what they are being paid large sums of money for, not for disseminating knowledge for its own sake. There are certainly many issues raised in the following pages which seem to us to have philosophical implications, but in fact they are not there for their own sakes; they are there in the service of a very practical purpose: getting on in public life.

How, finally, are we to evaluate the sophists? Certainly, their stock, after being very low for most of European history, has risen in recent generations, and contemporary scholars are tending increasingly towards more complex philosophical interpretations of their work – though a favourable judgement on them was delivered already by the great liberal Victorian ancient historian George Grote (in his *History of Greece*, 6th edn, 10 vols., London 1988, ch. 67). Nevertheless, the term 'sophist', in popular language, still bears much of the opprobrious connotation imposed on it so long ago by Plato. In our view, what should be said is that the sophists filled a necessary gap in Athenian education at the time, and that, by raising a multiplicity of questions in the fields of ethics, politics, psychology, epistemology, logic and linguistics, they provoked a great out-burst of inquiry into these subjects, which led to the many insights advanced, in the next generation, by such thinkers as Plato and Aristotle. Their own successors, in the Hellenistic and Roman worlds, confined themselves more closely to the teaching of rhetoric, but, in the persons of such great masters of both practice and theory as Cicero and Quintilian on the Latin side, and a long line of rhetoricians and composers of handbooks on the Greek side, they formed the tradition of European prose style, as well as that of formal oratory, which persists to this day.

SOURCES

Since most of the original works of the sophists have perished, we are dependent to a very large extent (as in the case of the early Greek philosophers) on the testimony of others for a knowledge of what they thought and wrote, and this circum-stance brings with it inevitable distortions and uncertainties. The first such source is Plato, whose chief relevant works have been mentioned just above. Plato is, of course, a declared foe of the sophists and all that they stand for, so that we cannot expect from him a sympathetic portrayal. However, he is also a great literary artist, and it does seem as though, on occasion, he allows one or other of the great sophists to speak more or less in their own words. One such occasion, it is generally agreed, is in the *Protagoras* (see ch. 1, §18, below), where Protagoras is allowed to set out his theory of the origins of human society in terms which may well reflect his own position in such a work as his *On the Original State of Things*. Other possible passages where sophists run true to form are Prodicus in *Protagoras* 337A–C (on the fine discrimination of meanings of words) and Hippias in *Protagoras* 337C–E (on the natural brotherhood of all men); while in the *Gorgias* Gorgias is probably allowed to state his view of the power of rhetoric with reasonable accuracy, and in the *Euthydemus* the eristic arguments of the sophistical brothers Euthydemus and Dionysodorus, while being wickedly satirized,

probably reflect well enough the sort of tricks they played. So
Plato is an important source, though always to be used with
caution.

Aristotle is also useful, at various points in his works, but
particularly in the *Rhetoric*, since he quotes a number of sophistic arguments and turns of phrase, normally with disapproval,
but not necessarily unfairly. Xenophon too, in his capacity as a
follower of Socrates, preserves a number of useful details in the
course of his *Memoirs of Socrates*, most notably, perhaps, his
reporting of Prodicus' famous discourse on the 'Choice of Heracles' (see ch. 3, §22, below), which probably preserves at least
its substance.

Other than these witnesses from the Classical period, we have
reports and quotations embedded in a wide range of later writers,
in general not overtly hostile and on occasion even sympathetic:
Cicero; Dionysius of Halicarnassus; Plutarch; the Sceptical philosopher Sextus Empiricus; the chronicler of the great second-
century AD sophists Philostratus; the anthologist and collector of
curious information Athenaeus of Naucratis; and various other
later rhetoricians and writers of rhetorical and lexicographical
handbooks. It is a tedious and painstaking task to assemble and
evaluate passages from such a wide range of authors, but it is one
that has been made a great deal easier by the monumental efforts
of Hermann Diels, in his definitive collection *Die Fragmente der
Vorsokratiker* (1903), as reworked by Walther Kranz (1934 and
1952). Only in the cases of Euthydemus (whose historicity Diels
appears to have doubted) and of Alcidamas have we been unable
to rely on guidance from that quarter. In all other cases, the
citation of the Diels/Kranz reference (A for testimonia, B for
fragments) is an indication of our indebtedness. Other modern
collections that we have found useful were those of a team
co-ordinated by Rosemary Kent Sprague, *The Older Sophists*
(1972), and *Early Greek Political Thought from Homer to the
Sophists* (1995), edited by Michael Gagarin and Paul Woodruff,
the former of which does include Euthydemus, while the latter
includes Alcidamas. The collection edited by Robin Waterfield
(known already for his many excellent translations of the works
of Plato, in particular), *The First Philosophers* (2000), which

includes the sophists as well as the Presocratic philosophers, appeared when this collection was virtually complete, but we have been able to check it with profit.

Of course, a number of original sophistic productions do survive, notably the two display-speeches of Gorgias, *The Encomium of Helen* and *The Defence of Palamedes*, and his remarkable treatise *On Not-Being*, or *On Nature* (preserved not quite verbatim by both Sextus Empiricus and the anonymous author of the treatise *On Melissus Xenophanes, Gorgias*); the *Tetralogies* of Antiphon, and the papyrus fragments of his treatise *Truth*; a section of a political speech, or pamphlet, composed by Thrasymachus; Alcidamas' diatribe *On Those who Compose Written Speeches*, or *On Sophists*, and his display-speech *Odysseus: Indictment of Palamedes for Treason*; the anonymous *Dissoi Logoi* (or *Double Arguments*), probably by a follower of Hippias or Protagoras, and a large portion of a sophistic treatise made use of by the Neoplatonic philosopher Iamblichus in his *Protrepticus* (or *Exhortation to Philosophy*), and known, therefore, as the *Anonymus Iamblichi*. We must be grateful for them all, even though they are far from the most important productions of members of the movement. In general, however, we are dealing with the ruins of a tradition. Even more, perhaps, than in the case of the Presocratic philosophers, whose primary doctrines are more extensively recorded in fragments and later sources, the intriguing question of what we have lost is always present in our encounters with the sophists.

In our translations of both the primary and secondary sources, we have not hesitated to consult good previous versions, but have provided new translations of all major passages. There have, of course, been many excellent translations of the relevant dialogues of Plato, such as the *Protagoras, Gorgias, Hippias Major* and *Euthydemus*, among which one may mention those of C. C. W. Taylor (*Protagoras*), Terence Irwin (*Gorgias*) and Robin Waterfield (*Hippias* and *Euthydemus*),[11] as well as the older ones of Jowett, Guthrie, Woodhead and Rouse. Xenophon's *Memoirs of Socrates* is also well served by Hugh Tredennick, as emended by Waterfield.[12] For such authors as Athenaeus, Cicero, Dionysius of Halicarnassus, Philostratus and Sextus Empiricus, we have benefitted from consulting the relevant editions of their works in the Loeb Classical Library. At all important points, however, we have made our own decisions.

LANGUAGE AND TRANSLATION

On a number of levels language itself plays a key role in sophistic thought, a fact which presents particular challenges to the translator. The sophists were part of an intellectual revolution which involved not only ideas, but also language – part of what makes their work so remarkable is its linguistic and stylistic innovation and experimentation. Rhetoric and also technical language were in their infancy and the sophists, though most renowned for their contribution to rhetoric, were crucially important within the development of them both.

As we have said, there are a number of different levels on which one can see language to be a crucial consideration, and which affect the process of translation. First, there is the matter of individual words, many of which convey far too broad a range of meanings to be restricted to any one particular English term. A few of the most significant examples are *logos, aretê, epistemê* and *technê*, all terms of great importance within sophistic thought. *Logos* is one of the most notoriously difficult words to tie down, with possible meanings ranging from 'word', 'speech' or 'discourse' to 'argument' and 'reasoning', or even to 'ratio' and 'calculation'. Moreover, it is often not possible to restrict the sense required in a particular instance to only one of these alternatives, given that *logos* may well have connotations not only of verbal discourse, for example, but also rationality. Likewise, *aretê* presents similar difficulties: should it be translated as 'virtue' or 'excellence'? 'Virtue' might suggest an overly moral understanding, while 'excellence' veers perhaps too much in a non-moral direction. Do we translate *epistemê* as 'knowledge', 'expertise' or 'science' and *technê* as 'art' or 'skill'? None of our words are entirely satisfactory – nor is the sense of the Greek words itself static. In cases where the meaning of such terms is particularly important we have drawn attention to the Greek term which is being translated.

In many cases it is very important for the point being made that a number of different senses of a word are alive. Perhaps the most marked example comes in Gorgias' treatise *On Not-Being* (ch. 2, §30, below), where the philosophical argument relies upon our understanding the Greek verb 'to be' in both its predicative and existential sense. As we explain below, it is this linguistic confusion which is manipulated to provide the grounds for philosophical questions about issues such as properties and existence.

Yet it is not only individual words which are important, but the style of the work in general. The sophist's rhetoric is interesting not from a solely stylistic point of view, but also in terms of the way in which it is often integral to their argumentation. We have therefore tried, insofar as is possible and without forcing the English, to maintain some of the stylistic character of the original, especially when dealing with primary sources.

Language is very much bound up with the sophistic enterprise: the innovations in language and style; the development, practice and theory of rhetoric; the philosophical questions raised by the exploration of language; and the philosophical questions concerning language itself and its use. We have tried to maintain at least some of the spirit of this in our translation and would like our readers to be aware of how important these many aspects of language are when considering sophistic thought.

Finally, we should point out that, although we have divided up the translations and commentaries, we are jointly responsible for this work as a whole.

Further Reading

GENERAL WORKS

Blass, F., *Die attische Beredsamkeit*, Leipzig, 1887–98.

Boudouris, K. J. (ed.), *The Sophistic Movement*, Athens: Athenian Library of Philosophy, 1982.

Classen, C. J. (ed.), *Sophistik* (Wege der Forschung 187), Darmstadt: Wissenschaftliche Buchgesellschaft, 1976. (Two useful collections of articles, some in English.)

Diels, H., *Die Fragmente der Vorsokratiker*, vol. II, W. Kranz (ed.), 10th edn, Zürich: Weidmann, 1952.

Gagarin, M. and P. Woodruff (eds.), *Early Greek Political Thought from Homer to the Sophists*, Cambridge: Cambridge University Press, 1995.

Gomperz, H., *Sophistik und Rhetorik*, Leipzig, 1912.

Guthrie, W. K. C., *In the Beginning: Some Greek Views on the Origins of Life and the Early State of Man*, London: Methuen, 1957.

—, *A History of Greek Philosophy*, vol. III: *The Sophists and Socrates*, Cambridge: Cambridge University Press, 1969. (A survey of basic importance.)

Havelock, E. A., *The Liberal Temper in Greek Politics*, London: Jonathan Cape, 1957.

Kennedy, G., *The Art of Persuasion in Greece*, London: Routledge & Kegan Paul, 1963.

Kerferd, G. B. *The Sophistic Movement*, Cambridge: Cambridge University Press, 1981. (An excellent and well-balanced survey and discussion; highly recommended.)

— (ed.), *The Sophists and Their Legacy*, Wiesbaden: Steiner, 1981.

Radermacher, L., *Artium Scriptores: Reste der voraristotelischen Rhetorik*, Vienna, 1951.

de Romilly, J., *The Great Sophists in Periclean Athens*, Oxford: Oxford University Press, 1992.

Sprague, R. K. (ed.), *The Older Sophists*, Columbia: University of South Carolina Press, 1972.

Untersteiner, M., *I Sofisti*, Torino, 1949 (English translation by Kathleen Freeman, *The Sophists*, Oxford: Blackwell, 1954). (A work of great learning, but also considerable eccentricity, vitiated mainly by a determination to see too coherent a philosophical position in many of the sophists.)

Waterfield, R., *The First Philosophers: The Presocratics and Sophists*, Oxford: Oxford Paperbacks, 2000.

INDIVIDUAL SOPHISTS

Protagoras

Adkins, A. W. H., '*Arete, Tekhne*, Democracy and Sophists', *Journal of Hellenic Studies* 93 (1973), 3–12.

Burnyeat, M. F., 'Protagoras and Self-refutation in Plato's *Theaetetus*', *Philosophical Review* 85 (1976), 172–95.

Cole, A. T., 'The Relativism of Protagoras', *Yale Classical Studies* 22 (1972), 19–45.

Kerferd, G. B., 'Protagoras' Doctrine of Justice and Virtue in the *Protagoras* of Plato', *Journal of Hellenic Studies* 73 (1953), 42–5.

Loenen, D., *Protagoras and the Greek Community*, Amsterdam: North-West Holland Publishing Co., 1941.

Saunders, T. J., 'Protagoras and Plato on Punishment', in Kerferd (ed.), *The Sophists and Their Legacy*, 129–41.

Schiappa, E., *Protagoras and Logos: A Study in Greek Philosophy and Rhetoric*, Columbia: University of South Carolina Press, 1991.

Woodruff, P. 'Protagoras on the Unseen: the Evidence of Didymus', in Classen (ed.), *Sophistik*, 80–87.

Gorgias

Adkins, A. W. H., 'Form and Content in Gorgias' *Helen* and *Palamedes*: Rhetoric, Philosophy, Inconsistency and Valid Argument in Some Greek Thinkers', in J. P. Anton and A. Preus, *Essays in Ancient Greek Philosophy* II, Albany: State University of New York Press, 1983, 107–28.

Harrison, E. L. 'Was Gorgias a Sophist?', *Phoenix* 18 (1964), 183–92.

Kerferd, G. B., 'Gorgias on Nature or That Which Is Not', *Phronesis* 1 (1955), 3–25.

MacDowell, D. M., *Gorgias, Encomium of Helen*, Bristol: Bristol Classical Press, 1982.

Verdenius, W. J., 'Gorgias' Doctrine of Deception', in Kerferd (ed.), *The Sophists and Their Legacy*, 116–28.

Wardy, R., *The Birth of Rhetoric: Gorgias, Plato and Their Successors*, London: Routledge, 1996.

Prodicus

von Fritz, K., 'Prodikos von Keos', in A. Pauly and G. Wissowa (eds.), *Realencyclopädie der Klassischen Altertumswissenschaft* (*RE*) 23, Stuttgart, 1957, 85–9.

Henrichs, A., 'Two Doxographical Notes: Democritus and Prodicus on Religion', *Harvard Studies in Classical Philology* 79 (1975), 93–123.

Kerferd, G. B., 'The "Relativism" of Prodicus', *Bulletin of The John Rylands Library* 37 (1954), 249–56.

Nestle, W., 'Die *Horen* des Prodikos', *Hermes* 71 (1936), 151–70 (reprinted in Classen (ed.), *Sophistik* 425–51).

Hippias

Johann, H. Th., 'Hippias von Elis und der Physis-Nomos-Gedanke', *Phronesis* 18 (1973), 15–25.

Morgan, M. L., 'The Continuity Theory of Reality in Plato's *Hippias Major*', *Journal of the History of Philosophy* 21 (1983), 133–58.

Schütrumpf, E., 'Kosmopolitismus oder Panhellenismus? Zur Interpretation des Ausspruchs von Hippias in Platons *Protagoras*', *Hermes* 100 (1972), 5–29.

Woodruff, P., *Plato, Hippias Major*, translated, with a commentary and essay, Indianapolis: Hackett Publishing Co., 1982. (Contains useful essay on the historical Hippias.)

Antiphon

Avery, H. C., 'One Antiphon or Two?' *Hermes* 110 (1982), 145–58.

Barnes, J., 'New Light on Antiphon', *Polis* 7 (1987), 2–5.

Dillon, J., 'Euripides and Antiphon on Nomos and Physis: Some Remarks', in Boudouris (ed.), *The Sophistic Movement*, 127–36.

Hourcade, Annie, *Antiphon d'Athènes: une pensée de l'individu*, Brussels, 2001.

Kerferd, G. B., 'The Moral and Political Doctrines of Antiphon the Sophist: A Reconsideration', *Proceedings of the Cambridge Philological Society* 4 (1956–7), 26–32.

Morrison, J. S., 'Antiphon', *Proceedings of the Cambridge Philological Society* 7 (1961), 49–58.

—, 'The *Truth* of Antiphon', *Phronesis* 8 (1963), 35–49 (reprinted in Classen (ed.), *Sophistik*, 519–36).

Pendrick, G., 'The Ancient Tradition on Antiphon Reconsidered', *Greek, Roman and Byzantine Studies* 34 (1993), 215–28.

Reesor, M., 'The *Truth* of Antiphon the Sophist', *Apeiron* 20 (1987), 203–18.

Saunders, T. J., 'Antiphon the Sophist on Natural Laws (B44 D-K)', *Proceedings of the Aristotelian Society* 78 (1977/8), 215–36.

Thrasymachus

Chappell, T. D. J., 'The Virtues of Thrasymachus', *Phronesis* 38 (1993), 1–17.

Kerferd, G. B., 'The Doctrine of Thrasymachus in Plato's

Republic', *Durham University Journal* 9 (1947), 19–27
(reprinted in Classen (ed.), *Sophistik*, 545–63).
Nicholson, P. P., 'Unravelling Thrasymachus' Arguments in the
Republic', *Phronesis* 19 (1974), 210–32.

Critias

Diehl, E., 'Kritias', in Pauly and Wissowa (eds.), *RE* 11, Stuttgart
1922, 1, 901–12.
Nestle, W., 'Kritias', *Neue Jahrbücher für das klassische
Altertum* 1903, 81–107 and 178–99 (reprinted in his *Griechi-
sche Studien*, Stuttgart, 1948, 403–29).
—, *Von Mythos zum Logos*, 2nd edn, Stuttgart, 1941, 400–
420.

Euthydemus and Dionysodorus

Chance, T. H., *Plato's Euthydemus: Analysis of What Is and
What Is Not*, Berkeley: University of California Press, 1992.
McCabe, M. M., 'Persistent Fallacies', *Proceedings of the
Aristotelian Society* 94 (1994), 73–93.

Alcidamas

Avezzù, G., *Alcidamante, Orazioni e Frammenti*, Rome: L'Erma
di Bretschneider, 1982.
Renehan, R., 'The Michigan Alcidamas-Papyrus: A Problem in
Methodology', *Harvard Studies in Classical Philology* 75
(1971), 85–105.
Solmsen, F., 'Drei Rekonstruktionen zur antiken Rhetorik und
Poetik, I: Alkidamas', *Hermes* 67 (1932), 133–44.
West, M. L., 'The Contest of Homer and Hesiod', *Classical
Quarterly*, n.s. 18 (1967), 433–50.

Double Arguments and *Anonymus Iamblichi*

Cole, A. T., 'The Anonymus Iamblichi and his Place in Greek Political Theory', *Harvard Studies in Classical Philology* 65 (1961), 127–63.

Kahn, C. H., 'The Origins of Social Contract Theory in the Fifth Century B.C.', in Kerferd (ed.), *The Sophists and Their Legacy*, 92–108.

Levi, A., 'On Twofold Statements', *American Journal of Philology* 61 (1940), 292–306.

Robinson, T. M., *Contrasting Arguments: An Edition of the Dissoi Logoi*, New York: Arno Press, 1979.

Taylor, A. E., 'Socrates and the *Dissoi Logoi*', in Taylor, *Varia Socratica*, Oxford: Parker, 1911, 91–128.

A Note on the Text

This volume employs a variety of abbreviated references, which should be explained at the outset. To each text quoted there is appended the author's name and the title of the work, and in many cases also a 'Diels-Kranz' reference. This normally consists of the letter B or A, followed by a number. The number is the number of the fragment in H. Diels and W. Kranz, *Die Fragmente der Vorsokratiker* (10th edn, Berlin, 1952), which is the standard edition of the fragments of the Sophists, as it is of the Presocratic philosophers. The letter B indicates that Diels and Kranz regarded the passage as a direct fragment of the author concerned; the letter A that it is only a testimony.

Apart from Diels-Kranz, the abbreviated references employed are the following:

Adler = A. Adler, *Suidae Lexicon*, Leipzig, 1928–38
Bowra = C. M. Bowra, *Pindari Carmina cum Fragmentis*, Oxford, 1935
CAG = *Commentaria in Aristotelem Graeca*, Berlin, 1882–1909
Cramer = J. A. Cramer, *Anecdota Graeca*, Oxford, 1834–7
Diehl = E. Diehl, *Anthologia Lyrica Graeca*, Leipzig, 1936
Diels = H. Diels, *Doxographi Graeci*, Berlin, 1879
— *Poetarum Philosophorum Fragmenta*, Berlin, 1901
FHSG = W. W. Fortenbaugh, P. M. Huby, R. W. Sharples and D. Gutas, *Theophrastus of Eresus: Sources for his Life, Writings, Thought and Influence*, Leiden, 1992.
Friedlein = G. Friedlein, *Procli Diadochi in Primum Euclidis Elementorum Librum Commentarii*, Leipzig, 1873

Gomperz = T. Gomperz, *Herkulanische Studien*, vol. II, Leipzig, 1866

Jacoby = F. Jacoby, *Fragmente der griechischen Historiker*, Berlin, 1923

Kaibel = G. Kaibel, *Comicorum Graecorum Fragmenta*, Berlin, 1899

Keil = H. Keil, *Grammatici Latini*, 8 vols., Berlin, 1885–1923

Kock = T. Kock, *Comicorum Atticorum Fragmenta*, 3 vols., Leipzig, 1880–88

Kühn = K.G. Kühn, *Medicorum Graecorum Opera*, 20 vols., Leipzig, 1821–33

Leone = P. Leone, *Oratori attici minori*, Torino, 1977

Lobeck = Phrynichus, *Eclogae*, ed. Ch. A. Lobeck, Leipzig, 1820

Maass = Aratus, *Phaenomena*, ed. E. Maass, Berlin, 1893

Nauck = *Tragicorum Graecorum Fragmenta*, 2nd edn, Leipzig, 1889

Pistelli = H. Pistelli, *Iamblichi Protrepticus*, Leipzig, 1888

Rabe = Hermogenes Tarsensis, *Opera*, ed. H. Rabe, Leipzig, 1913

Radt = S. Radt, *Tragicorum Graecorum Fragmenta*, vol. IV, Göttingen, 1977

Rose = V. Rose, *Aristotelis Fragmenta*, Leipzig, 1886

Sandbach = F.H. Sandbach, *Plutarch's Moralia*, vol. XV: *Fragments*, Loeb Classical Library, Cambridge MA & London, 1969

Schmid = W. Schmid, *Rhetores Graeci*, Leipzig, 1926

Snell = B. Snell, *Pindari Carmina cum fragmentis*, vol. II, Leipzig, 1975

Spengel = L. Spengel, *Rhetores Graeci*, Berlin, 1853–6 (revised C. Hammer, 1894)

Usener = H. Usener, *Epicurea*, Leipzig, 1887

Walz = C. Walz, *Rhetores Graeci*, 9 vols., Leipzig, 1832–6

Westerink = L. G. Westerink, *Olympiodorus, In Platonis Gorgiam Commentaria*, Leipzig, 1970

In presenting the passages, it has sometimes seemed desirable to supplement the text, if it is fragmentary, or if a gap is suspected in the manuscript, with conjectural material to complete the sense. Such supplements are marked with < >.

In the case of longer passages, we have divided up the text, for ease of reference, by inserting section divisions, or page numbers, in accordance with the accepted divisions of the original work (e.g. pages of the Stephanus edition in the case of Plato, or that of Bekker in the case of Aristotle). These are printed in italics, within square brackets.

1 PROTAGORAS OF ABDERA

Protagoras was born in Abdera, a Greek colony founded on the coast of Thrace in the northern Aegean by the city of Teos, in around 490–86 BC. He is repeatedly stated to have been a 'pupil' of the famous Atomist philosopher Democritus, probably simply because Democritus also came from Abdera, but in fact Democritus was by far the younger of the two and there is no observable connection between them, although they were doubtless acquainted. Another oft-repeated story is that his father, Maeandrius, one of the most prominent citizens of Abdera, entertained the Persian king Xerxes in his house during the Persian invasion of Greece in 481, and persuaded Xerxes to allow his son to be tutored by magoi, as the sages of Persia were called. This must be regarded as highly improbable (the young Protagoras would have been barely ten at the highest estimate, and hardly in a position to absorb the higher mysteries of Magism), but the background situation of family prominence and prosperity may be factual enough.

However he was educated, Protagoras became the first of a new wave of teachers who travelled about Greece giving both public lectures and private courses for fees, often large. He naturally gravitated, as did all the others, to Athens, perhaps first in the early 450s, but certainly early enough to have impressed himself upon Pericles, the leading Athenian statesman, sufficiently for Pericles to invite him in 444 BC to draft the law code for his experimental panhellenic colony in southern Italy, Thurii. This constituted an occasion for Protagoras to impress himself upon the western Greeks in general, which he duly did. He must have paid many visits to Athens, where we know, from

the setting of Plato's Protagoras and from a passing reference
in his Theaetetus (165A), that he enjoyed the hospitality and
legal protection of the millionaire Callias, son of Hipponicus.
However, apart from a story in Plutarch of an all-day philosophical discussion with Pericles, of unknown date (cf. §5
below), we only have evidence of two visits, the first (possibly a
literary fiction, but we have no reason to doubt its essential
accuracy) represented by Plato in his Protagoras as taking place
around 433, the second around 422, attested to by the comic
poet Eupolis in his play The Flatterers (I 297 Kock). This will
have been not long before his death, which we learn from a
reference in Plato's Meno (91D; cf. §4 below) to have taken
place when he was 'nearly seventy, having practised his craft for
forty years'. Another widespread, but probably apocryphal,
story is that he was condemned to banishment (or death) by the
Athenians for the irreverence of his Sceptical treatise On the
Gods, and that his books were officially burned in the market-
place, while he himself was drowned in a shipwreck on his way
to Sicily. Had this been the case, however, it is reasonable to
suppose that Plato would have made some allusion to it in
the passage of the Meno referred to above. There is nothing
intrinsically improbable, on the other hand, about death by
shipwreck, and the possibility of a vexatious, politically motiv-
ated law-suit cannot be ruled out (as in the case of Pericles'
other intellectual protégé, the philosopher Anaxagoras). As we
shall see, there are some details given as to who initiated it,
which lend a certain credibility to the story.

LIFE AND WORKS

'The Life of Protagoras' by Diogenes Laertius (c. AD 200), in
his Lives of the Philosophers, is a wretched compilation, but
worth quoting at length for the odd pieces of interesting information it contains, albeit frequently in garbled form:[1]

1. [50] Protagoras was the son of Artemon,[2] or, as Apollodorus[3]
and Dinon[4] in Book 5 of his History of Persia declare, of

Maeandrius,[5] and a citizen of Abdera (as we learn from Heraclides of Pontus in his treatise *On Laws*, who also tells us that he made laws for Thurii) ... He and Prodicus of Ceos gave public recitals and charged fees ... Protagoras was a disciple of Democritus ...

[51] He was the first to declare that there are two possible positions on every question, opposed to each other; and indeed he was the first to present arguments[6] along these lines. He began a book[7] as follows: 'Man is the measure of all things, of things that are that they are, and of things that are not that they are not.' He used to maintain that the soul was nothing apart from the senses, as Plato declares in the *Theaetetus*,[8] and that everything is true. And another book he began as follows: 'Concerning the gods, I am not in a position to know either that they exist, or that they do not exist; for there are many obstacles in the way of such knowledge, notably the intrinsic obscurity of the subject and the shortness of human life.' [52] Because of this beginning of his book, he was expelled by the Athenians; and they burned his books in the market-place, sending a herald round to collect them from each person who had acquired them.

He was the first to charge a fee of a hundred minae (for a course).[9]

He was the first to distinguish the tenses of the verb,[10] and to emphasize the power of the right moment (*kairos*),[11] and to establish debating contests, and to provide sophistic tricks for those presenting arguments. He disregarded the substance, and conducted his arguments on the basis of purely verbal distinctions,[12] thus becoming the progenitor of the crowd of sophistical disputants who are now prevalent[13] – so that, indeed, Timon says of him:[14]

'Protagoras the ready mixer,[15] knowing well the tricks of disputation.'

[53] He was also the first to institute the Socratic method of argument;[16] and he was the first, as we learn from Plato in the *Euthydemus*,[17] to make use of the argument of Antisthenes which seeks to demonstrate that contradiction is impossible;[18] and he was the first to demonstrate dialectical methods of attack

on any given thesis,[19] as Artemidorus the dialectician says in his
work *Against Chrysippus*.[20]

He was also the first to discover the so-called *tulê*, or shoulder-
pad, on which loads are carried, as Aristotle says in his work
On Education;[21] for he had been a porter by trade, as we are
told somewhere by Epicurus.[22] And it was in this way that he
was taken up by Democritus, when the latter saw him tying up
his bundles of wood.

He was the first to divide discourse (*logos*) into four parts:
entreaty, question, answer and command; *[54]* (others say into
seven: narration, question, answer, command, report, entreaty,
invitation);[23] these he called the foundations of discourse.[24]

The first of his works which he read in public was *On the
Gods*, the beginning of which we have quoted above. He read
it in Athens, in the house of Euripides, or, as some say, in
that of Megacleides; others say in the Lyceum, where his pupil
Archagoras, son of Theodotus, lent him his voice.[25]

The accuser [at his trial?][26] was Pythodorus, son of Polyzelus,
one of the Four Hundred; Aristotle, however, says it was
Euathlus.[27]

[55] The books of his that are preserved are the following:[28]

The Art of Controversy
On Wrestling[29]
On Mathematics
On the State
On Ambition
On Virtues
On the Original State of Things[30]
On What is in Hades
On the Misdeeds of Men
Instruction Book[31]
Law-suit about a Fee[32]
Opposing Arguments, two books.[33]

These were his works.[34] Plato also wrote a dialogue about him.[35]

Philochorus[36] tells us that, when he was sailing to Sicily, the
ship that he was on was sunk; and that Euripides makes a

covert reference to this in his *Ixion*. Some say that he died on a journey,[37] at the age of almost ninety. [56] Apollodorus,[38] however, says that he was seventy, that he practised as a sophist for forty years, and that he flourished in the eighty-fourth Olympiad.[39]

. . .

It is told of him that once, when he demanded a fee from his pupil Euathlus, on the latter declaring 'But I have not yet won the case!', he said: 'But if I win the case, I should get the fee because I have won it; if you win the case, I should get it because *you* have won it.'[40]

(Diogenes Laertius, *Lives of the Philosophers* IX 50–56 = 80A1)

Another account of his life and times, of almost equal unre-liability, is provided by the second century AD sophist Philo-stratus (c. AD 170–245). On the matter of Protagoras' early life, his source may be the Dinon of Colophon who is mentioned at the beginning of Diogenes' Life. If so, this reflects ill on the reliability of Dinon. The story about Protagoras' Persian education, we may note, is applied by Diogenes Laertius, with even less plausibility (from the chronological point of view) to Democritus. Philostratus bases some reckless speculations of his own on this tale, even as he weaves romance around the circumstances of Protagoras' death.

2. Protagoras of Abdera, the sophist, was a pupil of Democritus in his home town, and he consorted also with the *magoi* of the Persians, at the time of Xerxes' invasion of Greece. For his father was Maeandrius, who had become very wealthy compared to the majority of Thracians and who, through entertaining Xerxes in his house and giving him gifts, secured from him the company of the *magoi* for his son.[41] For the Persian *magoi* do not educate those who are not Persians, unless the King orders it.

As for his claim to be perplexed about whether gods exist or not, Protagoras seems to me to have committed this outrage because of his Persian education; for although the *magoi* commune with the gods in secret, in public they absolve themselves of any belief in the divine, as they do not want it to seem as though this is the root of their power.

So it is because of this that he was driven out from the whole earth by the Athenians;[42] according to some, having stood trial, while others believe that a decree was passed against him, although he had not been tried. Travelling between islands and mainlands, keeping a watch for the Athenian triremes, deployed on every sea, he drowned while sailing in a small boat.[43]

He was the first to practise conversing for a fee, and so was the first to hand down to the Greeks a practice not to be despised; for we value the things which we spend money on more than those we get for free.[44]

Plato, recognizing Protagoras' style as elevated, but self-indulgent in his dignity and disproportionately long-winded, characterizes this idea of him in a long tale.[45]

(Philostratus, *Lives of the Sophists* I 10 = 80A2)

Some further garbled details are provided by the late (fifth–sixth-century AD) lexicographer Hesychius of Alexandria. He too produces the 'porter' story.

3. *Protagoras, son of Artemon, of Abdera.* This man was a porter, but on meeting up with Democritus turned to philosophy, and specialized in rhetoric. He was the first to develop disputative arguments,[46] and charged his pupils a fee of a hundred minae, for which reason he was given the nickname 'Logos'.[47] Pupils of his were Isocrates the speech-writer, and Prodicus of Ceos.[48] His books were burned by the Athenians, for he said: 'About the gods, I have no means of knowing either that they exist or that they do not exist.' Plato wrote a dialogue about him. He died through being shipwrecked on a voyage to Sicily, being then ninety[49] years of age, having been a sophist for forty years.

(Hesychius of Alexandria, as quoted in Scholia on Plato, *Republic* 600C)

Two other testimonies relative to Protagoras' career may be included here.

First, an extract from Plato's Meno, where Socrates is provoking the politician Anytus by pretending to commend sophistic education (the overall topic is the question as to whether virtue, or moral excellence, is teachable). The passage may be taken as a fair portrayal of how such men as Protagoras were regarded by many 'right-thinking' Athenians. The Meno was probably composed in the mid-380s BC, about forty years after Protagoras' death. Its dramatic date is the very end of the fifth century, shortly before Socrates' trial and execution in 399 (in which Anytus, of course, had a hand).

4. SOCRATES: So, regarding this kind of excellence (*aretê*),[50] tell me to whom it would be correct for us to send him.[51] Or is it in fact clear from the argument we've just had that we should send him to those who profess to be teachers of virtue, and declare themselves available to any Greek who wants to learn, and who also set and charge a fee for this?

ANYTUS: And who are these men you're talking about, Socrates?

s: Actually, I presume you know that they are those men whom people call sophists.

A: Good Lord, mind your tongue, Socrates! May none of my acquaintances, relative or friend, citizen or stranger, be possessed by such madness that he goes to these men and ends up getting harmed. For it's quite evident that these men do harm and corrupt those who associate with them.

s: What do you mean, Anytus? Out of all those who lay claim to expertise in conferring certain benefits, are these really the only men who are so different from the others that, not only do they not help whatever anyone commits to them, like others do, but, conversely, they ruin it? And they think they have a right to charge money openly for this? After all, I know that one man, Protagoras, has acquired more money from this wisdom than Pheidias, who has crafted works of such manifest beauty, along with ten other sculptors.[52] Indeed, you're making a monstrous claim: if, on the one hand, it's the case that those who repair old shoes and mend old cloaks would not be able to escape detection, even for thirty days, if they sent back the items in worse condition than they had received them (in fact, if they did this, they'd soon starve to death); but, on the other, it went undetected by the whole of Greece, for more than forty years, that Protagoras was corrupting his associates and sending them away in worse condition than when he received them (for I think he was nearly seventy when he died, and had spent forty years in his occupation), and in all that time, right up to this very day, he has never stopped being well thought of;[53] moreover, not only Protagoras, but a whole lot of others, some before him,[54] others still around now.

(Plato, *Meno* 91B–92A = 80A8, expanded)

Secondly, Plutarch, in his Life of Pericles, *drawing on the late fifth-century (and thus near-contemporary) historian Stesimbrotus of Thasos, gives us a picture of the personal relations between Protagoras and the great Athenian statesman Pericles, who liked to be surrounded by intellectuals. (The tale, admittedly, is based on gossip spread about by Pericles' son Xanthippus, who was at odds with his father at the time, but there is no reason to doubt its basic accuracy.)*

5. For instance, a certain pentathlete had hit Epitimus the Pharsalian with a javelin accidentally, and killed him, and Pericles, Xanthippus said, spent an entire day discussing with Protagoras whether it was the javelin, or rather the one who hurled it, or indeed the judges of the contests, that 'in the strictest sense' ought to be held responsible for the accident.[55]

(Plutarch, *Life of Pericles* ch. 36 = 80A10)

Finally, we may include here the only substantial verbatim quotation we have of a work of Protagoras (the other two famous passages are of only a few lines each). This, quoted in the Consolation to Apollonius *and attributed, perhaps falsely, to Plutarch, is from an unidentified work, possibly a funeral speech for Pericles, such as Protagoras would have been pleased to compose, but of which we have no other evidence. Such a work would presumably have been composed in, or shortly after,* 429 BC. *The passage is in fairly simple and straightforward*

Ionic prose, not at all like the ornate efforts of his Sicilian contemporary Gorgias:

6. Pericles, who was called 'the Olympian' because of his surpassing power of reasoning and of understanding, learned that both his sons, Paralus and Xanthippus, had passed from life.[56] Protagoras describes his conduct in these words:

'Even though his sons were fine young men and died within seven days of each other, he endured it free from grief; for he maintained his calm, and this brought him great benefits every day, in terms of happiness, freedom from pain and good reputation amongst the multitude. For every man who saw Pericles bearing his sorrows in so steadfast a way thought that he was both high-minded and brave, and even more powerful than themselves, knowing very well that they themselves would be helpless in such circumstances.'[57]

For Pericles, immediately after the news about his two sons, none the less placed a garland on his head, according to the time-honoured custom at Athens, and, clothed in white robes, addressed the people, 'taking lead in good counsel',[58] and urging the Athenians on to war.

(Pseudo-Plutarch, *Consolation to Apollonius* 118EF = 80B9)

DOCTRINES

Man the Measure

We may begin with a series of passages from Plato's Theaetetus, *as being the oldest surviving testimonies to Protagoras' doctrine, although we should recognize their tendentious character. We simply do not know for certain what Protagoras meant by his famous dictum, which is attested as occurring at the beginning of his treatise entitled* Truth, *or* The Overthrowers,[59] *or how he argued for it. The supporting arguments attributed to him by Plato (and consequently by later writers), which seek to connect his position with that of Heraclitus, may well be fathered on him illegitimately by Plato.*

7. SOCRATES: Indeed, perhaps it's not just some trivial theory about knowledge that you've stated, but actually the one which Protagoras used to propound. He said the very same thing, although in some other way – for he says, you know, that man[60] is the measure (*metron*) of all things, of those which are, that they are, and of those which are not, that they are not. Presumably, you've read that?

THEAETETUS: Yes – a number of times.

S: So, does he mean this: that however each thing appears to me to be, this is how it *is* for me, and likewise, each thing *is* how it appears to you; and, you and I are both men?

TH: That's what he means.

S: Well, it's not likely that a wise man would talk nonsense – so let's go along with him. Sometimes, when the wind itself blows, does one of us become chilly, but not the other? Or one slightly chilly, but the other intensely?

TH: Yes, certainly.

S: So, will we say then that the wind is itself, by itself, cold or not cold? Or will we agree with Protagoras that it is cold for the man who is chilly, but not cold for the one who isn't chilly?[61]

TH: The latter seems reasonable.

S: So it also *appears* like this to each of us?

TH: Yes.

S: And '*appears*' is perceiving?[62]

TH: Yes, it is.

S: Then surely appearance and perception are the same thing in the context of heat and all such matters. For however each man perceives them to be, it's likely that this *is* the case for him.

TH: That's reasonable.

S: So perception is always of what really is and without falsehood, given that it's knowledge.

TH: So it seems.

S: Well, good Heavens, was Protagoras some omniscient fellow; and did he hint at this for us, the great rabble, but tell his pupils the truth[63] in secret?

TH: What do you mean by that, Socrates?

S: I'll tell you, and it's certainly no trivial theory:[64] namely, that nothing is one thing itself in itself, nor could you speak of it correctly as some thing, not even some *kind* of thing; but if you call it large, it will also appear small, or if heavy, then also light; and so on in all such cases, since nothing is one thing, neither some thing, nor some kind of thing. But all things really come about through change, movement and mixing with each other. We claim that these things actually *exist*, but we're wrong to say this about them. For nothing ever *is*, but is always *becoming*. And let all the wise men, except Parmenides, agree to this in turn: Protagoras and Heraclitus and Empedocles . . .

(Plato, *Theaetetus* 151E–152E = B1, in part)

The next passage comes from a later stage of the dialogue, where Socrates imagines the ghost of Protagoras popping up and confronting himself and Theaetetus with the 'true' meaning of his dictum. What follows is merely a section, but the core section, of his speech. In it, Protagoras addresses what might seem to be a major problem for him as an avowed teacher of excellence: if, as he maintains, all impressions are equally true and valid, on what basis does he offer his own impressions as superior and worthy of adoption by others – especially on payment of a considerable fee? Now Plato must be accounted in general a hostile witness, but here – as very probably in the case of Protagoras' statement of his political philosophy in the dialogue called after him (quoted below, §18) – it does seem as though he is allowing Protagoras to present a plausible account of his own position, and his evidence is therefore valuable. Protagoras' line is that, although all impressions are true for the person holding them, some are undoubtedly 'better' than others – 'better' in the sense, necessarily, of 'more useful', 'more effective' – and it is these impressions that Protagoras offers to inculcate, and make to seem, and be, true for the individual who submits to his instruction. There are still philosophical problems with this, notably the question of who decides what is 'better', and on what basis, but Protagoras had no difficulty, it seems, in arrogating to himself the capacity to judge on that. There is, however, one thing that Protagoras would not admit: any 'objective' criterion of goodness, such as that maintained by Socrates and Plato. He is left, then, with the concept of 'the most advantageous'.

8. 'For I declare that the truth is as I have written: that each of us is the measure of the things which are and those which are not, although one man differs vastly from another for this very reason: because, for one man, certain things are and appear to be, while for another man, other things do.[65] I am far from denying that wisdom and the wise man exist; but I do claim that the wise man is as follows: anyone who, when bad things appear to be and are for one of us, could change things around to make them both appear to be and be good.

'Now don't pursue my argument by picking up on some phrase of mine. Instead, get an even clearer understanding of what I mean. So, just as was said earlier, remember that for the invalid the things he eats appear to be, and are, bitter, while for the healthy man they are, and appear to be, the opposite. Well, we mustn't reckon either of them wiser – for that's not possible – nor must we accuse the man who is ill of being ignorant for believing such things, whereas the healthy man is wise because he has alternative beliefs. Instead, we must change one to the other, given that the latter condition is better.[66] So, in education as well, we must bring about a change from one condition to a better one; and while the doctor makes changes with drugs, the sophist does this with words.

'After all, it's not the case that anyone makes someone with false beliefs later have true beliefs. For it's not possible to believe in something which does not exist, nor in anything beyond the things which one experiences, and the latter are always true. Rather, I think that someone who, because their mind is in a bad condition, has some belief which is akin to it and is then made, through a good condition, to believe some other such things. And these are the appearances which some people, through a lack of skill, do indeed call true. I, on the other hand, call some things better than others, but in no way truer.'

(Plato, *Theaetetus* 166D–167B = A21a)

The following passages, from the late second-century AD physician and Sceptical philosopher Sextus Empiricus, may have some independent value, though the first sounds as though it may be simply an extrapolation from what is presented by Plato in the Theaetetus. *Especially the 'Heraclitean' theory of flux ascribed here to Protagoras is unlikely to have been held by him. However, it cannot be proved that it could not have been, so the testimony is worth presenting.*[67]

9a. Protagoras asserts that 'Man is the measure of all things, of things that are that they are, and of things that are not, that they are not'; and by 'measure' he means the criterion of truth,[68] and by 'things' [physical] objects,[69] so that what he is really claiming is that 'Man is the criterion of all objects, of those which are, that they are, and of those which are not, that they are not.' And in consequence of this he postulates only what appears (*ta phainomena*) to each individual, and thus he introduces relativity (*to pros ti*) . . .

What he declares, then, is that matter is in flux, and as it flows additions arise continuously in place of what flows out, and the senses are restructured and altered in accordance with the stages of life and all the other conditions of bodies. He says also that the reason-principles (*logoi*)[70] of all phenomena subsist in matter, so that matter, so far as depends on itself, is able to be all things that appear to all. And men, he says, apprehend different things at different times in accordance with their differing dispositions; for he who is in a natural state apprehends those things in matter which are able to appear to those in a natural state, and those who are in a state contrary to nature the things that appear to those in an unnatural state.

Furthermore, just the same account applies to the different stages of life, and to people according as they are asleep or awake, and to each distinct kind of condition. Thus, according to him, man becomes the criterion of what is the case; for all things that appear to men also are the case, and things that appear to no man are conversely not the case.

We see, then, that he dogmatizes about the fluidity of matter and about the subsistence in it of the reason-principles of all phenomena, these being non-evident matters which cause us[71] to suspend judgement.

(Sextus Empiricus, *Outlines of Pyrrhonism* I 216–19 = A14)

The second passage, from Book VII of his large work Against the Mathematicians, *does, however, appear to depend on independent knowledge of Protagoras' book* Truth, *or* The Overthrowers.

9b. Some authorities, also, have ranked Protagoras of Abdera among those philosophers who do away with the criterion, since he declares that all appearances (*phantasiai*) and opinions are true, and that truth is something relative (*pros ti*), by reason of the fact that everything that has appeared to be the case or been opined by someone is immediately real to that person. At any rate, at the beginning of his work *The Overthrowers* he has stated that 'Man is the measure of all things, of things that are that they are, and of things that are not that they are not.' And to the truth of this even the opposite assertion seems to testify; for if anyone claims that man is *not* the criterion of all things, he will simply be confirming the statement that man is the criterion, since the very person who is making the claim is himself a man, and in affirming what appears to him to be the case, he admits that this very claim is one of the things that appears to him.[72]

Hence, also, the madman is a reliable criterion of the appearances which occur in madness, and the sleeper of those in sleep, and the infant of those in infancy, and the elderly of those in old age.[73] Nor is it proper to disqualify one set of circumstances because of a different set of circumstances – that is to say, the appearances which occur in a state of madness because of the impressions received in a state of sanity, and those of sleep because of those in a waking state, and those of infancy because of those of old age. For as the latter do not appear to the former percipients, so also conversely the appearances perceived by these do not affect those. Consequently, if the madman or the sleeper is not a reliable judge of what appears to him because he is observed to be in a certain state of mind, then, since both the sane and the waking man are also in a certain state, they in turn will not be trustworthy for the determining of their percepts. In view of the fact, then, that no impression is received independent of circumstances, each man must be trusted in respect of those received in his own circumstances.

So this man [i.e. Protagoras], as some authorities have supposed, rejects the criterion, in so far as it claims to be a test of absolute realities and to distinguish the true from the false, whereas the aforementioned individual does not admit the existence either of anything absolutely real or of falsehood.

(Sextus Empiricus, *Against the Mathematicians* VII 60–64)

A further passage from Sextus' treatise Against the Mathematicians *is also worth quoting in this connection, since it makes mention of a strategy adopted, not only by Plato (cf.* Theaetetus *171A;* Euthydemus *286BC), but also, it seems, by Democritus before him, to counter Protagoras' position that appearance* (phantasia)*, or 'what appears to us', is the 'criterion':*

10. If appearance (*phantasia*) is accepted as the criterion, we must assert either that every appearance is true, as Protagoras used to claim, or that every one is false, as Xeniades the Corinthian[74] declared, or that some are true, some are false, as the Stoics and Academicians said, and the Peripatetics as well. But we ought not to say either that every one is true or that every one is false, or that some are true and some false; so we must not say that appearance is the criterion. One cannot say that every appearance is true, because this constitutes self-refutation (*dia tên peritropên*), as Democritus[75] and Plato[76] taught in opposing Protagoras; for if every appearance is true, the judgement that not every appearance is true, since it is based on an appearance, will also be true, and thus the judgement that every appearance is true will turn out to be false.

(Ibid., VII 388–90 = 80A15)

From the Protagoras *of Plato we can derive an interesting statement of Protagorean relativism. It is admittedly presented by Plato as being uttered by Protagoras in a rather peevish frame of mind, under pressure from some provocation by Socrates, but it nonetheless rings true as a piece of Protagorean argumentation,[77] and it would be more effective if Plato had in fact*

*borrowed from one of his works. Freed from its immediate
context, it could serve as a rhetorical introduction to a discourse
on the relativity of values.*

11. [Socrates] 'So, do you say that there are things which are
good?'

[Protagoras] 'I do.'

'And so,' I [Socrates] said, 'is it these things which are good,
namely, things which are beneficial to men?'

'For God's sake – they certainly are,' he said, 'and, even if
they're not beneficial to men, I still call them good.'

Then Protagoras appeared to be highly perturbed, anxious
and opposed to answering. So, when I saw the state he was in,
I took great care to be gentle in my questions. 'Do you mean',
I said, 'those things which are not beneficial to any *man*, or
those which are in no way beneficial? Do you call the latter
goods?'

'Not at all,' he said. 'But I do know many things which are
unbeneficial for men – foods and drinks and drugs and countless
others – but are still beneficial, and some which are neither
beneficial nor unbeneficial for men, but are beneficial for horses;
some only for oxen, and others for dogs. And then some which
are not beneficial to any of these, but are beneficial to trees; and
some which are good for the roots of the tree, but bad for its
branches, just as dung is good when it's laid on the roots of any
plant, but if you put it on the young branches and shoots, it
destroys everything. Then, also, oil is utterly bad for all plants
and is extremely damaging to the hair of all animals except man.
In fact, it's actually beneficial to men's hair, and to the rest of
the body. And the good is something so varying and manifold,
that this particular thing is good for men's bodies, externally,
while, internally, the very same thing is extremely bad. It's
because of this that all doctors tell those who are ill not to use
oil in what they are going to eat, except the very smallest amount
which can eradicate any smell from the bread and meat which
might offend the senses.'

(Plato, *Protagoras* 333D–334C)

Finally on this topic, a passage from Plutarch's Reply to Colotes
*(1108E–1109A), which may contribute an interesting perspec-
tive on what Protagoras' true position was on the objective existence of qualities – as well as affording proof of something that
we have already inferred to be extremely probable, that Democritus and Protagoras took some note of each other. Colotes of
Lampsacus (fl. c.270 BC) was a rather aggressive follower of
Epicurus, who composed a treatise entitled 'That following the
doctrines of the other philosophers actually makes life impossible', to which Plutarch writes two treatises in response.*

12. Colotes first charges him [i.e. Democritus] with asserting
that no object is any more of one character than of another, and
thus throwing our life into confusion. But so far is Democritus
from considering an object to be no more of one character
than another that he has attacked the sophist Protagoras for
making this assertion, and setting down many telling arguments
against him.
    (Plutarch, *Reply to Colotes* 1108E–1109A)

*This might seem at first a case of the pot calling the kettle black,
but in fact Democritus, though denying the reality of qualities,
maintained the objective existence of atoms; the implication
here is that he is condemning Protagoras for recognizing no
objective reality at all (e.g. the wind is neither hot nor cold, nor
do we even maintain the objective existence of wind). This has
considerable relevance to modern discussions of what Protagoras' true position was.*

'No Statement can be Contradicted'/ 'About Any Given Thing, Contradictory Statements may be Made'

*Connected with the claim that whatever appears to an individual
is 'true' for that individual are the assertions: (a) that it is
impossible to contradict any given statement; and (b) that it is
possible to make contradictory statements (antilogiai) about
any given state of affairs. Both these positions are variously
attributed to Protagoras. They may seem mutually exclusive,*

but this is not necessarily the case. Indeed, one could say that it is possible to make contradictory statements about any given thing or situation precisely because contradiction is impossible. Let us look at a few passages. The first is from Aristotle's Metaphysics:

13. It is from the same view[78] that the theory (*logos*) of Protagoras also stems, and it is necessary that both of them must either be true or untrue. For, if all beliefs and appearances are true, it is necessary that everything will simultaneously be both true and false; for many people hold beliefs opposite to those of others, and they consider that those who do not hold the same opinions as themselves are entirely mistaken: consequently, it is necessary that the same thing both is and is not. And, if this is the case, it is necessary that all beliefs are true; for those who are mistaken and those who speak the truth have opposite beliefs to each other. So if reality is of this nature, everyone will speak the truth.

(Aristotle, *Metaphysics* IV 5, 1009a7–16)

Protagoras would not, of course, accept that anyone has a 'wrong' opinion – simply that people have contradictory opinions, some of which are more useful *than others.*

The second passage is from Plato's Euthydemus, *where Protagoras is linked by Socrates with the clownishly contentious sophistical brothers, Euthydemus and Dionysodorus:*

14. And Dionysodorus said: 'Are you constructing your argument (*logos*), Ctesippus, as if contradiction existed?'[79]

'Yes, completely,' he said, 'absolutely so. But what about you, Dionysodorus, don't you think that contradiction exists?'

'Well,' he said, 'you certainly couldn't demonstrate that you've ever heard anyone contradicting someone else?'

'Oh really?' he said. 'Well, if I am to demonstrate it to you, let's now listen to Ctesippus contradicting Dionysodorus.'

'And would you be held to account for this?'

'Certainly,' he said.

'Well then,' he said. 'Are there descriptions (*logoi*) for each of the things which are?'

'Certainly.'

'So, of each thing as it is or as it is not?'

'As it is.'

'Yes, for if you recall, Ctesippus,' he said, 'just a moment ago we showed that nobody says "how it is not"; for it was clear that nobody says what is not.'

'So, what's that got to do with this?' replied Ctesippus. 'Are you and I contradicting each other any the less?'

'Well,' he said, 'would we be contradicting each other if we both gave the description (*logos*) of the same thing?[80] Presumably, we'd actually be saying the same thing?'

He agreed.

'But when neither of us gave the description of a thing,'[81] he said, 'is it then that we'd be contradicting each other? Surely, in this case, neither of us would have mentioned anything at all?'

He also agreed to this.

'Well, then, when I give the description of a thing, but you give a different description of a different thing; is it then that we contradict each other? Or then am I saying the thing, but you're not saying it at all? But how could someone who doesn't say something contradict someone who does?'

Then Ctesippus went silent, but I was astounded by this argument (*logos*), and said:

'What do you mean, Dionysodorus? Really, this argument always astounds me, even though I've heard it many times and from many people – for the followers of Protagoras also used to use it a lot, as well as others before them.[82] For to me it always seems an astounding thing, as it overturns not just others, but even itself. And I think we'll ascertain the truth about this most admirably from you. Is it impossible to say something false? That's what your argument indicates, isn't it? That, when somebody speaks, they either say what is true or they say nothing?'

He agreed.

'So is it impossible to say something false, but possible to believe it?'

'Not even to believe it,' he said.

(Plato, *Euthydemus* 285D–286C)

*A difficulty here is that the conclusion of Dionysodorus' argu-
ment is that contradiction (antilogia) is impossible, whereas
Protagoras is on record as having composed a work entitled
Antilogiai, which presumably consisted of opposite arguments
on a whole series of topics. A further complication is that
the doctrine that contradiction is impossible is fairly securely
attributed to Socrates' follower Antisthenes, the founder of the
Cynic school, and a man of whom Plato particularly disapproved (cf. e.g. Aristotle, Topics 104b20f: 'A thesis is a conception that is counter-intuitive (paradoxos) but propounded
by some well-known philosopher; for example, "Contradiction
is impossible" as Antisthenes maintained.'). So it may rather
seem here as if Plato, as on other occasions, is foisting upon a
philosophical opponent conclusions that seem to him to follow
from the opponent's stated position, but which the opponent
did not himself maintain. On the other hand, as has been pointed
out, Protagoras could have taken up this position precisely as
one half of an antilogia, the alternative being that everything
could be contradicted. And in any case, such a position would
suit his stance on the non-existence of objective truth. All we
can say is that, though it is plainly not his argument alone, it is
a position that he could have taken up.*

A further testimony of Aristotle bears on the question:

15. And next, if all contradictory statements (*antiphaseis*) are
true of the same thing at the same time, it is clear that everything
will be one. For a trireme, a wall and a man will be the same
thing, if anything can either be denied or affirmed of everything;
and this necessarily follows for those who accept Protagoras'
thesis. For, if someone believes that the man is not a trireme, it
is clear that he is not a trireme. Consequently, he also is a
trireme, if the contradictory statement is true.

(Aristotle, *Metaphysics* IV 4, 1007b18–23 = 80A19, in part)

*We see here, as in §13 above, the same position being described,
and attributed to Protagoras, as was being relied upon by Dionysodorus. Those who hold opinions opposite to one another
are entertaining* logoi *relating to different, opposed* pragmata

(antikeimena), *but truly reflecting those* pragmata, *so that all are cognizing and uttering things that are true.*

And lastly, this complex of arguments is linked up with Protagoras' famous dictum, in a later passage of the Metaphysics *which goes over the same ground as the earlier one:*

16. The saying of Protagoras is like the views described;[83] for he said that man is the measure of all things, whereby he meant no more than that what seems to any man to be the case really is the case. But if this is so, it follows that the same thing both is and is not, or is bad and good, and so with what is said in all other opposite statements; for things often appear to be beautiful to some and the contrary to others, and what appears to each man is the measure.

(Ibid. XI 1062b11–19)

Scepticism about the Gods

Protagoras' famous statement, from the beginning of his work On the Gods, *has been quoted above from Diogenes Laertius (§1 [51]).[84] However, it may be quoted again, separately, here. We may note that, despite the dim view that was taken of it, allegedly, by contemporary Athenians, and by many later critics, it is not really an assertion of atheism. It simply denies that there is any secure evidence about the nature of the gods available to the human intellect or senses. Indeed, if that were Protagoras' last word on the gods, it is hard to see what he put in the rest of his treatise. In fact, this utterance sounds more like an opening gambit, or even one side of a pair of contrary arguments about the gods.*

17. 'Concerning the gods, I am not in a position to know either that they exist, or that they do not exist; for there are many obstacles in the way of such knowledge, notably the intrinsic obscurity of the subject and the shortness of human life.'

(*ap.* Diogenes Laertius, *Lives of the Philosophers* (IX 51)

Political Theory: Origins of Civilization; Nature and Convention; the Teachability of Virtue, or Excellence

A major text in this connection is the so-called Great Discourse *of Protagoras in the Platonic dialogue called after him (320C–328D). Though this, in the form in which we have it, is doubtless the work of Plato himself, rather than a simple transcription of a work or works of Protagoras, nevertheless it is a reasonable supposition (held by most competent authorities) that it represents the substance of what Protagoras himself taught, perhaps as set out in his book* On the Original State of Things, *and/ or in a number of epideictic orations. The question of the authorship of the myth is particularly vexed, but there seems little point in Plato fathering a myth on Protagoras if he was not known to use them in illustrating his doctrines. In general, the speech seems to embody positions that Protagoras should have held – and that Plato certainly did not hold – so that it seems legitimate to make at least cautious and qualified use of it as a source for his political theory.*

The style of this speech tends to be somewhat repetitive and verbose, perhaps reflecting Plato's view of Protagoras as excessively 'long-winded'.[85] *The initial, 'mythical', narrative is very reminiscent, stylistically, of archaic narrative, with its simple structure and repetition. As the speech moves on to argument (*logos*), rather than myth (*mythos*) at 324e, it becomes increasingly rhetorical, with flurries of rhetorical devices verging, at points, on the bombastic, such as the string of ironical rhetorical questions at 325a. We have tried to capture some of the style in our translation, given that it is so integral to the spirit of the speech as a whole.*

18a. *[320C]* 'Well Socrates, I'll gladly do that.[86] But should I, as an older man addressing my juniors, demonstrate it to you by telling you a myth (*mythos*) or explaining it through an argument (*logos*)?'

The majority of those sitting around him replied that he should explain however he wished.

'In that case,' he said, 'I think it would be more agreeable to tell you a myth.[87]

'There was once a time when there were gods, but no mortal kinds.[88] Now when it came to the time allotted for their generation, the gods fashioned them within the earth, mixing together earth and fire and all compounds of earth and fire. And when they were about to lead them up into the light, they ordered Prometheus and Epimetheus[89] to arrange and allocate the appropriate capacities to each of them. Epimetheus begged Prometheus to be allowed to allocate them himself and said, "And when I have allocated them, you inspect."

'So, when he had persuaded Prometheus he carried out his allocation and, in this allocation, he conferred on some strength without speed, while he arranged for others to be weaker, but with speed. And some he armed, while others, to whom he had given a nature lacking arms, he equipped with some capacity for preservation. So, to those whom he had invested with smallness he allocated winged flight or underground dwellings; whereas those whom he had made strong through their size [321], it was this that provided their protection. In this way he also gave equal allocations to the others, taking care to equip them so that no kind should be destroyed.

'And when he had made sufficient their means of escaping each other, he equipped them with protection against the seasons which come from Zeus, clothing them with dense hairs or thick skin: sufficient to ward off the winter and capable of warding off the summer heat, but also there to provide their own natural bedding for each of them when they went to their rest. To some he gave hooves underfoot, to others claws and solid, bloodless skins. For each of them he then devised particular foods: for some, pasture from the earth; for others, the fruits from the trees; and, for others, roots; while there were yet others, for whom he resolved that their food should be meat from other animals. Upon these animals he conferred limited progeny, while he conferred a large progeny upon those whom they would devour, thereby providing a means of preservation for the species. However, Epimetheus, being somewhat lacking in intelligence, did not realize that he had used up the capacities on the brute animals. There was still the race of men which he had not equipped, and he was perplexed as to what he should do.

'And in his state of perplexity, Prometheus came to him in order to inspect the distribution, and he saw that while the other animals were well equipped in all respects, the race of men was naked: without shoes, without beds and without arms. Yet the appointed day had already come, on which even man must emerge from the earth into the light. So Prometheus, perplexed about what kind of security he could devise for man, stole the technical wisdom of Hephaestus and Athena along with fire – for neither its acquisition nor its use would be possible for anyone without fire – and, in this way, he gave them to man.

'So, although man now had wisdom concerning life, he did not have political wisdom: for this was in the hands of Zeus. However, Prometheus was no longer able to enter the high citadel where Zeus dwelt and, moreover, the guards of Zeus were terrifying. But the shared home of Athena and Hephaestus, where they would practise their favoured arts, he entered unobserved and, having stolen the fiery art of Hephaestus along with the other arts of Athena, he gave them to man. From this arose great resources for man's life [322], whereas Prometheus, on account of Epimetheus, is later said to have been prosecuted for theft.[90]

'So since man now had a portion of divinity,[91] firstly, because of his divine kinship, he was the only creature to worship the gods, and he endeavoured to set up altars and statues of the gods. Then, through his skill, he quickly articulated speech and words, and invented dwellings and clothes and beds and food from the earth. Equipped in this way, at first men lived spread apart and there were no cities. Thus, they were destroyed by beasts, because they were weaker than them in every way; and, much as the craftsman's art was of sufficient assistance for food, when it came to war against the beasts it was deficient – for they did not yet have the art of politics,[92] of which the art of war is a part. So they sought to gather themselves together and to save themselves by founding cities;[93] but when they had gathered together they began to wrong each other because they did not have the art of politics, and so, scattered once more, they began to perish.

'So Zeus, fearing for our species, lest it should be destroyed completely, sent Hermes to bring shame[94] and justice to men, so that there would be order in the cities and the uniting bonds of friendship. And so Hermes asked Zeus in what way he should give justice and shame to men: "Am I to allocate them, just as the arts have been allocated? For these have been allocated in such a way that one man who possesses the art of medicine is sufficient for many unskilled men, and likewise with other craftsmen. Now, should I place justice and shame amongst men in this way, or should I allocate them to everyone?"

'"To everyone," said Zeus, "and let all partake in them.[95] For there could not be cities if only a few partake of them just as with the other arts. And lay down a law issuing from me: the man who is unable to partake of shame and justice they must kill, since he is a plague on the city."

'And so, Socrates, for this reason both other peoples and the Athenians think that only a few should take counsel whenever there is a discussion concerning excellence in carpentry or some other craft, and whenever someone outside of this few takes counsel, they do not accept him, as you say[96] – and rightly so, as I say. However, when they go to counsel [323] concerning political excellence, which must proceed entirely through justice and sound-mindedness,[97] it is reasonable that they accept anyone, given that surely everyone has the ability to partake in this sort of excellence, or there would be no cities. This, Socrates, is the reason for it.

'And so that you do not think yourself mistaken in thinking that all men really do consider that every man partakes of justice and other political virtue,[98] again accept the following evidence. In other cases of excellence, just as you say, if someone claims to be good at playing the flute, or some other art, but is not, they either laugh at him or get angry, while his own family go up to him and chastise him as if he was mad. However, in the case of justice and other political virtue, even if they know that someone is unjust, if he himself tells the truth about himself in public,[99] the act of speaking the truth which, in the previous case, they considered to be sound-mindedness, here is thought to be madness; and they say that everyone must claim to be just, whether they are or not, or, alternatively, that he who does not feign justice is mad. For they think that everyone must partake in it in some way, at least to some degree, or they are no part of human society.'

(Plato, *Protagoras* 320C–323C)

'Protagoras' now turns (323C) to the question of the teachability of political virtue, a subject dear to his heart and important to his livelihood. In spite of the fact that all men have the capacity to share in aidôs and dikê ('shame' and 'justice'), and that society in general is perfectly capable of instilling an adequate degree of these virtues in all citizens, teachers like Protagoras still have an important role in bringing these capacities to a high degree of excellence. In this connexion, he introduces also an important, and enlightened, theory of punishment, which, if we can attribute it to the real Protagoras, anticipates in important ways that of Plato himself, in such works as the Gorgias (476A–479E) and, later, Laws IX (857A–864C). The key element in this theory is that punishment looks, not primarily to the past act, by way of retribution, but rather to the future, with the aim of preventing further wrongful acts, either on the part of the perpetrator himself or of others.

18b. 'As to the fact that it is reasonable for them to receive every man as an adviser concerning this type of virtue, given their belief that everyone partakes in it, this is what I have to say. Now, further, I will try to prove to you that they think that it occurs, in whomsoever it does occur, neither naturally nor by chance, but is teachable and stems from diligence. Now, in any case where men consider each other to be badly disposed either by nature or by chance, nobody gets angry, nor chastises, nor teachers, nor punishes those of such dispositions, in order that they should not be such as they are; rather, they pity them. For example, who would be so foolish as to attempt to do any of these things to those who are ugly or small or weak?[100] For they know, I presume, that these things arise in men by nature and by chance: goods and their opposites. Yet, where they think that men acquire goods through diligence and training and teaching,[101] if someone does not possess these, but the opposite evils, it is presumably in these cases that anger and punishments and chastisements occur.

'One such thing is injustice, impiety and *[324]*, in short, everything which is the opposite of political virtue. Indeed, in this case, everyone gets angry and chastises everyone, clearly because it is acquired through diligence and learning. For if you will consider, Socrates, that punishment can have some sort of effect on those who do wrong, this in itself shows that men think of virtue as acquirable. After all, nobody intelligent punishes those who do wrong, in relation to, and on account of, the fact that they did wrong, unless he is retaliating irrationally, like a beast. In fact, he who attempts to punish in accordance with reason does not retaliate on account of the past wrong (for he could not render something which has been done, undone) but for the sake of the future, so that neither the wrongdoer himself, nor others who see him being punished, will do wrong again. Now, if he has such a belief, he must believe that virtue is teachable; and so he punishes as a deterrent.

'So this is the opinion held by all those who retaliate both privately and publicly; and all men, not least the Athenians, your fellow citizens, retaliate against and punish those whom they consider to have done wrong. Thus, according to this argument, the Athenians are amongst those who think that virtue is acquirable and teachable. And so, in my opinion, I have given you sufficient proof that it is reasonable for your citizens to accept the counsel of a smith or a cobbler concerning politics, and to think that virtue is teachable and acquirable.'

(Ibid. 323C–324D)

The last, and longest, segment of The Great Discourse *addresses directly, if somewhat discursively, the problem raised by Socrates at 320A–C, that distinguished statesmen like Pericles, while seeing to it that their sons are taught all specialized subjects of which there are teachers, do not seem to be able to communicate to them the political virtue of which they themselves are past masters; from which he professes to conclude that virtue is not teachable. Protagoras maintains, reasonably, that at least the minimum quotient of virtue required to function in a state is in fact teachable, but that we must not expect that great statesmen like Pericles can communicate their peculiar excellence to their offspring, any more than a great painter like Polycleitus could communicate his genius to his sons. The sons of Polycleitus could doubtless be taught to paint in some fashion, but not to be great painters. This relates to Protagoras' otherwise attested principle (cf. §19 below) that 'natural ability' (physis) is required, as well as good teaching and practice, for successful learning – and physis is not necessarily inherited. Socrates' argument is thus exposed for what it is, a rhetorical gibe. The passage ends with a piece of self-advertisement by Protagoras, incorporating a 'special offer' of his to his pupils which we know from other sources (cf. §1 above) to have been a particular trademark. Overall, it seems probable that this part of the speech too incorporates genuine Protagorean material.*

18c. *[324D]* 'But you are still at a loss concerning good men: how can it be that good men teach their sons and make them wise about other subjects, of which there are teachers; but, when it comes to that virtue in which they themselves excel, they make them no better than anyone else? Now, about this, Socrates, I shall no longer tell you a myth (*mythos*), but an argument (*logos*).[102] Think about it in this way.

'Is there some one thing, or is there not, of which it is necessary that all citizens partake, if there is to be a city? For it is with this point, if anything, that we will release you from your confusion. Now if there is and this one thing is neither the craft of the carpenter, nor of the smith, nor of the potter; *[325]* but is justice and prudence and piety and, in short, this one thing which I call human virtue – if it is this of which everyone must partake and which every man must have and, even if he wishes to learn or to do something else, he must act with it, but not without – if whoever does not partake of this must be taught and punished, child, man and woman alike until, through punishment, they become better; and whoever does not submit to punishment and teaching must either be expelled from the city or executed, since they are effectively incurable – if this is the case, and even though its nature is such, good men still teach their sons other things, but not this, how remarkable these good men are! For we have shown that they do think it teachable, both in private and public matters. But then, even though it can be taught and cultivated, do they still teach their sons *other* skills, where death would not be the penalty of their ignorance; but, in the case of virtue, where the penalty for those children who have not learned nor been cultivated in virtue is death or exile (and, as well as death, confiscation of property and, so to speak, the entire overturning of their household), do they not teach it to them and exercise every care? Well, that's what we would have to think, Socrates.

'In fact, beginning right from infancy, for as long as they live, they teach and chastise them. As soon as they understand what is being said, their nurse, their mother, their teacher and their father himself strive that their child will be as excellent as possible; teaching and showing him in every act and word that this is right, but that is wrong; this is pious, but that impious; "do this", but "don't do that". That is if he obeys willingly; but if he doesn't, then, just like a twisted and bent piece of wood, they straighten him with threats and blows. After this, they send him to school and tell the teacher to pay far more attention to the orderly behaviour of their children than to their letters and lyre-playing. Then the teachers pay attention to this, and accordingly, when they have learned their letters and are coming to understand the written word, just as they had already done with speech, they provide them with the compositions of good poets to read out on their benches and they make them learn them. [326] These contain many warnings, and many accounts, praises and eulogies of the good men of the past; so that the child should copy them in emulation and strive to become like them. And again, the music teachers, in some similar way, pay attention to sound-mindedness, also so that the young do no wrong. As well as this, when they have learned to play the lyre, they then teach them the compositions of other good poets, composers of song, accompanying them on the lyre; and they make their souls habituated to the rhythms and harmonies, so that they become gentler and, as they become more rhythmical and harmonious, they are of more benefit,[103] in both their speech and their actions. For the whole life of man requires rhythm and harmony.

'Still then, as well as all this, they send their sons to a trainer, so that they may improve their body to serve their mind, now that this is in a good condition, and so that bodily weakness does not compel them to cowardice either in war or in other affairs. It is those who are most able who do this, and it is the richest who are most able. And their sons, who have begun going to school since earliest childhood, are the last to leave; and when they do leave school, the city then makes them learn its laws and to live in accordance with these, as if they were a pattern. This is so that they do nothing arbitrary but, just as the writing teachers trace lines with a stylus and give the tablet to those children who are not yet skilled at writing, and make them write by following their lines, so likewise, the city, having traced its laws, the inventions of the good law-givers of the past, makes them rule and be ruled in accordance with these. But whoever transgresses them, it punishes, and the name of this punishment, both amongst your people and in many other places, is "calling to account",[104] since justice is a calling to account. So, given that so much attention is paid to virtue both in private and public matters, do you wonder, Socrates, and are you perplexed as to whether virtue is teachable? But you shouldn't be wondering about that – it would be far more remarkable if it wasn't teachable!

'So why, then, do many sons of good fathers turn out worthless? Again, let me tell you. For it's no wonder, if I have been telling the truth, that, in this sphere, virtue, there can be no laymen [327], if there is going to be a city. Indeed, if what I say is true – and it is the truest thing of all – think about any type of practice or study you choose. If it was not possible for a city to exist, unless we were all flute-players, insofar as each person was able; and both in private and public, everyone was teaching everyone else this art; and was rebuking those who couldn't play well; and did not begrudge it – just as now with justice and law nobody begrudges each other nor do they conceal their abilities, as with other skills – for justice and virtue are, I think, of mutual advantage, and so, everyone readily talks about and teaches justice and law to everyone else – likewise, with flute-playing, if we were entirely ready and free to teach it to each other, do you think, Socrates, that the sons of good flautists would be more likely to become good flautists than sons of useless flautists? Well, I don't think that they would. Instead, whoever's son happened to be most naturally disposed towards flute-playing, this man would grow to be famous, while who-ever's son was talentless, would lack repute; and often a worth-less flautist would spring from a good one and, conversely, often good from worthless as well. But all would at least be adequate flute-players, compared to laymen and those who know nothing about flute-playing. Likewise now, you should consider that whoever seems to you to be the most unjust man of those brought up amongst laws and their fellow men would be just and a craftsman of the art of justice, if you had to judge him by comparison with those men who had neither education,[105] nor law-courts, nor laws, nor any comprehensive force making them pay attention to virtue, but were some uncivilized lot, like those whom the poet Pherecrates depicted at last year's Lenaea.[106] Indeed, surely if you were amongst such men, just like the misanthropes in his chorus, you'd rejoice if you came across Eurybatus and Phrynondas,[107] and you would lament with long-ing for the iniquities of the men here. But, as things are, you give yourself airs, Socrates, because all are teachers of virtue insofar as each is able, but to you it seems that nobody is one. Well then, just as if you were to ask who is a teacher *[328]* of Greek, not even one would emerge; and likewise, I think, if you were to ask who could instruct the sons of the craftsmen for us in that very skill which they have learned from their father, as far as the father and the father's friends who share his skill are able, I think it would not be easy, Socrates, to find a teacher for these men, while it would be all too easy to find one for those who are inexperienced; it is just so with virtue and all other things. But if there is someone amongst us who is outstanding even in some small respect, in leading us towards virtue, we must rejoice. Indeed, I think that I'm one such man, and that, standing out from other men, I help somebody towards becom-ing fine and good, meriting the fee which I charge, and even

more, as even my students themselves agree. Because of this, I
have constructed a certain system for charging my fees: when
someone has learned something from me, if he wishes he gives
me the money which I charge. But if he's unwilling, he goes to
the temple and, having sworn an oath as to how much value he
attributes to my teachings, he then pays out this amount.[108]

'I have told you, Socrates, such a story and argument, showing
how virtue is teachable and that the Athenians think it so; and
that it is not at all remarkable that the sons of good fathers
become worthless and the sons of the worthless, good, since
even the sons of Polycleitus, who are of the same age as Paralus
and Xanthippus here,[109] cannot be compared with their father,
and likewise with other sons of other craftsmen. But about these
two, it wouldn't be right to accuse them of this yet – there's still
hope for them – for they're young.'

(Ibid. 324D–328D)

That there was a work entitled The Great Discourse (Megas
Logos) *is revealed by an entry in a late doxographic source (=
80B3), though it did not necessarily bear much resemblance to
what we have in Plato's* Protagoras. *However, the subject matter
of the fragment (as mentioned above in the introduction to
§18c) does bear on a point made in the Platonic speech, to
wit, the importance of natural ability* (physis) *in education.
Protagoras would thus seem to be the originator of what in
later Greek philosophy (beginning with Aristotle, in* Eudemian
Ethics, *I 1, 1214a16ff.) became a much-utilized formulation:
natural ability, instruction and practice, as the three conditions
for successful education.*

19. Protagoras said, in the work entitled *The Great Speech*,
'Teaching requires natural ability and practice,' and 'In learning,
one must start from early youth.' But he would not have said
this, if he himself had been a late learner, as Epicurus used to
believe and say about Protagoras.[110]

(*Anecdota Parisiensia* I 171, 31)

Rhetorical Theory; Literary Criticism

Obviously, a very important aspect of Protagoras' teaching – as is the case with all the other major sophists – concerned the theory and practice of public speaking. The following extract from Plato's Phaedrus *actually concerns all the fifth-century teachers of rhetoric, but it may as well be included here as anywhere else,[111] since Protagoras (like Gorgias, Hippias, Prodicus and others) will have necessarily practised and taught rhetorical theory in general, not just the innovations explicitly attributed to him. One can see from this how sophisticated and elaborate the art of rhetoric had become even within a generation of its original development in Sicily by Corax and Teisias. Plato's purpose here, admittedly, is precisely to show how far short of being a science the rhetoric professed by the sophistic rhetoricians falls, in spite of its supposed sophistication; but in the process he reveals a good deal of useful information.*

20. SOCRATES: But now, tell me what we should call those who learn from you and Lysias; or is this that art of speech (*logoi*) which Thrasymachus[112] and the others have used to become clever speakers themselves, and also to make others so, as long as they are willing to give them gifts as though they were kings?[113]

PHAEDRUS: Well, they are kingly men, though they don't know the things which you're asking about. But while you do appear to give this other type its correct name, when you name it dialectic, rhetoric, on the other hand, appears to be eluding us.

S: What do you mean? Can there be anything valuable which lacks these things and is still acquired by an art (*technê*)? Surely then you and I must not disregard it, but must say what this remaining part of rhetoric actually is.

P: Well, Socrates, there's really a great deal in the books which have been written about the art of speaking.

S: Yes – you've done well to remind me. So, first of all, I think, the prologue (*prooimion*) must be spoken at the beginning of the speech – you mean these kind of things, don't you? The refinements of the art?

p: Yes.

s: Second, then, comes the narrative (*diêgêsis*), along with testimony (*martyriai*);[114] third the evidence (*tekmêria*); and fourth, the probabilities (*eikota*); and I think that proof (*pistôsis*) and counter-proof (*epipistôsis*) are also mentioned, by that man from Byzantium, a most excellent speech-crafter.

p: Do you mean the worthy Theodorus?[115]

s: Of course. And, he also speaks about how we must make a refutation (*elenkhos*) and supplementary refutation (*epexe-lenkhos*), in both the prosecution and the defence. And, aren't we going to bring in that wonderful Euenus of Paros,[116] who invented implicit allusion (*hypodêlôsis*) and indirect praise (*parepainoi*)? Some people say that he also wrote indirect cen-sures (*parapsogoi*), in verse, so as to aid memorization. What a wise man! But won't we wake up Teisias[117] and Gorgias, who saw that we must value probability over truth; used the strength of their speech to make the trivial seem important, and the important trivial, the new antiquated, but its opposite new; and discovered both conciseness and boundless length in speech on all subjects?[118] Once, when he heard me talking about these inventions, Prodicus laughed and said that he alone had dis-covered what is necessary in the art of speaking: namely, that speeches must be neither too long, nor too short, but of moderate length.

p: And very wise too, Prodicus!

s: But aren't we going to mention Hippias, that man from Elis? I think he'd probably support Prodicus.

p: Yes . . . why not?

s: Now, how will we talk about Polus'[119] school of speech and how he teaches how to say things twice (*diplasiologia*) and as maxims (*gnômologia*) and as images (*eikonologia*); and about his Licymnian words,[120] which that man gave him to help achieve eloquence?

p: And weren't there some similar Protagorean innovations, Socrates?

s: Yes, my boy, that *Correctness of Speech* (*Orthoepeia*),[121] and many other fine things.[122]

And when it comes to speeches which draw out pity for old age and poverty, it seems to me that it's this mighty Chalcedonian[123] whose skill is pre-eminent; and this man, as he claimed, was also skilled at rousing large groups to anger, and then, with his charms, calming them again once they had become angry; and it was in this way that he became most powerful in creating, but also eradicating, slander. But there seems to be a common consensus concerning the conclusions of speeches, although some do call it recapitulation (*epanodos*), while others give it another name.

P: Do you mean summarizing each point at the end of the speech, to remind the audience of what has been said?

S: Yes. And now if you have anything further to add about the art of rhetoric –

P: Just a few small, rather trivial, points.

S: Well, let's forget about these small points then . . .

(Plato, *Phaedrus* 266C–267D)

Three passages of Aristotle illustrate various aspects of Protagoras' concern for orthoepeia, *or 'correctness of speech', and reinforce what can be gleaned from Diogenes Laertius' doxographic account (§1) as to his pioneering role in the formulating of Greek grammar and syntax.*

The first is from the Rhetoric, *a passage in which Aristotle is asserting that 'the foundational principle (arkhê) of style is to speak correct Greek', and that there are five aspects of this: (1) the proper management of conjunctions; (2) the use of particular words, not general ones; (3) the avoidance of ambiguity (amphibolia); (4) attention to agreement of gender; (5) attention to agreement of singular and plural. Protagoras is mentioned only in connection with the fourth of these, but he probably had something to say about all of them.*

21. The fourth element is the way that Protagoras distinguished the genders of words, masculine, feminine and neuter;[124] one must make these agree correctly: e.g. 'she, having come and spoken,[125] went away.'

(Aristotle, *Rhetoric* 1407b6–9 = 80A27)

The second passage, from the Sophistical Refutations, *is concerned with* soloikismos, *'solecism', which Aristotle has defined earlier (4. 165b20–1) as 'to be un-Hellenic in expression' (*têi lexei barbarizein*).*

22. What solecism is has already been stated. It is possible to commit it, and not to commit it, yet to seem to do so, as well as to commit it, yet seem not to do so. If, as Protagoras used to say, *mênis* ['wrath'] and *pêlêx* ['helmet'] are [naturally] masculine,[126] according to him, he who calls 'wrath' a 'destructress' (*oulomenên*)[127] commits a solecism, though he does not appear to anyone else to do so, but he who calls it a 'destructor' (*oulomenon*) appears to commit a solecism, but does not do so. It is obvious, therefore, that one might produce this effect by art also; therefore, many arguments appear to infer a solecism when they do not really do so, as happens also with refutations.

(Aristotle, *Sophistical Refutations* 14, 173b17–25 = 80A28)

The third passage, from the Poetics, *concerns another topic to which Protagoras made a significant, if not even a basic, contribution, the distinguishing of the 'modes of discourse' (*skhêmata tês lexeôs*).[128] We learned from Diogenes (§1 [53]) that Protagoras 'marked off the parts of discourse into four, namely, wish, question, answer, command' (or possibly even seven), and we see that distinction being employed here. We may note also Protagoras' use of the beginning of the* Iliad, *once again, to make his point, in a manner critical of Homer.*

23. Next, as regards diction (*lexis*). One branch of the inquiry concerns the modes of discourse. But this area of expertise belongs to the art of delivery and to the masters of that science. It includes, for instance, what is a command, a prayer, a statement, a threat, a question, an answer and so on. Knowledge or ignorance of these things involves no serious criticism of the poet's art. For who can accept that Homer has erred in the way alleged by Protagoras, that in the words, 'Sing, goddess, of the wrath ...' he gives a command, thinking that he is uttering a prayer? For to order someone to do a thing or not to do it is, he

says, a command. We may therefore pass over this as a topic proper to another art, but not to poetry.

(Aristotle, *Poetics* 19, 1456b8–18 = 80A29)

It would seem that, over and above specifically grammatical criticism, Protagoras also engaged in a form of literary criticism. A fragmentary scholion on Homer, Iliad 21. 240 (Oxyrhynchus Papyri II, p. 68 = 80A30) reports Protagoras as declaring that the episode of the battle between Achilles and the River Xanthus is introduced to make a break in the battle narrative, and provide a transition to the Battle of the Gods (theomakhia). There is no apparent grammatical, nor yet any moral, dimension to this comment, but it is probable that most of Protagoras' 'literary' exegeses would have had a moral dimension. We may discern an example of this from later on in Plato's Protagoras, *where Protagoras is portrayed as embarking on a critical exegesis of an ode of Simonides. Once again, as with* The Great Discourse, *the language may be that of Plato, but there is little point in his portraying Protagoras as indulging in this sort of literary exegesis if that were not something that he was known to have done, so that it seems useful to quote it.*

24. So he [sc. Protagoras] began to ask questions in this kind of way . . . 'I think,' he said, 'Socrates, that the most important part of a man's education is to become skilled in verse: that is, to be able to understand the words of the poets, what has been composed correctly and incorrectly; and, to know how to distinguish this and give an account of it if one is asked. And so, my question is going to be about that very same thing which you and I were discussing just now, namely excellence (*aretê*);[129] but in the context of poetry – that will be the sole difference. Now Simonides somewhere says to Scopas, the son of Creon of Thessaly, that

> It is indeed hard for a man to become truly good,
> Foursquare in hand and feet and mind, fashioned without
>   reproach.

Do you know this ode, or should I go through all of it for you?'

And I replied that it was unnecessary: 'for I know it, and I happen to have paid a lot of attention to it'.

'That's good,' he said. 'So does it seem to you to have been well and correctly composed, or not?'

'Exceedingly well and correctly,' I said.

'But does it seem to you to have been composed well, if the poet says things which contradict himself?'

'No, not well,' I said.

'Well then, take a closer look,' he said.

'But, my dear man, I've already examined it sufficiently.'

'So do you know', he said, 'that as the ode continues he somewhere states:

Nor do I consider the words of Pittacus to be correct,[130]
Although they were said by a wise man, he said that it is hard to
    be good.

You understand that it's the same man who says both these words and those earlier ones?'

'I know it is,' I said.

'So, do you think', he said, 'that the latter is consistent with the former?'

'Well, it seems so to me.' (But even as I spoke I was afraid that there might be something in what he said). 'Why?' I said. 'Don't you think so?'

'Well, how could someone who says both these things seem to be consistent with himself, given that he first laid down that it is difficult for a man to become truly good; but then, as he proceeded a little way into the poem, he forgot and blames this Pittacus for saying the same things as himself, that it is difficult for man to be good; and he says that he does not accept him, even though Pittacus is saying the very same things as himself. And yet, whenever he blames this man for saying the same things as himself, it's clear that he's also blaming himself; and so, either his earlier or later statement must be incorrect.'

(Plato, *Protagoras* 338E–339D)

This leads to a protracted discussion with Socrates, during which Socrates, no doubt with tongue in cheek, produces some very strained exegeses indeed. But it is probable that in his teaching Protagoras made use of such exegesis of the poets as a lead-in to instruction in techniques of argument, and this passage provides some insight into that, despite its satirical quality.

Educational Method; Antilogic; Criticism of Mathematics

Near the beginning of the Protagoras, *the great sophist is made to give an account of how, specifically, he will improve a pupil who attaches himself to him. Once again, despite the satirical intent of Plato, we may glean something from it of what Protagoras thought he was doing (Socrates has just asked him how exactly he will make young Hippocrates 'better', as he promised to do.) What he professes here is to teach the sciences of household management and politics:*

25. 'Should Hippocrates come to me, he won't experience the type of things he would experience if he associated with some other sophist. For those others maltreat the young and they drive those who have fled from the arts back again against their will, as they involve them in the arts, teaching them arithmetic and astronomy and geometry and music.' (And as he said this, he glanced at Hippias.)[131] 'By contrast, whoever comes to me will learn nothing other than that for the sake of which he has come. This learning constitutes good management in one's own affairs, so that he can run his own house excellently and also, concerning the city, so that he becomes very capable of acting and speaking with regard to civic matters.'

(Ibid. 318D–319A)

This may have been the basic subject-matter of Protagoras' courses, but in the process of teaching the art of argument, he plainly ranged much more widely. We find in Plato's Sophist *an interesting account of the breadth of scope of the sophistic art of controversy, or* antilogikê, *of which Protagoras was more or*

*less the founder. We may therefore reasonably assume that we
have here a rough survey of what was contained in the two
books of Protagoras'* Antilogiai *(the Visitor from Elea is in
conversation with Theaetetus):*

26. VISITOR FROM ELEA: So, let us consider in what spheres
such people claim that they make others into controversialists
(*antilogikous*). Let's get down to its very roots in the following
way. Well then, do they make them adequate at controversy
concerning divine matters, those which are concealed from the
majority?

THEAETETUS: Well, certainly, that's what's said about them.

V: Then what about those aspects of earth and heaven which
are manifest, and the things which pertain to them?

T: Yes, of course.

V: Also, then, in private conversations, whenever something
is said about origin or existence in general,[132] should we take it
both that they themselves are skilful at disputation while others
also are, because they make them competent in the same skills
as themselves?

T: Absolutely.

V: Then, with respect to laws and all political matters, don't
they promise to make them good at disputing?

T: Well, unless they promised that, practically no one would
converse with them.

V: Those things which concern arts both in general and
specifically, and which are needed for arguing against any actual
practitioner, presumably these have been laid down in writing
and published for anyone who wishes to learn them.

T: I take it you mean Protagoras' works on wrestling[133] and
other arts.

V: And many others as well, my dear man. So doesn't this art
of controversy ultimately seem to be some power which is
capable of disputation in any area?

T: Well, at any rate, it doesn't seem to have left anything
out.

(Plato, *Sophist* 232B–E)

It would seem, from a passage of Aristotle's Metaphysics, *that Protagoras included mathematics within the scope of his antilogies. Here he is claiming that there is no such thing as a pure geometrical entity, such as a circle, which would touch a line at just one point; a real physical sphere will touch a real, physical measuring-rod at more than a single geometrical point. This is interesting, as implying that, already in the mid-fifth century, there were mathematicians who asserted that the objects of mathematics were not sense-objects:*

27. Nor at the same time is it true that mensuration is concerned with sensible and perishable magnitudes; for then it would perish when they do. Nor, again, can astronomy be concerned with sensible magnitudes or with this heaven of ours; for as sensible lines are not like those of which the geometrician speaks (since there is nothing sensible which is straight or curved in that sense; the circle touches the measuring-rod[134] not at a point, but (along a line),[135] as Protagoras used to say in refuting the geometricians), so the paths and orbits of our heaven are not like those which astronomy discusses, nor have the symbols of the astronomer the same nature as the stars.

(Aristotle, *Metaphysics* III 2, 937b32–998a4 = 80B7)

We have information from Aristotle, in a lost work (perhaps the dialogue Gryllus, *which concerned rhetoric), relayed by Cicero, that Protagoras made a collection of* topoi, *or rhetorical commonplaces – schematic set-pieces on various frequently utilized topics, such as patriotism, justice or avarice. Among his recorded works (see §1 [55] above), this may have been in the* Prostaktikos, *or* Instruction Book.

28. [Aristotle] further says that Protagoras composed and set out discussions of certain large general subjects, such as we now call commonplaces (*loci communes*).

(Cicero, *Brutus* 46)

Finally, it seems worth including a possible new fragment of Protagoras, derived from a work of the Christian theologian

Didymus the Blind,[136] and only published in 1969. Doubt has been cast on its authenticity, but we think without adequate grounds[137] – and its line of argument may find a curious confirmation in an (admittedly fragmentary) passage of the Double Arguments, *which may derive from Protagoras' own* Antilogies *(see below, ch. 10, §4, end).*

29. Protagoras says that being (*einai*), for things that are, consists in their being perceived (*phainesthai*). He says: 'It is clear to you, as being present, that I am sitting; to one who is not present, however, it is not clear that I am sitting; (therefore) it is unclear (*adêlon*) whether I am sitting or not sitting.'
    (Didymus the Blind, *Commentary on the Psalms* III)

Protagoras seems here to be making a (rather sophistical) point about the nature of certainty – which could be related to his remarks about his ability to be certain about the existence and nature of gods. In the Double Arguments *passage, the point seems to be that it is unfair to expect a jury in a law-court to judge as to the truth or falsity of statements about events of which they have not been eye-witnesses.*

2 GORGIAS OF LEONTINI

Gorgias (c. 483–376 BC), son of Charmantides, is generally held to be a number of years younger than Protagoras. He was born around 483 in the Sicilian city of Leontini. Leontini was founded in 729 – immediately from its fellow Sicilian city of Naxos, but ultimately from Chalcis in Euboea – not long after Syracuse to its south. It was therefore Ionian in sentiment, while Syracuse was Dorian. It flourished in the sixth century, but in Gorgias' lifetime it was generally subject to the political domination of Syracuse, from which it made periodic attempts to free itself, notably by forging alliances with other cities, including Athens. It was in connection with the renewal of its alliance with Athens that Gorgias burst upon the Athenian literary and intellectual world in 427, in the course of an embassy to Athens, when, in addition to his official speech before the Assembly, he delivered a number of 'show' speeches in the new Sicilian form of rhythmic prose. By this time he was already in his fifties. We know little about his earlier life, except that he learned his skill in rhetoric from the first generation of Sicilian rhetoricians, Corax and Teisias, both of Syracuse, presumably in the late 460s and early 450s, and was acquainted with the philosopher Empedocles of Acragas, who flourished in the same period. He also plainly knew of Parmenides of Elea, since he satirizes him quite effectively in a spoof philosophical oration, On Not-Being,[1] probably composed in the 440s. His brother Herodicus became a distinguished doctor.

Presumably following from his first appearance in mainland Greece, Gorgias delivered a number of notable epideictic orations at various Panhellenic Games, one at the Pythian, at a date unknown, in connection with which a golden statue was dedicated in his honour,[2] and one at the Olympian Games, probably of 420,[3] but these have not survived. What do survive are two short display-speeches, the Encomium of Helen and The Defence of Palamedes, which are brilliant examples of his style, along with a fragment of a funeral oration, in addition to the treatise on Not-Being mentioned above. The embassy of 427 was hardly his only visit to Athens, though we cannot definitely pinpoint any others. The dramatic date of Plato's dialogue called after him is beset by anachronisms (no doubt deliberate), but it may be assumed to have taken place some time in the later 420s, since the death of Pericles (429) is referred to at Gorgias 503C as recent. Certain references in the comedies of Aristophanes (cf. §8, below) seem to point to further periods of teaching in Athens in the late 420s. On the other hand, he is attested by Cicero (cf. §28 below) as being the teacher of the Athenian orator Isocrates (436–338 BC), presumably at some time around 415 (Isocrates is described as being still a youth – adulescens), in Thessaly, which would imply that he had already established himself there in the early teens of the century. Further, Xenophon tells us (Anabasis II 6, 16 = §7) that the Boeotian aristocrat Proxenus studied with Gorgias in his youth, at about the same time.

In Thessaly, the aristocratic ethos of which he must have found congenial, he based himself in Larisa, at the court of the Aleuad prince Aristippus, where he was available to tutor the young Pharsalian nobleman Menon (Plato, Meno 70B), as well as the numerous visiting students who congregated about him. There he remained, it would seem, for upwards of thirty-five years, but at some time subsequent to 380 BC, at the invitation of the tyrant Jason, he moved to Pherae, and ended his days at his court, in about 376, at an age generally reputed to have been between 105 and 109.

LIFE AND WORKS

For Gorgias, we do not have even the dubious benefit of a 'life'
from the hand of Diogenes Laertius, as, unlike Protagoras, he
did not consider him, or indeed any other of the great sophists,
to be in any sense a philosopher. However, the second-century
AD sophist Philostratus does give some account of him, along
with the other chief figures of the movement, in his Lives of the
Sophists. *Philostratus, we may note, regards him as the true*
founder of the sophistic movement, rather than Protagoras.

1. Sicily produced Gorgias of Leontini, and we should reckon
that the art of the sophists may be traced back to him, as if to a
father. For if we think about Aeschylus and how much he
contributed to tragedy, when he equipped it with its costumes,
the high buskin, the heroic types, messengers from far away and
from behind the scenes, and rules for what should be done on
and off the stage, such would be the contribution of Gorgias to
those who share his art. For it was he who set the sophistic
movement in motion: the extraordinary expressions (*para-*
doxologia); the rhetorical crescendoes; grandiose expressions
for grand subjects; sudden breaks (*apostaseis*) and transitions
(*prosbolai*), through which the speech became more pleasant
and more elevated; and he invested it with poetic diction for the
sake of ornamentation and dignity. How he improvised with
great ease I have already described at the beginning of my
discussion;[4] and when, already growing old, he talked in
Athens,[5] it is no wonder that he was admired by the masses,
though he also enthralled the most illustrious men, the young
Critias and Alcibiades, along with Thucydides and Pericles, who
were already old. Also Agathon, the tragic poet, whom Comedy
knows as 'wise' and 'of fine speech',[6] often uses Gorgianic style
in his iambics.

Moreover, he played a distinguished part at the religious
festivals of the Greeks, and declaimed his *Pythian Oration* from
the altar;[7] and for this his statue was dedicated in gold and was
set up in the temple of the Pythian god. His *Olympian Oration*

dealt with a theme of the highest political importance. For, seeing that Greece was divided against itself, he came forward as the advocate of reconciliation and tried to turn their energies against the barbarians and to persuade them not to regard one another's cities as the prize to be won by their arms, but rather the land of the barbarians.[8] The *Funeral Oration*, which he delivered at Athens, was spoken in honour of those who had fallen in the wars, to whom the Athenians awarded public funerals and panegyrics, and it is composed with extraordinary skill. For though he incited the Athenians against the Medes and Persians, and was arguing with the same purpose as in the *Olympian Oration*, he said nothing about harmony with the rest of the Greeks, for the reason that it was addressed to the Athenians, who had a passion for empire, which could not be attained without a policy of aggression. But he dwelt at length on their victories over the Medes, and praised them for these, thus indicating to them that victories over barbarians call for hymns of praise, but victories over Greeks for dirges.

It is said that, though Gorgias attained the age of 108, his body was not weakened by old age, but to the end of his life he was in sound condition, and his senses were those of a young man.

(Philostratus, *Lives of the Sophists* I 9, 492–3 = A1)

This passage comes from the introduction to Book I of Philo-stratus' work, and gives some useful information about Gorgias' methods.

2. Gorgias of Leontini founded the older type [sc. rhetoric] in Thessaly,[9] and Aeschines, son of Atrometus, founded the second, after he had been exiled from political life at Athens and had taken up his abode in Caria and Rhodes;[10] and the followers of Aeschines handled their themes according to the rules of art (*kata tekhnên*), while the followers of Gorgias handled theirs as they pleased (*kata to doxan*) ...

It was Gorgias who founded the art of extempore oratory (*skhedios logos*). For when he appeared in the theatre at Athens he had the confidence to say, 'Come, propose me a theme!'; and he was the first to make this bold move, indicating thereby that he knew everything and would speak on any subject whatever, trusting to his powers of improvisation (*kairos*).[11]

I think that this idea occurred to Gorgias for the following reason. Prodicus of Ceos[12] had composed a certain pleasant fable in which Virtue and Vice came to Heracles in the shape of women, one of them dressed in seductive and many-coloured attire, the other with no care for effect; and to Heracles, who was still young, Vice offered idleness and sensuous pleasures, while Virtue offered squalor and hard labour. This story Prodicus elaborated upon at some length, and then toured the cities and gave recitations of it for a fee, and charmed them after the manner of Orpheus and Thamyras. For these recitations he won a great reputation at Thebes and a still greater at Sparta, as one who benefited the young by teaching this fable. Thereupon Gorgias mocked Prodicus for handling a theme that was stale and hackneyed, and he devoted himself to improvisation (*kairos*).

Yet he did not fail to attract begrudgers. There was at Athens a certain Chaerephon, not the one who used to be nicknamed 'Boxwood' in comedies, because he suffered from anaemia due to hard study, but the one I now speak of had insolent manners and made scurrilous jokes.[13] This Chaerephon teased Gorgias for his efforts in this direction, and said: 'Gorgias, why is it that beans blow out my stomach, but do not blow up the fire?'[14] But Gorgias was not at all disconcerted by the question, and replied: 'This I leave for you to investigate; but here is a fact which I have long known, that the earth grows canes for such purposes.'[15]

(Ibid., Preface = 82A1a + 24)

Apart from Philostratus, we have a biographical notice on Gorgias in the Byzantine lexicon, the Suda. *The information that Gorgias was a pupil of the philosopher Empedocles of Acragas (c.493–433 BC) is provided also by other authorities,[16] and there seems no reason to doubt that he was at least acquainted with him. His own pupil Polus hailed from Acragas, giving further evidence of contact.*

3. Gorgias, son of Charmantides, of Leontini, orator, student of Empedocles, teacher of Polus of Acragas and Pericles and Isocrates and Alcidamas of Elaea,[17] who also took over direction of his school. He was the brother of the physician Herodicus. Porphyry places him in the Eightieth Olympiad (460–457 BC), but it is necessary to regard him as older.[18]

He was the first to give to the rhetorical genre verbal power and art of deliberate culture, and employed tropes and metaphors and figurative language (*allêgoria*) and hypallage and catachresis and hyperbaton and doublings of words (*anadiplôsis*) and repetitions (*epanalêpsis*) and apostrophes and clauses of equal length (*parisôsis*). He charged each of his students 100 minae.[19] He lived 109 years and wrote a great deal.

(*Suda*, s.v. Gorgias = A2).

Diogenes Laertius makes mention of Gorgias in his 'Life of Empedocles' relying on the authority of Satyrus (cf. above, n. 16) and of the chronographer Apollodorus of Athens (second century BC).

4. Satyrus in his *Lives* says that he [sc. Empedocles] was also a physician and an excellent orator: at all events Gorgias of Leontini, a man pre-eminent in oratory and the author of a treatise on the art, had been his pupil. Of Gorgias Apollodorus he says in his *Chronology* that he lived to be 109. Satyrus quotes this same Gorgias as saying that he himself was present when Empedocles performed magical feats.

(Diogenes Laertius, *Lives of the Philosophers* VIII 58–9 = A3)

Some background to the momentous visit of Gorgias to Athens in 427 is provided by the first-century BC historian Diodorus of Sicily, himself dependent on the late fourth-century BC Sicilian historian Timaeus of Tauromenium (c.356–260).

5. This year [sc. 427 BC – Archonship of Eucles in Athens] in Sicily the people of Leontini, who were colonists from Chalcis [in Euboea] and thus kinsmen of the Athenians,[20] were attacked,

as it happened, by the Syracusans. And being hard pressed in the war and in danger of having their city taken by storm because of the superior power of the Syracusans, they dispatched ambassadors to Athens, asking the Athenian people to send them immediate aid and save their city from the perils threatening it. The leader of the embassy was Gorgias the rhetorician, who in eloquence far surpassed all his contemporaries. He was the first man to devise rules of rhetoric and so far excelled all other men in the instruction offered by the sophists that he received from his pupils a fee of 100 minae.

Now, when Gorgias had arrived in Athens and been introduced to the people in assembly, he discoursed to them upon the subject of the alliance, and by the novelty of his mode of speech he astonished the Athenians, who are by nature clever and fond of oratory. For he was the first to use the rather unusual and carefully devised structures of speech, such as antitheses, sentences with equal members (*isokôla*) or balanced clauses (*parisa*) or similar endings (*homoioteleuta*) and the like, all of which at that time were enthusiastically received because of the exotic nature of the device, but are now looked upon as laboured and ridiculous when employed too frequently and tediously. The end result was that he won the Athenians over to an alliance with the Leontines, and after having gained admiration in Athens for his rhetorical skill, he made his return to Leontini.

(Diodorus of Sicily, *Universal History* XII 53, 1–5 = A4)

That this narrative derives from Timaeus is made clear by the testimony of Diodorus' approximate contemporary, the historian and literary critic Dionysius of Halicarnassus (fl. c.30 BC), in his Life of Lysias.

6. Gorgias of Leontini . . . wrote many of his speeches in a quite vulgar, inflated style, using language which was sometimes 'not far removed from dithyramb'.[21] His pupils Licymnius[22] and Polus and their associates composed in the same style. As Timaeus tells us, it was Gorgias who first made poetical[23] and metaphorical expression catch the imagination of Athenian orators, when he came as an ambassador to the city and astounded

his hearers with his rhetoric. The truth is, however, that this style had its admirers even earlier than this.[24]

(Dionysius of Halicarnassus, *Life of Lysias* 3 = A4)

A snippet of testimony from Xenophon in Anabasis *helps to date the beginnings of Gorgias' period of teaching in mainland Greece, since Proxenus seems to be at least in his early thirties when setting out from Sardis with Cyrus in 401 as one of the commanders of his Greek mercenaries in the famous 'March Up-Country'. He would have enrolled with Gorgias, then, presumably in Larisa, some time around 410 BC, and the suggestion is that a period of study with Gorgias gave him the conviction that he could manage men.*

7. Proxenus of Boeotia, when he was just a lad (*meirakion*), wanted to be a man who could do great things, and because of this desire he paid a fee to Gorgias of Leontini. After he had been with him for a time, he came to the conclusion that he was now capable both of commanding an army and, if he became friends with the great, of doing them no less good than they did him; so he joined in this adventure of Cyrus', imagining that he would gain from it a great name, and great power, and plenty of money.

(Xenophon, *Anabasis* II 6, 16–17 = A5)

On the other hand, there are two passages from comedies of Aristophanes which seem to give evidence of a period of instruction by Gorgias in Athens. The most significant, if chronologically later, is from The Birds, *produced in 414 BC, and seems to provide evidence of a Gorgianic school of rhetoric in place at this time.*

8a. There is in Phanae by the
    Waterclock[25] a ruffianly race
    Of tongue-twisters[26]
    Who reap and sow
    And gather in the vintage
    With their tongues, and figgerate.[27]

They are foreigners by race,
Gorgiases and Philips.
And when these Philips
Who live by their tongues
Are sacrificed, everywhere in Attica
The tongue is cut out and offered separately.[28]
(Aristophanes, *The Birds* 1694–1705 = A5a)

This Philip is referred to earlier, in The Wasps, *of 422 BC, in a manner implying that he is a pupil of Gorgias. He is unfortunately otherwise unknown to us, but must have been a reasonably notorious rhetorician and* sykophantês. *Such references as this and the later one from* The Birds *bear witness to a certain degree of notoriety of Gorgias and his teaching in Athens from the later 420s on, and seem to imply some protracted periods of residence. One of the 'tongue-twisters' of 414 may have been the young Isocrates, later one of his most famous disciples, though he studied with him also later, in Thessaly.*

8b. By Heracles, they have stings too! Do you not see, master?
    Stings by which in a law-suit[29] they destroyed Philip, the follower of Gorgias.[30]
    (Aristophanes, *The Wasps* 420–21 = A5a)

The famous statue of Gorgias at Olympia is described by the second-century AD travel-writer Pausanias, in his Guide to Greece.

9. Among some undistinguished dedications stand the figures of Alexinicus of Elis, the boy wrestling champion, by Cantharus of Sikyon, and Gorgias of Leontini, whose likeness at Olympia Eumolpus, the grandson of Deicrates, who married the sister of Gorgias, says he dedicated. This Gorgias was the son of Charmantides, and he is said to have been the first restorer of the study of language, which was utterly neglected and so forgotten that it had nearly vanished from mankind.[31] They say Gorgias was famous for his speeches both at the Olympic festival and when he went on an embassy to Athens with Teisias.[32]

Among Teisias' contributions to language was the speech he wrote (the most convincing of his time) in a money quarrel for a Syracusan woman: but Gorgias won even more respect than Teisias at Athens; and Jason the dictator in Thessaly put Gorgias before Polycrates, a considerable orator of the school of Athens. They say that Gorgias lived to be 105.

(Pausanias, *Guide to Greece* VI 17, 7–9 = A7)

The latter part of this passage is curiously disjointed and obscure. Pausanias jumps from 427 to about 380, when Gorgias moved to the court of Jason of Pherae, presumably at Jason's invitation. But what is meant by Jason's 'putting him before' the Athenian rhetorician Polycrates (c.440–370 BC)?[33] Was Jason looking for a court rhetorician, and did he turn down Polycrates in favour of the aged Gorgias?

There was also a gilded statue of Gorgias at Delphi, dedicated by himself, mentioned by Pausanias at X 18, 7, by Cicero, On the Orator III 32, 129, and by Pliny, Natural History XXXIII 83 – where, if we can emend the plainly corrupt date 'Seventieth Olympiad' to 'Ninetieth Olympiad' (by adding 2 Xs), we get a reasonably plausible date of 420 BC. Cicero and Pliny actually describe the statue as solid gold, but Pausanias is probably right that it was gilt.

The inscribed base of the statue erected at Olympia was actually found there in 1876. It comprises the dedication, followed by two quatrains of elegiac couplets, and runs as follows:

10. *Gorgias of Leontini, son of Charmantides*

    (a) The sister of Gorgias Deicrates took to wife
    And from her was born to him Hippocrates.
    From Hippocrates sprang Eumolpus, who dedicated this
        statue
    For two reasons: gratitude for education, and love.
    (b) Than Gorgias no one of mortals before discovered
    A finer art to fit the soul for contests of excellence;
    His statue stands too in the vale of Apollo
    Not as a show of his wealth, but of the piety of his ways.

(*Epigram* 875a, p. 534 Kaibel = A8)

*A little snippet from the early third-century AD antiquarian
Aelian gives us the significant information that sophists such
as Gorgias and Hippias assimilated themselves to rhapsodes
(traditional reciters of Homeric poems) by dressing in purple
robes – though probably only when attending festivals or giving
other public performances.*

11. Tradition records that Hippias and Gorgias went about in
purple clothes.

(Aelian, *Varia Historia* XII 32 = A9)

*A somewhat garbled passage from the Neoplatonic philosopher
Olympiodorus, in his commentary on Plato's* Gorgias, *gives,
despite its confusions, some further chronological information.*

12. Secondly, we shall say that they lived at the same time:
Socrates in the third year of the Seventy-seventh Olympiad
[470/69 BC],[34] and Empedocles the Pythagorean, the teacher of
Gorgias, studied with him.[35] And indeed Gorgias wrote a rather
witty treatise, *On Nature*, in the Eighty-fourth Olympiad [444–
441 BC]; so that Socrates is the earlier by twenty-four years or
a little more.[36] Moreover, Plato says in the *Theaetetus* [183E]:
'When I [sc. Socrates] was young I met Parmenides, who was
very old, and found him a most profound man.' This Parmenides
was the teacher of Empedocles, the teacher of Gorgias. Gorgias
lived to be an old man; for, as has been said, he died at the age
of 109.[37] So they lived at about the same time.

(Olympiodorus, *Commentary on the Gorgias*, Preface, 9,
p.7,25–8,12 Westerink = A10)

*Some anecdotes connected with his longevity are preserved by
the antiquarian Athenaeus (c. AD 200), in his literary miscellany,*
Deipnosophistae (Doctors at Dinner).

13. Gorgias of Leontini, about whom the same Clearchus[38] says,
in Book VIII of his *Lives*, that because he lived sensibly he
survived with all his faculties for nearly 110[39] years. And when
somebody asked him what his mode of life was, seeing that he

had lived so long a time so comfortably and with his senses
intact, he replied, 'I have never done anything for the sake of
pleasure.'

But Demetrius of Byzantium,[40] in the fourth book of his work
On Poetry, says: 'When Gorgias of Leontini was asked what
was the cause of his living more than 100 years, he answered,
"The fact that I have never yet done anything for the sake of my
gut [?]."'[41] (= A11)

(Athenaeus, *Deipnosophistae* XII 548CD = A11)

*There is a further detail on this topic in a treatise preserved
among the works of Lucian, but probably not by him,* On
Long-Lived Men:

14. Among the orators, Gorgias, whom some call a sophist,
lived to the age of 108, and died by abstaining from food. They
say that when he was asked the reason for his prolonged old age
and health with all his faculties, he said it was because he had
never allowed himself to be dragged around to other people's
parties.

(Lucian, *On Long-Lived Men* 23 = A13)

*As to his period of teaching in Thessaly, and the circumstances
of his life there, there are various testimonies – one from his
pupil Isocrates, in his* Antidosis.

15. Now, generally speaking, you will find that no one of the
so-called sophists has accumulated a great amount of money,
but that some of them have lived in poor, others in moderate
circumstances.[42] The man who in our recollection laid up the
most was Gorgias of Leontini. He spent his time in Thessaly
when the Thessalians were the most prosperous people in
Greece. He lived a long life and devoted himself to the making
of money. He had no fixed domicile in any city and therefore
paid out nothing for the public good, nor was he subject to any
tax. Moreover, he did not marry and beget children, but was
free from this, the most unremitting and expensive of burdens.
And yet, although he had so great an advantage towards laying

up more wealth than any other man, he left at his death only 1,000 staters.[43]

(Isocrates, *Antidosis* 155 = A18)

To this may be added a passage from the beginning of Plato's Meno, *useful despite the irony with which it is delivered. Menon is a young Thessalian nobleman, who came to Athens, probably on a diplomatic mission for his native city of Pharsalus, in around 403/2. He shortly afterwards (like Proxenus, cf. §7 above) joined the Persian prince Cyrus as a mercenary soldier in the famous 'March Up-Country'.*

16. SOCRATES: Menon, the Thessalians used to have a good reputation amongst the Greeks and were admired for their horsemanship and their wealth; while now, I think that they are also admired for their wisdom, not least the people of Larisa, the fellow citizens of your friend Aristippus. And Gorgias is responsible for this, since when he arrived in the city he captured the most prominent amongst both the Aleuadae, to whom your lover Aristippus belongs, and the Thessalians, as lovers of his wisdom. Moreover, he has given you a disposition accustomed to fearless and magnificent answers, whatever anyone might ask you, just as would be reasonable for those who do have knowledge; and this is because he offers himself to any Greek who wishes to ask him any question they like, and there is nobody to whom he declines to answer.[44]

(Plato, *Meno* 70AB = A19)

TEACHINGS AND METHODS

We are told a certain amount in various sources – some, unfortunately, hostile, such as Plato, but others neutral or even positive, such as Aristotle, Cicero and Philostratus – as to what Gorgias believed his art or expertise to consist of, and how it should be taught. He seems to have maintained that what he taught was not any set of doctrines,[45] but rather a method, *which in itself was value-free; it was not his concern or responsibility for what ends it was used (though he would prefer it used for just or moral purposes). He also was noted for claiming a most exalted status for the power of rhetoric – a capacity even to bewitch and enslave the reason (this is largely the theme of the display-speech Helen). He sought to adorn prose speech with many of the devices of poetry. Many particular rhetorical devices are credited to him, though in some cases in common with others, such as Thrasymachus of Chalcedon. We give a selection of passages below.*

First, a passage from the beginning of Plato's Gorgias, concerning his methods. This is, of course, fiction, but that does not necessarily disqualify it as a good representation of Gorgias' position.

17. SOCRATES: That's a good idea, Callicles.[46] But would he be willing to converse with us? For I would like to ascertain from him what constitutes the power of his art (*tekhnê*), and *what* it is that he offers and teaches; let him do the rest of his demonstration another time, as you[47] propose.

CALLICLES: Well, nothing would be like asking the man himself, Socrates, as this was one element of his demonstration. In fact, just now he was telling anyone inside to ask whatever they wanted, and he said that he would give answers to everything.

s: Excellent. Chaerephon, ask him.

CHAEREPHON: What should I ask?

s: Who he is.

CH: What do you mean?

s: Well, just as if he happened to be a craftsman of shoes, he would give you the answer that he is a shoemaker ... don't you understand what I mean?

CH: I do understand and I'll ask him. Tell me, Gorgias, was it true what Callicles here said, that you offered to answer whatever anyone asks you?

GORGIAS: *[448]* Yes, it's true, Chaerephon – just now I made this very offer, and I declare that up till now no one has asked me anything new for many years.

CH: Presumably, then, you'll find it easy to answer, Gorgias.

G: Well, it's up to you to try that out, Chaerephon.

*At this point, his follower Polus interposes, offering to answer
the question for him, as the great man is tired, but Polus quite
fails to grasp the point of the question, that Socrates is looking
for a definition of the subject-matter of the craft of rhetoric. We
resume at 448d1:*

s: Well, Gorgias, Polus appears to be very well prepared
for discourse (*logoi*). But he's not doing what he promised
Chaerephon.

G: How exactly, Socrates?

s: He doesn't really seem to me to have answered the question.

G: Well, then, if you want, you ask him.

s: Not if you are willing to answer yourself. I'd far rather ask
you. For Polus has made clear to me from what he's said that he
is far more practised in what's called rhetoric than in dialogue.[48]

POLUS: But why's that, Socrates?

s: Because, Polus, when Chaerephon asked you what craft it
is that Gorgias has knowledge of, you praised his art, as if
someone were attacking it, but you didn't give an answer as to
what it is.[49]

P: Well, didn't I answer that it is the very finest art?

s: Yes, indeed you did. Though nobody asked what Gorgias'
art is *like*, but what it *is*, and what we should call Gorgias. So,
just as Chaerephon offered you the previous examples, and you
answered him with correct and concise responses *[449]*; so now,
in the same way, tell us what this art is and what we should call
Gorgias. Or instead, Gorgias, you tell us yourself *what* we
should call you insofar as you have knowledge of *which* art.

G: Of the art of rhetoric, Socrates.

s: So, we should call you a rhetorician?

G: Yes, and a good one too, if you actually want to call me
'what I claim to be', in Homer's words.

s: Well, that is what I want.

G: So call me that.

s: So, should we say that you are able to make other people
rhetoricians too?

G: Yes, that's what I offer, and not only here, but also
elsewhere.

s: So, would you be willing, Gorgias, to continue this

discussion as we are now doing, with one asking and the other answering, but to postpone those long speeches, like Polus began, for another occasion? Now, don't renege on your promises. Be prepared to answer the question briefly.

G: There are some answers, Socrates, which must be made in long speeches. Nevertheless, I'll try to give as brief answers as possible. For this is another of my claims – that nobody is able to say the same things more concisely than me.[50]

s: Well, that's what's needed, Gorgias. So, give me a demonstration of this very thing, concise speech (*brachylogia*), but leave long speeches for another time.

(Plato, *Gorgias* 447C–449C = A20, expanded)

*Gorgias does produce something approaching a definition of the subject-matter of rhetoric at 449E, when he declares that it is knowledge of speech (*logoi*). When Socrates begins to chip away at this in his characteristic manner, showing that such crafts as medicine and gymnastics also require expertise in* logoi, *Gorgias makes a further distinction, in language which later commentators on the dialogue (as reported to us by the Neoplatonic commentator Olympiodorus, in* Commentary on the Gorgias, *Preface, p. 36, 25ff. Westerink) identified as distinctly Gorgianic.*[51]

18. SOCRATES: So why ever don't you call the other arts rhetoric, given that they concern speech, if what you call rhetoric is the art which concerns speech?

GORGIAS: Because, Socrates, each of the other arts concerns manual work or some such activity so to speak, while there is no such manual work in rhetoric. Instead, the whole activity and accomplishment is achieved through speech. It's because of this that I consider that the art of rhetoric concerns speech, and I'm correct to say this, as I claim.

(Ibid. 450BC = A27, expanded)

On the question of the definition of general concepts, a topic central to the concerns of Plato (and, if we may believe him, of Socrates), we have a most interesting piece of testimony relative to Gorgias' definition of aretê, *'virtue', or better, 'human excellence'. Gorgias declines to recognize that there is any such thing as* aretê, *distinct from the* aretê *of particular classes of person. For this he (through his proxy, Menon) is pilloried by Plato in the* Meno, *but then commended by Aristotle in the* Politics – *as he would be by many modern philosophers.*[52]

19a. SOCRATES: Well, I myself, Menon, am in the same predicament. For, along with the other citizens, I am impoverished in this regard, and I reproach myself for not knowing at all about virtue (*aretê*). And when I don't know what a thing is, how could I know what sort of a thing it is? ... Do you think that's possible?

MENON: I certainly don't. But you, Socrates, is it true that you don't know what virtue is, and should we take home this report about you?

S: Well, not only that, my friend, but also I've never even met anyone who knows, as far as I'm concerned.

M: What? Didn't you meet Gorgias when he was here?

S: Yes, I did.

M: Then didn't you think he knew?

S: I don't have a very good memory, Menon, and so I can't say now how he seemed to me then. But perhaps he does know and you know the things he said. So remind me what he said. Or if you want, tell it to me for yourself, as presumably you agree with him.

M: I certainly do.

S: So, then let's forget about him, as he's not here.[53] But, in Heaven's name, Menon, you tell me yourself, what do you claim that virtue is? Tell me and don't be grudging. Then I will have told a most fortunate lie, should you and Gorgias show that you do know, even though I said that I have never met anyone who knows.

M: But it's not a difficult thing to tell, Socrates. So first, then, if you want to know what virtue is for a man, it's easy to say that this is virtue for a man: to be adequate in civic affairs; to treat one's friends well, but one's enemies badly; and to be careful not to suffer any such thing oneself. But if you want to know virtue for a woman, it's not hard to explain that she must manage the household well, protecting its contents, and being obedient to her husband. And there is another virtue for a child, and for female, and for male, and for older men, and, if you want, both for a free man and for a slave.[54] And there are all sorts of other virtues; so that, concerning virtue, it's not a problem to say what it is. For, in each activity and age, for each of us in regards to each task, there is a virtue. And I think that the same is also true of vice (*kakia*).

(Plato, *Meno* 71B–72A)

Socrates, of course, satirizes this as 'a swarm of excellences', and demands a single definition of excellence; but Aristotle in the Politics *sees the case differently:*

19b. This conclusion also emerges clearly when we examine the subject more in detail, and in its different divisions. For those who speak in general terms, and maintain that excellence consists in 'a good condition of the soul', or in 'right action' (*orthopragein*), or in any thing of the kind, are guilty of self-deception. Far better than such general definitions is the method of simple enumeration of the different forms of excellence, as followed by Gorgias. We must therefore hold that what the poet said about woman, that 'a modest silence is a woman's crown',[55] contains a general truth – but a truth which does not apply to men. And in the case of children, since the child is immature, his excellence is obviously not a matter of relation to his present self, but of his relation to the end towards which he is developing, and to the authority which guides him. And similarly, too, the excellence of the slave is a matter of his relation towards his master.

(Aristotle, *Politics* I 13, 1260a24–8)

Gorgias, then, has views on the nature of moral excellence. However, unlike certain of his contemporaries, notably Protagoras, he did not purport to teach it. A later passage of the Meno *(95C) seems to bear witness to the 'value-free' nature of Gorgias' instruction.*

20. SOCRATES: How about these sophists? Do you think that they do teach virtue – an offer which they alone make?

MENON: In that regard, Socrates, I really admire Gorgias, as you would never hear him promising this [i.e. moral excellence, *aretê*], and he makes fun of others when he hears them promise it. Instead, he thinks that they should make people skilled at speaking.

(Plato, *Meno* 95C = A21)

On the other hand, we can see from a passage in the Gorgias, *where Gorgias is allowed to state his position very fairly, what his attitude to the moral or immoral use of the skills which he imparted probably was. The passage, admittedly, exhibits no trace of the distinctively Gorgianic rhythmic style (such as Plato was quite capable of imitating if he wished, as witness Agathon's speech at* Symposium *194E–197E), but it very likely represents his position.*

21. GORGIAS: So such is the nature and the extent of the power of this art. However, Socrates, rhetoric must be used in the same way as any other competitive skill. For other types of competitive skill must not be used against all men – and, just because a man learned boxing and mixed combat (*pankratiazein*) and fighting with armour, so that he is more powerful than both his friends and his enemies, this doesn't mean that he should strike or wound or kill his friends. But, by God, not even if someone who has attended the wrestling school, whose body is in good shape and who has become a fighter, then strikes his father or his mother or any other of his relatives or friends; not even for this reason must we revile the trainers and those who teach how to fight with armour, or expel them from the city. For they transmitted these skills to be used justly, against enemies and the unjust, and in defence, not as aggressors, whereas it is these subversives who use their strength and skill incorrectly. So it is not the teachers who are bad, nor does this mean that the art is responsible or bad, but rather, I think, those who use it incorrectly. The argument would be the same in the case of rhetoric. For the orator is able to speak against everyone, and on any

topic, so that in a crowd he is more persuasive, basically, about anything he chooses. But this does not make it any more justified to steal the doctors' reputation – just because he would be able to do so – nor that of the other craftsmen. No, he should rather use rhetoric correctly, just as with competitive skill. But I think that if someone has become an orator and then uses his ability and skill to do an injustice, we must not revile his teacher or throw him out of the city. For that man transmitted this skill for just usage, while the other put it to the opposite use. So, then, it is just to revile, to exile or to kill the one who has used it incorrectly, but not the teacher.

(Plato, *Gorgias* 456C–457C)

Just prior to this passage in the Gorgias, *we find a remark which seems to encapsulate Gorgias' view of the power of rhetoric.*

22. SOCRATES: And it's because I'm amazed at this, Gorgias, that I've been asking you for a while just what kind of power rhetoric has. For when I consider it in this way, its greatness appears superhuman.

GORGIAS: Well, if only you knew the whole truth, Socrates; that, in a word, it has all the powers collected together under its command. I'll give you good evidence. Many times already, when I myself have gone with my brother[56] and other doctors to someone who is sick, but refuses to drink medicine or to allow the doctor to cut or to cauterize him, I have persuaded him, with no skill other than rhetoric. And I claim that if a doctor and an orator go to whichever city you like, and must compete in argument either in the assembly or in any other gathering, as to which of them should be chosen as doctor, the doctor would not get anywhere, while the able speaker would be chosen, if he wanted to be.[57]

(Ibid. 456AB = A22, expanded)

There is another passage relevant to this theme in Plato's Philebus. *It is put into the mouth of Protarchus, who may or may not be a real person, but who is portrayed as being a follower of sophists. His mention of hearing Gorgias 'on many occasions' would seem to attest to a number of visits to Athens by the great man.*

23. PROTARCHUS: Many times I listened to Gorgias saying repeatedly that the art of persuasion greatly excels all the others. For it brings all things under its dominion, willingly and not by force, and it is by far the best of all the arts.

(Plato, *Philebus* 5BA)

As to the details of Gorgias' rhetorical instruction, we have some information, both from Plato and from the later rhetorical tradition, beginning with Aristotle. We refer the reader back, first of all, to the long passage of Plato's Phaedrus *quoted as §20 of Chapter 1, but the section relating particularly to Gorgias may be repeated here.*

24. SOCRATES: But we won't rouse from their slumbers Teisias and Gorgias, who realized that probability deserves more respect than truth, who could make trifles seem important and important points trifles by the force of their language, who dressed up novelties as antiques and vice versa, and discovered how to argue concisely or at interminable length about anything and everything.

(Plato, *Phaedrus* 267AB = A26)

We learn a little more from the same passage of Cicero (taken from a lost work of Aristotle) that was quoted in relation to Protagoras (ch. 1, §28, p. 41 above). The whole context may profitably be given here. Aristotle is presenting his theory of the origins of rhetoric as an art. It would seem that Gorgias, like Protagoras, published collections of topoi, *or schematic expositions of set topics, but that he also showed how to magnify or diminish the importance of any given topic. Aristotle himself doubtless learned something from these handbooks in composing his own* Topics *and* Sophistical Refutations.

25. And so Aristotle says that, once the tyrants had been expelled, there were legal claims in Sicily for the return of private

property after the long interval; and, owing to the sharp and adversarial nature of the people, it was then that the Sicilians Corax and Teisias first wrote down the precepts of the art – for, prior to this, nobody had been accustomed to use a particular method or art in their speech, even though many had spoken with care and order. He also says that Protagoras prepared and wrote down discussions on prominent topics, those which we now call commonplaces;[58] and that Gorgias did this as well, when he wrote in praise or criticism of particular things, since he considered that the most appropriate function of rhetoric was to be able to magnify something by praising it, and to bring it back down again by blaming it.[59]

(Cicero, *Brutus* 46–7)

Various passages of Cicero's Orator, *perhaps also deriving ultimately from Aristotle, describe further features of Gorgias' style, and detail his innovations.*

26. It is through this style [i.e. the epideictic] that one augments one's vocabulary and gains a greater degree of freedom in sentence structure and rhythm. It even facilitates the harmony and balance of sentences, and permits clear and rounded periodic sentences. This ornamentation is brought about deliberately, and is not concealed, but manifest and open, so that there is correspondence between words, as if the pairings had been measured. Accordingly, opposites are frequently juxtaposed and contraries paired together; while there is also equality and rhyme in the conclusions of clauses[60] ... Thrasymachus of Chalcedon and Gorgias of Leontini are said to have been the first to employ these devices, and subsequently, there was Theodorus of Byzantium as well as the many others whom Socrates calls 'cunning masters of speech' (*logodaidaloi*) in the *Phaedrus*.[61]

(Cicero, *Orator* 38–9 = A30, expanded)

Cicero returns to this topic later in the work.

27. Sentences are finished off, either, as if naturally, through the very arrangement of the words, or by certain types of words which have a certain degree of symmetry. If there are similar cases at the ends, correspondence of equal clauses, or the opposition of contrary ideas, the sentences then have natural rhythm, even if this has not been brought about deliberately.[62] Gorgias is said to have been the first to have striven for such symmetry (*concinnitas*).

(Ibid. 164–5 = A31, expanded)

And again, a little further on, in discussing the relationship between Isocrates and Gorgias – and Thrasymachus.

28. Those who have the greatest admiration for Isocrates give the highest degree of praise to this particular achievement – that he was the first to bring rhythm into prose. For when he saw that people listened to orators with seriousness, but poets with pleasure, it is said that he looked for rhythms which he could use even in oratory, both for the sake of pleasure and so that variety would prevent boredom. Their claim, however, is partly true, but not completely. For, although one must admit that there was no greater expert in this style than Isocrates, it was in fact Thrasymachus who first invented it. His writings are even too rhythmical. Moreover, as I said just before, it was Gorgias who first invented the juxtaposition of equal clauses, similar endings and contrary ideas in correspondence to contraries – those devices which mostly have a rhythmical cadence, even if this is not done deliberately – but he used them excessively . . .[63] Both Gorgias and Thrasymachus were predecessors of Isocrates, so that he excelled them, not in innovation, but in moderation. For just as he is more moderate in his use of metaphor and coining new words, he also shows more restraint in the rhythms themselves. But Gorgias is too keen on his own style and wantonly misuses his 'ornamentation' (as he himself considers it);[64] whereas Isocrates exercises more moderation in his use of them, even though it was when he was young that he heard the aged Gorgias in Thessaly.

(Ibid. 174–6 = A32, expanded)

Lastly, we have an interesting testimony from the second-century AD sophist Philostratus (cf. §1 above), in one of his letters, addressed to Empress Julia Domna.

29. The admirers of Gorgias were noble and numerous: first, the Greeks in Thessaly, among whom 'to be an orator' (*rhêtoreuein*) acquired the synonym 'to Gorgianize' (*gorgiazein*), and, secondly, all Greece, in whose presence at the Olympic Games he denounced the barbarians, speaking from the platform[65] in front of the temple. Aspasia of Miletus is said to have sharpened the tongue of Pericles in imitation of Gorgias, and Critias and Thucydides were not unaware of how to acquire from him grandiloquence and solemnity, converting it into their own work, the one by dexterity, the other by vigour of expression. Aeschines the Socratic, in whom you[66] were recently interested on the ground that he was clearly criticizing dialogues, did not hesitate to Gorgianize in the speech for Thargelia. For at one point he says: 'Thargelia the Milesian, coming to Thessaly, lived with Antiochus the Thessalian, who was king of all Thessaly.' The digressions (*apostaseis*) and transitions (*prosbolai*) of Gorgias' speeches became the fashion in many quarters and especially among the epic poets.

(Philostratus, *Letters* 73 = A35)

FRAGMENTS AND TESTIMONIES OF NAMED WORKS

In the case of Gorgias, we have what we do not have for any of his major rivals: some substantial surviving documents. In the case of the Helen and the Palamedes, we have the actual texts in full; in the case of the treatise On Not-Being something less than that, but certainly its substance. In the case of the Helen, at least, we have thought it suitable to arrange the text in quasi-poetical form, by dividing it according to the clausulae, to give some impression of the effect of the original. In fact, Gorgias is creating here a literary form some-

*where between prose and verse, as the Greeks themselves
appreciated.*

On Not-Being,[67] or On Nature

We begin, however, with his treatise On Not-Being, or On
Nature,[68] *which is reported to us by the second-century AD Sceptical philosopher Sextus Empiricus, and by the author of a curious
little work included in the Aristotelian corpus,* On Melissus,
Xenophanes, Gorgias *(hereafter MXG). It is not clear that either
the author of the MXG or Sextus is quoting absolutely verbatim,
but it seems likely that they are not altering very much. If this is
so, Gorgias has, for the purpose of satirizing Parmenides, Zeno
and – most specifically, in all probability – Melissus of Samos,
abandoned his characteristic high-flown style and adopted a
bald 'scientific/logical' mode suitable to the subject-matter.*

*There is, it must be said, a fair degree of controversy over
Gorgias' true purpose in composing this remarkable document.
Ancient authorities, beginning with Gorgias' own pupil Isocrates (*Helen 3*),[69] and including Sextus himself and many
modern authorities, are inclined to take it seriously,[70] while
others[71] have regarded it as an amusing spoof. We would agree
with George Kerferd that Gorgias is serious at least to the
extent of wishing to demonstrate that he, by the exercise of his
rhetorical skills of antilogic, can beat the Eleatic philosophers
at their own game. This would be consistent with his claims as
to the sovereign status of rhetoric.*

*Since neither Sextus nor MXG can be regarded as completely
accurate, we give their texts in turn, section by section.*

30(i)a. *[65]* Gorgias of Leontini belonged to the same party as
those who abolish the criterion,[72] although he did not adopt the
same line of attack as Protagoras. For in his book entitled *On
Not-Being, or On Nature*, he tries to establish successively three
main points – firstly, that nothing exists; secondly, that even
if anything exists it is inapprehensible (*akatalêpton*) by man;
thirdly, that even if anything is apprehensible, yet certainly it is
inexpressible and incommunicable (*anexoiston kai anher-
mêneuton*) to one's neighbour.

[66] That nothing exists he argues in the following fashion. If anything exists, either it is the existent that exists or the non-existent, or both the existent and the non-existent exist. But neither does the existent exist, as he will establish, nor the non-existent, as he will demonstrate, nor both the existent and the non-existent, as he will also make plain. Nothing, therefore, exists.

[67] Now the non-existent does not exist. For if the non-existent exists, it will at one and the same time exist and not exist; for in so far as it is conceived as non-existent it will not exist,[73] but in so far as it *is* non-existent, it will, in turn, exist.[74] But it is wholly absurd that a thing should both exist and not exist at one and the same time. Therefore the non-existent does not exist. Moreover, if the non-existent exists, the existent will not exist; for these are contrary the one to the other, and if existence is a property of the non-existent, non-existence will be a property of the existent. But it is not the case that the existent does not exist; neither, then, will the non-existent exist.

[68] Furthermore, the existent does not exist either. For if the existent exists, it is either eternal (*aidion*) or created (*genêton*), or at once both eternal and created; but, as we shall prove, it is neither eternal nor created nor both; therefore the existent does not exist. For if the existent is eternal, it has no beginning (*arkhê*); *[69]* for everything created has some beginning, but the eternal, being uncreated, has no beginning. And having no beginning, it is infinite (*apeiron*). But if it is infinite, it is nowhere. For if it is anywhere, that in which it is is different from it, and thus the existent, being encompassed by something, will no longer be infinite;[75] for that which encompasses is larger than that which is encompassed, whereas nothing is larger than the infinite; so that the infinite is not anywhere.

[70] Nor, again, is it encompassed by itself. For, if so, that in which it is will be identical with that which is in it, and the existent will become two things, place and body (for that wherein it is is place, and that which is therein is body). But this is absurd; so that the existent is not in itself either. Consequently, if the existent is eternal it is infinite, and if it is infinite it is

nowhere, and if it is nowhere it does not exist. So then, if the existent is eternal, it is not even existent at all.

[71] Nor, again, can the existent be created.[76] For if it has been created, it has been created either out of the existent or out of the non-existent. But it has not been created out of the existent; for if it is existent it has not been created, but exists already; nor out of the non-existent; for the non-existent cannot create anything, because what is creative of anything must of necessity partake of real existence. Neither, then, is the existent created.

[72] In the same way, it is not both together – at once eternal and created; for these are destructive the one of the other, and if the existent is eternal it has not been created, while if it has been created it is not eternal. So then, if the existent is neither eternal nor created nor both at once, the existent will not exist.

[73] Moreover, if it exists, it is either one or many; but, as we shall show, it is neither one nor many; therefore the existent does not exist.[77] For if it is one, it is either a discrete quantity (*poson*) or a continuous one (*synekhes*) or a magnitude (*megethos*) or a body (*sôma*). But whichever of these it be, it is not one; but if it be a discrete quantity it will be divisible, and if it be a continuous one it will be capable of being cut up; and similarly if it be conceived as a magnitude it will not be indivisible, while if it is a body it will be three-dimensional, for it will possess length and breadth and depth. But it is absurd to say that the existent is none of these; therefore the existent is not one.[78] *[74]* Yet neither is it many. For if it is not one, neither is it many; for the many is a sum of ones, and hence if the one is done away with, the many also are done away with along with it.

Well, then, it is plain from this that neither does the existent exist nor the non-existent exist; *[75]* and that they do not both exist – both the existent and the non-existent – is easy to prove. For if the non-existent exists and the existent exists, the non-existent will be identical with the existent so far as regards existing; and for this reason neither of them exists. For it is admitted that the non-existent does not exist; and it has been demonstrated that the existent is identical therewith; therefore it too will not exist. *[76]* And what is more, if the existent is identical with the non-existent, both of them cannot exist; for if the pair of them both exist, there is no identity, and if there is identity, there is no longer a pair. From which it follows that nothing exists; for if neither the existent exists nor the non-existent nor both, and besides these no other alternative is conceived, nothing exists.

(Sextus Empiricus, *Against the Mathematicians* VII 65–76)

Let us turn now to the version given in MXG, which certainly derives from the same original as Sextus, but is independent in certain details of vocabulary and argumentation (which will be noted). The author, it must be said, is much more interested than Sextus in the provenance of Gorgias' arguments, identifying them as emanating from Melissus or Zeno, or even the Atomists.

30(ii)a. *[979a12]* Gorgias claims that nothing exists; then, if anything does exist, it is unknowable (*agnôston*); and finally, if it is knowable, it cannot be revealed (*dêlôton*) to others. To show that nothing exists, he combines the claims of other people, all of those who seem to say contrary things about being (*ta onta*): some that it is one and not many, others, conversely, that it is many and not one; and some demonstrating that it is uncreated, others that it comes into existence.[79] He concludes this from a combination of both positions.

For it is necessary, he says, that if something exists it is either one or many and it is either uncreated or created. Indeed, if it turns out that it is neither one nor many, and neither uncreated nor created, it would be nothing. For if something did exist, it would be one or other of these. So, that there exists neither one nor many, and neither uncreated nor created, he tries to show partly as Melissus did and partly as Zeno did, after his own first proof, in which he states that it is impossible for either the existent or the non-existent to exist. For if the non-existent *is* non-existent,[80] then the non-existent (*to mê on*) would exist no less than the existent (*to on*). For the non-existent *is* non-existent, and the existent is also existent, so that things no more exist than do not exist.

On the other hand, if the non-existent exists, then the existent, its opposite, he says, will not exist. For if the non-existent exists, then the existent should not exist. And so, accordingly, he says, nothing would exist, unless the existent and the non-existent are the same. But if they are the same, in this way too, nothing could exist; for the non-existent does not exist, and nor does the existent, given that it is the same as the non-existent. Such, then, is his argument.

The author now proceeds (979a34–b20) to criticize this argument, rather ploddingly, but very reasonably, by emphasizing the distinction between the existential (which he calls the 'basic' – haplôs) and predicative senses of 'is'. In all this he shows no sign of recognizing (any more than does Sextus, after all) that this is all a rhetorical tour de force.

[979b20] After this argument, he says that, if anything exists, it is either uncreated (*agenêton*) or created (*genomenon*). If it is uncreated, he deduces, from the views of Melissus, that it is infinite (*apeiron*). Yet he also claims that the infinite is nowhere, given that it can be neither in itself nor in something else; for the latter would mean that there were two infinites, the one which is in something and the thing in which it is. But that which is nowhere must be nothing, he derives from Zeno's argument about space (*khôra*).[81]

So this is why it is not uncreated; but nor is it created. For nothing can come to be either out of what is existent or out of what is non-existent. For if it came into being from something existent, it would have changed, which is impossible; for if the existent were to change,[82] it would no longer be existent; just as, if the non-existent were to come into being, it would no longer be non-existent. Nor, on the other hand, could it come to be from the non-existent; for if the non-existent does not exist, nothing could come to be out of what is nothing; while if the non-existent *does* exist, once again it could not come to be from the non-existent, for the same reason that it could not come to be from the existent. So, if it is necessary that, if anything exists, it is either uncreated or created, and since both of these alternatives are impossible, it is impossible for anything to exist.

[979b36] Again, if anything exists, it must, he says, be either one or many; if it were neither one nor many, it could not exist. He says it cannot be one, because what is truly one would be incorporeal (*asômaton*), insofar as it has no magnitude (*megethos*) – this is removed from it by Zeno's argument.[83] If, however, it is not one, it could not exist at all. For if it is not one, neither can it be many;[84] and, he argues, if it is neither one nor is it many, then it does not exist at all.

[980a2] Again, he declares that nothing can be moved.[85] For if it were moved, it would not still be the same as it was, but what exists would become non-existent, while the non-existent would come into being. Furthermore, if it makes a movement, through which it changes place, not being continuous, it is divided,[86] and at the point where the existent is divided, it does not exist; so that if it moves in every part, it is divided in every part; and if this is the case, it does not exist in any part. For it lacks existence, he says, at the point where it is divided – using the term 'division' rather than 'void', as it is written in the treatises ascribed to Leucippus.[87]

(Pseudo-Aristotle, *Melissus, Xenophanes, Gorgias* 979a12–980a2)

We turn now to the second of Gorgias' propositions, first in the version of Sextus.

30(i)b. *[77]* In the next place it must be shown that even if anything exists it is unknowable and inconceivable (*agnôston te kai anepinoêton*) by man. If, says Gorgias, the things thought are non-existent, the existent is not thought. And this is logically valid: for just as, if it is a property of things thought to be white, then it would be a property of things white to be thought, so, if it is a property of things thought to be non-existent, then it will necessarily be a property of things existent not to be thought. *[78]* Consequently, it is logically sound and consistent to say: 'if things thought are not existent, then the existent is not thought'.[88] But things thought (for we must take them first) are not existent, as we shall establish; therefore, the existent is not thought. And in fact that the things thought are not existent is plain; *[79]* for if things thought are existent,[89] all the things thought exist, and in the way, too, in which anyone has thought them. But this is repugnant to reason; for if someone thinks of a man flying, or of chariots running over the sea, it does not straight away follow that a man *is* flying, or that chariots *are* running over the sea. So that the things thought are not existent.

[80] Furthermore, if the things thought are existent, the non-existent things will not be thought. For opposites are properties of opposites, and the non-existent is the opposite of the existent; and because of this, if 'to be thought' is a property of the existent, 'not to be thought' will most certainly be a property of the non-existent. But this is absurd; for Scylla and Charybdis and many non-existent things are thought. Therefore the existent is not thought. *[81]* And just as the things seen are called visible because of the fact that they are seen, and the audible termed audible because of the fact that they are heard, and we do not reject the visible things because they are not heard, nor dismiss the audible things because they are not seen (for each object ought to be judged by its own special sense and not by another) – so also the things thought will exist, even if they should not be viewed by the sight nor heard by the hearing, because they are perceived by their own proper criterion. If, then, a man thinks of a chariot running over the sea, even if he does not behold it he ought to believe that a chariot is running over the sea. But this is absurd; therefore the existent is not thought and apprehended.

(Sextus Empiricus, *Against the Mathematicians* VII 77–82)

Next, in the version of MXG:

30(ii)b. *[980a8]* And so, he gives these proofs that nothing exists, and he then goes on to give his proofs that, if anything exists, it is unknowable (*agnôston*). For then it would be necessary for all things thought to exist, while the non-existent, since it does not exist, could not be thought. But, if this is the case, he says that no one could say something false, not even if he were to say that chariots race in the sea. For everything would be in the same class. And, so, things seen and things heard will exist, because each of them is an object of thought; but if we reject

this reason, claiming that, just as what we see does not exist to
a greater extent because we see it, so what we see does not exist
to a greater extent because we think of it (for just as in that case
many would see these things, in this case too many people would
think these things), why would it be more clear whether such
things exist?[90] But it is very clear which type of things is true. So
that, even if things do exist, they must be unknowable, at least
for us.

(Pseudo-Aristotle, *Melissus, Xenophanes, Gorgias* 980a8)

*We turn now to the third stage of Gorgias' argument, first in
Sextus' version.*

30(i)c. *[83]* And even if it should be apprehended, it is incapable
of being communicated (*anexoiston*) to another person. For if
existent things, as objects of vision and of hearing and of the
senses in general, are by definition *externally* existent, and if
these visible things are apprehensible by sight and audible by
hearing, and not vice versa, how, in this case, can these things
be indicated to another person? *[84]* For the means by which
we indicate is speech (*logos*), and speech is not identical with
the really subsistent things; therefore we do not indicate to our
neighbour the existent things but speech, which is other than
what subsists. Thus, just as the visible things will not become
audible, and vice versa, so too, since the existent subsists externally, it will not become identical with our speech; and not being
speech, *[85]* it cannot be revealed to another person.

Speech, moreover, as he asserts, is formed from the impressions caused by external objects, that is to say, objects of sense;
for from the occurrence of flavour there is produced in us the
speech uttered concerning this quality, and by the incidence
of colour speech respecting colour. And if this be so, it is not
speech that serves to reveal the external object, but the external
object that proves to be explanatory of speech. *[86]* Moreover,
it is not possible to assert that speech subsists in the same fashion
as things visible and audible, so that the subsisting and existent
things can be indicated by it as by a thing subsisting and existent. For, he says, even if speech subsists, yet it differs from the

rest of subsisting things, and visible bodies differ very greatly from spoken words; for the visible object is perceptible by one sense-organ and speech by another. Therefore speech does not serve to indicate the great majority of subsisting things, even as they themselves do not reveal each other's nature.

(Sextus Empiricus, *Against the Mathematicians* VII 83–6)

And so back to MXG.

30(ii)c. [*980a19*] But even if they are known, how, he says, could anyone reveal them to someone else? For how could anyone express what they have seen in speech (*logôi*) or, how could it become clear to the hearer, if he has not seen it? For just as sight does not recognize sounds, so, likewise, hearing does not recognize colours, but only sounds; moreover, the speaker speaks, but he does not speak a colour or a thing. So, when some-one has no conception (*ennoia*), how could he conceive it through someone else's words, or through some sign which is other than that thing, unless he sees it, if it is a colour, or he hears it, if it is a sound? For, firstly, nobody speaks a sound or a colour, but only a word; so that it is not possible to think a colour but only to see it; nor to think a sound, but only to hear it. And even if it is possible to know and read a word, how can the hearer have a conception of the same thing? For it is impossible for the same thing to exist at the same time in a number of separate people; for then the one would be two. But even if the same thing was in a number of people, nothing would stop it from appearing differently in them, given that they are not completely alike, nor in the same place; for if there was such a thing, it would be one and not two. But not even the same man appears to perceive similar things in himself at the same time, but different things with his hearing and with his sight, and different again at the present moment and in the past, so that one man can hardly perceive the same as another. Thus it is impossible, if anything exists, for it to be known; and, if it is known, no one could reveal it to another; for the reason that things are not words, and because no one has the same conception as another.

(Pseudo-Aristotle, *Melissus, Xenophanes, Gorgias* 980a19)

Strangely, perhaps, in view of the totally negative nature of the treatise On Not-Being, *we do have two reports, in Plato's* Meno *(76Aff. = B4) and in Theophrastus'* On Fire *(73 = B5), of a piece of positive scientific doctrine by Gorgias, derived from his mentor Empedocles, on the nature of colour and light, namely that it impresses itself on our vision by means of 'effluences' (aporrhoai) emanating from the object seen, and fitting themselves into 'pores' (poroi) in our eyes. This must derive from some other source than the above, but provides interesting evidence of Gorgias' readiness to engage in physical speculations when it suited him.*

The Encomium of Helen

We may turn now, however, to something completely different, and much more characteristic of Gorgias: his two surviving display-speeches, The Encomium of Helen *and* The Defence of Palamedes. *Though they are obviously very different in style from* On Not-Being, *yet it could be argued that their purpose is not dissimilar, being, as it is, to demonstrate the all-conquering power of persuasive speech. In the case of the* Helen, *the purpose is not to mount a serious defence of Helen, but rather to hymn the power of persuasion; in that of the* Palamedes, *which has a much more explicitly forensic format, it seems to be to present a model for argument from probability. As we have said above, we have chosen to present the* Helen *in quasi-poetic form, distinguishing the cola, in an attempt to convey something of the impression it must have made on its hearers; we have also included in brackets a selection of the more striking alliterative flourishes of the Greek. In the case of the* Palamedes, *such extreme measures are not necessary. Firstly, the* Helen:

31.   [1] The adornment (*kosmos*) of a city   is manpower,
         of a body   beauty,
                   of a soul,   wisdom,
                            of an action,   virtue,
                                     of a speech,   truth;
      and the opposites of these make for disarray (*akosmia*).

Man and woman and speech and deed and city and object
should be honoured, if praiseworthy, with praise
                          and incur, if unworthy, blame,
for it is an equal error and mistake
    to blame the praiseable   and to praise the blameable.
[2] It is the part of one and the same man
    both to speak the needful rightly
    and to refute <what is said not rightly;
it is fitting, then,>[91] to refute those who rebuke Helen,
a woman about whom univocal and unanimous
    has been the testimony of inspired poets,
as has the ill omen of her name,
    which has become a memorial of misfortunes.
For my part, by introducing some reasoning into my
    speech,
    I wish to free the accused from blame (*pausai tês aitias*),
and, by revealing her detractors as liars and showing forth
    the truth,
    to free her from ignorance (*pausai tês amathias*).

[3] So then, that in nature and in ancestry
    the woman who is subject of this speech
    is pre-eminent among pre-eminent men and women
is not unclear, even to a few.
For it is clear that her mother was Leda,
    and her father was in fact (*genomenou*) a god, Zeus,
    but said to be (*legomenou*) a mortal, Tyndareus,
of whom the one was shown to be her father
                          because he was (*dia to einai*),
    and the latter was disproved,
                because he was said to be (*dia to phanai*),
    and the latter was the most powerful of men,
    while the former was lord of all things.

[4] Born of such stock,   she had godlike beauty,
which, taking and not mistaking (*labousa kai ou lathousa*),
    she kept;
In many did she work much desire for her love,

and with her one body she brought together many bodies
    of men
       thinking great thoughts for great goals,
of whom   some had greatness of wealth
             some the glory of ancient nobility,
             some the vigour of personal agility,
             some command of acquired knowledge;
and all came
    because of a passion which loved to conquer
(*philonikou*)
    and a love of honour which was unconquered (*anikêtou*).

[5] Who it was, and why and how he sailed away,
    taking Helen as his love, I shall not say.
To tell the knowing what they know already
       shows the right   but brings no delight.
Having passed over the time then in my speech now,[92]
I shall go on to the beginning of my future speech,
and I shall set forth the causes which made it likely
    that Helen's voyage to Troy should take place.

[6] For either it was   by the will of Fate
              and   the wishes of the Gods
              and   the votes of Necessity
that she did what she did,
             or   by force reduced
             or   by words seduced
          <or   by love possessed>.[93]
Now if through the first,
    it is right for the responsible to be held responsible;
    for God's predetermination (*prothymian*) cannot be
    hindered
              by human premeditation (*promêthiâi*).
For it is the nature of things,
    not for the stronger to be hindered by the weaker,
    but for the weaker to be ruled and drawn by the
    stronger,
    and for the stronger to lead   and the weaker to
    follow.

God is a stronger force than man
    in might   and in wit   and in other ways.
If then on Fate and on God one must place blame
(*anatheteon*)
   Helen from disgrace one must free (*apolyteon*).

[7] But if she was   by violence raped
           and   lawlessly forced
           and   unjustly outraged
it is plain that   the rapist, as the outrager, did the wronging,
        and   the raped, as the outraged, did the suffering.
It is right, then,
     for the barbarian who undertook a barbaric undertaking
        in word   and law   and deed
        to meet with blame in word,
        exclusion in law,
     and   punishment in deed.
And how would it not be reasonable for a woman
   raped   and robbed of her country   and deprived of her
friends
   to be pitied   rather than pilloried?
He did the dread deeds;   she suffered them.
It is just, therefore,
               to pity her,   but to hate him.

[8] But if it was speech   which persuaded her
                 and deceived her soul,
not even to this is it difficult   to make an answer
                 and to banish blame,
as follows:
Speech is a powerful lord, who
     with the finest and most invisible body
       achieves the most divine works:
       it can stop fear   and banish grief
       and create joy   and nurture pity.
I shall show how this is the case,
   for I must offer proof to the opinions (*doxêi deixai*) of
my hearers.
I both deem and define all poetry

as speech possessing metre.

[9] There come upon its hearers
                    fearful shuddering (*phrikê periphobos*)
            and   tearful pity (*eleos polydakrys*)
            and   grievous longing (*pothos philopenthês*),
and at the good fortunes and evil actions
        of others' affairs and bodies
through the agency of words
            the soul experiences suffering of its own.
But come, I shall turn from one argument to another.[94]

[10] Inspired incantations conveyed through words
            become   bearers of pleasure (*epagôgoi hêdonês*)
                and   banishers of pain (*apagôgoi lypês*);
for, merging with opinion in the soul,
    the power of the incantation beguiles it
                                and persuades it
                and alters it by witchcraft.
Of witchcraft and magic   twin arts have been discovered,[95]
                which are   errors of the soul (*psychês
                                hamartêmata*)
                    and   deceptions of opinion (*doxês
                                apatêmata*).

[11] All who have and do persuade people of things
        do so by moulding a false argument.
For if all men on all subjects
            had both   memory of things past
                and   <awareness>[96] of things present
                and   foreknowledge of the future,
speech would not be similarly similar,
    since, as things are now, it is not easy for them
                            to recall the past
                    nor   to consider the present
                    nor   to divine the future;
so that on most subjects most men
        take opinion as counsellor to their soul.
But opinion, being slippery and insecure,

casts those employing it into slippery and insecure successes.

[12] What cause, then,[97] prevents the conclusion
    that Helen similarly, against her will,
might have come under the influence of speech,
    just as if ravished by the force of pirates?
For the mode of persuasion is in no way like that of necessity,
    but its power is the same.
For the speech which persuades the soul
    constrains that soul which it persuades
                both to obey its utterances
                and to approve its doings.
The persuader, as constrainer, does the wrong,
and the persuaded, as constrained, is wrongly blamed.

[13] That persuasion, when added to speech,
                        can impress the soul as it wishes,
one may learn
        first   from the utterances of the astronomers
                 who, substituting opinion for opinion,
                 taking away one but creating another,
                 make what is incredible and unclear
                 seem true to the eyes of opinion;
        and second,   compelling contests in words,
                 in which a single speech,
                 written with art, but not spoken with truth,
                 may charm and persuade a large multitude;
        and third,   the struggles of philosophic arguments,
                 in which swiftness of thought is also shown
                 making belief in an opinion easily changed.

[14] The effect of speech upon the structure of soul
    is as the structure of drugs over the nature of bodies;
for just as different drugs dispel different secretions from
the body,
        and some bring an end to disease, and others to life,
so also in the case of speeches
                some distress, others delight,

some cause fear, others embolden their hearers,
and some drug and bewitch the soul with a kind of evil
persuasion.

[15] It has been stated, then, that,   if she was persuaded by
speech,
    she did not do wrong (*êdikêsen*), but was unfortunate
(*êtykhêsen*).
The fourth cause I shall discuss in a fourth section.
For if it was love which did these things,
    no difficulty will she have in escaping the charge
       of the sin which is alleged to have taken place.
For the things we see
      do not have the nature which we wish them to have,
       but the nature which each happens to have;
through sight the soul is impressed even to its core.

[16] For example,
    when enemy bodies fit themselves out against enemies,
      with warlike gear of bronze and iron,
        some for defence, some for offence,
if the sight sees this, it is alarmed, and alarms the soul,
      so that often men flee in terror
       from future danger as if it were present.
For strong as is the habit of obedience to the law,
    it is driven out by fear resulting from sight
      which, coming to a man, causes him to set at naught
       both the noble that is adjudged through law,
        and the good that comes about through victory.

[17] It has happened that people, having seen frightening
sights,
      have lost presence of mind for the present moment;
       even thus does fear extinguish and expel thought.
And many have fallen victim to
         useless labour (*mataiois ponois*)
    and   dread diseases (*deinais nosois*)
    and   madnesses hard to cure (*dysiatois
         maniais*).

In this way the sight engraves upon the mind
      images of things seen.
And many frightening impressions linger,
   and what lingers is very similar to what is said.

[18] Moreover, whenever pictures from many colours and
figures
   perfectly create a single figure and form,
they delight the sight;
while the crafting of statues and the production of
art-works
provide a pleasant vision to the eyes.
So it is natural for the sight
   to be grieved by some things and to long for
others;
and much love and desire for many things and bodies
   is wrought in many people.

[19] If, therefore, the eye of Helen,
   pleased by the body of Alexander,
   presented to her soul eager desire and contest of
love,
what is wonderful in that?
If, being a god, love has the divine power of the gods,
   how could a lesser being reject and refuse it?
But if it is a disease (*nosêma*) of human origin
   and a blind-spot (*agnoêma*) in the soul,
it should not be condemned as a sin (*hamartêma*),
   but considered a misfortune (*atykhêma*);
for she came – as she did come –
   by the snares of fate (*tykhês agreumasin*)
 not by the counsels of reason (*gnômês bouleumasin*),
 and by the constraints of love (*erôtos anangkais*),
 not by the devices of art (*tekhnês paraskeuais*).

[20] How then can one regard the blame of Helen as just,
 seeing as, whether she did what she did,
  by love o'ermastered
   or by speech persuaded

> or by force ravished
>> or by divine constraint compelled,
> she is utterly acquitted of all charge?

[21] I have through speech removed ill fame from a woman.

I have stayed true to the procedure that I set up
>> at the outset of my speech.

I have tried to end the injustice of blame (*mômou adikian*)
>> and the ignorance of opinion (*doxês amathian*).

My purpose was to compose a speech   as an encomium of
>> Helen
>>> and   an amusement for
>>> myself.[98]

Defence of Palamedes

The Defence of Palamedes, *as we have said already, while stylistically graceful, is not a prose poem in the way that the* Helen *is. It is rather an exercise in argument from probability,[99] transposed to the arena of myth. The story behind it is that of the 'framing' of Palamedes, at the siege of Troy, by Odysseus. Palamedes, who was reputed the cleverest of the Greeks after Odysseus himself, had incurred the enmity of Odysseus by exposing his trickery when Odysseus attempted to get out of serving in the expedition to Troy by feigning madness. In revenge, when the expedition reached Troy, Odysseus framed Palamedes by forging a letter to him from Priam, arranging for him to betray the Greeks, and hid a sum of gold in his tent. On this evidence, Palamedes was found guilty and put to death by the army.*

As a counterpart to this speech – not a direct response to it, but probably stimulated by it – see the Odysseus *of Gorgias' pupil Alcidamas, below ch. 9, pp. 303–9.*

32. *[1]* Prosecution and defence are not what is crucial in the judgement about death. No, it is Nature, with an open ballot, that casts a vote of death against every mortal on the day he was born. What is at issue is rather the question of dishonour and

honour, whether I am to die justly, or whether I must die violently with the greatest reproaches and the most shameful accusation. *[2]* These being the two alternatives, you have the latter[100] within your power, I the former; for justice is in my hands, violence in yours. You will be able to kill me, if you wish, easily, for you have power in this sphere, over which, as it happens, I have no power.

[3] If, then, the accuser, Odysseus, made his accusation, either clearly knowing that I was betraying Greece or conjecturing somehow that this was the case, out of good will towards Greece, then he would be the best of men; how would this not be true of one who saves his homeland, his parents and all Greece, and in addition punishes a wrongdoer? But if he has compounded this allegation out of envy or conspiracy or knavery, just as in the former case he would be the finest of men, so in this case he would be the worst of men.

[4] In my exposition of these matters, where shall I begin? What shall I say first? To what part of the defence shall I turn my attention? For an unsupported accusation creates evident perplexity, and because of the perplexity it follows that I am at a loss in my speech, unless I learn something from the truth itself and the present necessity, having come upon teachers more productive of danger than solutions.[101] *[5]* Now I clearly know that my accuser accuses me without clear <knowledge>;[102] for I know in my heart clearly that I have done no such thing; and I do not know how anyone could know what did not happen. But in case he made the accusation thinking it to be so, I shall show you in two ways that he is not speaking the truth; for I could not if I wished, nor would I if I could, put my hand to such works as these.

[6] I turn first to this argument, that I lack the capacity to perform the act. There must, after all, have been some starting-point of the treason, and that starting-point would have been speech, for before any future deeds there must first be discussions. But how could there be discussions unless there had been some meeting? And how could there have been a meeting unless the other party sent to me or someone went from me to him? For no message arrives in writing without a bearer.

[7] But this, you may say, can be conveyed by speech. So then, suppose he gets together with me, and I with him – how does this work? How do we communicate with each other – Greek with foreigner? How do we listen and talk to each other? Just on our own? But we do not understand each other's language. So with an interpreter? That would be adding a third person in a situation where things need to be secret.

[8] But let us assume that this event has happened, even though it has not. The next thing requisite is to give and receive some pledge of faith. What would the pledge be? Would it be an oath? Who was going to trust me, traitor that I would be? But perhaps an exchange of hostages? And who could those be? For instance, I might have handed over my brother (for I had no one else),[103] and the foreigner one of his sons; in this way the pledge would have been most secure from him to me and from me to him. But such action, if it happened, would have been manifest to all of you.

[9] Now it may be alleged that we made the contract for money, he giving it, and I receiving it. Was it, then, for a small sum? But it is not probable that a man would take a small sum for a great service. So, then, a large sum? What, in that case, was the means of conveyance? How could one person have carried it? Or are we to suppose many? But if many brought it, there would have been many witnesses to the plot, while if one brought it, what was brought could not have amounted to anything much. [10] And again, did they bring it by day or by night? But, in the latter case, there is the difficulty of the great number of guards and the frequency of their patrols, so that there is no possibility of evading them. By day, then? But the light plainly militates against such activities. So much for that, then. Next, did I go out to receive this bribe, or did he who was bringing it come into the camp? But both alternatives are impossible. If I had in fact gone out and got it, how would I have concealed it both from those within the camp and those outside it? Where would I have put it? How would I have kept it safe? If I had made use of it, I would have been unmasked; if I did not, then of what advantage was it to me? [11] But let us assume that what did not happen in fact happened. We met

up, we came to an agreement, I received money from them, I managed to avoid detection, I hid the money. I then had to deliver that about which these deliberations had taken place. This, however, is more troublesome still than what I have already described. For in acting, I had to act either by myself or with others. But this is not work for one man. Then in concert with others? But who? Clearly those with whom I associate. These would have to be free men or slaves, would they not? Well, the free men with whom I associate are you yourselves. Who, then, among you had any awareness of this? Let him speak. As for slaves, is it not incredible that I would use them? For they are prepared to inform both in the hope of freedom and when hard-pressed by necessity.[104]

[12] As for the action, how would it have been carried out? Clearly the enemy had to be introduced into the camp in greater numbers than yourselves, which is impossible. How could I have introduced them? Through the gates? But it is not my job to shut or open these – there are special officers in charge of that. Well then, perhaps over the walls, with a ladder? But surely <I would have been detected>.[105] The whole area is full of guards. Well, how about through a hole in the wall? No, it would have been obvious to all. Life under arms is carried on outdoors (this is a camp, after all!), where everyone sees everything, and everyone is seen by everyone. In every circumstance, then, and by every means it was impossible for me to do any of these things.

[13] Consider, all of you, the following point as well. What reason did I have to want to do this, even granting to the full that I had the capability? For no one wishes without due reward to run the greatest dangers, or to plumb the depths of wickedness. So what reason was there? (Again I revert to this point.) Was it to gain absolute rule? Over you, or over the foreigners? But over you I would have no prospect of ruling, so many as you are and of such a nature, considering the many great resources at your disposal, noble ancestry, material wealth, distinguished achievements, strength of intellect, royal status in your cities. [14] So, over the foreigners then? But who is going to be their betrayer? By employment of what power shall I, a Greek, take

over the foreigners, I being one and they many? By persuasion, pray, or force? They would not be willing, I think, to be persuaded, and I would hardly be in a position to apply force. But perhaps there are those willing to betray them to a willing accomplice, accepting a reward for their betrayal? But to believe and accept this is the height of foolishness; for who would choose slavery instead of kingship, the worst in place of the best?

[15] Now someone might say that I have entered on this through a passion for wealth and money. But I possess a modest sufficiency of money, and I have no need of much. It is the big spenders who have need of much money, not those who are in control of the pleasures of nature, but those who are enslaved to pleasures and are seeking to acquire honours from wealth and conspicuous consumption. None of this applies to me. To the truth of this claim I offer my past life as witness, and to this you yourselves can be witnesses. You have been my companions, so you know where the truth lies.

[16] Nor indeed for the sake of honour would anyone with even a moderate degree of wit set his hand to such an enterprise. For honours derive from virtue, not from wickedness. How would honour accrue to the betrayer of Greece? And in any case, I am not in want of honour; for I am in fact held in the highest honour, by the most honourable of men, that is to say yourselves, for my wisdom. [17] Nor, furthermore, would one do these things on grounds of security. For the traitor is the enemy of all: the law, justice, the gods, the great multitude of mankind. He transgresses the law, he dissolves justice, he destroys the multitude, he dishonours divinity. But he whose life is beset with the greatest dangers can have no security. [18] But perhaps I wanted either to help my friends or harm my enemies? After all, one might commit injustice for these reasons. But in my case quite the opposite situation obtained: I was harming my friends and helping my enemies. The action involved no acquisition of goods; but no one enters upon a crime with the aim of doing badly. [19] The remaining alternative is that I did what I did to escape some terror or trouble or danger. But no one could say that any of these motives apply to me. All men do all things in pursuit of these two aims: either in search

of some profit, or to escape some punishment; and whatever villainy is committed for reasons other than these <is likely to involve the perpetrator in great evils. But that I would most of all>[106] do harm to myself by committing these acts is quite clear. For in betraying Greece I was betraying myself, my parents, my friends, the honour of my ancestors, the cults of my native land, the tombs of my family and my fatherland which is the greatest in Greece.[107] Those things that mean most to all men I would be handing over to wrongdoers.[108] *[20]* And consider this also. How would my life not be unliveable if I had done these things? Where could I have turned for help? To Greece? Only to suffer the due penalty from those that I had wronged? Who, indeed, of those who had suffered could keep his hands off me? So then was I to stay among the foreigners? Abandoning everything of most importance to me, deprived of the finest honour, spending my days in the most shameful ill-repute, casting aside the labours performed in the cause of virtue throughout my past life? And that through my own fault, though to fail through one's own fault is the greatest shame for a man. *[21]* Moreover, not even among the foreigners would I be trusted. How could I be, seeing that they were aware that I had done something supremely untrustworthy, in having betrayed my friends to my enemies? Life is not worth living if one loses one's credibility. One may lose one's money, or be deposed from absolute rule, or be exiled from one's fatherland, and still pick oneself up, but once one has lost one's credibility one can never get it back.

So then, that I would not, <if I could, nor could not, if I would>,[109] betray Greece I have now sufficiently demonstrated. *[22]* I next wish to turn to a direct address to my accuser. In what, I wonder, do you put your faith when, having such a character as you have, you direct an accusation at one such as me? It is worthwhile learning what sort of a man it is who makes these allegations, such as you are unworthy to make, and I am unworthy to receive.[110] Are you attacking me on the basis of sure knowledge or of conjecture? If on the basis of knowledge, you presumably know what you know either from seeing the deed yourself, or from participating, or through learning the facts from someone who participated. If, then, you saw yourself, tell the judges here the manner, the place, the time – when, where, how you saw. If you participated, you are liable to the same questions. And if you heard the facts from a participant, we must know who he is – let him come forward, let him show himself, let him bear witness! For the accusation will gain much in credibility if you can produce a witness. As it is, neither of us can produce a witness.

[23] But perhaps you will claim that it is fair for you not to produce witnesses of what you allege happened, but that it is for me to produce witnesses for what did not happen. But this is precisely not fair; for as to what did not happen it is, surely, impossible to produce witnesses, whereas for what happened it is not only not impossible, but is actually easy, and not only easy, but <actually required. But>[111] for you it was not possible to find, never mind witnesses, but even false witnesses, while for me it was possible to find neither of these. [24] That you do not possess knowledge about the subject-matter of your accusation is obvious, then. It follows, therefore, that since you do not have knowledge, you must have an opinion. Do you then, most reckless of men, on the basis of opinion, that most untrustworthy thing, and having no knowledge of the truth, dare to bring a man up on a capital charge? Who do you know of that has done any such thing? It is open, surely, to all men to have opinions on any subject you please, and as to this you are no wiser than anyone else; but it is not right to repose trust in those who express opinions, but rather in those who have knowledge, nor to hold opinion to be more trustworthy than truth, but on the contrary, truth more trustworthy than opinion.

[25] You have accused me in the indictment we have heard of two most contradictory things, wisdom and madness, things which cannot coexist in the same man. When you claim that I am artful and clever and resourceful, you are accusing me of wisdom, while when you claim that I betrayed Greece, you accuse me of madness. For it is madness to attempt actions which are impossible, disadvantageous and disgraceful, the results of which would be such as to harm one's friends, benefit one's enemies and render one's own life contemptible and precarious.

And yet how can one have confidence in a man who in the course of the same speech to the same audience makes the most contradictory assertions about the same subject? [26] I would like to hear from you whether you think that wise men are witless or intelligent. For if you think they are witless, your argument is innovative, but not true; whereas if you think they are intelligent, then surely it is not appropriate to intelligent men to commit the grossest mistakes, and to prefer evils to the goods in their possession. If therefore I am wise, I have not made mistakes; if I have made mistakes, I am not wise. So in either case you would be wrong.

[27] I have no desire, though I could do so, to bring up against you in turn the many abominations, both old and new, that you have committed in your time;[112] for I do not wish to escape this indictment on the ground of your misdeeds, but on the basis of my virtues. So much, then, for you.

[28] To you, however, gentlemen of the jury, I want to say something about myself which may seem invidious, but is true, something that would not be appropriate to one who is not under indictment, but quite fitting to someone who is. For I am now undergoing scrutiny[113] before you, and presenting an account of my past life. I therefore implore you, if I remind you of some of my past good deeds, not to be offended at what I say, but rather to accept that it is incumbent on one who is under grave and false indictment to say something about his true virtues among you who know them already – which indeed I regard as a most pleasant task. [29] First, then, and second and most of all, all through from beginning to end my past life has been blameless, free from any accusation; for no one has been able to fix any true accusation of wrongdoing against me with you. Indeed not even my accuser has presented any proof of anything that he has alleged; thus his speech, lacking any proof, has the effect of mere abuse. [30] I might indeed claim, and in doing so I would not be lying, nor could I be refuted, that I am not only blameless but actually a major benefactor of you and of the Greek nation and of mankind in general, not only of the present generation but of all those to come. For who else but I made human life viable instead of destitute, and civilized

instead of uncivilized, by developing military tactics, a major contrivance for progress; written laws, the guarantees of justice; writing, the instrument of memory; weights and measures, the convenient means of commercial exchange; number, the guardian of goods; powerful beacons and very swift messenger services – and, last but not least, draughts, a harmless way of passing the time?[114] *[31]* I mention these by way of demonstrating that it is to this sort of thing that I apply my attention, using this as an indication that I abstain from shameful and wicked deeds. For when one puts one's mind to such things as the former, it is impossible that one concern oneself with the latter. And I claim the right, if I on my part have done you no harm, not myself to suffer harm at your hands. *[32]* And indeed for none of my other activities am I deserving of ill-treatment, at the hands of either young or old. For to older men I cause no offence, to younger ones I am not without usefulness, while to the fortunate I bear no grudge, and for the unfortunate I am full of sympathy. I do not despise poverty, nor do I honour wealth above virtue, but rather virtue above wealth. I am not useless in council, nor am I lazy in battle, but I do what I am assigned, in obedience to those in command. In truth, it is not my habit to praise myself, but the present emergency compels me, since I have been accused of these things, to make my defence in every possible way.

[33] It remains to me now to speak to you about yourselves, and with that I will end my defence. Appeals to pity and entreaties and the intercession of friends are of use when the trial takes place before a mob;[115] but among you, the most distinguished of the Greeks, and deservedly so regarded, it is not proper to resort to persuasion by means of the intercession of friends or entreaties or appeals to pity, but it is right for me to escape this charge by relying on the most perspicuous justice, explaining the truth, not seeking to deceive you. *[34]* And you in your turn should not direct your attention to words in preference to deeds, nor give more credence to accusations rather than their refutation, nor deem that a short time affords wiser judgement than a long time, nor believe that slander is more reliable than your experience of me. For in all cases good men must

take great care not to make mistakes, and much more in cases that admit of no remedy than in those that do; for these can be dealt with by those who exercise foresight, but are beyond cure to those who must resort to hindsight. And this is the case when men judge a man on a capital charge, as is the situation facing you now. [35] If, then, through words the truth of deeds could become transparent and manifest to one's hearers, judgement would now be easy on the basis of what has been said. Since, however, that is not the case, put a guard on my body, wait for a longer time and make your judgement on the basis of truth. For you run the great risk, through appearing unjust, of losing one reputation and gaining a different one. To good men death is preferable to a shameful reputation; for the one is the natural end of life, while the other is a disease within life. [36] If you kill me unjustly, it will become obvious to many; for I am not unknown, and your wickedness will become known and perspicuous to the whole of Greece. And the blame for this injustice, as will be clear to all, will rest with you, not with my accuser; for the outcome of the trial rests with you. But no greater error could be committed than this. For you will not only be sinning against me and my parents if you deliver an unjust verdict here, but you will have on your consciences the commission of a dreadful, godless, unjust, lawless deed, in having put to death a man who was an ally, useful to you, a benefactor of Greece, and a fellow Greek, convicting him on the basis of no clear wrongdoing or reliable accusation.

[37] I have said what I have to say, and I rest my case. For while to recapitulate what has already been said at length may be sensible before bad judges, it is not appropriate to assume that a body comprised of the most eminent of the Greeks does not pay attention nor remember what has been said.[116]

Funeral Speech

Other than these two orations, we have one considerable passage of a Funeral Oration, *designed to be spoken over the Athenian dead at some point during the Peloponnesian War, preserved by Dionysius of Halicarnassus (= B6), as an example*

of the 'grand style', in the course of his essay On the Style of
Demosthenes. *As with the* Helen, *and unlike the* Palamedes, *this
oration is couched in Gorgias' most high-flown style, so we have
chosen once again to arrange it according to cola. Dionysius
introduces it as follows:*

33. Thus I have not come across any forensic speeches (*dikanikoi
logoi*) by him: apart from a few political (*dêmêgorikoi*) speeches
and some handbooks (*tekhnai*), most of those which I have read
are epideictic. The following passage shows the characteristic
qualities of his speeches in the genre. He is celebrating the valour
of the Athenians who distinguished themselves in war.

'What was absent to these men
                              which should be present to men?
And what was present,
                                        that should not be present?
Would that I could say what I wish,
                     and would that I wish what I should,
avoiding divine displeasure,
                                        and escaping human envy.
For these men attained
                              an excellence which is divine
                     but   a mortality which is human,
                              often preferring
                                 gentle fairness to inflexible justice
                              often
                                 to exactness of law   straightness of
                              speech,
believing that the most godlike and universal law was
this:
    in time of duty
         duly to speak out and to remain silent,
             to act and <to leave undone>,[117]
cultivating two needed qualities especially,
    judgement   <and vigour>[118] (*gnômên kai rhômen*),
    the one for deliberating,   the other for accomplishing
    (*tên men bouleuontes, tên de apotelountes*),

the servants of those unjustly languishing,
the punishers of those unjustly flourishing
bold in regard to the expedient,   gentle in regard to what
is fitting,
   by the prudence of judgement
            checking the irrationality <of vigour>,[119]
            insolent with the insolent,
            decent with the decent,
            fearless with the fearless,
            terrible among terrors.[120]
As evidence of these qualities,
         they set up trophies over their enemies,
                              as honours to Zeus
                     but glories to themselves;
not being inexperienced
   either in inborn valour,
      or in lawful loves,
         or in armed strife,
            or in honourable peace,
reverent to the gods through justice,
   respectful to their parents through tendance,
      just towards their fellow citizens through equity,
         pious towards their friends through keeping faith.
Wherefore   though they have died   desire for them has
not died,
      but lives on,
         though they live not,
            immortal in bodies not immortal
(all' athanatos ouk en athanatois sômasi zêi ou zôntôn).'
(*Funeral Oration*, Dionysius of Halicarnassus,
Demosthenes 1)

*We have a few other notable expressions or phrases culled from
this and from other speeches. From this, the characterization of
vultures as 'living tombs' (*empsykhoi taphoi*) and a phrase,
relayed by Philostratus, revealing that Gorgias, like his pupil
Isocrates after him, made a pitch for panhellenic unity:*

34. 'Victories over the barbarians call for hymns, over Greeks for laments.'

   (Philostratus, *Lives of the Sophists* I 9, 5)

Then, a fine characterization of the generosity of the Athenian statesman Cimon, which may have formed part of an encomium of Athens in general:

35. 'Cimon acquired money in order to make use of it, and he made use of it in order to gain honour (*ktasthai hôs khrôito, khrasthai de hôs timôito*).'

   (Plutarch, *Life of Cimon* 10)

And from an unknown work, a characterization of tragedy, relayed by Plutarch, as producing

36. 'a deception in which the deceiver is more justly esteemed than the non-deceiver, and the deceived is wiser than the undeceived'.

   (Plutarch, *On the Glory of the Athenians* 348C)

Again, from an unknown work, two notable phrases, disapproved of by Aristotle in his Rhetoric, *where he is detailing types of bad taste (*psykhrotês*) in style. Here he is condemning outlandish metaphors:*

37. For instance, Gorgias talks of 'events that are green and full of sap',[121] and says 'foul was the deed you sowed, and evil the harvest you reaped.'[122] These phrases smack too much of poetry.

   (Aristotle, *Rhetoric* III 3, 1406b5–11)

Traces survive of his speeches at the Olympian and Pythian Games, and of his Encomium for the People of Elis, *as well as of his* Art of Rhetoric, *but nothing worth quoting.*

   Just one fragment, quoted by the Neoplatonist philosopher Proclus, in his commentary on Hesiod's Works and Days, *is intriguing, since it seems at first sight to embody a philosophical*

*thought. This, however, is probably an illusion; Gorgias is much
more likely to be making a purely rhetorical point.*

38. What Gorgias said is not absolutely true. He said, 'Being (*to
einai*) is obscure (*aphanes*) if it is not graced by seeming (*to
dokein*), and seeming is feeble (*asthenes*) if not graced by
being.'[123]

(Proclus, *Commentary on Hesiod*, 758)

3 PRODICUS OF CEOS

*Prodicus was born some time in the decade 470–460, in Iulis,
the chief of the 'four cities' (tetrapolis) of the island of Ceos, the
most northerly of the Cyclades, in the Aegean not far from
the coast of Attica, and home also, in the previous generation,
to the distinguished lyric poets Simonides and his nephew Bacchylides. Since his homeland was an early member of the Delian
League and, through its proximity to Attica, very much within
the orbit of Athenian culture, it was natural that Prodicus should
gravitate in that direction; and, indeed, he seems to have spent
a good deal of his career in Athens. We know remarkably little
about his life. As we have no clear indication of his date of birth,
so we have no idea when or how he died – though it does seem
safe to dismiss the garbled report in the Suda that, like Socrates,
he was put to death by the Athenians for corrupting the youth!
He survived Socrates, at any rate, since he is attested in the
Apology (19E) to have been still alive at the time of Socrates'
trial in 399.*

*It would seem that, like Gorgias, he first came to Athens as
an ambassador for his native city (cf. §2 below) – and apparently
somewhat earlier than Gorgias[1] – but, if so, he quickly established himself as a popular public speaker and teacher of rhetoric, commanding high fees, and specializing, so far as we can
discern, in the correct use of words and the fine discrimination
of synonyms. His particular patron seems to have been the
millionaire Callias, son of Hipponicus, in whose house we find
him staying, along with Protagoras, in Plato's Protagoras (cf.
§3 below). Plato makes Socrates refer to him with ironic respect,
and a reference in Aristophanes' The Clouds suggests that he was*

linked in the public mind with Socrates. Among his followers are reported as being the playwright Euripides and the moderate oligarch Theramenes; and the youthful Xenophon is reported, in rather remarkable circumstances, as attending his lectures, probably in Thebes, and probably in the 410s (cf. §2 below).

LIFE AND TEACHING METHODS

We may start with the biographical notice in the Suda, *wretched though it is.*

1. Prodicus was a Cean from the island of Ceos, of the town of Iulis, natural philosopher and sophist, a contemporary of Democritus of Abdera and Gorgias, a student of Protagoras of Abdera.[2] He died in Athens by drinking hemlock, having been charged with corrupting the youth.

(*Suda*, s.v. Prodikos = 84A1 D–K)

We find a somewhat more copious, though no more informative, notice in Philostratus' Lives of the Sophists.

2. Prodicus of Ceos had so great a reputation for wisdom that even the son of Gryllus,[3] when he was a prisoner in Boeotia, used to attend his lectures, after procuring bail for himself. When he came on an embassy to Athens and appeared before the Council, he proved to be the most capable ambassador possible, though he was difficult to hear, since he spoke with a deep voice.[4] He used to hunt out well-born youths, and those who came from wealthy families, so much so that he even had agents employed in this pursuit, for he had a weakness for money, and was addicted to pleasures. Xenophon, we may note, did not disdain to relate the fable of Prodicus called *The Choice of Heracles . . .*[5] As for the language of Prodicus, why should I describe its characteristics, when Xenophon has given so complete a sketch of it?[6] (= A1a).

(Philostratus, *Lives of the Sophists* I 12 = A1a)

Next we may turn to Plato's description of him in the Protagoras, *along with his fellow sophists Protagoras and Hippias of
Elis, at the house of Callias, son of Hipponicus, at a gathering
of sophists and their followers, in around 433 BC, just before
the beginning of the Peloponnesian War. The dialogue gives a
very vivid, and presumably essentially accurate, picture of how
the great sophists fitted into Athenian society. We may note that
Prodicus, although he has his followers, is represented as being
much inferior in distinction to Protagoras (which is, of course,
reasonable), and perhaps slightly lower in the pecking order
than Hippias.*

3. SOCRATES: 'And then also did I behold Tantalus'[7] – well,
Prodicus of Ceos was staying there too. He was in some room
which Hipponicus had previously used for storage; but now,
because there were so many staying, Callias had emptied it out
and turned it into a bedroom for his guests.[8] So Prodicus was
still lying down, wrapped up in what seemed to be a large
number of sheepskins and blankets. Then Pausanias of Cerames
was lying beside him on the next bed and, with Pausanias, some
lad, quite young and of a good nature, I think – certainly very
attractive. I think that I heard his name was Agathon, and I
wouldn't be surprised if Pausanias turned out to be in love with
him.[9] So there was this lad, as well as both Adeimantuses, the
sons of Cepis and of Leucolophides, and there appeared to be
some others. But I wasn't able to ascertain what they were
discussing from outside, even though I was very intent on hearing Prodicus; for I consider him to be an exceedingly wise man
– quite divine! Still, his voice was so deep that it produced a
booming sound in the room, which obscured what was said.
   (Plato, *Protagoras* 315D–316A)

We also find a significant reference to him in Plato's Hippias
Major, *the dramatic date of which is generally agreed to be c.420
BC. Socrates is talking to Hippias, ironically congratulating him
on his ability to combine the private and public spheres of
activity (that is, using the occasion of coming on an embassy as
an opportunity to make money for himself by giving lectures*

*and courses), and comparing him in that to his chief rivals,
Gorgias and Prodicus.*

4. SOCRATES: Or take that friend of ours Prodicus – he often
went to other places on public business; and the climax was
when he arrived recently from Ceos on public business: he spoke
in the Council and gained himself a good reputation,[10] while
at the same time, through giving private demonstrations and
associating with young men, he earned an incredible amount
of money.
(Plato, *Hippias Major* 282C)

*Despite what may seem to us obvious differences, there was
plainly some degree of association made in the public mind
between Prodicus and Socrates, possibly because of a perceived
affinity between Prodicus' concern for making fine distinctions
between the meanings of kindred words and Socrates' search
for exact definitions of key moral terms. Aristophanes plays
on this in* The Clouds *(produced in 423 BC). The Clouds are
speaking:*

5. 'To no other of the transcendentalists[11] would we pay heed
save only Prodicus, for his wisdom and wit, and you –
because you strut through the streets, rolling your eyes,
and shoeless put up with much hardship,
and direct at us your haughty gaze.'
(Aristophanes, *The Clouds* 360–64 = A5)

*For this sort of reason Plato is concerned to distance Socrates
from him, making his master adopt an ironic, though generally
affectionate, tone when speaking of him;* Theaetetus *151B is a
case in point (Socrates is talking about young associates whom
he comes to feel he cannot help):*

6. SOCRATES: And that's what happens to these people. But
sometimes, with those whom I don't consider to be mentally
pregnant, as I know that they don't need anything from me, I
try, with all good will, to match them up with someone; and,

God willing, I guess well enough whose company will benefit them. I've handed a number of them over to Prodicus, and many to other wise and inspired men.

(Plato, *Theaetetus* 151B)

He also gets a mention in the Apology, *along with his surviving fellow sophists, incidentally revealing that he was still alive and flourishing in 399:*

7. SOCRATES: As this does actually seem to me to be a fine thing, when someone is able to educate men, just like Gorgias of Leontini, Prodicus of Ceos and Hippias of Elis. For each of them, gentlemen, is able to go into any city and persuade those young men who can associate freely with whichever of their fellow citizens they choose that they should leave this company and associate with them, giving them money and even thanking them as well.

(Plato, *Apology* 19E–20A)

A number of passages throw some light, albeit distorted to varying degrees, on Prodicus' relations with his patrons and pupils. First, Socrates speaking to his follower Antisthenes in Xenophon's Symposium, *commending him, teasingly, as an excellent pander:*

8. 'I know that you acted the pander between Callias here and Prodicus, when you saw that the one had a passion for philosophy and the other needed money. And I know that you introduced him to Hippias of Elis, from whom he learned the art of memorizing . . .'

(Xenophon, *Symposium* 4, 62 = A4a)

Then a passage from Athenaeus' Deipnosophistae, *alluding to a dialogue of Aeschines of Sphettus, another follower of Socrates and younger contemporary of Prodicus:*

9. His [i.e. Aeschines'] *Callias* contains the quarrel between Callias and his father Hipponicus,[12] and abuse of the sophists

Prodicus and Anaxagoras. For he says that Prodicus was to blame for his pupil Theramenes,[13] and the latter for Philoxenus the son of Eryxis[14] and Ariphrades the brother of Arignotus the fiddler, his intention being to show up the kind of instruction given by these teachers from the baseness and itch for depravity in those whom he named.[15]

(Athenaeus, *Deipnosophistae* V 220B = A4b)

Then a report from Dionysius of Halicarnassus, in his Life of Isocrates *(§1) on Isocrates, whom we have already come across as a pupil of Gorgias:*

10. He was a pupil of Prodicus of Ceos and Gorgias of Leontini and Teisias of Syracuse – the men having at the time the greatest fame among the Greeks for (rhetorical) expertise – and, as some report, of Theramenes the rhetorician, whom the Thirty put to death for seeming too democratic.

(Dionysius of Halicarnassus, *Life of Isocrates* 1 = A7)

And lastly, a passage from Aulus Gellius' Attic Nights:

11. Euripides was a pupil of Anaxagoras the natural philosopher and Prodicus the rhetorician, and, in moral philosophy, of Socrates.

(Aulus Gellius, *Attic Nights* XV 20, 4 = A8)

DOCTRINE

*To a large extent all the great sophists taught the same thing – skill in public speaking – but we can discern significant differences of method and of emphasis between them. In the case of Prodicus, though he plainly gave instruction in a wide variety of subjects, there seems to have been a special emphasis on the correct use of words (*orthoepeia*) and fine discrimination between similar words. A number of passages bear on this. First, one from Plato's* Cratylus:

12. SOCRATES: Moreover, the study of names happens to be no trivial matter. So, if I had already heard the fifty-drachma demonstration (*epideixis*) from Prodicus,[16] which he claims will give the listener a sufficient education on this topic, there would be nothing to prevent you[17] from knowing right now the truth about correctness of names. Still, I didn't actually hear that one, but only the one-drachma one.

(Plato, *Cratylus* 384B = 411)

Aristotle also makes reference to the fifty-drachma lecture in the Rhetoric, *suggesting that it contained instructions as to how to arrest your audience's attention:*

13. Moreover, calls for attention, when required, may come equally well in any part of a speech; in fact, the beginning of it is just where there is least slackness of interest. It is therefore ridiculous to put this kind of thing at the beginning, when everyone is listening with most attention. Choose, therefore, any point in the speech where such an appeal is needed, and then say, 'Now I beg you to note this point – it concerns you quite as much as myself' or 'I will tell you something more terrible [or "more astonishing"] than you have ever heard before.' This is the time, as Prodicus said, when your hearers are dozing, to throw in something from the fifty-drachma speech.

(Aristotle, *Rhetoric* III 14, 1415b8–17 = A12)

A testimony from the late rhetorician Marcellinus, in his Life of Thucydides, *confirms what was Prodicus' most distinctive subject of instruction:*

14. For a short time, as Antyllus[18] says, he [i.e. Thucydides] showed an enthusiasm for the balanced clausulae (*parisôseis*) and verbal antitheses practised by Gorgias of Leontini, which were at that time much in vogue among the Greeks; and also the exact definition of words taught by Prodicus of Ceos.

(Marcellinus, *Life of Thucydides* 36 = A9)

Plato, at various points in the dialogues, pokes fun at this characteristic of Prodicus. First, let us take two passages from the Protagoras. *In the first an impasse has been reached between Protagoras and Socrates, and various of those present have intervened with suggestions for a resolution. The last of these has been Plato's cousin Critias (himself no mean sophist, cf. below, Ch. 7). Prodicus is presented as responding to him.*

15. Then Prodicus said, 'I think you speak very well, Critias. For it's necessary that those who attend such a discussion are a *joint* (*koinous*), but not *equal* (*isous*) audience for both speakers – that's not the same thing. For one must listen to both *jointly*, yet not give *equal* credit to each of them, but more to the wiser one and less to the more unintelligent one. Now I myself, Protagoras and Socrates, think that you should agree to *debate* (*amphisbêtein*) with each other about your arguments, but not to *wrangle* (*erizein*) – for friends debate with friends, even through good will, whereas it's those who disagree with and are hostile to each other who wrangle. And it's in this way that we might have the finest meeting, as you the speakers would *gain a* very *good reputation* (*eudokimoite*) amongst us the listeners – yet you would not be *praised* (*epainoisthe*); for gaining a good reputation occurs without deception in the souls of those who listen, but being praised often comes in the words of those who lie, contrary to their true opinion. And again, it's in this way that we the listeners would *derive* maximum *enjoyment* (*euphrainoimetha*), although we would not *feel pleasure* (*hêdoimetha*); for one who derives enjoyment learns something and partakes in wisdom through thought itself, whereas one who feels pleasure eats something or experiences some other pleasure through the body itself.'

(Plato, *Protagoras* 337A–C = A13)

There is certainly a large measure of satire in this portrayal, but it nonetheless points to the type of distinctions that Prodicus liked to make. The same is true of the second passage, which involves Socrates' spoof exegesis of a poem of Simonides. It seems worth quoting this at length, as it satirizes what seems

to have been a favoured sophistic procedure (the 'moralizing'
exegesis of Homer or one of the other poets), as well as
employing Prodican techniques of etymology.

16. [Socrates] 'Then, to tell you the truth, so that I should have
time to consider what the poet might mean, I turned to Prodicus
and, calling on him, I said, 'Prodicus, Simonides was actually a
fellow citizen of yours – so it's right for you to help the man.
And so I am resolved to call for your help . . . for to re-establish
Simonides certainly needs the help of your artistry, with which
you distinguish *wishing* from *desiring*, showing how they are
different; and also those many other fine distinctions which you
made just now.[19] Now consider whether you are in agreement
with me; for Simonides doesn't seem to me to be contradicting
himself. Now, Prodicus, you state your opinion first: do you
think that becoming and being are the same thing or different?'
      'Different, by God,' said Prodicus.
      'So, in the first passage is Simonides not revealing his own
opinion; that it is hard for a man to *become* truly good?'
      'Yes, that's true.'
      'Whereas he reproaches Pittacus,' I said, 'not, as Protagoras
believes, for saying the same things as himself, but for saying
something different. For Pittacus did not say that *becoming*
good is hard – just like Simonides – but *being* good. Now
Protagoras, as Prodicus here says, being and becoming are not
the same thing and, unless being is the same as becoming,
Simonides does not contradict himself. Perhaps Prodicus and
many others might say, along with Hesiod,[20] that it is difficult
to become good,

> For the gods have laid hard labour on the approach to virtue
> But when somebody reaches its summit
> It is then easy to keep, though it was difficult to obtain.'

So Prodicus praised me when he heard this, but Protagoras
said, 'Your correction, Socrates, contains a mistake which is
worse than the one you are correcting.'
      And I replied, 'Then it seems I've done a bad job, Protagoras,

and I am a ridiculous doctor, as I've made the illness worse by curing it.'

'Yes, that's true.'

'How so?'

'The poet would be very ignorant if he says that possessing virtue, which all men consider to be the very hardest thing of all, is some easy matter.'

And I said, 'Yes, by God, it's really opportune that Prodicus here is present in our discussion. Indeed, Protagoras, it's likely that Prodicus' wisdom is something divine and ancient, originating from the time of Simonides, or even earlier.[21] But, although you are skilled in many other areas, you seem to be unskilled in this type of wisdom – you do not share the skill which I possess through studying with Prodicus. So now it seems to me that you don't understand that perhaps Simonides does not understand "hard" just as you understand it; but it's like when Prodicus here reproaches me on every occasion concerning "terrible" (*deinos*): whenever, in praising you or someone else, I say that Protagoras is a terribly wise man, he asks whether I am not ashamed to call good things "terrible". For the terrible, he says, is bad ... So, perhaps again with "hard", the Ceans and Simonides take it to be something bad or some other thing which you don't understand. So, let's ask Prodicus, as it's right to ask him about Simonides' dialect. Prodicus, what did Simonides mean by "hard"?'

He replied, 'Bad.'

'So, it's for this reason, Prodicus,' I said, 'that he blames Pittacus for saying that it is hard to be good; for it's as if he had heard him saying that it is bad to be good.'

(Ibid. 339E–341C = A14, expanded)

This is of course quite absurd, and acknowledged to be so just below, where Socrates ironically suggests that Prodicus must have been joking, but it serves to illustrate another aspect of Prodicus' instruction in orthoepeia, *or the correct use of language. The foolery in Aristophanes'* The Clouds *(658ff.) about correctness in the gender of nouns is very probably also a parody of Prodicus' efforts in this field. We find a number of other*

*significant references to Prodicus in the dialogues. First, a pass-
age from the* Euthydemus, *where the sophist brothers have just
been tying the young Cleinias in knots, by 'proving' to him that
he can learn neither what he knows nor what he does not know,
and Socrates is consoling him, ironically, by explaining that
they are just softening him up with preparatory exercises, 'like
the enthronement of the neophyte in Corybantic rites'.*

17. [Socrates] 'So, now consider that you are hearing the opening
of the sophistic mysteries. For first, as Prodicus says, it's necessary to learn about the correct use of words.[22] Now, that is just
what our two visitors are showing you: that you don't know
that 'learning' (*manthanein*) is what men call it when, on the
one hand, someone who has no knowledge about a particular
thing at the outset then subsequently obtains knowledge of it,
and, on the other hand, they also use this very same term when
someone who already has knowledge uses this knowledge to
examine the same thing. Although they tend to call this "understanding" (*xunienai*), rather than "learning", there are times
when they call it "learning".'

(Plato, *Euthydemus* 277E–278A = A16)

There is another amusing passage in the Laches, *where Socrates
is discussing the nature of bravery (*andreia*) with the distinguished generals Nicias and Laches. Nicias has declared that
bravery is a kind of knowledge (of what is truly to be feared), and
Socrates, quizzing him on this, asks whether he considers that
animals can be brave. In reply to this, Nicias makes a 'Prodican'
distinction between 'bravery' and 'rashness' (*thrasytês*), which
does not require knowledge; whereat Laches jumps on him for
making illegitimate distinctions. Socrates defends him.*

18. [Socrates] 'No, don't say anything, Laches. For you appear
not to have realized that he has acquired this wisdom from our
friend Damon,[23] and that Damon often associates with Prodicus,
who certainly seems to be the best of the sophists at distinguishing such terms.'

(Plato, *Laches* 197B–D = A17)

Also in the Charmides (163B–D), and in the Meno (75E), we find reference made to Prodicus as the author of fine linguistic distinctions; in the former passage between 'doing' (prattein) and 'making' (ergazesthai), in the latter between 'end' (teleutê), 'limit' (peras) and 'last bit' (eschaton) – though it is not clear that Prodicus himself made precisely these distinctions. Aristotle, however, in the Topics (II 6, 112b12ff.) does mention a genuine distinction made by Prodicus – and one of some interest, since it anticipates one made later by the Stoics, when they distinguished 'joy' (chara), as a rational emotion, from the irrational passion 'pleasure' (hêdonê).

19. Furthermore, you must see whether your opponent has stated something as an accidental attribute of itself, taking it as something different because it bears a different name, just as Prodicus divided pleasure (*hêdonê*) into 'joy' (*chara*), 'delight' (*terpsis*) and 'merriment' (*euphrosynê*); for these are all names for the same thing, namely pleasure. If, therefore, anyone should assert that joy is an accidental attribute of merriment, he would be saying that it is an accidental attribute of itself.

(Aristotle, *Topics* II 6, 112b22–8 = A19)

Of course, the fine discrimination of the meanings of similar words could not constitute the whole of a sophist's course of instruction. It is to be regarded rather as Prodicus' trademark, or 'secret weapon', in teaching his charges how to think clearly and speak effectively, and that is why we hear so much about it. Not much else, however, has come down to us, but views of Prodicus are attested on the dangerous question of the origin of religion and the nature of gods, a topic, as we have seen, dealt with also by Protagoras. Indeed, Prodicus would seem to be the true inventor of the theory later attached to the name of Euhemerus, that men originally deified essential aspects of their daily life, such as bread and wine, water and fire, and similarly honoured early inventors of arts and sciences. We have testimonies to Prodicus' theory in various sources, the earliest extant one being Cicero (De Natura Deorum I 37, 118), but we also learn that he was quoted with approval by the early Stoic philosopher Persaeus (fl. c.275 BC), a pupil of Zeno. The testimony occurs in the Epicurean Philodemus' (c.110–35 BC) treatise On Piety.

20. Persaeus appears in reality to be prepared to dispense with a divinity, or at least take up an agnostic position; seeing as, in his treatise *On the Gods*, he says that Prodicus was not unpersuasive in writing that things that provided nourishment or other help to us were the first things to be acknowledged and honoured as gods, and later that persons who first found new means of obtaining food or providing shelter, or invented other arts and crafts were called names like Demeter, Dionysus and the like.

(Philodemus, *On Piety* cols 9, 7, pp. 75–6 Gomperz = B5)

Sextus Empiricus gives some further details.

21. Prodicus of Ceos says that 'the ancients accounted as gods the sun and moon and rivers and springs and in general all things that are of benefit for our life, because of the benefit derived from them, even as the Egyptians deify the Nile.'[24] And he says that it was for this reason that bread was worshipped as Demeter, and wine as Dionysus, and water as Poseidon, and fire as Hephaestus, and so on with each of the things that are good for use.

(Sextus Empiricus, *Against the Mathematicians* IX 18 = B5, continued).

This doctrine on the origins of the gods is doubtless what is being referred to by Aristophanes in The Birds *(produced in 414), when, in the course of the* parabasis, *the birds, in the process of giving their own (spoof-Orphic) version of cosmogony, remark (692): 'Having now learned the truth from us, you can tell Prodicus to go to hell!'*

FRAGMENTS OF KNOWN WORKS

*Only two titles of works by Prodicus have come down to us,
and neither appears, on their face, to have much to do with
grammar or correct usage of words. One is* Horai, *or Seasons,
in which occurred his famous fable of the 'Choice of Heracles',
of which we have an extended account by Xenophon in his*
Memoirs of Socrates *(II 1, 21–34). What the title signifies is
quite uncertain, but perhaps 'addresses, or thoughts, for all
seasons' – or it may have been that the (personified)* Horai
figured in it, in an introductory role.[25] *We know of the title from
a scholion on Aristophanes'* Clouds:

22. There is extant a book of Prodicus entitled *Horai*, in
which he portrayed Heracles interviewed in turn by Virtue
and Vice, each soliciting him to elect the manner of life represented by herself, with Heracles ultimately choosing the hardships offered by the former over the fleeting pleasures promised
by Vice.
   (Scholion, Aristophanes, *The Clouds* 361)

*Of this story of the 'Choice of Heracles' we have an extended
account in Xenophon's* Memoirs of Socrates, *put into the mouth
of Socrates, as part of an exhortation to his follower Aristippus
(later the founder of the Cyrenaic school of hedonist philosophy)
to practise moderation of the passions. From Socrates' method
of introducing it, one might conclude that, while Prodicus had
written this work down, he had not published it, but rather used
it for public recitations. Certainly, what we have does not seem
to be an entirely verbatim quotation, appearing at the outset
not far from Xenophon's normal style, though the employment
of balanced clausulae becomes increasingly noticeable towards
the end. What may after all be the case is that Prodicus, who
survived Socrates, published the work only posthumously, so
that it would be dramatically correct for Socrates only to have
heard it – and for Xenophon to quote it somewhat loosely; but
there is little reason to doubt that we have here, in substance, a*

*genuine piece of Prodicus. In this use of mythological material
for epideictic purposes he is at one with his colleagues Protagoras and Gorgias, as we have seen. The theme he will doubtless
have borrowed from the epic* Judgement of Paris, *giving that a
suitably moralistic twist. Partly, at least, due to this fable
of Prodicus (though the adoption of Heracles as a role model
by Antisthenes, founder of the Cynic movement, would also
have been influential), Heracles becomes a hero for the later
Stoic school.*

23. [Socrates] 'The same view of virtue (*aretê*) is also presented
by the sophist Prodicus in the story of Heracles, which is one of
his most popular display topics (*epideixeis*). It goes like this, as
far as I can recall.

'When Heracles was just developing from childhood towards
manhood, at the age when the young begin to take an independent line, and show whether they are going to turn their lives to
the path of virtue or to that of vice, he went out to a quiet place
and sat down to consider which path he should take. *[22]* While
he was so engaged, he saw, as in a vision, two women approach
him. Both were tall, but one of them was handsome in appearance with a natural air of distinction, her skin adorned with
purity, her eyes with modesty, her figure with self-control and
clad in white garments; while the other was well nourished to
the point of fleshiness and softness, made up to have a com-
plexion both too white and too red to be genuine, and with a
figure more upright than was consistent with nature, the eyes
shamelessly highlighted, and clad in a way that revealed as much
as possible of her charms. She kept on admiring herself, and
watching to see if anyone else was admiring her, and often even
glancing at her own shadow. *[23]* When they came nearer to
Heracles, the first of the two continued to advance in the same
steady way, but the other, wishing to get in ahead of her, ran up
to him and said:

' "I see, Heracles, that you are in doubt as to which way of
life to adopt. If you take me as your friend and follow me, I will
lead you by the most pleasant and easiest road; you will leave
no pleasure untasted, and you will live out your life without any

experience of hardship. *[24]* In the first place, you will not be concerned with wars or public responsibilities, but rather your constant concern will be what food or drink you can find to suit your taste, or what sight or sound might please you, or what scent or touch might delight you; which beloved's society might gratify you most, how you may sleep most softly and how you can achieve all these objects with the least trouble. *[25]* And if there is ever any suspicion of a shortage of any of these benefits, you need not fear that I shall involve you in any physical or mental effort or distress in procuring them; you shall enjoy the fruits of other people's labours, and you shall refrain from nothing from which you can derive any advantage. For I grant my followers permission to draw benefit to themselves from all quarters."

[26] 'When Heracles heard this, he asked, "Lady, what is your name?" She replied, "My friends call me Happiness (*eudaimonia*), but those who dislike me give me the begrudging title of 'Vice' (*kakia*)."

[27] 'Meanwhile, the other woman came forward and said, "I too have come to meet you, Heracles, because I know your parents[26] and have carefully studied your natural qualities in the course of your education, and this has led me to hope that, if you will only take the path that leads to me, you may become an excellent performer of fine and noble deeds, and I may win much greater honour still, and brighter glory for the blessings that I bestow. I will not deceive you with anticipations of pleasure; instead, I shall set out for you truly just how the gods have ordained things to be. *[28]* Of those things that are really good and admirable, nothing is granted by the gods to men without some effort and application. If you want the gods to be gracious to you, you must worship the gods; if you wish to be loved by your friends, you must confer benefits on your friends; if you desire to be honoured by a state, you must be of help to that state; if you expect to be admired for your excellence by the whole of Greece, you must try to benefit Greece. Likewise, if you want your land to produce abundant crops, you must cultivate your land; if you expect to make money from your livestock, you must take care of your livestock; if you have an

urge to extend your influence by war, and want to be able to liberate your friends and subdue your enemies, you must both learn the actual arts of war from those who are expert in them, and practise the proper way of applying them; and if you want to be physically efficient, you must train your body to serve your reason, and exercise it with toil and sweat."

[29] 'Here Vice, as Prodicus tells us, interrupted. "Do you realize, Heracles," she said, "what a long and difficult road to enjoyment this woman has laid out for you? I will lead you by a short and easy road to happiness."

[30] ' "You shameless creature!" said Virtue. "What good have you to offer? Or what do you know of what is really pleasurable, seeing as you will do nothing to earn even that? You don't even wait to feel the desire for what is pleasant, but stuff yourself with everything before you want it, eating before you are hungry and drinking before you are thirsty. To make eating enjoyable you invent refinements of cookery, and to make drinking enjoyable you provide yourself with expensive wines and, in the summer, rush about searching for ice. To make going to sleep pleasant you provide yourself not only with soft blankets, but also with bases for your beds, for it is not work but having nothing to do that makes you want to go to bed. You force the gratification of your sexual desires before they demand it, employing all kinds of devices and treating men as women. That is the sort of training you give to your friends – exciting their passions by night, and putting them to sleep for the best part of the day. [31] Immortal though you are, you have been thrown out by the gods, and you are despised by decent men. You are denied the hearing of the sweetest of all sounds – praise of yourself – and you are denied the seeing of the sweetest of all sights; for you have never beheld any act of yours that was admirable. Who would trust anything you would say? Who would come to your assistance if you needed someone? What person of sound mind would dare to join your band of devotees?

When[27] they are young,
   (your followers) are feeble in body,

and when they get older,
   they are foolish in mind;
in effortless comfort are they maintained in their youth,
but in laborious squalor do they pass their old age,
          disgraced by their past actions
      and   weighed down by their present ones;
for in their youth they have run through all that was pleasant,
and for their old age they have laid up what is hard to bear.

[32] '"I associate with gods, and I associate with good men;
no fine action, human or divine, is done independently of me. I
am held in the highest honour both among gods and among
those men who are akin to me.

      I am a welcome fellow-worker to the craftsman,
         a faithful guardian to the householder,
           a kindly protector to the servant;
     an efficient helper in the tasks of peace,
       a staunch ally in the operations of war,
         and the best partner in friendship.

[33] '"My friends can enjoy food and drink with pleasure
and without effort, because they abstain until they feel a desire
for them. Their sleep is sweeter than the sleep of the easy-living,
and they neither are annoyed when they have to give it up, nor
do they make it an excuse for neglecting necessary tasks.

The young enjoy the praise of their elders,
   and the older people are happy in the respect of the young.
They recall their past achievements with pleasure,
   and rejoice in their present successes,
because through me they are dear to the gods,
         loved by their friends,
     and   honoured by their fatherlands.
And when their appointed end comes,
    they do not lie forgotten in obscurity,
      but flourish celebrated in memory for all time.

'"So, Heracles, child of good parents, if you submit to toil in the way that I have described, you may come to possess the most beatific happiness."'

'That, then, is roughly how Prodicus describes the education of Heracles by Virtue, except that he actually dressed up the sentiments in language still more splendid than I have used now.'

(Xenophon, *Memoirs of Socrates* II 1, 21–34 = B2)

Apart from this display-speech from his work Horai, *we have some evidence, from Cicero and from Galen, of a treatise by Prodicus entitled* On the Nature of Man. *We find brief mentions of such a treatise in Galen,* On the Elements I 9 *(as part of a list of those who wrote treatises* On Nature, *which includes Melissus, Parmenides, Empedocles, Alcmaeon and Gorgias), and another in Cicero,* On the Orator III 32, 128 *(as one of three sophists who have written* On the Nature of Things, *the other two being Thrasymachus and Protagoras). Such a title was, of course, the standard in later ages for the 'book' which early philosophers were credited with, but a further piece of evidence from Galen (*On the Physical Faculties*) seems to put it beyond doubt that Prodicus discoursed on the nature of man. What Galen is here quoting him for, however, is rather his characteristic linguistic nitpicking than any degree of medical expertise.*

24. Prodicus said in his work *On the Nature of Man*, 'Phlegm is that portion of the humours which has been subject to heat and as it were "overcooked". He got at this by deriving the word from the verb "to burn" (*pephlekhthai*),[28] since he tends to use words in special senses, although he keeps the same meaning for the thing itself as do other people. The man's innovative nitpicking attention to words is well enough attested in Plato.[29] On the other hand, that which everyone else calls "phlegm", that is to say the white variety, he calls *blenna* ("mucus"), which, being a cold and damp humour, is found in greatest quantity in the aged and in those who have caught cold

from any cause whatever, and no one in his senses would call
this anything but cold and damp.

   (Galen, *On the Physical Faculties* II 9)

*Other than this, what positions Prodicus may have taken up in
his treatise* On the Nature of Man *we have no idea.*

4 HIPPIAS OF ELIS

*The dates of Hippias' life cannot be fixed with any accuracy,
but he is generally regarded as being the youngest of the great
sophists. In the longer of Plato's dialogues called after him, he
represents himself as being 'much younger' than Protagoras
(below, §7), so we may take it that he was an approximate
contemporary of Socrates (i.e. born about 470 BC). Along with
Protagoras and Prodicus, he figures in Plato's Protagoras, the
dramatic date of which is shortly before the beginning of the
Peloponnesian War (c.433 BC). Like his fellow sophists, he
seems to have been much in demand from his native Elis as an
ambassador, and in that capacity visited many of the states of
Greece, giving lectures and seminars at the same time. Plato, in
the two dialogues bearing his name, presents him, albeit with
heavy irony, as professing a wide variety of arts and sciences:
mathematics, astronomy, music, linguistic science, literature,
handcrafts and mnemonics (which last he seems to have been
the first to develop in a scientific way), and this is confirmed
from such other sources as we have. In the field of mathematics,
he is declared by Proclus (below, §18) to have been the co-
discoverer of the curve known as the quadratrix, which was
used for the trisection of rectilinear angles and for the squaring
of the circle. Very little of anything he wrote has survived, but
we find mention of a Trojan Dialogue, an Elegy (for a boy's
chorus from Messana in Sicily which was drowned) and a List
of Olympic Victors. We have no idea when he died, though a
reference to him in Plato's Apology (19E) – already mentioned
in connection with Prodicus – implies that he was still alive in
399. However, there is a fleeting reference in the Church Father*

*Tertullian (Apology, 46) to his having been killed while organiz-
ing a plot against the state (presumably of Elis). If that has any
substance (Tertullian is hardly a reliable source), he cannot have
lived much past the end of the fifth century, or he would have
been too old, one would think, for any active plotting.*

LIFE AND TEACHING METHODS

*We have various rather miserable biographical notices of him.
First, the entry in the* Suda.

1. Hippias of Elis, son of Diopeithes, sophist and philosopher,
pupil of Hegesidamus who defined the end of life (*telos*) as
self-sufficiency (*autarkeia*).[1] He wrote a great deal.
   (*Suda*, S.V. Hippias = 86A1)

Then a more substantial discussion in Philostratus' Lives of
the Sophists, *though much of the information in it seems to be
borrowed from Plato's* Hippias Major *285Bff. (below, §§9–10).*

2. Hippias of Elis, the sophist, had such powers of memory,
even in his old age, that after hearing up to fifty names only
once he could repeat them in the order in which he had heard
them. He introduced into his discourses discussions on geometry, astronomy, music and rhythms, and he also lectured on
painting and the art of sculpture. These were the subjects that
he dealt with in other parts of Greece, but in Sparta he discoursed
on the different types of state and on the foundations of cities
and their achievements, because the Spartans, owing to their
desire for ruling, took pleasure in this kind of subject-matter.
There is also extant by him a *Trojan Dialogue*, which is not an
oration – Nestor in Troy, after it has been captured, expounds
to Neoptolemus, the son of Achilles, what course he ought to
pursue in order to win a good reputation.[2]
   On behalf of Elis he went on more embassies than any other
Greek, and in no case did he fail to maintain his reputation,
whether by making public speeches or lecturing, and at the same

time he amassed great wealth, and was enrolled in the tribes of cities both great and small.³ In order to make money he even visited Inycus, a small town in Sicily, to whose people Plato makes sarcastic allusion.⁴ Attaining fame, during the rest of his career he charmed the Greeks by such practices as delivering speeches at Olympia, elaborate in subject-matter and carefully crafted. His style was never defective, but copious and natural, and he seldom took refuge in poetical turns of phrase.

(Philostratus, *Lives of the Sophists* I 11, 495 = A2)

A further detail is provided in the Lives of the Ten Orators, *falsely attributed to Plutarch, in connection with the life of Isocrates (839B).*

3. Then (Isocrates) married the daughter of the orator Hippias, Plathanê, who had three sons, one of whom, Aphareus, he adopted.⁵

(Pseudo-Plutarch, *Lives of the Ten Orators* 839B = A3, in part)

A reference in Xenophon's Symposium *(4, 62, quoted earlier in connection with Prodicus (ch. 3, §8 above), credits Socrates' follower Antisthenes with having introduced Hippias as well as Prodicus to the millionaire patron of sophists Callias, son of Hipponicus. At any rate, he is represented as being present at the famous gathering of sophists in Plato's* Protagoras *(314C, 315C, etc.).*

4. [Socrates]: ' "And after him I recognized", as Homer says [*Odyssey* XI 582], "Hippias of Elis, sitting on a chair in the opposite colonnade. And Eryximachus, son of Acumenus,⁶ Phaedrus from Myrrhinus, Andron, son of Androtion, and several foreigners, fellow-citizens of Hippias as well as some others, were sitting around him on benches. They appeared to be asking Hippias certain questions concerning physics and astronomy, while he, sitting on his chair, distinguished and explained to each of them the things which they asked about." '

(Plato, *Protagoras* 315C)

Somewhat later in the dialogue (337C–E), when an impasse
has been reached between Protagoras and Socrates, Hippias
endeavours to patch things up with some well-chosen words,
which may well represent sentiments that he was known for
uttering in real life (this follows directly on a very characteristic
utterance of Prodicus', quoted above, ch. 3, §15).

5. Very many of those present accepted what Prodicus had said.
And, after Prodicus, the wise Hippias said, 'You men who are
present, I think that you are all related and kinsmen and fellow
citizens by nature, not by convention.[7] For like is related to like
by nature, while convention, being a tyrant over men, forces
many things on us which go beyond our nature. So it is shameful
for us to know the nature of things (being wisest amongst the
Greeks, and having gathered together for this very reason at the
central assembly (*prytaneion*)[8] itself of Greek wisdom and here,
at the greatest and most blessed house within this city) and yet,
like the most vulgar of men, to quarrel with each other.'
(Ibid. 337C–E)

However, the most extensive portrayal of Hippias by Plato
occurs, as mentioned above, in the two dialogues called after
him. To get the full flavour of that portrayal, one should really
read the whole of each dialogue,[9] but those passages most likely
to contain factual details are collected here. In general, Plato is
not concerned in these dialogues with expounding any doctrines
of Hippias, but rather with using him as a foil for developing
Socrates' search for definitions (of which Hippias is portrayed
as quite failing to grasp the significance).
First, the opening of the dialogue:

6. SOCRATES: Noble and wise Hippias,[10] what a long time it is
since you've stopped off at Athens.
HIPPIAS: I've not had time, Socrates. For whenever Elis needs
to conduct any affairs with other cities, she always comes to me
first out of all the citizens and chooses me as an ambassador,
considering me to be the ablest judge and messenger of what
each of the cities says. So, very often, I have been on an embassy

to other cities, especially Sparta, on many affairs of great significance.[11] And that's why, in answer to your question, I don't often come here.[12]

SOCRATES: Well, Hippias, that's certainly the occupation of a man who's truly wise and accomplished. For you are able, privately, to take a great deal of money from the young and then provide them with a greater benefit than that which you obtain; while also, in public, you are able to do good for your city, as needs be for one who intends not to be looked down on, but to have a good reputation amongst the masses.

(Plato, *Hippias Major* 281A–C = A6, expanded)

Socrates then goes on to congratulate Hippias ironically on his ability to mix private with public business, 'unlike the wise men of old', and to suggest that, really, those old sages would look rather naive if they were resurrected now. Hippias' reply, blending self-satisfaction with diplomacy, leads to a most interesting passage, comparing him with his rivals:

7. HIPPIAS: Yes, it's just as you say, Socrates. And yet, I'm inclined to praise the ancients and our predecessors before and more than our contemporaries, taking care to avoid the envy of the living, but also the anger of those who have died.[13]

SOCRATES: In my opinion your discussions and thoughts about them are excellent, Hippias. And I am able to testify that you speak the truth, and that your art really has made advances towards being able to deal with public matters at the same time as private. Well, that man Gorgias, the sophist from Leontini, arrived here from his home as an ambassador on public business,[14] since he was the ablest of the men of Leontini at conducting communal affairs, and he seemed to speak excellently in public; yet also, in private, by giving demonstrations (*epideixeis*) and associating with the young men, he made and received a great deal of money from our city. Or take that friend of ours Prodicus[15] – he often went to other places on public business; and the climax was when he recently arrived from Ceos on public business: he spoke in the Council and gained himself a good reputation, while at the same time, through giving private demonstrations and associating with young men, he earned an incredible amount of money. By contrast, none of the men of old ever thought fit to earn a fee of money, nor to give demonstrations of their own wisdom amongst all different peoples; they were so foolish they didn't even realize how valuable money was for them. But both of these men have made more money from their wisdom than any other craftsman from any art whatsoever. And, even before them, there was Protagoras.

HIPPIAS: Socrates, you don't know anything about just how good this is. For if you knew how much money I have made, you'd be amazed. Forget about the other instances; but once, when I came to Sicily,[16] even though the old and distinguished Protagoras was staying there, I, a much younger man, earned more than 150 minae in a short space of time;[17] and also, from one very small place, Inycum, more than 20 minae. And when I came home with this I gave it to my father, so that he and my other fellow citizens were utterly amazed. Now I really think that I have earned more money than whichever two of the sophists you choose.

(Ibid. 282A–E = A9, expanded)

Hippias' visits to the Olympic Games were the subject of much comment. Here is a passage from the Hippias Minor, *of the same dramatic date as the* Hippias Major. *Hippias has just delivered an* epideixis, *in the school of Pheidostratus (cf.* Hippias Major 286B, §9 below),[18] *at the invitation of a certain Eudicus, consisting of an exhortation by Nestor to Achilles' son Neoptolemus, urging him to follow his father's example and to avoid that of Odysseus. This comparison of the characters of Achilles and Odysseus – reminiscent, in its use of mythological subject-matter, of Prodicus'* Choice of Heracles – *probably reflects an actual* epideixis *of Hippias'. Socrates has been listening to this, at Eudicus' invitation, and (naturally) wants to ask Hippias some questions arising out of it.*

8. EUDICUS: But it's clear that Hippias won't begrudge you an answer, if you ask him something. Surely, Hippias, if Socrates asks you something, you'll answer? Won't you?

HIPPIAS: Well, I'd be doing something really terrible if, on this occasion, I evaded Socrates' question, Eudicus, considering that whenever it's the Olympics, I travel to the solemn assembly of the Greeks at Olympia,[19] to the sacred precinct there, from my home at Elis, and present myself at the sanctuary as both a speaker, on whatever subject anyone wishes from those which I have prepared for demonstration, and as ready to answer whatever anyone wishes to ask me.[20]

SOCRATES: Your experiences certainly are blessed, if you arrive at the sanctuary at each Olympiad, feeling so full of good hope for wisdom in your soul. And I'd be amazed if any of the athletes go there to compete with as much fearlessness and confidence in their body as you claim to have in your intellect.

HIPPIAS: Yes, and it's reasonable that I have this experience, Socrates. For, from the time when I began to compete at the Olympics, I have never come across anyone superior to me in anything.[21]

(Plato, *Hippias Minor* 363C = A8, expanded)

In the passage of the Hippias Major *mentioned above we learn more about this* epideixis.

9. HIPPIAS: And by God, Socrates, just recently I've gained a good reputation there,[22] concerning noble pursuits, by giving an explanation of the practices which young men must pursue. I have a thoroughly excellent speech composed on these matters; its style is particularly good. This is the layout and the beginning of the speech: I recount how, when Troy had been captured, Neoptolemus asked Nestor what type of noble pursuits could give the one who practises them a fine reputation, even if he is young. And, in response, Nestor laid out for him a whole collection of very noble customs. This is the speech which I delivered there, and I intend to give it here in two days' time, at the school of Pheidostratus, along with many other points which are worth hearing – Eudicus the son of Apeimantus has requested this. So make sure to be there yourself, and bring some others, any listeners who'll be able to assess what I say.

(Plato, *Hippias Major* 286B = A9)

*We can derive some impression of the full range of Hippias'
professed expertise from a passage of the* Hippias Major
*immediately preceding the above, as well as from another later
in the* Hippias Minor. *Hippias has just been boasting about how
well he gets on with the Spartans, who would be no friends
of the more theoretical aspects of sophistry. We find mention
here of astronomy, mathematical studies, metrics, historical
studies (genealogies and accounts of foundations of cities) and
mnemonics.*

10. SOCRATES: By Heavens, then, Hippias, what sort of thing
is it that they [i.e. the Spartans] praise you for and like to hear?
Or is it obvious that it's those things which you know best,
matters of astronomy and the movements of the heavens?

HIPPIAS: Not in any way – they can't even stand to hear
them.

S: But they like to hear something of geometry?

H: Not at all, as many of them, so to speak, don't even know
how to count!

S: So, they're certainly not going to endure you lecturing on
arithmetic?

H: Certainly not, by God.

S: So it must be those matters of which you give the very
best explanations: the value of letters, syllables, rhythms and
harmonies?[23]

H: My dear man! Harmonies and letters indeed!

S: So what is it, then, that they are glad to hear from you and
praise you for? Tell me yourself, as I can't work it out.

H: They delight to hear about genealogies of heroes and
men, and the founding of cities, how they were established in
antiquity, and, in general, about the whole of antiquity (*archai-
ologia*); so that I am forced to learn it by heart for them, and to
make a very diligent study of all such matters.

S: By God, Hippias, you're lucky that the Spartans don't
rejoice to hear about our archons starting from Solon – you'd
certainly have a job learning that by heart!

H: Why's that, Socrates? I can recall fifty names, when I've
heard them just once.

s: You're right – I wasn't taking account of your mnemonic abilities. So now I understand: probably the Spartans take pleasure in you because of your vast knowledge, and they treat you just like children treat old women, as a source of pleasant stories.

(Ibid. 285B–286A = A11)

In the Hippias Minor *passage, Socrates alludes also to Hippias' remarkable strategy of self-advertisement at the Olympic Games.*

11. SOCRATES: Come on, then, Hippias. Quite simply, in this way examine whether this is true in all of the sciences or not.[24] Certainly you're the wisest man in most of the arts, as I once heard you boasting, when you described your great and enviable wisdom in the agora, by the bankers' tables. You claimed that you once arrived at Olympia with only those things on your person that you had made yourself.[25] First – you began with this – the ring which you had was your own work, as you knew how to engrave rings, and another seal was your work, and an oil-flask and strigil, which you made yourself. Then you claimed that you yourself had cobbled the shoes which you wore, and that you had woven your cloak and tunic. And then – it's this that everybody thought was the most remarkable thing and clear evidence of superlative wisdom – you claimed that the girdle which you wore on your tunic was of the same type as the most expensive Persian girdles, but that you had woven it yourself. In addition to all this, you said that you had come bringing poems, epics, tragedies and dithyrambs, and a whole number of varied prose writings; and that you had arrived as the pre-eminent expert concerning both those matters which I mentioned just now, and the correctness of rhythms, harmonies and letters, and, as well as these, many other matters, as I seem to recall. But still, I seem to have forgotten your skills of memory, in which field you consider yourself to be truly outstanding; and I think I've forgotten all sorts of other things as well!

(Plato, *Hippias Minor* 368B–D = A12)

This is more or less all the information we have on Hippias' life and attainments. There is a protracted passage of Xenophon's Memoirs of Socrates (IV 4, 5–25), where Hippias is represented in conversation with Socrates, but in fact Socrates does most of the talking, and no distinctive doctrine is attributed to Hippias, so it is not worth quoting here.[26] It is not easy to see, in fact, why Xenophon introduced him in the first place.

REFERENCES TO IDENTIFIED WORKS

As mentioned in the introductory section, we know of the names of a few compositions by Hippias, but no fragment is preserved of any of them.

First, the Elegy *which he composed on a boys' chorus from Messana in north-eastern Sicily, which was drowned in crossing over the straits to perform in Rhegion, on the mainland opposite. This was composed to be inscribed on a monument in their memory dedicated by the city of Messana at Olympia. The second-century* AD *travel-writer Pausanias gives us the details.*

12. On that occasion the Messanians went into mourning for the loss of the boys, and, among other works carried out in their honour, they dedicated bronze statues of them at Olympia, together with their chorus-director and flute-player. The original inscription showed that they were dedications from the Messanians on the straits, but later on, Hippias, the well-known Greek wise man, composed the elegiac verses on them. The statues are the work of Kalôn of Elis.

(Pausanias, *Guide to Greece* V 25, 4)

We also find mention (in a scholion on Apollonius of Rhodes' Argonautica, *III 1179) of a work on the names of tribes, or nations (*Ethnôn Onomasiai*), in which Hippias listed an* ethnos *called* Spartoi, *'the Sown Men'. In the context, which is a mention of Cadmus and the origin of the dragon's teeth which Aeetes is providing for Jason to sow, this might reasonably be thought to refer to the well-known 'Sown Men' of Thebes, but* *we cannot be sure that Hippias was not adducing some other more obscure tribe of the same name.*

Another similar work was his List of Olympic Victors, *about which Plutarch, at the beginning of his* Life of Numa, *makes the following rather dismissive remark:*

13. Chronology, however, is hard to fix, and especially that which is based on the names of victors in the Olympic Games, the list of which is said to have been published at a late stage[27] by Hippias of Elis, who had no properly authoritative basis for his work.

(Plutarch, *Life of Numa* 1)

And lastly, a work with the implausibly vague title of Synagôgê *(*Collection*). All we know of this (from Athenaeus'* Deipnosophistae*) is that it included a reference to a woman of remarkable beauty, Thargelia of Miletus.[28] What the book was a 'collection' of is hard to conjecture.*

14. Among women famous for their beauty was Thargelia of Miletus, who had been married fourteen times, and who was very beautiful in looks as well as clever, according to the sophist Hippias in his work entitled *Collection*.

(Athenaeus, *Deipnosophistae* XIII 608F)

REFERENCES TO UNIDENTIFIED WORKS

A passage from an unidentified work, but possibly from the introduction to this Synagôgê, *is quoted by Clement of Alexandria in his* Stromateis.

15. Come then, let us adduce the witness of the sophist Hippias of Elis, who made the same statement regarding the question before me,[29] writing as follows:

'Of these things some may have been said by Orpheus, some by Musaeus briefly in various places, some by Hesiod and Homer, some by other poets, others in prose works of Greek

and non-Greek writers; but by putting together the most significant and kindred items, I shall compose a discourse that is both
new and varied.'

(Clement of Alexandria, *Stromateis* VI 15)

*Other than this, we have intriguing references in various authors
to snippets of information by Hippias on various matters mythical, historical or geographical, thus giving us some insight into
the sort of discourses he delivered – particularly in places such
as Sparta, which liked 'hard facts' and distrusted rhetoric (cf.
§10 above). In many cases, a second authority is referred to
along with Hippias, which would suggest that this second authority is the original source for the reference to Hippias.*

*Diogenes Laertius quotes Hippias, along with Aristotle, as
an authority for the assertion that:*

16. Thales ascribed soul even to inanimate things, arguing from
the magnet and from amber.[30]

(Diogenes Laertius, *Lives of the Philosophers* I 24 = B7
D–k)

Proclus, in his Commentary on the First Book of Euclid, *after
crediting Thales with first introducing geometry into Greece,
records that:*

17. After him, Mamercus, brother of the poet Stesichorus, is
mentioned as having applied himself to the study of geometry;
and Hippias of Elis records that he acquired a reputation in it.

(Proclus, *Commentary on the First Book of Euclid*, p. 65,
11–14 Friedlein = B12)

*Another passage of Proclus' Commentary testifies to an impress-
ive degree of proficiency in geometry on Hippias' part. Proclus
is discussing the problem of the trisection of an angle:*

18. Nicomedes[31] made use of conchoids – a form of line whose
construction, kinds and properties he has taught us, being himself the discoverer of their peculiarities – and thus succeeded

in trisecting the rectilinear angle generally. Others have done the same thing by means of the quadratrix of Hippias and that of Nicomedes, they too using mixed lines, namely the quadratrices.[32]

(*Ibid.* p. 272, 3–10 Friedlein)

Turning to a geographical detail, the twelfth-century AD commentator Bishop Eustathius of Thessalonica tells us that:

19. Hippias derives the names of the continents (sc. Asia and Europe) from Asia and Europa, the daughters of Oceanus.

(Eustathius, *Paraphrasis of Dionysius Periegetes* 270 = B8)

We also learn from a scholion on Aratus, Phaenomena *172 (p. 369, 27 Maass = B13) that Hippias and Pherecydes declared that the group of stars known as the Hyades (normally reckoned to be five) were seven in number; and from a scholion on Pindar,* Nemean *7, 38 (where Pindar has just talked of Neoptolemus coming to Ephyre in Thesprotia = B15), that Hippias mentions an Ephyre in Elis – perhaps in some patriotic connection.*

The second hypothesis to Sophocles' Oedipus the King *(= B9) contributes the following detail of terminology (apropos the Greek title of the play* Oidipous Tyrannos*):*

20. The poets after Homer have adopted a peculiar usage in referring to the kings before the Trojan War as 'tyrants' (*tyrannoi*). For this term was passed on to the Greeks rather late, in the time of Archilochus, as the sophist Hippias says. Homer, at any rate, calls Echetus, who was the most lawless of all of them, not a 'tyrant', but a 'king':

   to King Echetus, the bane of mortals [*Odyssey* 18.85]

It is said that the word 'tyrant' is derived from the name 'Tyrrhenians', for they were notoriously troublesome as pirates.[33]

(Hypothesis in Sophocles, *Oedipus Tyrannus*)

Next a snippet of historical information that would have gone down well in Sparta, from Plutarch's Life of Lycurgus, *perhaps*

*derived from some work of Hippias on chronology, or on consti-
tutions:*

21. Hippias the sophist says that Lycurgus himself was of a
warlike disposition and experienced in many campaigns.
    (Plutarch, *Life of Lycurgus* 23 = B11)

*Then a detail related to mythology, again from a scholion on
Pindar:*

22. Pindar in his *Hymns* says that the stepmother of Phrixus
was Demodice, but Hippias says that her name was Gorgopis.[34]
    (Scholion, Pindar, *Pythian* 4, 242 = B14)

*Lastly, some snippets of a more linguistic nature, somewhat akin
to the concerns of Prodicus. First, a detail from the surviving
summary of the* Attikistês *of the second-century AD grammarian
Phrynichus:*

23. They say that Hippias and a writer named Ion[35] used the
term *parathêkê* (for 'deposit'). We prefer to say *parakatathêkê*,
following Plato, Thucydides and Demosthenes.
    (Phrynichus, *Attikistes* p. 312 Lobeck = B10)

Then two reports from an essay of Plutarch's On Slander, *of
which only fragments are preserved. They may have formed
part of an ethical discourse.*

24. Hippias say that there are two kinds of envy (*phthonos*) – the
just, when one envies or begrudges bad men their honours, and
the unjust, when one envies the good. And envious persons suffer
twice as much as those who are not, since they resent not only
their own troubles, like others, but also other men's prosperity.
    (Stobaeus, *Anthology* III 38, 32 = Plutarch, *Fragments* 155
    Sandbach = B16)

25. Hippias says that slander (which he calls *diabolia*) is a
dreadful thing, because there is no penalty described in the laws

for slanderers as there is for thieves. Yet they steal the best of possessions, friendship, so that violence (*hybris*), damaging though it is, is more honest than slander, because it is not underhand.

(Stobaeus, *Anthology* III 42, 10 = Plutarch, *Pragments* 156 Sandbach = B17)

5 ANTIPHON[1]

An adequate treatment of Antiphon of Rhamnus, the only Athenian among the major sophists (apart from the ambiguous figure of Plato's cousin Critias, who will be dealt with below, ch. 7) is made difficult by uncertainty as to how many Antiphons we are actually faced with. The author of the Tetralogies and of certain forensic speeches, who can probably be identified with the anti-democratic politician who masterminded the establishment of the regime of the Four Hundred in 411 BC, and who was condemned to death and executed by the restored democracy as a result, has been distinguished by some from the author of the treatises On Truth and On Concord (which two treatises have also been thought by some to have different authors). But there are also in the picture the following: a good democrat who was executed by the Thirty in 403, and for whose daughter the orator Lysias wrote a speech;[2] a tragic poet who fell foul of the tyrant Dionysius the Elder of Syracuse, and was executed by him (some time in the early fourth century); a diviner and dream-interpreter, who wrote a book on the latter subject; and an individual who set up a psychiatric clinic in Corinth (probably in the mid-fifth century). We are persuaded that at least the two 'main' Antiphons can in fact be accommodated within the same skin, despite the palpable differences in style between the forensic speeches and the Tetralogies[3] and the On Truth or the On Concord. As we have seen in the case of Gorgias, a master of style can change his style to suit the subject-matter. As for the diviner and the psychiatrist, we have grave doubts that they can be accommodated, but many authorities accept them, so it seems best to include them, with due caution.[4]

Our Antiphon, then, is an Athenian, son of Sophilus, of the deme Rhamnus. He is said by Caecilius of Caleacte (reflected in the reports of Hermogenes of Tarsus, Pseudo-Plutarch, Philostratus, Photius and the anonymous Life *prefixed to his speeches in the manuscripts, see §§2–4 below) to have been a little younger than Gorgias, which would seem to imply a birth-date in the early to mid-470s. He would thus be a slightly older contemporary of Socrates, with whom Xenophon represents him in conversation (Memoirs of Socrates I 6 = §9). His father ran a school, and is said to have been his first teacher. Though undoubtedly influenced in later life by Gorgias, Antiphon may be credited with being the pioneer of the art of rhetoric at Athens, both through his teaching and through his writings. He also seems to have pioneered the art of speech-writing, and his three surviving forensic speeches (which will not be included in this volume, as not being properly sophistic productions) have a claim to be among the earliest examples of Attic prose, while his three* Tetralogies *constitute a most interesting example of the tools of rhetorical instruction.*

He was also active in politics, in the conservative interest, and became prominently involved in the anti-democratic coup of 412, which established the regime of the Four Hundred – which in turn led, as mentioned above, to his being executed by the restored democracy in 411.

LIFE AND WORKS

First, a confused and confusing sequence of biographical notices in the Suda, *listing three different Antiphons, all of whom are possibly the same man.*

1. (a) Antiphon, an Athenian, diviner[5] (*teratoskopos*) and epic poet and sophist. He was given the nickname of 'speech-cook' (*logomageiros*).

(b) Antiphon, son of Sophilus, an Athenian, of the deme of Rhamnus. No teacher of him is known.[6] Nevertheless, he embarked on the forensic type of speech after Gorgias. He is

said actually to have been the teacher of Thucydides. He was
given the nickname of 'Nestor'.

(c) Antiphon, an Athenian, an interpreter of dreams. He wrote
a book on the interpretation of dreams.

(*Suda*, s.v. Antiphon = 87A1)

*This is very minimal, but we have a number of more copious
sources, all probably dependent on a life of Antiphon which we
know to have been composed in the first century BC by the
rhetorician Caecilius of Caleacte. First, that of the second-
century AD rhetorician Hermogenes of Tarsus.*

2. When one comes to speak of Antiphon, one must first remark
that, as Didymus the grammarian[7] and several others have
noted, and in addition to that from what one can discover
oneself, there would seem to have existed a number of Antiphons, two of whom practised the art of sophistry, and therefore
fall within our purview. One of these is the rhetorician who
composed the murder speeches[8] and public addresses and others
of this sort.[9] The other is the so-called diviner and interpreter of
dreams, to whom are said to belong the books *On Truth* and
On Concord and the *Politikos*.[10]

I must confess myself in something of a quandary on this
matter. On the one hand, the difference of genres tends to
persuade me that there were two Antiphons; for really there is
a great discrepancy between *On Truth* and the other books. But
on the other hand the testimony of Plato[11] and other authors
tells in the other direction; for I am told by many that Thucydides
was a pupil of Antiphon of Rhamnus, and while I know that it
is to the Rhamnusian that the forensic speeches belong, I am
also conscious that Thucydides has a very different style from
him, and one that has much in common with the treatise *On
Truth*. So I am not convinced by Didymus.

Nonetheless, whether there is just one Antiphon, employing
two styles differing so radically as they do from one another, or
in fact two, each practising a different style, we must deal
with each separately; for there is, as I have said, a pronounced
distinction between them.[12]

The Antiphon from Rhamnus, then, of whom we have the forensic speeches, while showing political acumen in the clarity and practicality and, in other respects, the expressive quality of his style, all of which contribute to persuasiveness, nevertheless shows these qualities to a lesser degree than the other orators – for he is, of course, the first to have pursued this kind of speaking, and is the absolute inventor and originator of the political genre of oratory, being chronologically the eldest of all the ten orators. He employs grand language to a large extent, but yet in a rather fine way this grand language is worked into the context of the speech, and does not seem out of place, as in the case of Hyperides, nor, as in the case of Aeschines, is his language sophistically elaborated, although his style is often high-flown; yet he takes care not to let it bore the reader. Nevertheless, his style is rather forbidding, albeit clever at the same time.

The other Antiphon, on the other hand, to whom is attributed the book *On Truth*, is not at all political, but comes across as grand and pompous, particularly in his way of dealing with every question by categorical assertions, characteristic of a style which is dignified and aiming at grandeur; but he is lofty in his diction and rough, so as to end up not far from harshness, and he indulges in amplifications without achieving clarity, so as to confuse his argument and to be generally obscure. But he is at the same time painstaking in his composition, and takes delight in the even balancing of clauses (*parisôsis*). It is not, however, the case that the author possesses expressive character (*êthos*) or true quality, and I would not say either that he is endowed with cleverness (*deinotês*), except of a superficial kind which is not really cleverness at all. Critias, too, is similar to him in style; and for this reason we will discuss Critias immediately after him.[13]

(Hermogenes of Tarsus, *Peri Ideôn*, B399, 18 Rabe)

A rather fuller account, also dependent on Caecilius of Caleacte, is to be found in the Lives of the Ten Orators, *falsely attributed to Plutarch, but probably of the first or second centuries AD.*

3. Antiphon was the son of Sophilus, of the deme of Rhamnus. He studied under his father (for he was a sophist, with whom

Alcibiades also is said as a boy to have studied), and having achieved competence in speaking – as some consider, through his own natural ability – he entered upon a political career. He set up a school (*diatribê*), and engaged in a dispute with Socrates on the subject of words, not in a spirit of contention, but in that of dialectical inquiry, as Xenophon presents it in his *Memoirs of Socrates*.[14] And he composed some speeches for citizens who requested them for their contests in the law-courts, being the first who turned to this profession, according to some authorities. At any rate, no forensic oration is attested for any of those who came before him, nor for his contemporaries either, because it had not yet become the custom to write speeches; there is none by Themistocles, Aristides or Pericles, although their circumstances provided them with many demands and also occasions for such speeches. And it was not by reason of incompetence that they failed to compose such speeches, as is plain from what is said by the historians about each of the above-mentioned statesmen. Yet all those whom we are able to record as having practised this kind of speech, going back to the earliest times, will be found to have had some contact with Antiphon when he was already old; I mean people like Alcibiades, Critias, Lysias and Archinus.[15] He was also the first to publish manuals of rhetoric (*rhêtorikai tekhnai*), being a man of acute intelligence; and for this reason he was given the nickname of 'Nestor'.

Caecilius, in his treatise about him, deduces, from the terms in which Antiphon is praised in the works of the historian Thucydides, that he was the latter's teacher.[16] In his speeches, he is accurate and persuasive, clever in invention and ingenious in presenting difficult cases; he tends to take an unexpected line, and he aims his arguments at both the laws and the emotions, aiming above all at what is suitable to each occasion.

He was born at the time of the Persian wars and of the sophist Gorgias, than whom he was somewhat younger;[17] and his life extended until the dissolution of the democracy by the Four Hundred,[18] in causing which he seems himself to have had a part, at one time by being a trierarch of two ships, at another by being general and gaining many victories for the Four Hundred, by arming men of military age and by manning sixty

triremes, and by being on every occasion their envoy to Lacedaemon at the time when Eëtioneia had been fortified.[19] And after
the Four Hundred were overthrown he was indicted, along with
Archeptolemus, one of the Four Hundred, and was condemned;
being subjected to the penalties prescribed for treason, he was
thrown out unburied, and posted up as an outlaw, along with
his descendants . . .[20]

There are extant sixty orations ascribed to this orator, twenty-
five of which Caecilius declares to be spurious. He is mocked
for his love of money by Plato in his *Peisander*[21] . . .[22] He
composed a manual for the cure of grief (*tekhnê alypias*), on the
analogy of the treatment of the sick by doctors and, getting
himself a dwelling (*oikêma*) in Corinth near the market-place,
he advertised that he was able to cure those suffering from grief
through the power of words (*logoi*); and discovering the causes
of their sickness by inquiry he gave consolation to sufferers. But
he came to consider the art beneath his dignity, and turned
instead to rhetoric.[23] He is commended most for his oration
concerning Herodes, that against Erasistratus about the pea-
cocks, that on the indictment (*eisangelia*), which he wrote in his
own defence, and that against the general Demosthenes for
making an illegal motion in the assembly. He wrote also a
speech against the general Hippocrates and caused him to be
convicted by default.[24]

(Pseudo-Plutarch, *Lives of the Ten Orators* 832B–834B)

*The account of his life and works here presented, derived from
Caecilius of Caleacte, is to be found also in two other sources,
the* Bibliotheca *of Photius, the learned patriarch of Constanti-
nople, composed around AD 858 (codex 259, p. 485b9ff.), and
in the life of Antiphon prefixed to his works in the manuscript
tradition, but, although neither of these texts is obviously dependent on Pseudo-Plutarch,[25] they contain nothing different of
any significance, so we merely note them. The evidence of Philostratus, however, in his* Lives of the Sophists, *though also probably dependent on Caecilius, does seem worth including, if only
for the literary reflections with which he adorns his narrative.
Philostratus accepts without question the identification of the*

*orator and politician with the sophist, but he also tries to weave
in not only the psychiatrist in Corinth, but even the tragic poet
executed by Dionysius of Syracuse – which latter, at least, says
little for his judgement.*

4. *[498]* As for Antiphon of Rhamnus, I am not sure whether
he ought to be called a good or a bad man. On the one hand, he
may be called a good man, for the following reasons. He was
very often appointed a general, and very often won victories; he
increased the Athenian navy by sixty fully equipped triremes;[26]
he was regarded as the most capable man of his time, both in
the art of speaking and in originality of invention. On these
grounds, then, he deserves praise from me or any other. On the
other hand, he could be regarded as a bad man for the following
reasons: he overthrew the democracy; he enslaved the Athenian
people; he was a partisan of Sparta, secretly at first, but openly
later on; and he let loose on the Athenian political scene the
mob of the Four Hundred Tyrants.

Some say that Antiphon invented the art of rhetoric when it
did not exist before him, others that it was already invented, but
that he developed it; some say that he was self-taught in his art,
others that he owed it to his father. For they say his father was
Sophilus, who was a teacher of rhetoric, and educated the son
of Cleinias,[27] as well as other prominent individuals. Antiphon
developed great powers of persuasion, acquiring the nickname
'Nestor' because of his capacity to convince his audience, on
whatever topic; and he announced a course of 'grief-assuaging'
lectures (*nêpentheis akroaseis*), asserting that no one could
tell him of a grief so terrible that he could not root it out of
the mind.[28]

[499] Antiphon is lampooned by the comic poets for his
cleverness in forensic pleading, and for charging large sums of
money, particularly to clients who were under indictment,[29] for
composing speeches to frustrate the course of justice. I should
make clear what is involved here.[30] In the case of other sciences
and arts, men honour those who have excelled in any of these
areas; for instance, they respect doctors who are skilful more
than those who are less skilful, while in the arts of divination

and music they admire whoever is more expert, and for carpentering and all the vulgar crafts they cast the same sort of vote; only in the case of rhetoric, even as they praise it, they distrust it as being crooked and mercenary and dedicated to the frustration of justice. And it is not only the general public who have such a view of this art, but also the most distinguished members of society. At any rate, they call 'clever rhetoricians' those who demonstrate a degree of skill in invention and exposition, thus bestowing upon such excellence a thoroughly ill-sounding epithet. This being the case, it was only to be expected, I think, that Antiphon, like the rest, should become a butt of comedy; for it is just things that are notable that comedy holds up to mockery.

[*Philostratus, like all the other sources dependent on Caecilius, now relates the story of the tragic poet who fell foul of Dionysius I, expatiating on the moral of the story at some length. He then concludes:*]

A good many of his legal speeches survive, and in them his rhetorical power (*deinotês*) and all the aspects of the art are manifest.[31] There are also others of a sophistic type, but more sophistic than any is the speech *On Concord*, in which are brilliant and profound maxims and elevated diction, adorned, moreover, with poetical language; and their diffuse style makes them resemble the smoothness of a plain.

(Philostratus, *Lives of the Sophists* I 15)

An anecdote concerning his speech in his own defence is relayed to us by Aristotle in the Eudemian Ethics, *in connection with his analysis of 'great-spiritedness' (*megalopsychia*), betokening considerable sympathy on Aristotle's part for Antiphon.*

5. And a great-spirited man would consider more what one virtuous man thinks than what many ordinary men think, as Antiphon after his condemnation said to Agathon[32] when he praised his speech for his defence.

(Aristotle, *Eudemian Ethics* III 5, 1232b6–9)

ANTIPHON AS TEACHER

Plato allows Socrates, in the Menexenus, *to make mention of Antiphon as a teacher of rhetoric (though ranking him, with his usual irony, as inferior to his own teacher, whom he claims to have been Aspasia, the mistress of Pericles). Despite the wild anachronisms contained in Socrates' speech, the dialogue is supposed to take place during the lifetime of Aspasia, so probably in the 420s, and thus attests to Antiphon's activity as a teacher of rhetoric in this period.*

6. 'So it is not surprising that a man who is trained like me should be clever at speaking. But even a man less well taught than I, who had learned his music from Lamprus and his rhetoric from Antiphon the Rhamnusian – even such a one, I say, could nonetheless win credit by praising Athenians before an Athenian audience.'

(Plato, *Menexenus* 236A)

Cicero, in the Brutus, *attests to the fact that Aristotle included Antiphon in his history of rhetoric[33] (we give here a continuation of the passage quoted above in ch. 2, §25).*

7. Antiphon of Rhamnus produced similar writings [i.e. to those of Gorgias], concerning whom we have the trustworthy assurance of Thucydides that no man ever pleaded his case better, when in his hearing Antiphon defended himself on a capital charge.[34]

(Cicero, *Brutus* 12, 47)

Antiphon is linked significantly with Thrasymachus and Theodorus of Byzantium (both of whom figure in Socrates' ironic survey of the masters of rhetorical theory in Phaedrus *266Cff.) by Dionysius of Halicarnassus, in his* Letter to Ammaeus, *as part of an historical argument to prove that Demosthenes was not dependent on the precepts of Aristotle's* Rhetoric, *as some foolish contemporary Peripatetic had apparently claimed.*

8. This I have done, my excellent Ammaeus, both out of a concern for the truth, which I think should be the aim of every inquiry, and for the edification of all those who are seriously committed to study of political oratory. It is important that they should not assume that all the principles of rhetoric are covered in Peripatetic philosophy, and that nothing significant has been discovered by Theodorus, Thrasymachus, Antiphon and their associates . . .

(Dionysius of Halicarnassus, *First Letter to Ammaeus* 2)

Lastly, we have the portrayal of him by Xenophon in his Memoirs of Socrates, *where Xenophon alleges that he was trying to attract the followers of Socrates away to himself. If Xenophon is being honest in claiming that he was present at these exchanges (he lists three separate confrontations), it must date from Antiphon's last years, since Xenophon was only born c.430 BC. The account, it must be said, is not of as much relevance as one would like, since it tells a good deal more about Socrates than it does about Antiphon, but it seems worth including nonetheless.*

9. *[1]* It is befitting to Socrates not to pass over the conversations that he had with Antiphon the sophist. On one occasion, this man, wishing to seduce Socrates' associates (*synousiastai*) over to himself,[35] accosted him in their presence and said: *[2]* 'Socrates, I always thought that those who practised philosophy ought to become happier by reason of that,[36] but it seems to me that you have derived the opposite result from it. At any rate, you lead the sort of life that no slave would tolerate, if imposed on him by his master. The food and drink you consume is of the worst possible kind, and the cloak you wear is not only of wretched quality, but is the same summer and winter; and you are always without shoes or tunic. *[3]* Then, you never take money, which is cheering to those who possess it, and which allows people to live with more freedom and pleasure. So if you are going to influence your associates in the same way as the teachers of other skills, who seek to produce pupils after their own model, you should consider yourself a teacher of misery (*kakodaimonia*).'

[4] To this Socrates replied: 'You seem to have persuaded yourself, Antiphon, that I live such a miserable life that I am persuaded that you would rather die than live like me. Come on, then: let us consider what you see as so harsh about my way of life. *[5]* Is the problem that those who accept money are stuck with performing the service for which they've been paid, whereas I, since I don't take money, am not constrained to discourse with anyone that I don't wish to? Or do you turn up your nose at my diet on the ground that I eat food less wholesome than you do, and less productive of vigour? Is it that my means of subsistence are more difficult to get hold of than yours, as being rarer and more expensive? Is it that you enjoy your provisions more than I do mine? Don't you know that that man eats most pleasantly who least desires sauces to spice up his food, and that he most enjoys drinking who craves the least for a drink that he hasn't got?[37] . . . *[10]* You seem to me, Antiphon, to consider happiness to reside in luxury and extravagance; but I have always thought that to need nothing is divine, and to need as little as possible is the nearest thing to the divine; and that the divine is best, and what is nearest to the divine is nearest to the best.'

[11] And another time again, when Antiphon was conversing with Socrates, he said: 'Socrates, I certainly consider you a righteous man, but not at all a wise one. And you actually seem to me to recognize this yourself; at least, you don't charge anyone money for consorting with you. And yet if you thought that your cloak or your house or any other bit of your property was worth money, rather than giving it away free, you wouldn't even take a price for it less than its value. *[12]* So it's plain that if you thought that your company was worth anything, you would demand for that nothing less than its value. You may therefore be honest, since you don't try to make a profit by false pretences; but wise you surely are not, seeing as your knowledge is worth nothing.'

[13] To this Socrates replied: 'Amongst us,[38] Antiphon, the same standards in respect of what is honourable and what is shameful are thought to apply equally to the disposal of physical beauty and of wisdom. Someone who sells his youthful beauty

to anyone who wants it is called a prostitute; but if one contracts a friendship with someone whom he knows to be of excellent character, we consider him to be acting with prudence. And similarly in the case of wisdom, those who sell it to anyone who wants it are called sophists; but if anyone makes a friend of one whom he knows to be naturally gifted by sharing any worthwhile knowledge that he happens to have, we consider that he is doing what an upright citizen should. *[14]* And as for myself, Antiphon, I must say that, even as other people take pleasure in a good horse or dog or bird, I take as much pleasure, or even more, in good friends, and if I have anything good to impart, I let them know of it, and I put them in touch with any others from whom I think they will get any assistance towards the acquisition of excellence. And together with my friends, I unroll and read through the books in which the wise men of past times have written down and left to us their treasures; and anything we see that is good, we pick out for ourselves; and we regard it as a great benefit that we have become friends with one another.'

To me, as I heard him say this, it certainly seemed that he was himself a man blessed with good fortune, and that he was leading his hearers on towards true nobility.

[15] And then again, when Antiphon asked him how he expected to make others into successful politicians when he himself, in spite of this presumed expertise of his, did not take part in public affairs,[39] Socrates replied: 'Which way, Antiphon, would I more effectively practise politics – by doing so on my own, or by seeing to it that as many people as possible are made capable of practising it?'

(Xenophon, *Memoirs of Socrates* I 6 = A3)

Aristotle, in his lost dialogue On Poets,[40] *confuses the issue by seeming to identify the protagonist of the foregoing conversations with Socrates as 'Antiphon the diviner' (teratoskopos, cf. §1a above). Aristotle is not necessarily referring to this passage of Xenophon, but that does not dissolve the problem, since Xenophon himself may be reflecting a well-known confrontation. It may be best after all to accept that 'our' Antiphon also professed himself a* teratoskopos. *But if so, why not also a dream-interpreter (cf. §1c above) and even a psychiatrist?*

10. He [sc. Socrates] was argued against contentiously, according to Aristotle in the third book of his treatise *On Poetry*, by Antilochus of Lemnos and by Antiphon the diviner, just as Pythagoras was by Cylon of Croton . . .
    (Aristotle, Fr. 75 Rose)

ANTIPHON AS POLITICIAN

Assuming the identity of sophist and politician, we may adduce the testimony of Thucydides and others to his political prowess and tendencies. First, Thucydides.

11. The man who made this proposal [i.e. for the setting up of the Five Thousand], and who in all other respects was most conspicuous and enthusiastic in contriving the dissolution of the democracy, was Peisander. However, the individual who put together the whole project so as to bring it to fruition, and who devoted the most thought to it, was Antiphon. He was a man second to none among the Athenians of his time in ability (*aretê*), being pre-eminent both in intellectual power and in capacity for self-expression. He did not willingly put himself forward either in the public assemblies or in any other forum of debate, but was regarded with suspicion by the mass of the people because of his reputation for cleverness. However, if anyone was involved in a contest either in the law-courts or in the political arena, he was the man who was able to give the best and most helpful advice to those who sought it. And when the democracy was restored and the regime of the Four Hundred[41] was put on trial, and he himself was brought to ruin and given harsh treatment by the people,[42] of all those who up to my time have been accused on the same grounds, he seems to me to have given the best account of himself when on trial for his life.
    (Thucydides, *History of the Peloponnesian War* 8, 68)

*Aristotle also speaks with respect of Antiphon, as one would
expect, in his account of the establishment of the regime of the
Four Hundred.*

12. In this way, therefore, the oligarchy was set up, in the
archonship of Callias (412/11 BC), about a hundred years after
the expulsion of the tyrants, the chief movers being Peisander,
Antiphon and Theramenes, men of good birth and of distinguished reputation for wisdom and judgement.

　　(Aristotle, *Athenian Constitution* 32.2)

FRAGMENTS OF KNOWN WORKS

On Truth

*This work comprised two books. The overall thrust of it seems
to have been to demonstrate that reality, or 'truth' (alêtheia),
does not lie on the surface of things – in what is accessible
to the senses, or within the ambit of conventional belief – but
is often in conflict with this. However, it must be said that it is
not always easy to accommodate the surviving fragments to
this position. The first book seems to concern primarily
epistemological or ethical questions (the reality of time, the
construction of the circle, the nature of justice, the reality of
the distinction between Greek and non-Greek), while the
second seems to have dealt with the creation of the world and
of living things, though with what relevance is often far
from clear.*

*First, a general characterization of the tendency of the work,
admittedly from a thoroughly tendentious source, the Church
Father Origen, in his treatise* Against Celsus. *However, despite
its rhetorical content, it does testify both to the continuing
reputation of Antiphon (here plainly regarded as both sophist
and politician/speech-writer), and to the impression given of the
overall theme of the work.*

13. Even if an orator was a Demosthenes, with all the sinfulness
characteristic of him, and with the deeds resulting from that

sinfulness; or even if another is thought to be an Antiphon, who even denied the existence of providence (*pronoia*) in his work entitled *On Truth* – a title similar to that of Celsus' own work – nonetheless they are worms wallowing in some patch of the mud of stupidity and ignorance.

(Origen, *Against Celsus* IV 25 = B13)

Next, a rather mysterious quotation relayed by Galen suggesting that there is no objective correlation either of sight (and presumably of the other senses) or of intellectual activity (gnômê). This seems not unlike the position being taken up by Gorgias in On Not-Being,[43] *and may reasonably be regarded as programmatic for the whole work.*

14. And in the second book of the *Lectures*[44] Critias, in making a distinction between thought (*gnômê*) and sense-perception, often speaks in the same terms as Antiphon does in the first of the two books of *On Truth*: 'If you have grasped this[45] you will understand that there is nothing out there corresponding either to what the most powerful beholder sees with his sight, nor of the things which the most powerful knower knows with his mind.'[46]

Galen, *Commentary on Hippocrates' 'The Doctor's Workshop'* XVIII B 656 Kühn = B1–2)

A second extract from the same work, quoted by Galen just after the first, seems to accord a more positive role to the gnômê, *but may just be emphasizing its dominant position in the life of the individual.*

15. And again: 'For in the case of all men the mind is the ruler of the body both in matters of health and disease and everything else.'

Ibid. = B2)

Two little linguistic snippets from Harpocration seem to relate to the main theme of the unreality of appearances.

16. 'Unseen' (*aopta*): for 'invisible (*aorata*) and not actually seen, but seeming to be seen', Antiphon, in the first book of *On Truth*.

(Harpocration, *Lexicon*, s.v. *aopta* = B4)

17. 'Non-experiences' (*apathê*)[47]: for 'experiences (*pathê*) which did not really take place', Antiphon, in the first book of *On Truth*.

(Ibid., s.v. *apathê* = B5).

More substantially, we have an interesting testimony from Aristotle, in the Physics,[48] *as to Antiphon's proposal for squaring the circle. This, as we learn from Simplicius (Commentary on Aristotle's Physics, p. 54, 12 Diels), involved inscribing a square within a given circle, and then progressively constructing chords on each side of the square which halved the sides so as to make a polygon of ever more and smaller sides, getting closer and closer to the circumference of the circle. Aristotle has, as we can see, no patience with this proposal, which he (quite justifiably) condemns as not based on geometrical principles, but he may have missed (or simply disregarded) Antiphon's true point, which may have been not to contribute to the science of geometry, but rather to suggest that, by such a device as this, appearance can be made to equate to 'truth'. This would, then, be somewhat analogous to Protagoras' point about the line touching the circle, in ch. 1, §27 above (where Protagoras is engaged, according to Aristotle, in 'refuting the geometricians').*

18. Let us note that we are not obliged to answer every kind of objection we may meet, but only such as are validly deduced from the accepted principles of the science in question; those that are not, we need not bother with. Thus, it is appropriate for the geometer to refute the squaring of the circle that proceeds by way of equating the segments,[49] but he does not have to consider Antiphon's solution, as it is not in accord with geometrical principles.

(Aristotle, *Physics* I 2, 185a14–17 = B13)

A rather different point of contrast between appearance and reality is reported by Aristotle elsewhere in the Physics – *once again disregarding Antiphon's probable point.*

19. Now it is the view of some that the nature and essence (*physis kai ousia*) of natural products is their primary inherent stuff, on its own and unmodified, as for instance the 'nature' of a bed is its wood, and of a statue its bronze. Antiphon claimed it as evidence of this that, if a man buried a bedstead and the resulting rotting process was activated so as to put out a shoot, what would come up would be not a bedstead but a tree, since the artificial (*kata nomon*) arrangement of the material is merely incidental to it, whereas the essential reality (*ousia*) is that which persists and is constant under these accidental modifications.

(Ibid. II 1, 193a9–17 = B15).

This is certainly a rather far-fetched and improbable example, but Antiphon's purpose here is plainly to contrast nomos *and* physis *('convention' and 'nature') in general. That this comes from the* On Truth *is assured by an entry in Harpocration's* Lexicon, *plainly taken from Antiphon's original version of this argument:*

20. 'Alive' (*embios*): Antiphon, in Book I of *On Truth*: '. . . and the rotting process should become alive', instead of 'be in a living state', that is, should live, and not dry up and die.

(Harpocration, *Lexicon*, s.v. *embios* = B15)

A number of other individual words and turns of phrase from the Truth *are preserved by Harpocration, but they cast no real light on its contents. One, however, has taken on a crucial importance by virtue of coinciding, providentially, with the contents of an otherwise anonymous papyrus, found at Oxyrhynchus in the late nineteenth century (Oxyrhynchus Papyri XI 1364), which has become our main evidence for* On Truth. *First Harpocration:*

21. 'Regards' (*agei*): Antiphon, in Book I of *On Truth*: 'were to regard (*agoi*) the laws as important', instead of 'were to consider (*hêgoito*) . . .'

(Ibid., s.v. *agei*)

Next, the papyrus. We omit small scraps, and indicate only major supplements. The subject-matter, once again, is the contrast between nature and convention, particularly in the sphere of justice. It is probably misguided to try to derive an ethical position, immoralist or otherwise, from the text; Antiphon, rather, is simply observing the facts of life as he sees them.[50]

22a. [*Fragment A*]
[*Col. 2*] . . .[51] We recognize and respect <the laws[52] of nearby communities>, whereas those of communities far away we neither respect nor revere. In this, however, we have become barbarized[53] towards one another, whereas in fact, as far as nature is concerned, we are all equally adapted to being either barbarians or Greeks.

We have only to think of things which are natural and necessary to all mankind; these are available to all in the same way, and in all these there is no distinction between barbarian or Greek. For we all breathe out into the air by the mouth and the nostrils, and we laugh when we are pleased [*col. 3*] in our mind, or we weep when we are grieved, and we receive sounds with our hearing, and see by the light of our vision, and we work with our hands, and we walk with our feet . . .[54]

(*Papyrus Oxyrhynchus* XI 1364)

22b. [*Fragment B*]
[*Col. 1*] Justice, then, is a matter of not breaking the laws and customs (*nomima*) of the city in which one is a citizen.[55] So a man would make use of justice most advantageously for himself if he were to regard the laws as important when witnesses are present, but, when on his own without witnesses, the demands of nature. For the demands of the laws are adventitious (*epitheta*), but the demands of nature are necessary (*anangkaia*); and the demands of the laws are based on agreement, not nature, while the

demands of nature [*col.* 2] are not dependent on agreement. So if a man transgresses the demands of law and is not found out by those who are parties to the agreement, he escapes without either shame or penalty;[56] but if he is found out, he does not.

If, on the other hand, a man – *per impossibile* – violates one of the inherent demands of nature, even if all mankind fails to notice it, the harm is no less, and even if everyone is aware of it, the harm is no greater. For the injury which he suffers is not a matter of appearance (*dia doxan*) but of truth (*di' aletheian*).

This is just what the present course of argument is about, to show that many of the things which are just according to the law are at odds with nature. For it is laid down by law for the eyes, what [*col.* 3] they may see and what they may not, and for the ears, what they may hear and what they may not, and in the case of the tongue, what it may say and may not, and what the hands may do and not do, and where the feet may go and where they may not go, and in the case of the mind (*nous*), what it may desire and what it may not. But as far as nature is concerned, none of these things is more in accord or conformity with it than any other, either the things from which the laws discourage men or the things towards which they steer them.[57]

Again, life is in accordance with nature, and so is death, and life is one of the advantages (*sympheronta*) for human beings, while death is one of the disadvantages. [*Col.* 4] But the 'advantages' which are prescribed by the laws are shackles upon nature, whereas the advantages prescribed by nature make for freedom.[58] It is not the case that things which bring pain can be properly claimed to benefit man's nature more than things which bring pleasure; nor indeed is it the case that the things that bring sorrow are more advantageous than the things that produce enjoyment. For the things that are truly (*tôi alêthei*) advantageous ought not to harm us but help us. So then the things that are advantageous by nature are . . .[59]

(Ibid.)

22c. [*Col.* 5] . . . and people who defend themselves when attacked, while not initiating action themselves; and people who behave well to their parents, even when their parents mistreat them; and those who offer their opponents an oath, while they themselves do not swear one:[60] of the cases here mentioned, many one would discover to be at variance with nature; they lead to greater pain when less is possible, and less pleasure, when more is possible, and to suffering misfortune, when it was possible to avoid it.

If some assistance accrued from the laws to those who give up their rights in such ways, and disadvantage to those who do not give them up, but put up resistance, [*Col. 6*] then obedience to the laws would hold some advantage; but as it is, it is clear that justice in accordance with the law does not give adequate assistance to those who give up their rights in such ways, since it leaves the sufferer to suffer and the doer to act, and not even when the act has been committed is it in any position to prevent the sufferer from suffering or the doer from acting.[61] When justice is introduced to effect punishment, it is no more particularly on the side of the sufferer than the committer of the act. For he who is seeking redress must persuade [the jury] that he has suffered wrong, and must plead for the opportunity to gain a favourable verdict; but it is also left open to the doer to deny the charge . . .[62]

(Ibid.)

22d. [*Fragment C*]

. . . to bear witness truthfully for one another is conventionally considered to be just and, furthermore, useful in the conduct of human affairs. But the one who does this is not just, at least if justice means not harming anyone who has not done you harm.[63] For necessarily the man who gives evidence, even if his evidence is true, in a sense harms ('wrongs') another man, and may well be himself harmed in turn later, on account of what he has said, insofar as the man against whom his evidence has been given is found guilty because of his evidence, and loses either money or life, through the agency of this man whom he has never himself harmed. So in this respect he harms the man against whom he gives evidence, because he harms someone who never did him any harm, and the result is that he himself is liable to be harmed by the man against whom he gives evidence, having earned his hatred because of his true evidence. And not only is he harmed by this hatred, but also because he must forever afterwards be on his guard against the man against whom he gave evidence; since he now has an enemy, such as will speak and do any harm that he can to him.

So these, then, are plainly no small harms, both that which he suffers and that which he commits; for there is no way that the justice of this procedure[64] can be reconciled with the principle that one should do no harm if one has not suffered it beforehand.[65] No, either one or the other of them is just, or both are unjust.

Further, it is apparent that the whole process of going to court and giving judgement and proceeding to arbitration in order to come to a settlement is contrary to justice. For what helps one set of people injures another; in this process, those who are helped do not suffer harm, certainly, but those who are injured[66] are harmed . . .

(Ibid.)

We now turn to Book II of the work, which seems (as has been noted earlier) to have concerned topics related to cosmogony and zoology, and is represented only by a series of short references (B22–43), not all of which are worth presenting. How these topics were fitted into an overall theme of the conflict between convention and nature, or appearance and reality, is not at all clear. It is possible, however, that Book II contained a straightforward account of the natural world in the Ionian physicist tradition, following on the analysis of the conventional, artificial world of human society in Book I, and that this was the nub of Antiphon's position: 'truth' lies in the world of nature, not in that of convention. As for the particular theories attributed to him, there is little or nothing that is original, as we shall see; but then it was no part of Antiphon's purpose to propound new-fangled cosmological theories, but rather to adopt, if possible, generally agreed ones.

First, then, a number of snippets of a cosmogonical nature, all from lexicographical sources (Harpocration, Photius, the Suda), or from the doxographer Aetius.

23. 'Everlastingness' (*aeiestô*): Antiphon, in the second book of *On Truth* [uses this term for] eternity (*aidiotês*) and remaining always in the same state, on the model of the word *euestô* ('happiness').

    (Harpocration, *Lexicon*, s.v. *aeiestô* = B22)

This is most interesting, both as suggesting a theory of the eternity of the universe as a whole, but also as indicating Antiphon's readiness to coin new terms.

24. 'Distension' (*diastasis*): Antiphon, in the second book of *On Truth*: 'concerning the distension which now prevails', referring to the ordering (*diakosmêsis*) of the universe.

    (Ibid., s.v. *diastasis* = B23)

25. 'Undistended' (*adiastaton*): Antiphon spoke thus of what has not yet been separated or distinguished.

    (Ibid., s.v. *adiastaton* = B24)

This is presumably a reference to the prevailing separation of the various elements into distinct objects (by contrast to an original blending of everything?). The use of the term diastasis, *at any rate, seems to imply a theory of original mixture. As for* adiastatos, *Antiphon is by far the earliest attested user of the word, and may have coined it himself.*

26. 'Disposition' (*diathesis*): Antiphon used *diathesis* in the sense of 'state of mind' (*gnômê*) or 'thought' (*dianoia*); the same author used it for the 'arrangement' of a speech, that is, in the sense of expounding something. In the second book of *On Truth*, however, the same author uses it for the arrangement of the world (*diakosmêsis*).

    (*Suda*, s.v. *diathesis* = B24a)

27. 'By means of the whirl' (*dinôi*): Antiphon, in Book II of *On Truth*, for 'by means of whirling' (*dinêsei*).

    (Harpocration, *Lexicon*, s.v. *dinôi* = B25)

*This is an intriguing testimony, since it introduces the possibility
that Antiphon may be being at least glanced at by Aristophanes
in his comedy* The Clouds, *produced in 423 (ll. 379–80), where
he makes Dinos the supreme deity in the system of his comic
creation 'Socrates'. On the other hand, the scholiast ad loc.
attributes the term to Anaxagoras, and most commentators
attribute it more immediately to his follower Diogenes of Apollonia, whose doctrine of Air as the supreme deity is certainly
being parodied in the play. At any rate, Antiphon would seem
to have adopted the 'whirl' (dinos) as the mechanism by which
the cosmos evolved.*

*We now turn to some details of cosmology, all of which seem
thoroughly in accord with the Ionian physical tradition.*

28. (*Concerning the nature of the sun.*) Antiphon says that it
is fire which feeds upon the damp air around the earth, and
creates risings and settings by progressively leaving behind
the burned-up air, and always taking up the moistened air
beneath it.[67]

(Aetius, II 20, 15 Diels = B26)

29. Antiphon says that the moon shines by her own light,[68] but
is obscured and made dim by the superimposition of the sun,
since it is the nature of the stronger fire to dim the weaker; and
that this happens also in the case of the other stars.[69]

(Aetius, II 28, 4 Diels = B27)

30. (*Concerning the eclipse of the moon.*) Alcmaeon, Heraclitus,
Antiphon (say that the moon is eclipsed) because of the revolution of the bowl-shaped (*skaphoeides*) body and its decli-
nations (*perikliseis*).

(Aetius, II 29, 3 Diels = B28)

*Both in this theory, and in that of the dependence of the sun
on exhalations from the earth, Antiphon would seem to be
following Heraclitus, for whom both of these doctrines are
attested. Heraclitus seems to have envisaged the sun and moon
as bowl-shaped figures (skaphai), like polished concave mirrors,*

the latter of which turns progressively during the month, revealing more and more of its dark side.

31. So also in Antiphon, in the second book of his *On Truth*, we can find this term [i.e. *eiloumenon*, 'close-packed'], in the following passage:

'Whenever, then, there come about in the air rain and winds opposed to each other, then the water is compacted and condensed in many places; and whenever any of the colliding bodies is overcome [sc. by another], it is condensed and compacted, close-packed by the wind and the force [sc. of the collision].'

Here he too seems to use the term *eiloumenon* in the sense of 'confined' or 'compacted into itself'.

(Galen, *Commentary on Hippocrates, Epidemics* XVII A 681 Kühn = B29)

This appears to be an attempt to explain the genesis of hailstones, or possibly snow. It is in fact not unlike the theory of Anaxagoras on the subject (cf. 59A85).

32. 'Wrinkled' (*grypanion*): Antiphon, in Book II of *On Truth*: 'for by burning the earth and fusing it it makes it wrinkled'.

(Harpocration, *Lexicon*, s.v. *grypanion* = B30)

33. 'Become wrinkled' (*grypanizein*): for the earth to quiver and shake, and to be as it were shrivelled (*rhysousthai*) by earthquake: thus Antiphon.

(*Etymologium Genuinum*, s.v. *grypanizein* = B31)

These two entries pose a slight problem, as they seem to refer to different processes, using the same term (both adjective and verb, we may note, are attested only for Antiphon), but this may not after all be so. §32 has a neuter subject, presumably fire, and it has been assumed to refer to the fire of the sun, but the sun's rays do not after all produce such a drastic effect upon the earth. It seems much more probable that the reference is to the fire associated with seismic, particularly volcanic activity, which does indeed produce this effect; and thus both adjective and verb would refer to the influence of seismic activity on the shaping of the earth as we know it.

34. (*Concerning the sea, how it arose and how it comes to be salty.*) Antiphon's view is that [the sea is] the sweat resulting from <the primordial wet element being vaporized by the>[70] hot, from which process the remaining wet element is separated off, being made salt by evaporation, which is what happens in the case of sweat in general.

(Aetius, III 16, 4 Diels = B32)

This comes in a doxographical sequence listing Anaximander, Anaxagoras and Empedocles, all of whom propound views similar to those of Antiphon, so that once again we can see that he is not aspiring to originality. The text is interesting, though, in seeming to indicate that Antiphon is working with a four-element system like that of Empedocles.

There follow a few snippets concerning the composition of the human body.

35. 'To be covered in skin' (*pephoriôsthai*): that the term *phorinê* ('hide') may be used of human skin, Antiphon makes plain in Book II of *On Truth*.[71]

(Harpocration, *Lexicon*, s.v. *pephoriôsthai* = B33)

36. 'Headache' and 'heaviness in the head' . . . and food and drink which causes heaviness of the head. For what causes this Antiphon uses the verb *karoun* ('to stupefy').

(Pollux, *Onomasticon*, II 41 = B34)

37. 'Red-blooded' (*enaimon*): also *enaimôdes*, in Antiphon.[72]
(Ibid. II 215 = B35)

38. And Antiphon also has said: 'that in which the foetus grows and is nourished is called the membrane (*khorion*)'.

(Ibid. II 223)

39. The term *epiplous* ('intestinal membrane, the fold of the
peritoneum'): Antiphon also uses this, making it both masculine
and feminine.[73]

(Ibid. II 224)

*There are a few other reported words, but they add nothing to
our understanding of the contents of the work. As it is, we are
left with a problem: Antiphon in Book II is plainly engaged in
an account of the origins and composition both of the world
and of man, but is he still concerned with the opposition between
convention and 'truth'? If he is, there is certainly no surviving
sign of that.*

On Concord

*'Concord' (*homonoia*), like talk of the 'ancestral constitution',
had become something of a buzzword in conservative political
circles in the later fifth century. It came to denote a willingness
on the part of the lower orders to accept the wise and benevolent
guidance of their betters, its opposite being* stasis, *or factional-
ism. There is a good expression of this view in Xenophon's*
Memorabilia *(IV 4, 16), put into the mouth of Socrates,[74] quoted
by Diels-Kranz under B44a, and worth repeating:*

'Moreover, concord is agreed to be the greatest good for states,
and very commonly in various states the senates[75] and the best
people call upon the citizens to 'be of one mind' (*homonoein*);
and everywhere in Greece there is a law which prescribes that the
citizens should take an oath to 'be of one mind', and everywhere
this oath is taken. The purpose of this, I take it, is not that the
citizens may come to the same decision in choral competitions,
or commend the same flute-players, or choose the same poets, or
take pleasure in the same things, but that they may obey the laws;
for it is when the citizens abide by these that states become
strongest and happiest, but without concord a state cannot be
well organized nor even a household well administered.'

*It is tempting to conjecture that Antiphon's treatise on this
subject was composed in the context of the coup of 412/11,*

though it must be said that nothing in the surviving fragments of the work lends itself to that hypothesis. Thucydides, in his account of the regime of the Four Hundred, refers to homonoia *on one occasion (VIII 93), but only at a stage when the regime is collapsing, reporting that, after disturbances in the Piraeus, the Four Hundred and the hoplites in the Piraeus 'came to an agreement to hold a meeting of the Assembly on a stated day to discuss concord (*homonoia*)'. This in fact resulted in the decommissioning of the Four Hundred, and the (brief) establishment of the Five Thousand, which Thucydides characterizes as 'the best regime which the Athenians ever enjoyed within my memory' (VIII 97).*

As with On Truth, *a number of the surviving references seem at first sight to have little to do with the subject. We have references, for instance, to various bizarre races, the 'Shadow-Feet' (Skiapodes), the 'Long-Heads' (Makrokephaloi) and the 'Troglodytes, who live beneath the earth', as being mentioned by Antiphon in this work (= B45–7, all from Harpocration's Lexicon), and this seems baffling, but it has been plausibly suggested by Morrison[76] that they are being produced, by way of introduction, as examples of peoples for whom custom, even in these weird forms, has become second nature, and this may encourage us to believe that the habit of* homonoia *can become natural to us too.*

However that may be, the main theme of the work seems to be the human condition, and how it can be improved by the practice of concord. Morrison seeks to distinguish the topics dealt with as falling under the headings of education, psychology and sociology, and arranges the fragments in accordance with that assumption, but there is really no indication that Antiphon intended any such distinction. The content of the fragments preserved to us are conditioned rather by the interests of John of Stobi, from whose Anthology *most of the fragments derive (attesting to the continuing popularity of the work in late antiquity).[77] We prefer in this edition to follow the order offered by Gagarin and Woodruff,[78] which stays closer to the order of fragments presented in Diels-Kranz (while improving somewhat the logical sequence of thought),*

rather than following the more imaginative grouping adopted
by Morrison.

The first fragment (after those concerning the various bizarre
races) seems to set up a contrast between the godlike form or
appearance of men, and their actual behaviour. The next two
continue this pessimistic vein. They may, however, have formed
part of an introductory protreptic address.

40. 'Most godlike' (*theeidestaton*): having the appearance (*idea*)
of a god. Antiphon speaks as follows in the *On Concord*: 'Man,
who claims, on the one hand,[79] to be the most godlike of all
beasts . . .'
    (= B48, from Photius, 'The Library')

41. [Antiphon] 'The whole of life is wonderfully easy to find
fault with, my good fellow;[80] it has nothing in it special or great
or wonderful, but everything is small and weak and of short
duration and mixed with great sorrows.'
    (Stobaeus, *Anthology* IV 34, 56 = B51)

42. 'To take back' (*anathesthai*): Antiphon, *On Concord*: 'One
cannot just take back one's life like a piece at draughts.'
    (Harpocration, *Lexicon*, s.v. *anathesthai* = B52)

We now turn to the longest preserved fragment, which concerns
married life, its problems and advantages. Here the connection
with the theme of homonoia *is easier to discern, though it is not*
actually stated. We may note that this passage exhibits a much
higher degree of literary artistry, of a Gorgianic type, than did
On Truth; but we have seen the same phenomenon in the case
of Gorgias himself, so this need not be taken as an indication of
difference of authorship.

43. [Antiphon] 'Well, then, let his life progress further, and let
him want marriage and a wife.[81] That day, that night, is the
beginning of a new destiny (*daimôn*), a new fate. For marriage
is a great test (*agôn*) for a man. If the wife turns out to be
incompatible, how should he deal with the situation? Divorce

is a troublesome process, making enemies of your friends, people who have the same thoughts, the same feelings, as yourself, whom you respect and who respect you.[82] But it is difficult, too, to keep such a possession, to bring home pains when you expected to acquire pleasures.

'But come, let us not speak of the untoward, let us talk instead of the most compatible of alliances. What is pleasanter for a man than a wife after his own heart? And what is sweeter, especially when he is young? But in that very place wherein dwells the pleasure, the painful is lurking somewhere close by. For pleasures do not come in on their own, but there follow along in their train pains and toils. Indeed, even victories in the Olympian or Pythian Games and contests of that sort, and various skills and intellectual accomplishments,[83] and all pleasures, tend to come only at the cost of great pains. For honours, prizes, those snares which God has granted to men, place them under the necessity of great toil and sweat.

'For I, if I had a second body which needed as much care as I give to myself, could not live, considering all the trouble I give myself, what with tending to the health of my body and earning my daily livelihood, and seeing to my honour and temperance and reputation and good fame. What, then, if I actually had a second body like this one, for which I would be equally responsible? Is it not obvious, then, that a wife, even if she is after one's own heart, would nevertheless give a man as much happiness and as much pain as he gives himself, what with the concern for the health of two bodies and the gathering of a livelihood and temperance and good fame?

'Well then, let us suppose that children are born. Now indeed everything is full of worries, and the carefree flourish of youth[84] departs from one's mind, and the expression on one's face is no longer the same.'

(Stobaeus, *Anthology* IV 22, 66 = B49)

The sequence of thought, especially in the latter part of the passage, is somewhat murky, as is its relevance to the overall theme, but presumably what Antiphon is working up to is an argument that homonoia *makes all these responsibilities and anxieties easier to bear. Stobaeus, after all, has included this extract in a chapter entitled 'That it is not a good idea to get married', so he is selecting what interests him.*

44. [Antiphon] 'Primary among human activities, I think, is education (*paideusis*); for when a man makes a right beginning of any matter whatsoever, it is likely that the end, too, will turn out right. For example, according to the type of seed one plants in the earth, one should expect the harvest to be of like kind; and thus, whenever one implants good education in a young body, this lives and flourishes throughout the whole of life, and neither rain nor drought will destroy it.'

(Ibid. II 31, 39 = B60)

This seems to form part of a discussion of the education of children, and so might be taken to follow on from the previous passage, though, once again, how it relates to the theme of homonoia *is less than clear.*

45. [Antiphon] 'There is nothing worse for men than lack of discipline (*anarkhia*). Appreciating this, the men of former times accustomed their children to being disciplined and doing what they were told from the outset, so that, when they grew to manhood and experienced great change in their lives, they should not be thrown into confusion.'

(Ibid. II 31, 40 = B61)

Antiphon here sounds very much the conventional conservative – rather like the Just Argument in Aristophanes The Clouds, *indeed, or like Plato, later, in Book III of the* Laws *(698Bff.).*

46. [Antiphon] 'With whomever a person consorts for most of the day, such he will necessarily come to be like himself in his habits.'

(Ibid. II 31, 41 = B62)

This extract follows in Stobaeus immediately on the preceding, and the reference probably therefore is to children – the recommendation being that they consort with the right people.

47. 'For taking care of the aged (*gêrotrophia*) is very like taking care of the young (*paidotrophia*).'
    (Clement, *Stromateis*, VI 19 = B66)

This banality may form part of an argument for preserving homonoia by paying proper attention to the older generation. It is notable that Antiphon is the first attested user of either of the terms in brackets.

48. [Antiphon] 'Life is like an all-day watch-duty (*phroura*), and the length of a life is like a single day, so to speak, in which we look up at the light, and then pass on our watch to others who come after us.'
    (Stobaeus, *Anthology* IV 34, 63 = B50)

This interesting remark is mildly reminiscent of the 'secret doctrine' mentioned by Socrates at Phaedo *62B, to the effect that we men are set on this earth by the gods 'as on a kind of guard-duty' (en tini phrourâi), but there it is part of an argument against suicide, as being a 'desertion of one's post', whereas here it is not clear quite what Antiphon's point is. Plainly Stobaeus found it edifying, though.*

49. [Antiphon] 'There are some who are not content with living their present life, but are constantly in a state of eager preparation as if they were going to live some other life, not the present one; and as they are thus engaged time passes them by and runs out.'
    (Ibid. III 16, 20 = B53a)

This is a shrewd and perceptive remark, but its relevance to the overall theme is thoroughly obscure.

50. [Antiphon] 'Those who work and are thrifty and suffer privation in order to increase their property derive the sort of pleasure from that which one would expect them to derive. On the other hand, if people diminish their possessions and use them up, they suffer such pain as if they had lost their own flesh.'

(Ibid. III, 16, 20 = B53)

Again, what is the point of this remark?

51. [Antiphon] 'The story is told of a man who observed another man acquiring a large sum of money, and asked him to lend it to him at interest; but he refused, being the sort of man who distrusted others and never helped anyone. Instead, he took the money and stored it away. Another man observed him doing this, however, and stole the money. Some time later the man who had stored it away went to collect it, and found it gone. Greatly distressed by this disaster, particularly because he had not lent it to the man who had asked for it, which would both have kept the money safe for him and brought in more as well, on meeting the man who had wanted to borrow from him, he lamented his misfortune to him, saying that he had made a mistake and was sorry that he had not obliged him, but had refused, since the money was now entirely lost. The other told him not to worry about it, but rather to make believe that he still had the money in his possession and had not lost it, and to put a stone in the place where the money had been. "For you made no use of it at all when you had it, so there is no need now to think that you have lost anything."

'And indeed, when a man has not made use of something nor intends to make use of it, it makes no difference to him whether he has it or not, nor is he harmed either more or less by not having it. For when God does not wish to bestow benefits unreservedly upon a man, he provides him with wealth in material things, but makes him poor in good judgement, and thus, by taking away the latter, he deprives him of both.'

(Ibid. III 16, 30 = B54)

This little story puts one in mind of the New Testament 'Parable of the Talents' (though comparison with an Aesopian fable would be more apposite), but once again its relevance to the theme of homonoia is by no means clear. The moral is perhaps that one should cooperate with one's fellow men, but the point seems really to be that one should make the most of the advantages one is given, irrespective of cooperation.

52. [Antiphon] 'A man who, when proceeding against his neighbour to do him injury, is deterred by fearing that, failing to achieve what he wishes, he may end up with what he does not wish, is more prudent.[85] For while he is afraid he delays action, and while he delays, often the passage of time diverts his mind from his purpose. When the deed is done, after all, there is no question of this, but as long as there is delay, there is a possibility of the deed also not being done. The man who thinks that he will succeed in doing his neighbour injury, and suffer none himself, is lacking in prudence. High hopes are not always a good thing; for such hopes have cast down many into incurable misfortunes, where they have turned out to suffer just those things which they thought they would inflict on their neighbours. Prudence might be predicated more correctly of no other man than one who, by putting a block on[86] the immediate pleasures of his spirit, is able to dominate and conquer himself. He who wishes to gratify his spirit immediately, wishes what is worse instead of what is better.'

(Ibid. III 20, 66 = B58)

Again, this sequence of gnomic sentiments, constituting as it does an encomium of prudence (sôphrosynê), while replete with wisdom, has no very obvious relevance to the subject of the treatise; but we may reflect that we lack the context.

53. [Antiphon] 'Someone who has neither desired nor embarked upon shameful or evil acts cannot be described as "self-controlled" (sôphrôn); for there is nothing which he has had to overcome in order to make himself orderly (kosmios).'

(Ibid. III 5, 57 = B59)

This is interestingly reminiscent of the account of 'continence' (enkrateia) that Aristotle gives in Book VII of the Nicomachean Ethics, but its relevance to the present theme is once again unclear. The same is true of the next few snippets, from lexicographical sources.

54. 'Very light on the reins' (*euêniôtata*): Antiphon in the treatise *On Concord*. Someone who is gentle and moderate and not troublesome is 'light on the reins'. The metaphor is from horses.
   (Harpocration, *Lexicon*, s.v. *euêniôtata* = B70)

55. Flattery (*thôpeia*): Antiphon, in the treatise *On Concord*: 'Many people do not recognize the friends they have, but take on as companions flatterers (*thôpes*) who fawn on wealth and good fortune.'
   (*Suda*, s.v. *thôpeia* = B65)

56. [Antiphon] 'Recent friendships are compelling, but old friendships are more compelling.'
   (*Excerpta Vindobonensia* 64 = B64)

The Politikos

Of the contents of this treatise we have virtually no indications, though from its title it would be reasonable to conjecture that it contained sundry reflections on 'the state of the nation', no doubt of a critical nature. It was presumably a political pamphlet,[87] rather similar to the anti-democratic broadside published among the works of Xenophon, and attributed to a figure, writing probably near the beginning of the Peloponnesian War, now nicknamed 'the Old Oligarch'; and to the speech or pamphlet by Thrasymachus, of which we have an extract preserved by Dionysius of Halicarnassus (below, ch. 6, §11). However, all we have are a few individual words and phrases, many giving further proof of Antiphon's linguistic innovativeness.

First, a significant word, probably referring to the prevailing state of Athenian politics, preserved by an anonymous lexicographer:

57. *Apeitharkhia* ('lack of discipline'): Antiphon in the *Politikos*.
   (Antiatticista, *Bekker's Anecdota* 78, 20 = B72)

Then a sentence from Athenaeus, again probably embodying a criticism of Athenian society – perhaps in this case the tendency of young aristocrats (like Alcibiades, whom we know Antiphon to have attacked) to turn to demagoguery after squandering their patrimonies.

58. The verb *kataristân* ('to squander one's property by lunching') is used by Antiphon in the *Politikos* thus: 'When, then, one has lunched away his own property or that of his friends . . .'
   (Athenaeus, *Deipnosophistae* X 423A = B73)

Then a term preserved by the lexicographer Harpocration, which may concern excessive readiness to make contributions to communal feasts (also a weakness of extravagant young aristocrats), though on the face of it it has a positive connotation – 'ready to stand one's round'.

59. *Eusymbolos* ('ready at contributing'),[88] in the sense of 'contributing readily and generously', that is to say, 'good at contributing': Antiphon in the *Politikos*.
   (Harpocration, *Lexicon*, s.v. *eusymbolos*)

And another term from Harpocration, of obscure reference, but possibly relating to the same criticism as above:

60. *Hêmioliasmos* ('adding half as much again'):[89] Antiphon in the *Politikos*: 'of doubling and adding-half-as-much-again', with the meaning of 'giving one and a half times the amount in one's reckonings'.[90]

Lastly, a note from the grammarian Priscianus.

61. The Greeks use the verb *katamelein* ('neglect') with either a genitive or an accusative, e.g. Antiphon in the *Politikos:* 'not to

be called a boozer (*philopotês*) and to seem to neglect one's affairs through a weakness for wine'.[91]

(Priscianus, *Institutio de arte grammatica* 18, 230)

On the Interpretation of Dreams

This work is attributed to Antiphon in a variety of sources, including Cicero, in his treatise On Divination, *without any suggestion that it might belong to a different Antiphon from our sophist/politician, so we may accept it. Especially if one is prepared to accept the identity of the psychiatrist in Corinth with our man, an interest in the significance of dreams would follow naturally enough – as it did in the case of Sigmund Freud. The dream-interpreter is also to be identified, presumably, with the* teratoskopos, *or diviner.[92] This complex of interests is not, after all, incoherent with those of a rhetorician, especially one who was the author of the* Tetralogies, *printed below.*

First, an entertaining anecdote, from the Stromateis *of Clement of Alexandria, which shows that Antiphon was as much concerned with omens as with dreams:*

62. The story about Antiphon is amusing. A certain man took it as an omen[93] when a sow ate her litter; but, noticing that the sow was thin with lack of food by reason of the meanness of its owner, Antiphon declared: 'You should be encouraged by the omen. She is so hungry she might have eaten *your* children!'

(Clement, *Stromateis* VII 24 = A8)

And a dictum of Antiphon's from a late gnomology, which is of value as indicating Antiphon's basic approach to these phenomena:[94]

63. Antiphon, on being asked what divination consisted in, replied: 'the conjecture of a wise man (*anthrôpou phronimou eikasmos*)'.

(*Gnomologia Vindobenensis* 50 = A9)

Then a slightly mysterious mention by the second-century AD dream-interpreter Artemidorus in his treatise The Interpretation of Dreams. *Artemidorus is expounding the symbolic significance of dreaming about various types of fish (a rather improbable subject of dreams, one would have thought). It is not clear that Antiphon had anything to say on anything but the cuttle-fish, but it seems best to give the whole context anyhow.*

64. Soft fish signify benefits for criminals only; for, indeed, they hide by changing their colours and by making themselves resemble the places in which they are. But for other men, they signify obstacles and delays because of their ability to grasp on to objects and because of their viscosity. They also indicate great slackness in business, since they do not have any bones – bones being the strength of the body. Into this category fall the octopus, the squid, the sea-anemone, the paper nautilus, the musk-octopus, the purple polyp and the cuttle-fish (*sêpia*). This last, in particular, signifies assistance to those running away because of the inky fluid which it often employs to make its escape. Antiphon of Athens makes mention of this dream.
   (Artemidorus, *The Interpretation of Dreams* II 14 = B78, expanded)

Next we turn to a series of references by Cicero in his On Divination, *showing that Antiphon's treatise held an important place in the tradition of dream-interpretation, and was made use of by the Stoics (who, of course, did believe in providence). Cicero's brother, Quintus, is speaking.*

65. 'But let us leave oracles and come to dreams. In his treatise on this subject, Chrysippus, just as does Antipater,[95] has assembled a large collection of trivial dreams, which he explains according to Antiphon's rules of interpretation – a procedure which displays the acumen of the author,[96] certainly, but it would have been better if he had cited illustrations of a more serious type.'
   (Cicero, *De Divinatione* I 39 = B79)

What Antiphon's principles of interpretation were we learn in a later passage.

66. 'Here we may bring in that theory of Antiphon's concerning the interpretation of dreams, according to which interpreters of dreams depend upon technical skill and not upon natural inspiration; and the same goes for the interpretation of oracles and of prophecies – for they all have their interpreters, just as the poets have their commentators. Divine nature, after all, would have acted in vain if it had simply created iron, copper, silver and gold, and had not taught us how to reach the veins of those metals; nor would he have usefully given field crops and orchard fruits to the human race without a knowledge of how to cultivate them and prepare them for food; and timber would be of no service without the carpenter's art to convert it into lumber. So, with everything that the gods have given for the benefit of humanity, there has been joined some art through which its usefulness may be grasped. The same is true of dreams, prophecies and oracles: since many of them were obscure and doubtful, appeal was made to the explanations of professional interpreters.'

(Ibid. I 116 = B 80, expanded)

There is a definite and interesting theory here of, basically, a sort of cosmic sympathy, according to which the divinity provides for men a means of utilizing all the phenomena presented in nature. But can this be the theory of an Antiphon who is alleged to have denied the existence of providence?[97] It seems to us that it can – even if one gives full weight to Origen's tendentious allegation. Antiphon need only be denying the personal intervention of gods in human affairs; he need not be denying that the universe has an order, laid down by the divinity, the secrets of which can be discerned by the skilled interpreter (anthrôpos phronimos, cf. §63 above).

The third passage from the De Divinatione *provides some interesting examples of Antiphon's principles of interpretation. Cicero himself is now speaking, from a New Academic perspective.*

67. 'Furthermore, do not the conjectures of dream-interpreters rather reveal their authors' ingenuity than provide any proof of

a relation between dreams and the laws of nature? There is, for example, the story of a runner planning to set out for the Olympic Games, who dreamed that he was riding in a four-horse chariot. The next morning he goes off to an interpreter.[98] The interpreter says to him: "You will win, for that is implied in the speed and the strength of the horses." Later the same runner went to Antiphon.[99] He, however, said: "You are bound to lose, for do you not see that four ran ahead of you?" And there is the story of another runner – for the book of Chrysippus and that of Antipater are full of such dreams – but I go back to the runner: he reported to an interpreter that he had dreamed of being changed into an eagle. The interpreter said to him: "You have as good as won, for no bird flies faster than the eagle." This runner also consulted Antiphon. "You fool," said he, "do you not see that you are beaten? For that bird is always chasing and driving other birds before it, and is thus itself always last."

(Ibid. II 144)

Cicero uses these examples to make a sceptical point, that the dream-interpreter's art is only based on human conjecture; Antiphon's original point would in fact not have been much different from this, except to claim that his conjecture (confirmed, no doubt, by events) was superior to that of other people.

Next, a mention by Seneca the Elder, in his Controversiae, *of a witty comment by a friend of his, which shows at least that Antiphon's book was still well known in the first century AD.*

68. Junius Otho . . . edited four books of *Styles* (*Colores*), which our friend Gallio aptly described as 'books of Antiphon' – so full of dreams are they!

(Seneca, *Controversiae* II 1, 33 = B81)

And lastly, an extract from a late writer on divination, Melampus, seeming to indicate that Antiphon also dealt with the significance of such phenomena as a twitching eyelid.

69. If the right eye twitches, the man will triumph over his enemies, according to Phemonoe,[100] the Egyptians and Antiphon;

and he will have people coming home from abroad. If the upper
eyelid of the right eye twitches, that is always a sign of gain, and
according to Antiphon of success in business and health; for a
slave, of a plot against him; for a widow, of a journey abroad.

(Melampus, *On Palpitations* 18–19)

The Tetralogies

*Finally, it seems appropriate to include in this collection the
series of model arguments which Antiphon composed, presumably for the instruction of his students in rhetoric. They consist
of three sequences of four skeleton speeches, two each for the
prosecution and the defence, in a series of imaginary, but representative, forensic situations.*[101] *A certain degree of circum-
stantial detail is presented, to enhance realism, and some
interesting issues of causality, responsibility and probability
(eikos) are raised. The ingenuity of this tour de force, of which
we have no other examples from the classical period, should
not be underestimated; it is comparable to playing chess against
oneself. The nearest surviving analogy is perhaps the so-called
Double Arguments (Dissoi Logoi), which will be included later
in this volume (ch. 10), but they do not have a specifically
forensic subject-matter, being concerned with more philosophical issues. Of course, every teacher of rhetoric taught his pupils
to argue both sides of the question (and Protagoras, as we
know, composed* Antilogiai *(Contrary Arguments), which were
doubtless similar to these), but this collection of examples by
Antiphon is all that survives to us.*

First Tetralogy

*This involves a situation where a man has been murdered, but
his slave is found still alive by passers-by, though dying, and,
before he dies, identifies as the murderer the defendant, who is
known to be an enemy of the deceased, and who was about to
be taken to court by him in a potentially very damaging law-case.
The prosecution is undertaken by friends of the deceased.*

70. (i) Opening Speech for the Prosecution

[1] Such plots as are concocted by ordinary people are not hard
to unmask; but in the case of criminals who have natural ability,

who are experienced in affairs, and have reached an age when they are at their peak of mental efficiency, detection and exposure is difficult. *[2]* Owing to the greatness of the danger involved, they give much thought to the problem of carrying out the crime in safety, and they do not embark on it until they have entirely assured themselves against suspicion. Taking account of all this, you must give the utmost weight to any indication whatever of probability (*eikos*) that is presented to you. We, on the other hand, who are prosecuting in this case of murder, are not prosecuting the innocent, while letting the guilty go free; *[3]* for we recognize clearly that, as the whole city is polluted by the criminal until he is prosecuted, the impiety becomes ours and the penalty for your error reverts upon us, if our prosecution is wrongly directed. Thus, as the whole pollution (*miasma*) reverts upon us, we shall try to demonstrate to you as clearly as we can that the defendant killed the dead man.

[4] <It is not likely that professional criminals murdered this man,>[102] as nobody who was prepared to undergo the greatest of dangers would give up the benefit accruing from it when it was securely within his grasp; and the victims were found still in possession of their cloaks. Nor again did anyone kill him in a drunken brawl; for such a person would be identified by his drinking companions. Nor again did his death result from a quarrel;[103] they would not have been quarrelling in the dead of night or in a deserted place. Nor was it a case of someone hitting the dead man when aiming at someone else; for he would not in that case have killed him along with his slave.

[5] Since every basis for suspicion (sc. that the crime was unpremeditated) has been removed,[104] the mode of death itself indicates clearly that the victim was killed deliberately. Now who is more likely to have attacked him than an individual who had already suffered great injuries at his hands and who could expect to suffer greater ones still? That man is the defendant. He was an enemy of the victim from of old, and had brought several serious cases against him of which he had won none, *[6]* while on the other hand he himself has been indicted [i.e. by the dead man] on even more numerous and more serious charges, and has not once gained acquittal, so that he has lost a considerable

portion of his property.[105] Further, he had recently been indicted by the dead man for embezzling sacred funds, at a penalty of two talents.[106] He knew that he was guilty, had experience of the effectiveness of his opponent and he bore a grudge for past events. It was natural for him, then, to plot against him, and it was natural for him to seek protection from his enmity by killing his opponent. [7] His desire for revenge made him unmindful of the dangers, while fear of the ruin bearing down on him roused him on to attack all the more urgently. By doing this he hoped not only to avoid detection in murder, but to escape the indictment. [8] Nobody, he reckoned, would pursue the suit, and he would get a judgement by default; and even if he did after all lose his case, he deemed it better to have gained revenge than, like a coward, to be ruined by the indictment without striking back. And he clearly was convinced that he would lose it, or he would not have thought the present trial the safer option.[107]

[9] These, then, are the considerations which impelled him to this impious act. Had there been many witnesses to the act, we would have produced many witnesses; but as the dead man's servant was the only one present, those who heard his statement will bear witness; for he was still alive when rescued from the scene, and in response to our questioning stated that the only one of his attackers whom he had recognized was this fellow.[108]

[10] Since, then, conclusions from probability (eikota) and from eye-witnesses have alike proved the defendant's guilt, there is no way that in accordance with either justice or expediency you can acquit him. For those who concoct such plots would be immune from conviction, if they are not to be convicted either by eye-witnesses or by probable inferences: but it is against all your interests that this fellow, in the state of disgusting pollution that he is in, should profane the precincts of the gods by entering them, or communicate his defilement to the innocent by sitting at the same tables with them.[109] It is this sort of thing that causes blights (aphoriai) and public disasters. (11) You must therefore regard the avenging of the dead as a personal duty, and, by punishing the defendant for the sin which is his alone, and imposing suffering on him alone, render the city as a whole pure from guilt.

(ii) *Opening Speech for the Defence*

[1] I would not be far from the mark, it seems to me, in regarding myself as the most unfortunate of all men. In the case of others who meet with misfortune, if, for instance, they are caught in a storm, when calm weather returns they have relief from their trouble; when they fall ill, they are saved by recovering their health; if some other misfortune overcomes them, they gain relief from the supervening of its opposite. *[2]* In my case, however, this is not so; not only did this man overthrow the peace of my household during his lifetime, but, even if I escape conviction on this occasion, he has inflicted a host of woes and worries upon me after his death. For I have reached such a pitch of misfortune that even a pious and honest life is not adequate to save me, but unless I can actually find and convict his murderer, whom the dead man's avengers have proved incapable of finding, I shall myself be found guilty of murder and be visited with an unholy death.

[3] Now they declare, on the one hand, that it is very difficult to prove my guilt because of my cleverness, but at the same time, in maintaining that my actions themselves prove me to have done the deed, they assume me to be a fool. For if now, because of the magnitude of my enmity, you find me guilty on the grounds of probability (*eikotôs*), it was still more natural for me to foresee before committing the crime that suspicion would devolve upon me as it has done, and, if I knew of anyone else who was plotting the murder, I was likely to go so far as to stop them, rather than deliberately to fall under obvious suspicion by committing the crime myself. For if I was detected in the act of committing the crime, I was doomed; while if, on the other hand, I was not caught in the act, I knew clearly that I would fall under suspicion, as indeed has been the case.

[4] Truly, my fate is a wretched one: I am forced not only to defend myself, but to expose the true murderers as well. Still, I must set my hand to this; nothing, it seems, is more bitter than necessity. But I have no other means of exposing the criminals than by following the methods employed by my accuser, who first exempts everyone else from guilt, and then declares that the actual manner of the death reveals me as the murderer. For

if, when everyone else appears to be innocent, that serves to fasten suspicion upon me, then, if suspicion falls upon these others, it is only reasonable for me to be freed from guilt.

[5] It is not, as the prosecution alleges, improbable, but probable, that a man wandering about in the middle of the night should be murdered for his clothes. The fact that he was not stripped of them proves nothing. If his assailants did not have time to strip him, but were frightened off by passers-by and abandoned him, they showed good sense, not madness, in preferring their lives to their booty. [6] But on the other hand, how can we know that he was not in fact murdered for his clothes, but may have seen others committing some quite different crime, and been killed by them to prevent him informing on them? Again, what about those who hated him not much less than I did – and there were many – is it not more likely that they murdered him rather than I? It was obvious to them, after all, that I would end up as the prime suspect; while I in turn knew that I would fall under suspicion because of them.

[7] Now to turn to the evidence of his servant – why should that be regarded as worthy of belief?[110] Terrified as he was by the danger he was in, it is hardly likely (*ouk eikos*) that he would recognize the murderers; it is likely (*eikos*) rather that, at the instance of those who were his masters,[111] he would assent to whatever they suggested. When we give little credence to the evidence of slaves in general – otherwise we would not submit them to torture – how is it just for you to convict me on the evidence of this one? [8] Furthermore, if one allows probabilities (*ta eikota*) the status of facts when they tend towards convicting me, one must on the same principle consider the following as bearing witness to my innocence: it was more likely (*eikoteron*) that, with a view to carrying out my plot in safety, I should take particular care not to be present at the scene of the crime than that the slave should recognize me correctly just as he was being slaughtered.

[9] I will now demonstrate that, unless I was out of my mind, I must have thought the danger which I am now in far greater, instead of less, than that arising from the indictment. If I were convicted on this charge, I knew that, though I should be

deprived of my property, yet I would not lose my life or civic rights. I should still have been living, and left to enjoy those rights; even though dependent on contributions of money[112] from my friends, I would not have been plunged into the worst possible situation. On the other hand, if I am found guilty now and executed, I shall leave the stain of disgrace and pollution upon my children; if instead I go into exile,[113] I shall become an old man without a country, begging my bread in a strange land.

[10] Of the charges brought against me, then, all are devoid of credence. But even if probability, in conflict with actuality,[114] tends towards my having killed the man, I still deserve that much the more to be acquitted by you.[115] It is clear, after all, that I would have been taking action only after severe provocation; had that not been so, I would never have been a reasonable suspect in his murder. At any rate, it is those who did kill him, and not those who had every reason to, that you would do right to convict.

[11] So then, cleared as I am of the charge in every particular, it is not I who will pollute the purity of the gods by entering their precincts, nor do I act impiously in urging you to acquit me. It is those who are prosecuting me, an innocent man, while they let the guilty escape, who will be the cause of any blight (aphoria) that ensues;[116] it is they who deserve to suffer all the penalties which they say I should be liable to, for urging you to commit impiety towards the gods.

[12] Since, then, the prosecution have rendered themselves liable to such accusations, you should put no credence in them. I myself, on the other hand, as you will see by examining my past achievements, do not concoct plots or seek after what does not belong to me.[117] On the contrary, I have made several substantial tax contributions (eisphorai); I have served many times as trierarch; I have fitted out choruses in splendid style; I have often contributed money to friends;[118] and I have frequently paid out large sums as sureties (engyai) for many. My wealth derives not from litigation, but from application;[119] I observe my religious duties, and I abide by the law. As I am the man I am, then, you should not adjudge me guilty of anything unholy or disgraceful.

[13] If I were being prosecuted by a living opponent, I would not be satisfied with merely defending myself;[120] I would have demonstrated the villainy both of this man himself and of those who, while professing to be championing his cause, are in fact pursuing advantage for themselves at my expense by prosecuting me.[121] However, more out of a sense of propriety than justice to myself, I shall forego the opportunity. Instead, I entreat you, gentlemen, you who are the judges and arbiters of the most serious of matters: take pity on my misfortune and become its healers; and do not, by associating yourself with my opponents' attack, allow me to be destroyed by them without regard for either justice or the gods.

(iii) *Second Speech for the Prosecution*

[1] He is committing outrage upon the term 'misfortune',[122] when he uses it to cover up his crime, in the hope of concealing his unholy behaviour. Neither does he deserve your 'pity', since he has involved his victim in a doom he never asked for, whereas it was with full deliberation that he placed himself in danger. That it is he who committed the murder we have proved in our first speech; that his defence is invalid we shall now undertake to demonstrate by refuting it.

[2] Let us postulate that the murderers were disturbed by people approaching and made off in haste, leaving their victims before they had stripped them. Then, even if the persons who came upon them found the master dead, they would have found the slave still conscious, as he was rescued alive and was able to give evidence, and, through questioning him, would have informed us clearly who had done this deed; and thus this fellow would not have been in the dock. Or postulate, on the other hand, that others, who had been seen by the two committing some similar crime, murdered them to avoid being unmasked. Then news of that crime would have been publicized at the same time as the news of the present murder, and suspicion would have been directed towards those concerned. *[3]* Again, I do not see how persons who were less at risk should have plotted against the dead man sooner than persons who had more to fear. The fears and sense of injustice of the latter were enough

to overcome prudence; whereas with the former the risk and disgrace involved, which would weigh more heavily with them than their grievance, would have been sufficient, even if they had contemplated doing the deed, to control the rage that was dominating their reason.[123]

[4] Further, they are wrong when they say that the evidence of the slave is unworthy of trust. Where evidence of this sort is concerned, slaves are not tortured: rather, they are given their freedom. It is when they deny a theft or enter into a conspiracy of silence with their masters that we judge that they will only tell the truth under torture.[124]

[5] Nor is it more likely that he was absent from, rather than present at, the scene of the crime. For if he was absent, he was going to be liable to the same risks that he would run if present – for any of his accomplices, if caught, would have pointed the finger at him as the originator of the plot – and he would have carried out the task less effectively; for there would not be one of those taking part who would not have been more hesitant about it than he was himself.

[6] Furthermore, he did not believe the danger arising from the indictment to be less serious, but actually much greater, than that in which he now stands, as I shall now show. Let us grant that he had equal hopes of conviction or acquittal in one case as in the other. But he had no hope of the indictment being abandoned as long as this man was alive; for he would never have persuaded him to that. He did not, on the other hand, expect to be brought to trial on the present charge, as he reckoned that he could get away with the killing.

[7] Again, in claiming that he should not be condemned by you on the ground that he is so obviously the suspect, he is arguing illegitimately. If this fellow, involved as he was in the greatest dangers, could be turned from his purpose by the knowledge that suspicion would fall upon himself, nobody at all would have plotted the crime; for everyone who was involved in less danger than him would also be less likely than him to have undertaken the crime, since they would still have been more frightened by the certainty of being suspected than by that danger.[125]

[8] As for his tax-contributions and his financing of choruses, they may be sufficient indication of his wealth, but they are far from being evidence for his innocence. For it is precisely his fear of losing his wealth that makes him a likely candidate to have committed this murder, unholy as it is. When he claims that murderers are not those who are likely to have killed, but who have actually killed, he is of course quite right about those who have actually killed – if it were the case that those who actually killed him were known to us; but as they are not, proof must be based on what is probable, and that shows that the defendant, and no one else but the defendant, is the murderer. Crimes of this kind, after all, are committed in secret, not in the presence of witnesses.

[9] Since, then, he has been proved guilty of the murder so plainly on the basis of his own defence, he is asking nothing else of you but to transfer his own pollution on to yourselves. We, on the other hand, ask you for no favours; we simply put it to you that if neither arguments from probability nor the evidence of witnesses serve to prove the defendant guilty on this occasion, it will no longer be possible to prove any defendant guilty. *[10]* When there is no doubt about how the murder took place, when the tracks of suspicion lead plainly in the direction of the defendant, and when the evidence given by the slave is entirely trustworthy, how can you in justice acquit him? And if he is acquitted by you unjustly, then it is not upon us that the dead man's curse will lie: it is upon you that he will bear down. *[11]* In due consciousness of this, then, come to the dead man's aid, take vengeance on his murderer, and purify the city from pollution. Do this, and three benefits will follow: you will reduce the number of those who plot such crimes; you will increase the number of those who observe piety; and you will rid yourselves of the defilement which rests upon you because of this fellow.

(iv) *Second Speech for the Defence*
[1] See, I am voluntarily putting myself in the hands of that misfortune, which they claim that I am blaming unfairly,[126] and of the enmity of these people, on the one hand fearing the comprehensiveness of their slander of me, but on the other

trusting in your good judgement and in the truth of my account of my actions. But if I am deprived by them even of the right to lament before you the misfortunes that beset me, I do not know to what other refuge I can turn.

[2] The methods being used to misrepresent me, after all, are most remarkable – not to say most villainous! They present themselves to you as prosecutors and avengers of murder; yet they are in effect putting up a defence of all the real suspects, and then, because they cannot find the real killer, declaring that I am the murderer.[127] The fact that they are doing the opposite to the task enjoined upon them shows that they are seeking not so much to punish the murderer as to have me wrongfully executed. [3] I conceive it to be my job simply to respond to the evidence of the servant, for I am not here either to identify the murderers or to prove their guilt, but am defending myself against the charge brought against me. Nevertheless, I must go further than this, in order to demonstrate both that these people are plotting to destroy me and that I should be freed from all suspicion. [4] I ask only that my misfortune,[128] which they are using against me, you may transform into good fortune; and I call upon you, by acquitting me, to make me a happy man, rather than, by condemning me, to render me an object of pity.

They assert that those who came upon them being assaulted were in all cases more likely to inquire as to the identity of their attackers, and then bring the news back to the victim's home, rather than running away and abandoning them.[129] [5] On the contrary, I do not believe that there exists a man so impulsive or so brave that, on coming in the middle of the night upon corpses breathing their last, would not turn and run away rather than put himself in danger of his life by stopping to inquire who had committed this crime. Now since it is more likely that the passers-by did the natural thing,[130] those who murdered these people for their clothes can no longer reasonably (*eikotôs*) be let off, and I am free and clear of suspicion.

[6] Whether or not any other crimes were reported at the same time as this murder, who knows?[131] It was nobody's business to look into this; and in the absence of any clear announcement, it

is not incredible that those involved in such a crime should have committed this murder too.

[7] And then again, why should the evidence of the slave be considered more trustworthy than that of free men?[132] Free men are liable to fines and loss of civic rights, if their evidence is deemed not to be true; whereas this slave, who did not provide us with a chance to cross-examine or torture him – what sanction can there be for him? Or what means of disproving him is left? He was going to be able to give testimony without any sanctions at all, so it is not surprising that he was persuaded to make false accusations against me by his masters, who are my enemies.[133] On the other hand, it would be nothing short of impious if I were executed by you on the basis of such unsafe evidence as this.

[8] These people assert that it is less plausible that I was absent from the murder than that I was present at it. But I myself, not relying on probability but on facts, will prove that I was not present. All the slaves in my household, male and female, I am prepared to surrender to you for torture;[134] and if I am revealed not to have been at home in bed that night, or to have left the house for any reason, I admit that I am the murderer. The night was no ordinary one; for the murder was committed at the Diipoleia.[135]

[9] On the subject of my wealth, the fear of losing which they allege as a plausible motive for killing him, the situation is just the opposite from what is assumed. It is rather the unfortunate who have something to gain from causing mayhem,[136] as their current unfortunate state may be expected to profit from changes; the fortunate, on the other hand, are well advised to preserve their prosperity by maintaining the status quo, for if there is change their good fortune may turn into bad.[137]

[10] Again, whereas they claim to convict me on the basis of probability (ta eikota), they maintain that I am, not the probable, but the actual[138] murderer. But the other probabilities in the case have been shown to be in my favour – for not only has the witness who denounced me been shown to be unreliable, but there is now no means of cross-examining him. Likewise, I have shown that the evidence[139] supports me, and not them; and the traces of the murder have been proved to lead not to me,

but those whom the prosecution are absolving. So, then, since all the charges made against me have been shown to be unfounded, it is not the case that there is no way of convicting criminals, if I am acquitted; rather, it would follow that no defence will be effective for persons accused, if I am condemned.

[11] You see how unjustly my accusers are attacking me. Yet despite the fact that it is they who are striving to have me put to death in so impious a way, they maintain that they are free from guilt, and that I, who am urging you to act with piety, am acting impiously. But as I am innocent of all their charges, I solemnly beg you on my own behalf to respect the piety of those who have done no wrong, just as on the dead man's behalf I remind you of his claim to vengeance, and urge you not to punish the guiltless, and thus let the guilty escape; for once I am dead, no one will seek further for the truly guilty. [12] So, having due regard for these considerations, do you, in a spirit of both piety and justice, grant me acquittal, and do not wait until you are forced to repent by recognizing your mistake; for repentance in cases such as this brings with it no remedy.

Second Tetralogy

Antiphon now turns to a case of involuntary manslaughter. One young man, practising the javelin in a gymnasium, has accidentally struck and killed another youth, who ran in front of his throw. The parents of the dead youth wish to claim that, although he is innocent of intentional killing, the killer is nonetheless polluted with blood-guilt, and should be exiled for the prescribed period (at least one year). The defence argues that, since the death took place through carelessness on the part of the victim, all responsibility rests with the victim, and no guilt or pollution accrues to the doer of the deed. Presumably what interested Antiphon about this case was the problem of responsibility – a question which we have seen Protagoras debating for a whole day with Pericles (above, ch. 1, §5).

71. (i) *Opening Speech for the Prosecution*[140]
[1] When there is agreement as to the facts, cases may be settled in advance by the relevant law and by those who voted it into law in the Assembly, which together are sovereign over every

aspect of the constitution; but if there is any matter in dispute, this, gentlemen of the jury, devolves on you to decide. However, I do not think that the defendant will in fact enter into any dispute with me. My son was struck in the side, in the gymnasium,[141] by a javelin thrown by this young man here, and died on the spot.

[2] I do not accuse him of killing my son deliberately, but of killing him by accident[142] – though the loss to me is not less from an accidental than from a deliberate killing. If he has not caused upset[143] to the dead boy himself, he has certainly caused it to the living. I ask you accordingly to pity the childlessness of his parents, show sorrow for his own untimely end, prevent his killer from setting foot where he should not set foot, and not permit the whole city to suffer defilement on his account.

(ii) *Opening Speech for the Defence*

[1] It is now clear to me that misfortunes and necessities can of themselves force even those who avoid litigation into court, and those who value their peace to assume a pose of daring and generally to go against their nature in both word and deed.[144] For I myself, who am least of all such a one nor wish to be, if I am not very much mistaken in myself, have now been compelled by the misfortune in which I find myself, quite contrary to my normal tendency, to come forward as a defendant in a case in which I found it difficult enough myself to acquire any actual knowledge, and in which I am in still greater difficulty as to how I shall explain it to you. [2] However, constrained as I am by harsh necessity, I too, gentlemen of the jury, take refuge in your pity, and beg of you, if I seem to you to speak with more subtlety than is usual, do not allow the aforementioned circumstances to prejudice you against my defence to the extent of inducing you to base your judgement on appearance rather than reality.[145] Appearance as regards actions tends to the advantage of those skilled in speaking; the reality, on the other hand, tends to the advantage of those who act with justice and piety.

[3] It was my belief that, in educating my son in those activities from which the state derives most advantage, benefit would accrue to both of us; but the outcome has been very much

counter to what I had expected. For the boy – not as a result of insolent or intemperate behaviour, but while practising the javelin in the gymnasium with his age-mates – struck a blow, certainly, but killed no one, at least if one considers the *truth* of what he did:[146] he became unwittingly involved in blame for a mistake which another person committed against himself.

[4] If it had been the case that the javelin had wounded the boy through being directed towards him outside the bounds of the designated throwing area, then no argument would be left to us that we had not caused his death. But since in fact the lad ran into the path of the javelin, and placed himself in its way, <my son was prevented>[147] from hitting his target, while the other, moving into the path of the javelin, was struck, and thus burdened us with the blame for something we did not do. [5] Since it was because he ran in front of the javelin that the boy was struck, my lad is not justly accused, as he did not strike anyone who was standing out of the way of the target. If, however, it is clear to you that the boy was not struck while standing still, but only after deliberately moving into the path of the javelin, you have a still clearer demonstration that his death was due to his own error;[148] for he would not have been struck if he had stayed where he was and not run across.

[6] Since, you see, it is agreed on both sides that the boy's death was accidental (*akousios*), it is by discovering which of the two was guilty of making a mistake that we should arrive at a yet clearer proof of who was the true killer. For it is those guilty of a mistake in carrying out their intentions who are the cause of accidents; even as it is those who voluntarily do a thing or allow it to be done to them who become responsible for what happens to them.

[7] Now my lad, on his side, did not make any mistake in relation to anyone: in undertaking his practice, he was not doing anything forbidden, but what he had been ordered to do, and he was not involving himself with those who were exercising when he threw his javelin, but was in his proper place among the other javelin throwers; nor was it through throwing wide of the target and sending his javelin into the bystanders that he hit the boy, but through doing everything correctly, as he intended. He was

not therefore the cause of any accident, but rather the victim of one, in that he was prevented from hitting the target.

[8] The boy, on the other hand, in deciding to run forward, missed the critical moment (*kairos*) at which he could have run across without being hit, and became involved in a situation which was far from what he wished. Accidentally committing an error (*akousiôs hamartôn*) which affected himself, he has thus met with a disaster for which he has himself alone to blame. He has brought punishment upon himself for his mistake, and has therefore duly paid the penalty – not that we rejoice at or approve of this outcome; we actually feel both sympathy and sorrow!

The mistake thus reverts upon this dead boy; so the act which caused his death is not to be regarded as ours, but as that of the person who committed the mistake: and thus the result of the action, reverting as it does upon the agent, not only frees us from blame, but has caused the agent quite justly to be punished, at the same time as he committed the mistake.

[9] Furthermore, we are also absolved by the law on which he relies in prosecuting me for killing the boy, forbidding as it does the taking of life whether wrongfully or otherwise.[149] For the mistake perpetrated by the victim himself clears the defendant here of having killed him by accident, while the prosecutor does not even suggest that he is guilty of deliberate homicide. Thus he is freed of both accusations, that is to say, of killing the boy either accidentally (*akôn*) or deliberately (*hekôn*).

[10] Both the truth of the situation and the statute in accordance with which he is prosecuted absolve my son from guilt; but our way of life does not justify our being involved in such a misfortune as this.[150] Not only will my son suffer an appalling injustice if he is made to bear the guilt of such a mistake as this, but I myself, who am to no greater degree, but just equally, free from guilt, will encounter misfortunes many times worse than he. Once my son's life is ruined,[151] the remainder of my life will not be worth living, and in my childlessness I will be, as it were, confined still living in a tomb.[152]

Have pity, then, on this child, who is suffering a misfortune none of his fault; and have pity on me, old and wretched as I am, for my sudden and unexpected sorrow. Do not by your condemnation bring us to a miserable fate, but rather show your piety by acquitting us. The dead boy is not deprived of vengeance for the misfortune he has suffered,[153] and we in turn cannot in justice be expected to share the blame for errors committed by the other side. So have respect for the truly pious response that is appropriate to these actions, and for justice, and acquit us in due accord with piety and justice; do not impose upon a father and a son, a most wretched pair, miseries inappropriate to the time of life of either of us.[154]

(iii) Second Speech for the Prosecution

[1] That the grip of necessity can induce all men to speak and to act in a way contrary to their nature is a fact of which the defendant seems to me to be giving you proof in very deed.[155] Whereas hitherto he was a man least likely to exhibit shamelessness or audacity, today he is being compelled by his actual misfortune to say things such as I certainly never thought he would say. [2] I was foolish enough to imagine that he would not make any reply; otherwise I would not have delivered just one speech instead of two, and thus deprived myself of half of my allotted time for prosecution;[156] and he, but for this audacity of his, would not have had a twofold advantage over me by using one speech to answer the one speech for the prosecution, and then being able to make accusations of his own without fear of an answer.[157]

[3] Seeing that he has gained such an advantage over us in respect of the speeches, and an even greater one by his methods of procedure, it is outrageous that this fellow should beg you to listen sympathetically[158] to his defence. I, on the other hand, having done no one any harm, but having myself suffered cruel misfortunes, and now suffering even more cruel ones, come with real justification[159] to appeal to your sympathy, and to make my own request of you, gentlemen: you, who are the proper avengers of impious deeds, while determining what is righteous, do not let rascally subtleties of argument divert you from recognizing the truth of the situation, so that you regard it as false; [4] for such subtleties are composed more for plausibility than for

truth, while the truth will be told with less trickery, and will thus be less powerful to convince.[160]

Trusting in justice as I do, I hold his defence in contempt; but my distrust of the harshness of fate instils terror into me lest I not only lose the benefit of my child, but may see him convicted by you in addition to being the cause of his own death. [5] For this fellow has reached such a pitch of audacity and shamelessness as to assert that he who threw the javelin and killed neither wounded nor killed, while he who neither touched the javelin nor had any intention of throwing it, missing all the rest of the earth and every other body on it, thrust the javelin through his own ribs. I would actually seem to have a better case in charging the lad with wilful murder than the defendant in claiming that the lad neither struck nor killed anyone.[161]

[6] My son was ordered at that moment by the trainer, who was collecting the javelins of the throwers, to go and pick them up;[162] but by reason of the lack of discipline of the thrower of the cast, he fell into the path of the offensive weapon of this lad; and so, without having done anything wrong to anyone in any respect, he died a miserable death. The other lad, however, who failed to note the designated time for picking up the javelins, was not prevented from striking his target, but indeed struck a target sad and bitter for me; he did not kill my son deliberately, certainly, but it would be truer to say that he acted deliberately than that he neither struck nor killed him.

[7] They[163] killed my son, then, no less by acting unwittingly than if they had acted deliberately; but, in seeking to deny that he killed him at all, they wish to maintain that they are not liable to the law which forbids the taking of life whether justly or unjustly. So, then, who struck the blow? To whom is the killing to be referred? To the spectators, or perhaps to the boys' attendants – whom no one has dreamed of accusing of anything? My boy's death is no mystery, but, for me at least, only too plain. I believe that the law is correct in ordering the punishment of those who have killed; not only is it just that he who killed without meaning to kill should be liable to punishments that he did not mean to incur, but it is also the case that the victim, whose injury is not lessened by the fact that it was involuntary

rather than deliberate, would be unjustly treated if he were deprived of retribution.

[8] Nor does the defendant deserve to get off because of the bad luck involved in the commission of his error. For if, on the one hand, the bad luck is not due to any divine involvement, then, as an error, it is only right that it should be a misfortune for the person who committed it; but if, on the other hand, the curse of God has fallen upon the doer of this deed by reason of some previous act of impiety on his part, then it is not right for us to stand in the way of divine visitations.

[9] They declared, too, that it is not fitting for those who have lived as decently as they have to be visited with ill treatment. But what about us, in that case? How would we be receiving right treatment, if we are punished with death when our way of life has been in no way inferior to theirs?[164]

When he argues that he is free from wrongdoing, and claims that ill consequences must fall upon those who have done wrong, and not be misdirected towards the innocent, he is actually taking our side. For it would be both an injustice to my son, who was killed by this lad here, though he had done nothing wrong towards anybody, if he were left unavenged; and I myself would suffer outrageous treatment if I, being even more guiltless than he, fail to gain from you the satisfaction granted to me by the law.

[10] Furthermore, on the basis of what the defence themselves admit, the accused cannot be acquitted of wrongdoing or of accidental killing, but, if anything, he and my son are equally liable to both charges, as I shall now demonstrate.[165] Granting that, because my son ran across in front of the javelin and did not remain still, he may justly be taken to be his own killer, then this lad is not free from blame either; he would only be innocent if he had been standing still and not throwing his javelin when my boy was killed. The killing was therefore due to both of them, but my boy, whose fault rebounded on himself, has punished himself even more severely than the fault deserved (for he has died); so how can it be right that his accomplice, who joined him in committing an offence against an innocent party, should get away scot-free?

[11] Since, then, the accused have themselves testified in their

defence to the fact that the lad had some involvement in the killing, you can hardly, in accordance with justice and piety, acquit him. If we, whose lives have been destroyed through the defendant's mistake, were found guilty of having brought death upon ourselves, we would suffer not piety but impiety at your hands; and if those who have brought death upon us are not banned from the customary rites and places of worship,[166] you will be showing disrespect to the gods no less than you would by acquitting those who are unholy.[167]

Since the pollution as a whole, from whatever source it derives, ultimately devolves upon you, you must exercise the greatest caution with respect to this issue. If you find him guilty and ban him from setting foot where the law forbids him to set foot, you will be free from liability to any charges;[168] but if you acquit him, you will become liable to them. [12] So for the sake of both your righteousness and the laws, take this fellow away and punish him; and do not on your own account take a share in his pollution, but let us, the parents whom he has condemned to a living death,[169] at least appear to have our misery alleviated.

(iv) *Second Speech for the Defence*

[1] It seems to me that, as is only to be expected, my opponent was so caught up with his own speech of prosecution that he did not understand my defence; you, on the other hand, should bear in mind that, while we, as the contestants, take a partial view of the case, each of us naturally considering that his own version of it is the just one, your duty is to consider the facts conscientiously,[170] since it is from what is said that the truth of the matter must be deduced. [2] As far as I am concerned, if I have said anything which is false, I am content that you should bring under equal suspicion whatever truth I have spoken. On the other hand, if I have spoken the truth, but have also used precise and subtle arguments,[171] it is not I who uttered them, but he whose action made them necessary, to whom any annoyance they may cause should justly be directed.

[3] I want you first of all to grasp that a man is not a murderer just because somebody says he is, but only if someone can prove it. Now the prosecution accepts that the event happened as we

describe it, but he disputes as to who properly is to be regarded as the killer, despite the fact that there is no other means of demonstrating this than by examining what happened. [4] He indignantly complains that his son has been slandered, if he should be proved a killer when he neither threw the javelin nor had any intention of doing so; but that is not a response to my argument. I am not claiming that his son threw the javelin or struck himself; but simply that, since he moved within range of the javelin, his death was caused, not by my lad, but by himself – for he was not killed when standing still. Since this running across was the cause of his destruction, it follows that, if it was at the command of his trainer that he ran across, his trainer would be the person who killed him; but if he moved into the path of the missile on his own impulse, then his destruction was caused by himself.

[5] I do not wish to embark on any other argument until I demonstrate still more clearly which of the two[172] was responsible for this event. My lad did not miss his target any more than those who were practising with him, nor did he, through his own mistake, commit any of the acts of which he is accused. The other boy, on the other hand, did not do the same as his fellow onlookers, but moved into the path of the javelin, and thus clearly demonstrates that it was through his own mistake that he suffered worse misfortunes than those who stayed where they were. The former, in throwing, would not have been guilty of an error of any sort, if no one had moved into the path of his missile; while the latter would not have been hit, if he had remained where he was among the spectators.

[6] I will now proceed to show that my son was not more involved in the boy's death than any one of his fellow javelin-throwers. For if it was because of the fact that my son was throwing a javelin that the boy was killed, then all those practising with him would participate in the blame, for it was not because of their failure to throw that they did not strike him, but simply because he did not come within range of the javelin of any one of them. Similarly, my lad, who made no greater mistake than they, would not have hit the boy any more than they did, if he stayed where he was among the spectators.

[7] Again, not only is the original error to be imputed to the boy alone, but also a degree of negligence.[173] Since my son saw no one running across, how could he have taken care not to hit anyone? Your boy, on the other hand, when he saw the javelin-throwing going on, might easily have taken the precaution of not running across; for he was perfectly free to stand still where he was.

[8] As for the law which they appeal to, it is a perfectly commendable one; it is indeed right and just that it should impose upon those who have killed unintentionally unintended punishments. But my lad is not guilty of error, and so cannot be justly punished for the error of another; it is enough that the latter should bear the consequences of his own errors. On the other hand, the boy, who was destroyed through his own error, simultaneously committed his error and punished himself for it. And as the killer has been punished, his killing has not gone unavenged.

[9] Since, then, the killer has paid the penalty, it is not by acquitting us, but rather by condemning us, that you will impose a burden on your consciences (*enthymion*). The boy, who is bearing the brunt of his own error, will leave behind him nothing that calls for atonement (*prostropaion*) from anyone; but if my son, who is innocent of the charge, meets with destruction, there will be that much the greater burden on the consciences of those who have condemned him.

If the dead boy is proved to have been his own killer by the arguments that have been presented to you, it is not we who have stated them who are responsible for that, but the nature of his own actions. *[10]* Since investigation proves conclusively that the boy was his own killer, the law, in acquitting us of blame, lays the condemnation on the true killer. Do not, then, plunge us into miseries which we do not deserve, nor do you yourselves go against the will of God in coming to the aid of our opponents in their misfortunes. Remember, as it is right and just that you should, that the accident was caused by the one who moved into the path of the javelin, and acquit us; for we are not to blame for his death.

Third Tetralogy

We now have a situation where a killing takes place in consequence of a drunken brawl. This case has a certain amount in common with the second, in that the plea of the defence is justification, and in the fact that the dead man caused his own death. The difference here is that the defendant did intend to aim a blow at the victim, if only to defend himself; the issue is whether his use of force was justified, or excessive.[174] *As in the previous case, a complication as regards laying the blame is introduced, in the person of a doctor, to whom the badly injured victim was entrusted by his relatives, and under whose care he died (although a passing attempt is made to blame the trainer in the Second Tetralogy).*

Another difference worth noting between this and the previous cases is that the evidence of witnesses is important, as it would be in most real-life cases, and is referred to by both prosecution and defence,[175] *though it is of course not included in the text.*

Finally, this sequence exhibits an oddity (which may, indeed, be reflective of real-life cases): the defendant decamps before the end of the trial, leaving the second speech for the defence to be delivered on his behalf by his friends.

72. (i) Opening Speech for the Prosecution[176]

[1] It is the custom – and a good one too – in cases of murder that juries must take particular care that litigants observe justice both in conducting their case and in presenting their evidence, neither letting the guilty go free nor bringing the innocent to trial. [2] For when God wished to create the human race and brought the first of us into existence,[177] he endowed us with the earth and sea as our nurturers and preservers, that we might not perish for lack of the necessities of life before our natural end in old age. Whoever, then, when our life has been found worthy of such consideration by God, unlawfully kills another human being both sins against the gods and casts confusion upon the laws of man. [3] For the victim, deprived of the gifts which God has given him, naturally leaves behind him the ill will of his spirits of vengeance (*alitêrioi*), the agents of God's

punishment,[178] which they who prosecute and testify in defiance of justice introduce into their own homes, defiling them with a defilement that is not proper to them, since they associate themselves with the sin of him who committed the offence. *[4]* And accordingly, if we, as avengers of the dead, should accuse innocent persons because of some private enmity, not only will our failure to avenge the murdered man lay us open to being haunted by the awful spirits of vengeance, to whom the dead will appeal for justice, but by unjustly causing the death of the innocent, we are liable to be punished for murder, and, because we have persuaded you to act contrary to law, we too become liable for your error.

[5] I certainly fear this, and thus it is that I bring the true sinner before you, so that I may stand clear of any of the above charges; and if you in turn give such attention to the trial as is commensurate with the points that I have just made, and impose upon the criminal a sentence appropriate to the injury which he has done, you will ensure that the entire city is free of defilement.

[6] If the defendant had killed his victim accidentally (*akôn*), he would be deserving of some degree of mercy. But in fact he committed, with outrageous wantonness, a drunken assault upon an old man, striking him and throttling him until he deprived him of life. So for killing him he is liable to the penalties laid down for murder; and for overturning all the customary rights to respect enjoyed by the aged, it is only just that he not be exempt from the full punishment usual in such cases. *[7]* It is accordingly correct that the law hand him over to you for punishment; and you have listened to the witnesses who were present at his drunken outburst.[179] You must, then, in exacting recompense for the lawlessness of his behaviour, and punishing his arrogant violence as harshly as the injury which it has caused demands, deprive him in his turn of a life which contrived the death of another.

(ii) *Opening Speech for the Defence*
[1] I am not at all surprised that the prosecution's speech was brief; after all, for them the danger is not that they may suffer

some harm, but that they may fail to satisfy their enmity by bringing destruction on me contrary to justice. On the other hand, that they should want to put this incident, in which the victim had himself to blame rather than me, on a level with cases of the highest seriousness gives me, I think, reasonable cause for indignation. By initiating violence, and making a drunken assault on a man in a far more sober state than himself, he has been responsible not only for his own disaster, but also for this accusation against me.

[2] It is my view that these people are behaving with neither justice nor piety in laying a charge against me. Their man initiated the violence; and even if I had used iron or stone or wood to repel him, I would not even thus have been at fault – for aggressors are liable to receive in return, not the equal of what they hand out, but more and worse. In fact, when struck by him with his fists, I simply used my own to retaliate for the blows which I received. Was I not justified in that?

[3] All right, then. 'But', he will object, 'the law, in forbidding either justified or unjustified killing, exposes you as liable to the penalty laid down for murder; for the man is dead.' But I maintain, for a second and a third time, that I did not kill him. If the man had died straight away from the blows which he received, his death might have been imputed to me, though even then I would have been justified – aggressors deserve to be repaid not just equally but more severely – [4] but in fact he died many days later, having been entrusted to the care of an incompetent doctor,[180] his death being due to the incompetence of the doctor, not to the blows which he received. The other doctors warned him that, though he was curable, he would die if he followed this particular treatment; but nonetheless, thanks to your advice, he did die, and thereby caused an outrageous charge to be brought against me.

[5] Furthermore, the law under which I am being prosecuted actually tends to my acquittal, since it lays down that the party who acted with premeditation is guilty of the murder.[181] Now how could I have acted with any premeditation against him that he would not have had against me? I resisted him on his own terms, and returned him blow for blow; so it is clear that

I had only the degree of premeditation against him that he had against me.

[6] And again, if anyone thinks that his death occurred because of the blows which he received, and that therefore I am his murderer, let him consider, on the other hand, that it was the initiator of the conflict who was the cause of those blows, and that therefore they reveal him, and not me, as the cause of his death. I would not have defended myself, after all, if I had not been struck by him first.

Thus I am acquitted both by the <law and by the fact that he is the>[182] aggressor; in no way am I his murderer. As for the dead man, if his death was due to misfortune (*atykhia*), he had only himself to blame for that misfortune: he was unfortunate in striking the first blow. Or again, if his death is to be blamed on some failure of judgement (*aboulia*), it was through his own failure of judgement that he perished; for he was not in a sound state of mind when he struck me.

[7] That I have been accused in contravention of justice, I have now proved. But I want to demonstrate also that my accusers are themselves answerable to all the charges that they are directing against me. By accusing me of murder when I am guiltless, and by seeking to rob me of the life which God has given me, they are committing impiety against God; by seeking to bring about my death unjustly, they are confounding the laws of man and are becoming in effect my murderers; and by trying to persuade you to execute me impiously, they themselves become subverters[183] of your righteousness.

[8] As for these fellows, then, may God lay on them the punishment they deserve. You, on the other hand, must consider your own position, and be more prepared to acquit me than to condemn me. If I am acquitted unjustly, in the event that I get off because you have not been properly informed of the facts, then it is on whoever failed to inform you, not on you, that I shall cause the dead man's avenging spirit (*prostropaios*) to descend; whereas if I am wrongfully condemned by you, then it is upon you, and not upon my accuser, that I shall turn the anger of my avenging daemons (*alitêrioi*).

[9] In this realization, then, let the consequences of their

impiety recoil on the prosecution; clear yourselves of blame; and acquit me as piety and justice demand; for thus all of us, as citizens, will best stay clear of guilt.

(iii) *Second Speech for the Prosecution*

[1] It does not surprise me that this fellow, having committed so shocking a crime, has spoken in a similar vein to his acts; and at the same time I quite understand your readiness, in your concern to discover the exact nature of what happened, to put up with listening to such utterances as should properly be rejected out of hand. Thus, he admits that he administered the blows which caused the other's death, yet he denies that he is the murderer of the dead man, and actually asserts, alive as he is and looking upon the light of day, that we, who are seeking to avenge the victim, are in fact his own murderers. I want now to demonstrate that the remainder of his defence is on a similar level.

[2] To start with, he claimed that, even if the man did die as a result of his blows, he did not kill him; for it is the aggressor who is to blame for what results, and is condemned as such by the law; and the aggressor was the dead man. First, let me tell you that young men are more likely to be the aggressors and behave provocatively when drunk than the old.[184] The young are roused by their natural arrogance, the fullness of their physical strength and their lack of experience with wine to indulge their anger; while older men tend to greater sobriety though their experience of the effects of drink, the weakness of age and their fear of young men's strength.

[3] Furthermore, it was not with the same weapons, but with quite opposite ones, that the accused defended himself, as the facts show.[185] The one killed through employing hands at the peak of their strength, while the other defended himself ineffectively against one stronger than himself, and died without leaving on his opponent any indication of his attempts at defence. Moreover, if it was with his hands and not with a weapon of iron that the defendant did the killing, then in so far as his hands are more a part of him than is steel, by that much the more is he a murderer.

[4] Again, he had the temerity to assert that the one who struck the first blow, even though he did not succeed in killing, is more truly the murderer than he who killed; for, he says, it is the aggressor who wills the murder. But I would maintain very much the opposite. If our hands are the instruments which carry out what each of us intend, he who struck and did not kill was the intentional author only of the blow, whereas he who struck the blow with deadly result[186] was the intentional author of the murder; for it was as the result of the act that the defendant performed with intent that the man was killed.

Again, while the striker of the blow may be said to have suffered a misfortune (*atykhia*),[187] the receiver of the blow suffered a disaster (*symphora*); for the latter was killed as a result of the other's act, so that it was not through his own error (*hamartia*), but through that of the man who struck him, that he died. The former did more than he intended, and, by his own misfortune, killed a man whom he did not intend to kill.[188]

[5] I am surprised that, when the defendant alleges that the man's death was due to the doctor,[189] he should place the responsibility of that upon us, on whose advice it was that he received medical care. For after all, if we had failed to put him under a doctor's care, the defendant would surely have maintained that his death was due to lack of medical attention. But even if his death was due to the doctor, which it was not, the doctor is not his murderer (for the law frees him from blame);[190] on the other hand, as it was only by reason of the blows administered by this fellow that we entrusted the dead man to a doctor at all, how can the murderer be anyone else but the one who made it necessary for us to employ the services of the doctor?

[6] So then, despite the fact that it has been proved so clearly and so thoroughly that he killed the dead man, this fellow has risen to such a pitch of impudence and shamelessness that he is not content with defending his own misdeeds; he is actually accusing us, who are taking steps to expiate the defilement generated by him, of committing lawless and unholy acts.

[7] Utterances as shocking as this, or even more so, are quite in character for one guilty of such a crime as he has committed. We, on the other hand, have clearly demonstrated how the death took place;[191] we have shown that the blow which caused it is freely admitted; and we have proved that the law fixes the responsibility for death on the striker of the blow. So therefore, in the name of the victim, we lay upon you the solemn duty of appeasing the anger of the spirits of vengeance by executing the defendant, thus cleansing the whole city of pollution.

(iv) *Second Speech for the Defence*[192]

[1] The defendant, not because he deemed himself to be guilty, but rather in fear of the aggressiveness of his prosecutors, has withdrawn into exile. We, his friends, feel that we are doing our duty to him more profitably by helping when he is alive than by defending his memory when dead. Certainly, it would have been best if he could have pleaded his own case; but since the present course of action appeared to him less dangerous, it remains for us, to whom his loss would be a very great sorrow, to complete his defence.

[2] It is my view, certainly, that it is with him who struck the first blow that the blame for the action rests. The prosecution is simply not being plausible in arguing that the defendant was the aggressor.[193] If outrageous behaviour (*hybrizein*) on the part of the young and self-control on the part of the old were as natural as seeing with the eyes and hearing with the ears,[194] then there would be no need for you to deliberate at all; their very age alone would serve to convict the young. As things are, however, since many young men are self-controlled, and many old men become violent when drunk, their argument does not support the prosecutor any more than the defendant.

[3] If this argument be recognized to support us as much as it does the dead man, we have the entire advantage; for according to the witnesses, it was he who started the brawl.[195] Since that is the case, the defendant is cleared of all the other charges brought against him as well. For if it is the case that it is the one who struck a blow, which is what ultimately caused you to seek

the assistance of a doctor, who is the murderer, rather than the person who actually killed,[196] it follows that the murderer is he who struck the first blow. For it was he who forced both his victim to strike back in self-defence, and himself, when struck, to have recourse to the doctor. The defendant, then, would suffer quite outrageous injustice, if he, being neither the killer nor the initiator of the fight, should be declared a murderer in place of the real killer and the real aggressor.

[4] Nor again is the defendant any more than the prosecutor likely to have been the one with the intention to kill.[197] If it had been the case that he who struck the first blow had intended not to kill, but merely to strike, while he who was defending himself had intended to kill, then it would indeed have been the latter who was possessed of murderous intent. But as it was, he who was defending himself also merely intended to strike, but not to kill; however, he made a mistake, and struck with an effect which he did not intend. [5] He was thus, admittedly, the intentional author of the blow; but how can he have intended the killing, seeing as he struck not as he intended (akousiôs)? In fact, responsibility even for the mistake belongs to the one who began the conflict rather than to the one who was defending himself. For the latter was seeking to return equal measure for what he had suffered, and committed his mistake under compulsion from his attacker; whereas in the case of the other, it was by reason of his own lack of self-control that he gave and received the blows that he did; and so deservedly bears the responsibility[198] both for his own mistake and for that of his victim.

[6] Again, he did not defend himself more strongly than warranted by the attack made upon him, but much more mildly, as I shall proceed to demonstrate.[199] His opponent was offensive, drunken, and violent; he took the initiative, and was not in any sense defending himself. Our friend was seeking to avoid his blows and ward him off – what he suffered, he suffered through no choice of his own (akousiôs) – and the blows he gave were given in his own defence against an aggressor, being a much milder response than the aggressor deserved; indeed, he himself took no aggressive action at all. [7] And even if his defence did

turn out more vigorous than the attack made upon him, by reason of the strength of his hands, he cannot justly be condemned by you for that. For in all cases severe penalties are imposed on an aggressor, but nowhere is any penalty prescribed for one who is acting in self-defence.

[8] The point that the taking of life, whether justifiable or unjustifiable, is forbidden,[200] has been responded to: for it was not the actual blows, but the ministrations of the doctor that led to the man's death, as is attested to by the witnesses. Further, the accident was caused by the aggressor, not by the one who was acting in self-defence. The latter gave and received all the blows which he did through no choice of his own (*akousiôs*), and therefore the accident which occurred was not of his making. The other acted in all respects voluntarily (*hekousiôs*), and it was by his own actions that he brought the misfortune upon himself; hence his mistake arose from his own misjudgement.

[9] It has been demonstrated, then, that the defendant is not liable to any of the charges brought against him. But even if both the action and the mischance which led to it are deemed to be the joint responsibility of both parties, and the defendant be considered on the basis of the arguments no more deserving of acquittal than of condemnation,[201] he should still by rights be acquitted rather than condemned.[202] Not only is it not just that his accuser should secure his conviction without clearly demonstrating that he has been wronged, but it is an offence to religion that the accused should be condemned, if the charges against him have not been conclusively proven.

[10] So then, as the defendant has been cleared from every angle of the charges made against him, we lay upon you, on his behalf, a request with more claim to righteousness than our opponents, that, in seeking to punish a murderer, you do not put an innocent party to death. For the avenging spirit[203] of the dead man will bear down nonetheless on those truly responsible, and this man, if wrongly done to death, will bring down a double pollution of avenging spirits on those who kill him. Be duly afraid of that, and consider it your duty to absolve the innocent from blame. Whoever is truly guilty you may let time

reveal, even as you may leave his punishment to those closest to the dead man. It is thus that you will best observe both justice towards men and piety towards the gods.

6 THRASYMACHUS OF CHALCEDON

LIFE AND WORKS

Thrasymachus is a figure of whom not much is known. He came from the Greek colony of Chalcedon[1] on the Bosporus, being born around 460–455 BC. At any rate, he was well known before 427, when Aristophanes refers to him in his Banqueters *(below, §4), and survived, probably, to at least the end of the century, when he composed a speech for the people of Larisa in Thessaly against King Archelaus of Macedon, who reigned from 413 to 399, and who attacked Larisa in 400. He is best known for his appearance in Book I of Plato's* Republic, *in what may be a very tendentious portrayal of his character and doctrines; otherwise he is known primarily as a rhetorical stylist rather than a thinker. He appears to have died in Chalcedon; at any rate, a monument was raised to him there after his death (cf. §11).*

First, an entry in the Suda:

1. Thrasymachus of Chalcedon: sophist, from Chalcedon in Bithynia. He first developed the use of the period and the clause, and introduced the style of rhetoric currently prevailing.[2] He was a pupil[3] of the philosopher Plato, and of the rhetorician Isocrates. He wrote *Deliberative Speeches* (*Symbouleutikoi* [i.e. *Logoi*]), *Handbook of Rhetoric, Trifles* (*Paignia*),[4] *Starting-points for Speeches* (*Aphormai Rhētorikai*).

(*Suda*, s.v. Thrasymakhos = 85A1)

To this we may append a passage from the conclusion of Aristotle's Sophistical Refutations, *in which he is contrasting, with his accustomed modesty, his own revolutionary role in the development of logic with the gradual development of rhetoric. It is interesting for the pivotal position which he assigns to Thrasymachus in this, ignoring the claims of those whom we would regard as bigger names in the sophistic movement. In Plato's* Phaedrus *(266Cff.),[5] we may note, we find a more comprehensive conspectus of rhetorical theory, which features Teisias, Thrasymachus and Theodorus, but also Gorgias, Polus, Prodicus, Hippias, Protagoras and Evenus of Paros.*

2. When, however, the initial step in discovery has been made, it is easier to add to it and develop the rest. And this is just what happened in rhetorical composition, and also with practically all the other arts. Those who made the initial discoveries in all cases progressed just a little way, whereas the famous modern practitioners of the art, entering into the inheritance, one might say, of a long series of predecessors who had gradually advanced it, have brought it to its present perfection – Teisias following the first inventors,[6] Thrasymachus following Teisias,[7] Theodorus following Thrasymachus, while many others have made numerous contributions; hence it is in no way surprising that the art has gained considerable scope.

   (Aristotle, *Sophistical Refutations* 183b28–34 = A2, extended)

Next, a useful evaluation of his style by Dionysius of Halicarnassus, in the course of a discussion of that of Lysias. There is a further evaluation of Thrasymachus' style by Dionysius given below, along with a specimen passage (§13).

3. The next virtue I find in Lysias is a most admirable one, the inventor of which Theophrastus[8] declares to be Thrasymachus, but I consider it to be Lysias. I believe, actually, that Lysias was the senior in age of the two[9] – granting that both reached their prime at the same age – and, even if this view is not accepted, then he deserves priority in that he engaged in more real forensic contests than Thrasymachus. Nevertheless, I do not wish to press the argument about priority in this virtue; for the present

purpose all I need to assert is that Lysias excelled in it, and I can do this with confidence. But what is this virtue to which I am referring? It is a style (*lexis*) in which ideas are reduced to their essentials and expressed tersely, a style most appropriate, and indeed necessary, in forensic speeches and every other form of practical contest.

(Dionysius of Halicarnassus, *Lysias* 6 = A3, extended)

A passing reference in a play of Aristophanes, the lost Banqueters *produced in 427, indicates that Thrasymachus was a well-known figure by this time – the year in which Gorgias of Leontini first came to Athens. It is part of a dialogue between a father and son.*

4. FATHER: Well, you'll get your come-uppance in time, my lad!
SON: Ha! That 'get your come-uppance' is from the rhetoricians.
FATHER: Where will all these fine phrases of yours land you in the end?
SON: 'Land you in the end' – you got that from Alcibiades!
FATHER: Why do you keep making insinuations (*hypotekmairei*) and slandering people who are just trying to practise decency?
SON: Oho, ho! O Thrasymachus! Which of the law-men came up with that piece of jargon?[10]

(Aristophanes, Fr. 198 Kock, from *The Banqueters*)

Next, a reference by Aristotle in the Rhetoric, *in the course of a discussion of simile and metaphor, to a fine turn of phrase by Thrasymachus.*

5. A simile works best when it is in effect a metaphor, for it is possible to say that a shield is *like* the drinking-cup of Ares, or that a ruin is *like* the tattered rag of a house, and to say that Niceratus is *like* a Philoctetes bitten by Pratys[11] – the simile made by Thrasymachus when he saw Niceratus, who had been beaten by Pratys in a recitation competition, still going around with his hair uncut and unkempt.

(Aristotle, *Rhetoric* III 11, 1413a5–10 = A5, extended).

Another reference in Aristotle's Rhetoric, *where he is engaged in listing types of enthymeme, may help to explain why Plato chose Thrasymachus to be the combative and bombastic propounder of the 'might is right' theory in Book I of the* Republic *– the suitability of the name attracted him. Before Plato, Thrasymachus' name had been punned on, it seems, by the physician Herodicus of Selymbria (late fifth century), a man somewhat fond of such word-play.*

6. Another procedure is to draw meaning from a name. Sophocles, for instance, says: 'O steel in heart as thou art Steel in name.'[12]

This is a device much used by people in praises of the gods. Thus, too, Conon called Thrasybulus[13] 'rash in counsel' (*thrasyboulos*), and Herodicus said of Thrasymachus, 'You are always bold in battle (*thrasymakhos*)!'; of Polus,[14] 'You are always a colt (*pôlos*)!'; and of the law-giver Draco[15] that his laws were not those of a human being but of a dragon (*drakôn*) – for they were extremely harsh.

(Ibid. II 23, 1400b17–23 = A6, extended)

A passage from Cicero's De Oratore, *in which the speaker, Quintus Lutatius Catulus, has just been commending Hippias' encyclopedic range of expertise (using the story about his appearance at the Olympic Games,[16] cf. above, ch. 4, §11), gives some indication of the range of Thrasymachus' interests as well.*

7. 'What shall I say of Prodicus of Ceos, or of Thrasymachus of Chalcedon, or of Protagoras of Abdera – each of whom both lectured and wrote what was, for their time, a great deal on natural science (*de natura rerum*) as well?'

(Cicero, *De Oratore* III 128 = A9)

Next, some representative passages from Book I of Plato's Republic *(336B), the dramatic date of which is generally reckoned to be about 411–410 (though Plato is never too concerned with chronological accuracy). What is of primary interest*

here, in fact, is not Plato's satirical portrait of Thrasymachus,
which, vivid and amusing though it is, may or may not bear any
relation to reality, but the fact that, like the other great sophists,
he is a respected guest in a rich Athenian household, in this case
that of the Syracusan metic Cephalus, one of whose sons was
the well-known speech-writer Lysias, about whose relation to
Thrasymachus we have seen Dionysius of Halicarnassus specu-
lating (§3). Significantly, perhaps, Plato does not represent
Lysias as being present at this gathering, though his elder brother
Polemarchus is, and is made by Plato to lead off the discussion
on the nature of justice.

8. [Socrates] 'Now Thrasymachus on many occasions during
our discussion had been trying to interrupt us and lay hold of
the argument, but he had always been restrained by those who
were sitting next to him, who wished to hear the discussion out.
But when we did come to a pause, and I had asked this question,[17] he could no longer contain himself, but, gathering himself
up like a wild beast, he hurled himself at us as if to tear us to
pieces.

'Polemarchus and I sprang apart in terror, but Thrasymachus
bawled out in the midst of us, "What rubbish is this, Socrates?
Why are you giving way to each other like simpletons? If you
really wish to know what justice is, then don't merely ask
questions and pride yourself on refuting any and every reply
that anyone gives to you, because you have grasped the truth
that it's easier to ask questions than to answer them. No, give
an opinion yourself, and say what you think justice is. And
don't just tell me that it is what is needful or beneficial or
profitable or gainful or advantageous; for I won't accept from
you any such drivel as that." I was struck with terror at his
words, and was filled with fear as I looked at him, and I think
that if I hadn't seen him before he saw me, I'd have been struck
dumb.[18] As it was, however, when he had at first begun to get
aggravated at the discussion, I had glanced at him first, and so I
was able to reply to him.'

(Plato, *Republic* I 336B)

This satirical portrayal goes on to the end of Book I (354B), but this extract gives a flavour of it. Just one more passage should be quoted, however, since it attributes to Thrasymachus a version of the 'might is right' doctrine that he may conceivably have held, although probably in a more reasonable form than here presented. He asserts, with characteristic bluster,

9. 'I affirm that the just is nothing else than the advantage of the stronger (*to tou kreittonos xumpheron*) –'
   (Ibid. I 338c)

a definition which Socrates then proceeds immediately to pick apart. It is possible, however, to maintain reasonably that 'justice' means no more than 'the interests of the stronger', in the sense that any system of government legislates in accordance with its overall view of society, and expects its subjects to obey its laws; and thus such obedience will constitute 'justice' within that social system – and there is no other, transcendental perspective from which one can declare laws or conduct to be just or unjust. This, though Plato profoundly dislikes it, is a perfectly plausible position to hold.

Under pressure from Socrates, Thrasymachus recasts his definition later, at 343C, as 'the other fellow's good' (allotrion agathon), but this is a more vulgar, 'locker-room' version of the theory – alleging that the honest man will always come off worse in private contracts, and so on – that he does not have to maintain to make his basic point.

The only other indication of Thrasymachus' views on political or ethical questions that we have is contained in a fragment of a political speech of his preserved by Dionysius (below, §13), and that reveals no very clear philosophical position, nor is Dionysius quoting it for that purpose, but for stylistic reasons. Otherwise, all our reports of Thrasymachus concern only details of his stylistic innovations.

We may continue with another passage from Aristotle's Rhetoric, where he is discussing the rhythms suitable to oratorical prose – he has just dismissed the 'heroic' (i.e. dactylic hexameter), iambic and trochaic metres as unsuitable.

10. There remains the paean,[19] the use of which began with Thrasymachus, though people had then no name to give it. The paean is a third class of rhythm, very similar to those just mentioned; it has in it a ratio of three to two, whereas the other two kinds have a ratio of one to one and two to one respectively. Between these two last ratios there comes the ratio of one-and-a-half, which is that of the paean.

(Aristotle, *Rhetoric* III 8, 1409a2–6 = A11, extended)

Then, we may refer back to some passages from Cicero's Orator, *quoted already in connection with Gorgias (ch. 2, §§26–8), where Thrasymachus is linked with him as the inventor of the consciously balanced period.*

On the other hand, we may quote Dionysius of Halicarnassus, in the course of his essay on the orator Isaeus (Isaeus 20), where he evaluates Thrasymachus among a number of others, including Antiphon and Critias.

11. As for those who made a profession of functional discourse and practised forensic oratory, like Antiphon of Rhamnus, Thrasymachus of Chalcedon, Polycrates of Athens,[20] Critias the leader of the Thirty, Zoilus who left the studies criticizing Homer[21] and other writers of this type, I found none more incisive or more charming than Lysias. As for Antiphon, he cleaves to the severe, old-fashioned style, and does not engage personally in either political debates or in law-suits.[22] Polycrates is ineffective in his speeches for actual lawsuits, frigid and vulgar in his display-speeches (*epideiktikoi*) and lacking in charm when charm is required. Thrasymachus is pure, subtle and inventive, and able, according as he wishes, to speak either with terseness or with an abundance of words; but he occupied himself entirely with the writing of handbooks and display-speeches, and has left no forensic speeches. The same might be said about Critias and Zoilus, except in so far as they differ from one another in the individual characteristics of their styles.

(Dionysius of Halicarnassus, *On Isaeus* 20 = A13, expanded)

Finally, a curious little notice in Athenaeus about the inscription on his funerary monument, in a context concerned with alphabet-riddles. If we could be sure that Thrasymachus composed this epitaph himself, it would be of some significance, but we cannot be.

12. Neoptolemus of Parion[23] says in his *Epitaphs from Chalcedon* that the following epitaph is inscribed on the memorial to the sophist Thrasymachus:

'My name: *Theta, rho, alpha, san, y, my, alpha, chei, ou, san*;
My native city Chalcedon; my profession, Wisdom (*sophiê*).'
(Athenaeus, *Deipnosophistae* X 454F = A8)

FRAGMENTS AND REFERENCES
TO KNOWN WORKS

It is Dionysius of Halicarnassus, in his essay On the Style of Demosthenes, *who preserves for us the only substantial fragment that survives of Thrasymachus' prose. It is the beginning of a political speech, apparently composed for delivery by a young upper-class Athenian of conservative sympathies. The speaker is sentimental about the good old days and the 'ancestral constitution', and critical of the current war. Dionysius, however, is primarily concerned, not with the content, but with the style, which for him is an excellent example of the 'middle' style, a mixture of the 'grand' and the 'simple'. The speech was probably composed in the early 420s, as the war does not seem to be long in progress. It does not necessarily express the views of Thrasymachus himself.*

13. <*Reflections on the Present Situation?*>
The third type of style was a mixed one, which was a combination of the other two. Whether the first to unite them and establish the product in its present form was Thrasymachus of Calchedon,[24] as is the view of Theophrastus,[25] or someone else,

I cannot say. But those who took this style over from him, developed it and pretty well perfected it were, among the orators, Isocrates the Athenian, and, among the philosophers, Plato the Socratic; it is impossible to find any other writers, except Demosthenes, who practised the essential and practical virtues of this style to greater effect, or who gave a better demonstration of beautiful language and adorned it more skilfully with additional artistic touches. The style of Thrasymachus, if it is really the source of the middle type, appears to possess an admirable grasp of the theory[26] of it: for it contains a well-tempered blend of the merits of the other two. But it does not exhibit a power equal to its purpose, as is exemplified by the following passage from one of his political speeches:

'I would have preferred, men of Athens, to have shared in the political life of olden times, when it was proper for young men to keep quiet, since the political situation made their participation in debate unnecessary, and their elders managed the affairs of state correctly. But since fortune has assigned us to an age in which we witness <the rule of the city by others>,[27] while we ourselves suffer the consequences (for the worst of these are not the work of gods or of chance, but of human agents), I am compelled to speak.[28] For that man is either quite devoid of wit or greatly forbearing who will permit himself to be continually exploited by anyone who wishes to, and will himself take the blame for the treachery and cowardice of others.

'We have had enough of the immediate past and the change from peace to the dangers of war; in the times we are in, we hanker after the day that is gone and live in dread of the day that is to come. Enough also of the change from concord (homonoia)[29] to mutual hostility and turbulence. In the case of others, it is excess of good fortune that makes them arrogant and seditious; we, on the other hand, in good times practised moderation, but have gone mad when faced with misfortunes, which normally have a sobering effect upon others.[30]

What, then, is a man to think or to say who is on the one hand burdened with grief over the present state of affairs, and at the same time feels that he has some proposals for preventing its continuance into the future? The first thing I would point out is that those politicians and others who are currently squabbling with one another have arrived at a paradoxical situation, such as is inevitable for those who indulge in witless wrangling; for while they imagine that they are expressing opposing views, they do not perceive that they are carrying out the same policies, and that their opponents' speeches contain the same arguments as their own.

For consider, for a start, what either side is seeking after. The first object of contention is the ancestral constitution (*patrios politeia*), though it is very easy to understand and most commonly accessible to all our citizens. For events which are beyond our personal knowledge we must rely on accounts provided by earlier generations, but as to events which were actually witnessed by our elders, we must learn of these from those who know.'[31]

Such, then, is the style of Thrasymachus, a well-blended mean of the two extreme styles, and a suitable starting-point for the study of both.

(Dionysius of Halicarnassus, *On the Style of Demosthenes* 3)

Next, the Speech for the Larisaeans. *Of this we have only one short extract, preserved by Clement of Alexandria in his* Stromateis, *in the course of a disquisition on the proneness of the Greeks to plagiarize one another. On the basis of this one cannot be certain whether, as in the Athenian speech, Thrasymachus is speaking in character, or in his own person. In the latter case, this may have been delivered during a visit to Larisa in Thessaly, and commissioned by an opponent of an alliance with Archelaus, at some time after the accession of Archelaus to the throne of Macedon in 413, and probably in close proximity to Archelaus' actual attack on Larisa in 400.*

In this connection, an interesting puzzle presents itself. There is also in existence a speech composed for a (small) Thessalian city, very probably Larisa, and attributed to the second-century AD *Athenian sophist Herodes Atticus, which concords very much in spirit with the extract which we have here. This does sound in many ways authentically fifth-century, and shows a good deal of detailed knowledge of the political scene in Thes-saly.*[32] *It has been attributed to Critias, on the grounds that Herodes was a great admirer of Critias' style, but since we know that Thrasymachus composed a speech for the Larisaeans, it seems improbable that Critias composed one as well (though he did spend some time in the region in the period from 406 to 404, just before returning to Athens to assume headship of the quisling regime known as 'the Thirty Tyrants'). However, in view of the apparent anachronism recorded in n. 32 above, it may be best to conclude that the speech is just a very good sophistic effort composed by Herodes himself in the style of Critias (we know of many themes of comparable obscurity treated by various of the great second-century sophists), rework-ing the existing speech by Thrasymachus.*[33]

14. And while Euripides says in the *Telephus*,[34] 'Shall we who are Greeks be slaves to barbarians?', Thrasymachus says in his speech *For the People of Larisa*, 'Shall we become slaves to Archelaus, Greeks as we are, to a barbarian?'

(Clement of Alexandria, *Stromateis* VI 1)

Next, we have some notices of a work entitled the Megalê Tekhnê *(Great Art), the title of what was presumably Thrasy-machus' chief manual of rhetoric; this is no doubt to be identified with the* Tekhnê Rhetorikê *listed in §1. The reference to it, which is found in a scholion to Aristophanes'* The Birds, *where Aristophanes is parodying a public prayer for the welfare of Athens and its allies, does not make a great deal of sense as it stands, but Thrasymachus may have used the Chians as an* exemplum *of some sort in a specimen speech.*

15. Thrasymachus, too, says the same as Theopompus,[35] in his *Great Art*.

(Scholion, Aristophanes, *The Birds*, 880 = B3)

The following passages also may in fact come from the Megalê Tekhnê, *though they are given other titles. First, an amusing item from Athenaeus, stated to be from Thrasymachus'* Prooimia, *or*

'Preludes'. *It concerns the early fifth-century poet and athlete Timocreon of Rhodes, who was also a notorious glutton. Once again, we can only imagine that Thrasymachus used him as an exemplum* in some connection.

16. Thrasymachus of Chalcedon, in one of his *Preludes*, relates how Timocreon went to the court of the Great King[36] and while being entertained by him stuffed himself with much food. Asked by the King how he proposed to function after such a start,[37] he claimed that he could thrash any number of Persians. Next day, after winning against many opponents, one by one, he began to shadow-box. When he was asked the reason for that, he replied that he still had left over an equal number of knock-out blows, in case anyone else wanted to take him on.

(Athenaeus, *Deipnosophistae* X 416A = B4)

Then we find references in Aristotle, and probably also Plato, to a work called Eleoi, *which might most appropriately be rendered, perhaps,* Methods of Arousing Pity, *and which may or may not have also formed part of the* Megalê Tekhnê. *In this passage, Aristotle is discussing the topic of delivery (lexis), which he tells us has been little studied hitherto.*

17. When the techniques of delivery have been developed, they will produce the same effect as on the stage. But only very slight attempts have been made to deal with them, and by a few people, as by Thrasymachus in his *Methods of Arousing Pity*.

(Aristotle, *Rhetoric* III 1, 1404a 13–15)

It is probably this work to which Plato is referring in the passage of the Phaedrus *previously quoted in connection with Protagoras (ch. 1, §20), but which may suitably be repeated in part here.*

18. 'And when it comes to speeches which draw out pity for old age and poverty, it seems to me that it's this mighty Chalcedonian whose skill is pre-eminent; and this man, as he claimed,[38]

was also skilled at rousing large groups to anger, and then, with his charms, calming them again once they had become angry; and it was in this way that he became most powerful both in creating, but also eradicating, slander.'

(Plato, *Phaedrus* 267C)

We also have a passing reference in Plutarch, in his Table Talk, *to a work entitled* Overthrowing Arguments *(*Hyperballontes Logoi*), in the context of seating guests at dinner, the precise relevance of which to the subject being less than clear. At any rate, to judge both from the conjunction with Aristotle's* Topics, *and the mention of practising an* hypothesis synkritikê, *the* Hyperballontes Logoi *must have comprised hints as to how to overturn an opponent's position. They could have formed part of a more general* Tekhnê, *but need not have. It does at least show that the work was still available at the end of the first century* AD.

19. 'Moreover, the decision is not an easy one, seeing as the guests differ in age, in influence, in intimacy and in kinship; on the contrary, one must have to hand, like someone practising a theme of comparison (*hypothesis synkritikê*), the *Topics* of Aristotle, or the *Overthrowing Arguments* of Thrasymachus – although he is accomplishing nothing useful, but rather transferring empty fame from the market-place and theatre to social gatherings.'

(Plutarch, *Table Talk* I 2 616D = B7)

Finally, a curious testimony in the Neoplatonic philosopher Hermeias' Commentary on Plato's Phaedrus, *on the reference to Thrasymachus at 267C, quoted just above, §17, to which reference may be made. Since Hermeias' commentary is essentially a transcription of the seminar of his master Syrianus, who was also a considerable authority on the history and theory of rhetoric, it is possible that at least Syrianus had access to a copy of Thrasymachus'* Methods of Arousing Pity *(*Eleoi*), to which Plato is also probably referring.*

20. 'But to pass now to the application of pathetic language . . .'

For the Chalcedonian, that is to say, Thrasymachus, taught this, that one must rouse the juror to sympathy, and drag in pity, old age, poverty, wailing children and so on. He used the term 'mighty man', either with reference to the power of his oratory, or indeed because in one of his speeches he wrote something to the effect that 'The gods do not direct their gaze to human affairs; for in that case they would not have overlooked the greatest of goods for men, justice. For we see that men make no use of it.'

It is ironic, perhaps, that we should have this remark on the disregard of justice from Thrasymachus' lips (if we may take this to be a substantially verbatim quotation), in view of the pillorying of him for his Nietzschean views on justice in Plato's Republic.

7 CRITIAS OF ATHENS

Critias, son of Callaeschrus, is, apart from Antiphon (if he is indeed one person!), the only substantial member of the sophistic movement who actually hails from Athens itself, despite the centrality of Athens to the activities of all the figures at whom we have looked so far. He was in fact of noble Athenian ancestry, tracing his descent from Dropides, a kinsman of the famous statesman and lawgiver Solon (c.640–560 BC). He was also a first cousin of Plato's mother Perictione, and, despite his evil reputation among supporters of Athenian democracy, it is notable that Plato does not hesitate to present him in a fairly positive light in his dialogue Charmides, *as an associate of Socrates already in the late 430s – an association which he continued all his life, and which contributed greatly to the prejudice against Socrates which led to his execution in 399.*

He is most notorious for having served as the head of the puppet regime set up by the Spartans in Athens after its defeat in 404, the so-called 'Thirty Tyrants', but long before that he had been mixed up in anti-democratic politics. He was implicated, rightly or wrongly, in the scandal of the mutilation of the Hermae on the eve of the great Athenian expedition to Sicily in 415, but was freed on the evidence of Andocides.[1] He was no doubt involved in the oligarchic coup of 412 (the Four Hundred), in which Antiphon was prominent, but took no major part. However, in the aftermath of that, he proposed the return from exile of Alcibiades (who would have been an old friend of his), and when Alcibiades was once again exiled in 406, Critias too was forced into exile, in Thessaly, where he would have had guest-friends. On the defeat of Athens, he returned, as has been said, to take up the leadership of the 'Thirty Tyrants', under which all democratic liberties were suppressed. The regime, however, lasted only about fifteen months, being overthrown by the returning democrats under Thrasybulus in the summer of 403, Critias himself being killed in the process.

He was quite a prolific author, in both prose and verse. In prose, he composed various Constitutions (Politeiai), of the Thessalians, the Spartans and possibly also of the Athenians: On the Nature of Love; Lectures (Homiliai); Aphorisms; and Proems for Public Speakers (Dêmêgorika Prooimia). In verse, he composed didactic and praise poetry in both hexameters and elegiacs, including an ode to his friend Alcibiades, a verse Constitution of the Spartans, and a number of tragedies, of which we have fragments of the Tennes, the Rhadamanthys and the Pirithous, as well as a play commonly spoken of as a satyr-drama, Sisyphus[2] – this latter being particularly notorious for its views on the gods and the origins of religion.

Critias was not really a professional sophist; rather, he was an Athenian gentleman, of reactionary political sympathies (very much like the Callicles portrayed in Plato's Gorgias), who entered thoroughly into the sophistic tradition. His reputation was naturally blackened after his death, but he found great favour, in the second century AD, with the distinguished Athenian sophist and grandee Herodes Atticus, and this led to something of a revival of his fortunes, though no works of his survive.[3]

LIFE AND WORKS

We begin with an extended discussion by Philostratus, in his Lives of the Sophists (I 16), which embodies quite a judicious evaluation, though somewhat inflated in expression.

1. Critias the sophist, even if he was instrumental in over-throwing democracy at Athens, is not yet necessarily to be declared evil – the democracy, after all, might have been over-thrown by its own impetus, since it had become so overbearing

that it would not take heed even of those who were trying to govern it according to its own laws – but seeing that he conspicuously went over to Sparta, and betrayed the sacred sites; that he was instrumental, through the agency of Lysander, in demolishing the city walls; that he deprived the Athenians whom he drove into exile of any haven in all Greece by warning that any harbouring of the Athenian exiles would mean war with Sparta; that in savagery and bloodthirstiness he was outstanding even among the Thirty; that he sided with the outrageous plan of Sparta to give Attica the appearance of a mere pasture for sheep by emptying her of her human herd: for all this I hold him to be the basest of all men who have a name for baseness.

Now if he had been a man of no education, led astray into these excesses, there would be some force in the argument of those who assert that he was demoralized by Thessaly and the society that he frequented there;[4] for characters that lack education are easily led in any direction in their choice of life-style. But since he had been highly educated and frequently delivered himself of philosophical maxims, and traced his ancestry back to Dropides, who was archon at Athens next after Solon,[5] he cannot be acquitted in the sight of most men of the charge that these crimes were due to his own natural wickedness.

Then again it is remarkable that he did not come to resemble Socrates, son of Sophroniscus, in company with whom above all others he engaged in philosophy, and who had the reputation of being the wisest and the most just man of his time; but he did grow to be like the Thessalians, who affect an insolent arrogance, and behave tyrannically even in their wine-drinking. However, not even the Thessalians neglected the pursuit of wisdom, but all the cities great and small in Thessaly were fans of Gorgias (*egorgiazon*), and looked to Gorgias of Leontini; and they would have changed over and become fans of Critias (*kritiazein*), if Critias had given any exhibition (*epideixis*) in their country of his own special skill. But for this kind of success he cared nothing, and instead tried to increase the oppressiveness of their oligarchies, by conversing with the men in power there, and disparaging all popular government, and by attacking the Athenians as being the most perverse of mankind; so that, taking all this into consideration, it would seem that Critias was a corrupting influence for the Thessalians, rather than the Thessalians for Critias.

He was killed by Thrasybulus and his party who restored the democracy from Phyle,[6] and there is a school of thought which maintains that he behaved honourably at the end, because his tyranny became his winding sheet. But in my view it is quite clear that no human being can be said to have died nobly for a cause that he took up for no right reason. And I believe that this is why this man's expertise and his writings are held in low regard by the Greeks; for unless our public utterances and our moral character are in accord, we shall seem to speak with a tongue not our own, just as in the case of flutes.

As regards his style of oratory, Critias was characterized by brief and sententious utterances, and he was well skilled in the use of elevated language, but not of the dithyrambic variety, nor such as relies on words taken over from poetry; but his was the kind of elevated language that is composed of the most appropriate words and is not artificial. I see him, moreover, as a master of conciseness, and as one who, even in the context of a defence speech, was accustomed to make vigorous attacks on an opponent; and as one who atticized, but in moderation,[7] not employing outlandish words – for bad taste in atticizing is truly barbarous – but allowing his Attic words to illuminate his discourse like the rays of the sun. He also achieves grace by passing without connectives from one part of speech to another.[8] Then also, Critias aims for surprising effects both in thought and expression, yet his eloquence is somewhat lacking in force, though it is pleasant and smooth, like the breath of the west wind.

(Philostratus, *Lives of the Sophists* I 16 = 88A1)

Next, some biographical information, of a typically muddle-headed nature, from Diogenes Laertius, at the beginning of his 'Life of Plato'. In particular, Diogenes seriously telescopes the number of generations between our Critias and the Dropides who was the relation of Solon.

2. Plato, son of Ariston and Perictione (or Potone),[9] who traced back her ancestry to Solon; a citizen of Athens. For Solon had a brother, Dropides,[10] from whom sprang Critias, who was the father of Callaeschrus, who was the father of Critias, one of the Thirty, as well as of Glaucon,[11] who was the father of Charmides and Perictione; from whom and Ariston sprang Plato, in the sixth generation from Solon.

(Diogenes Laertius, *Lives of the Philosophers* III, 1 = A2)

Then, two passages from Plato's Charmides, *which features Critias as one of the main characters (as a sort of chaperone of his younger cousin Charmides), in a manner not entirely complimentary, but still affectionate enough. The dramatic date of the dialogue is 432 BC, just before the outbreak of the Peloponnesian War. Socrates is portrayed as just having returned from a military tour of duty at Potidaea, in Thrace. Critias would seem to be in his early twenties.*

3. [SOCRATES] 'Then Critias, glancing towards the door, as he saw some youths coming in making fun of each other, and a further crowd of people following in their train, said: "As regards the beauties, Socrates, I rather think you will find out at once; for these entering now are in fact the outriders and lovers of the person who is held, for the while at least, to be the greatest beauty; and he himself, I rather think, must by now be nearly with us."

'And he, I asked, is who, and the son of whom?

' "You actually do know him," he replied, "but he was not yet of age when you went away – Charmides, son of our uncle Glaucon, and my cousin." '

(Plato, *Charmides* 154A = A2, expanded)

4. [SOCRATES] 'Indeed, I said, it is only fair, Charmides, that you should outshine the rest in all these ways; for I don't imagine there is anyone else here who could easily identify any two Athenian families united together which would be likely to produce finer or nobler offspring than those from which you originate.[12] For your father's house, which traces its ancestry to

Critias, son of Dropides, has been celebrated by Anacreon[13] and
Solon and many other poets, so that it is celebrated by tradition
amongst us as foremost in beauty and virtue and everything else
that is regarded as conducive to happiness; and then the case is
the same with your mother's house, for of Pyrilampes, your
uncle,[14] it is said that no one in all the continent [i.e. of Asia]
was regarded as superior to him in beauty or stature, as often
as he came on an embassy to the Great King, or anyone else in
Asia, and his house as a whole is in no way inferior to the other.'

   (Ibid. 157E–158A = A2, expanded)

*Plato, in his works, makes no attempt at a direct apologia
for the association of his notorious cousin with Socrates, but
Xenophon does address this problem, in the preface to his*
Memoirs of Socrates, *from which some passages may be quoted.
This work is composed partly, at least, in answer to a polemical
pamphlet composed in the 390s by a sophist called Polycrates,
which was presented in the guise of the speech at Socrates' trial
by one of his accusers, Anytus, and dwelt at some length on
Socrates' association with Critias and Alcibiades – which had,
indeed, been one of the prime motivating factors in bringing
him to trial. Polycrates is therefore the 'accuser' referred to here.*

5. *[12]* However, the accuser alleges, Critias and Alcibiades,
who had belonged to the circle of Socrates, did more harm to
their country than any others. Critias developed into the most
thievish and violent and murderous of all the oligarchs, and
Alcibiades in his turn became the most dissolute and arrogant
and violent of all the democrats. *[13]* I certainly do not propose
to defend any evil that these men did to the state; my only
concern is to explain how their relationship with Socrates
came about.

   [14] These two men were the most naturally ambitious of all
the Athenians, determined that all affairs of state should be
under their personal control, and that they should acquire a
name above all others. They realized that Socrates lived with
entire self-sufficiency on very little money, that he was supremely
self-disciplined in respect of all pleasures, and that in argument

he could do as he liked with anyone who conversed with him. [*15*] Knowing these facts as they did, and being such as I have described, should one say that they sought Socrates' society because they desired his way of life and his degree of self-discipline, or because they thought that, if they consorted with him, they would gain supreme proficiency in both speech and action? [*16*] It is actually my view that if God had offered them the choice between living their whole lives as they saw Socrates living his, and dying, they would have chosen rather to die. Indeed they demonstrated this by their subsequent conduct: as soon as they sensed that they were superior to the rest of those who frequented his company, they broke up with Socrates and went into politics, which was the reason why they had sought his society in the first place.

[*This, it must be said, seems less than effective as a defence of Socrates, as Xenophon admits that it was possible for these two reprobates to learn techniques of dialectic from him without adopting the ethical standards that should have gone with that. He feels, however, that he has an answer to that difficulty. We continue a little lower down.*]

[*24*] Critias and Alcibiades, then, as long as they consorted with Socrates, were enabled with his support to control their base desires. But when they had left him, Critias, being driven into exile in Thessaly, fell in with men who were more attached to lawlessness than to justice.[15] Alcibiades, in turn, because of his good looks was sought after by many women of distinction, and, because of his power in the city and among the allies, he was both pampered by many influential men and held in honour by the people, and easily rose to the top; and, just as athletes who easily come first in athletic competitions tend to neglect their practice, so he neglected himself.

[*25*] Since this is what befell those two characters, and since they were exalted by their birth, elated by their wealth, puffed up with their power and spoiled by many people, how can one be surprised that, when they were corrupted for all these reasons and long separated from Socrates, they became overbearing? [*26*] So then, when they erred, is Socrates' accuser going to hold him responsible for that, but does he find nothing to praise in

the fact that in their youth, when it was to be expected that they should be most irresponsible and undisciplined, Socrates induced them to behave decently? That is not how other cases are judged.

[*Xenophon now launches into some rhetorical generalizations, returning to specifics a little further down.*]

[29] However, even if he himself did nothing bad, if he commended these men when he saw them behaving badly, he might reasonably have incurred blame. But in fact, when he observed that Critias was in love with Euthydemus[16] and was trying to seduce him, in the manner of one seeking to gratify his sexual appetite, Socrates tried to put him off by maintaining that it was slavish and unsuitable to a man of decency to solicit his favourite, on whom he wished to make a good impression, appealing to him like a beggar and imploring him to grant his favours, especially as he would be begging for nothing good. And when Critias ignored such remonstrances, and was not turned aside from his purpose, Socrates is said to have remarked, in the presence of several persons including Euthydemus himself, that Critias seemed to be suffering from pig's itch: he wanted to scratch himself against Euthydemus like little pigs do against stones.[17]

This incident caused Critias to develop a dislike for Socrates, so that when, as a member of the Thirty, he took charge of legislation along with Charicles, he held a grudge against Socrates, and introduced a law against teaching 'the art of debating (*logôn tekhnê*)', doing this out of spite towards Socrates, since he had no means of getting at him other than traducing him in the public view by applying to him the usual layman's allegation against all philosophers.[18] I must say that I never myself heard Socrates engaging in this practice, nor did I ever come across anyone who claimed to have heard him doing so.

[*There follows a rather fanciful dialogue between Socrates and Critias and Charicles (33–8), in which Socrates is forbidden to conduct his usual activities. Xenophon then sums up:*]

[39] So much, then may be said about the nature of the association of Critias with Socrates and the relations between them. I myself would actually deny that there is any possibility of being instructed by a person of whom one disapproves; and

it was not by reason of their approval of him that Critias and Alcibiades associated with Socrates when they did associate with him, but rather because from the outset they had resolved to attain prominence in public affairs.

(Xenophon, *Memoirs of Socrates* I 2, 12–39)

Xenophon, as we say, does not appear to see that he is hardly absolving Socrates from the charge levelled against him. Critias and Alcibiades are in fact asserted to be associating with him precisely for the reason that any bright young aristocrat would associate with a sophist: to develop skill in public speaking through sharpening their wits.

It would seem that in the oligarchic coup of 411, in which Antiphon was prominently involved, Critias, if anything, played (perhaps opportunistically) a pro-democratic role, if we may deduce this from a reference in the speech of the prominent fourth-century politician Lycurgus in Against Leocrates, *delivered in 330 BC. Lycurgus is reminding the jury how they did things 'in the good old days'.*

6. 'When Phrynichus[19] was cut down at night beside the fountain in the osier beds by Apollodorus and Thrasybulus,[20] and they were later apprehended and imprisoned by the friends of Phrynichus, the people, on learning what had happened, released the prisoners, and instituted an inquiry with torture.[21] On inquiring into the matter, they discovered that Phrynichus had been trying to betray the city,[22] and that those who killed him had been unjustly imprisoned. The people then issued a decree, on the motion of Critias, that the corpse should be tried for treason, and that if it was their decision that this was a traitor who had been buried in the country, his bones should be dug up and cast beyond the borders of Attica, so that there should not be lying within the land even the bones of someone who had betrayed his country and his city.'

(Lycurgus, *Against Leocrates* 113 = A7, expanded)

On the other hand, a reference in a speech in the Demosthenic corpus (not by Demosthenes, but also from the late fourth century), Against Theocrines, which speaks of Critias as one of the leaders of the Four Hundred, is certainly confused, and not worth quoting.

However, a snippet of information from Aristotle's Rhetoric is of interest, as attesting to an attack on Critias by the democratic leader Cleophon (who was dominant in Athenian politics in the period after 411 up to the end of the war), which is no doubt connected with Critias' being driven into exile in 406. Aristotle is discussing the use of witnesses. It sounds as if this gibe of Cleophon's formed part of a comprehensive assault on Critias' moral character, as part of a prosecution speech in a law-case (which may well have been published, since Aristotle has knowledge of it).

7. As regards witnesses, they are of two kinds, the historic and the recent; and these latter, again, either are or are not liable to the consequences of the trial. By 'historic' witnesses I mean the poets and all other notable persons whose views are clearly discernible. Thus the Athenians appealed to the witness of Homer on the question of Salamis; and the people of Tenedos quite recently appealed to the evidence of Periander of Corinth in their dispute with the people of Sigeum; and Cleophon, in the course of his indictment of Critias, made use of the elegiacs of Solon, in order to make the point that the house of Critias had long been known for its indiscipline, or Solon would never have written, 'Come, bid the red-haired Critias take heed of his father.'[23]

(Aristotle, *Rhetoric* I 15, 1375b26–34)

The events of 404–403 are related in some detail by Xenophon in Book II of his Hellenica. Here, he gives a bald announcement of the setting up of the Spartan-sponsored puppet regime.

8. In the following year [sc. 404/3], the people resolved to elect thirty men, who would codify the ancestral laws (*patrioi nomoi*), in accordance with which they would administer the state. And the following were elected: Polychares, Critias . . . [twenty-eight more names follow].

(Xenophon, *Hellenica* II 3, 1–2)

This makes the process sound rather more democratic than it was. The assembly met under the shadow of the presence of the Spartan army and its commander, Lysander. What they elected was ostensibly only a constitutional committee to revise the laws, but was in fact an oligarchic junta, which was to rule indefinitely and with absolute powers. The Thirty never did revise the laws, but turned immediately to executing, first, notorious democratic troublemakers, but then, progressively, rich citizens and resident aliens (such as Lysias' brother Polemarchus, see below §11), to raise funds from confiscating their assets. They also called in a Spartan garrison to back them up. Xenophon chronicles their activities from II 3, 3–14, and then turns to the split between Critias and Theramenes (a rather ambiguous figure, a moderate oligarch, who emerged as the leader of the 'moderate' faction in the junta), which led ultimately to Theramenes' arraignment and execution at the instigation of Critias (15–56). All this is much too long to quote in full in the present context, being rather peripheral to Critias' career as a sophist. One remark of Theramenes, however, in his defence speech before the Council, is worth noting, as making a rather paradoxical allegation about Critias' time in Thessaly:

9. 'Still, I am not surprised at Critias' misunderstanding the situation.[24] When this was taking place, he was not around, but was up in Thessaly establishing democracy along with Prometheus, and arming the serfs against their masters.'[25]

(Ibid. II 3, 36)

The execution of Theramenes took place, probably, in January 403, but by this time a group of exiled democrats under Thrasybulus had occupied the fort of Phyle on the Boeotian border, and were using it as a base for operations against the junta. A mid-winter expedition failed to dislodge them, as did another one in early May, and then Thrasybulus moved down and seized the Piraeus. Once again, the Thirty launched an attack, but were defeated, and in this battle Critias himself was killed (Xenophon, Hellenica II 4, 1–19).

This did not end the rule of the junta, who had established a

secure base for themselves at Eleusis, and unity and democracy
was not restored until September. In the immediate aftermath
of the battle in Piraeus, however, we learn (from a scholion on
Aeschines, Against Timarchus *39) that the Thirty erected a*
memorial to Critias:

10. This is an example of the government of the Thirty. When
Critias, one of the Thirty, had been killed, they erected by way
of memorial a statue of Oligarchy, with a torch in her hand,
setting fire to Democracy, and the following inscription:
    'This is a monument to good men and true, who for a short
      while
    curbed the arrogance of the cursed common people of Athens.'
                 (Scholion, Aeschines, *Against Timarchus* 39)

Another perspective on the Thirty is provided by the speech-
writer Lysias, who came of a family of wealthy resident aliens
(his father's house in the Piraeus is the scene of Plato's Republic*).*
When the Thirty, in the winter of 404/3, set about confiscating
the property of wealthy citizens, one of the junta, Eratosthenes,
picked on the property of Lysias and his brother Polemarchus.
Polemarchus was murdered, but Lysias escaped and joined the
democratic rebels in Phyle. After the restoration of democracy,
he prosecuted Eratosthenes. He is not explicitly attacking Crit-
ias, since Critias is dead, but obviously Critias had to have
approved the confiscation. Critias, indeed, must have known
Lysias personally; they shared an interest in rhetoric, and are
often mentioned together in the sources (see below). Lysias is
here supplying some background.

11. 'Now his life [i.e. Eratosthenes'] in the intervening period I
will leave aside; but when the sea-battle [i.e. at Aegospotami, in
405] took place, and the consequent disaster to the city, while
the democracy was still in place (this being the point at which
they started their sedition), five men were set up as 'overseers'
(*ephoroi*) by the so-called 'club-members' (*hetairoi*),[26] to marshal the citizens, as well as to be leaders of the conspirators and
to work in opposition to the mass of the people; and among

these individuals were Eratosthenes and Critias. They placed
tribal administrators (*phylarkhoi*) over the tribes, and prescribed what measures should be voted in and who were to be
magistrates; and they had absolute discretion for any other
measures they chose to take.'

(Lysias, *Against Eratosthenes* 43 = A11)

*We may turn now to a few notices of his literary and other cultural
activities. First, a significant detail relayed by Athenaeus.*

12. But all Greeks in the old days were very keen on music; in
which connection, flute-playing in particular was very popular.
Chamaeleon of Heraclea,[27] at any rate, in his *Protrepticus*,[28]
says that all Spartans and Thebans learned to play the flute, as
did also the Heracleots of Pontus in his time, as well as the most
distinguished Athenians – Callias, the son of Hipponicus, and
Critias, the son of Callaeschrus.

(Athenaeus, *Deipnosophistae* IV 184D = A15)

*Whatever the case may be for Callias – a great patron of sophists,
as we have seen – Critias' love of flute-playing may be accounted
a mark of his pro-Spartan tendencies. It is interesting, also, that
in the Peripatetic tradition stemming from Aristotle, Critias was
still a name to be conjured with, despite his leadership of the
Thirty.*

*In this connection, a slightly ambiguous, but on the whole
favourable, reference in Aristotle's* Rhetoric *may be noted. He
is discussing that part of a speech which is called the narration
(*diêgêsis).

13. Well-known deeds you will not have to do more than recall
to people's minds; because they are well known, most people
usually need no narration of them; for instance, if your object
is the praise of Achilles, you will need none, for all know the
facts of his life – what is required is that you apply them properly.
But if your object is the praise of Critias, you must give an
account of his deeds, for not many people know of them.

(Aristotle, *Rhetoric* III 16, 1416b26–29 = A14)

Here the contrast seems to be, not between Achilles the great hero and Critias the great villain, but rather between Achilles, whose achievements are well known, and Critias, whose achievements are not. It really sounds as if Aristotle thought of Critias as a sadly underrated figure, and that this attitude to him was inherited by the later Peripatetic school.[29]

Next a series of passages placing Critias in the history of Greek oratory. First, a testimony from Pseudo-Plutarch, Life of Antiphon, ranking Critias among those of a younger generation who learned speech-writing from Antiphon.

14. Yet all those of whom we have any record as having tried their hand at this kind of speech, going back to the earliest instance, one will find to have based themselves on Antiphon, when he was already old; I mean such persons as Alcibiades, Critias, Lysias and Archinus.[30]

   (Pseudo-Plutarch, *Life of Antiphon* 832DE = A16)

Then a passage from Cicero's De Oratore. *The orator Marcus Antonius, one of the interlocutors in the dialogue, is speaking.*

15. 'Why do you think it is that more or less every period of history has produced its own particular style of oratory? We can estimate the correctness of this judgement less easily in the case of our own orators, since they have left, in truth, only very few writings on which to base such a judgement, than in that of the Greeks, from whose writings the method and tendency of the oratory of every age may be appreciated. The very earliest of whom we have any secure texts are Pericles and Alcibiades, with Thucydides as their contemporary,[31] all of them accurate, pointed, terse and more copious in ideas than in diction. There followed on these such figures as Critias, Theramenes and Lysias.[32] We possess many writings of Lysias; of Critias a few; of Theramenes we only have reports.'

   (Cicero, *De Oratore* II 92–3 = A17, expanded)

Philostratus, in one of his letters, links Critias with Thucydides, as being influenced by Gorgias.

16. Critias and Thucydides are not unknown, as having taken over from Gorgias both grandness of conception and gravity of style,[33] but refashioning these into a mode proper to themselves, in the one case through fluency of speech, in the other through force of expression.[34]

(Philostratus, *Letters* 73 = A17)

Once again the names of Lysias and Critias are linked (as well as that of Critias' relation Andocides), by Dionysius of Halicarnassus in his Life of Lysias.

17. He [i.e. Lysias] is entirely pure in his diction, and is the perfect exemplar of the Attic dialect – not the archaic variety employed by Plato and Thucydides, but that which was in general use in his day, as one may judge from a study of the speeches of Andocides, Critias and many others.

(Dionysius of Halicarnassus, *Life of Lysias* 2 = A18)

He mentions Critias again, in an interesting context, in his essay On Isaeus – *a passage quoted above in ch. 6, §11, since it concerns also Antiphon and Thrasymachus. Of more importance for the analysis of Critias' style, however, is the evaluation of the second-century AD rhetorician Hermogenes, in his treatise* On Types of Style *(*Peri ideôn*)*.

18. *On Critias:* He also has a style which is stately (*semnos*), much like Antiphon's, and sublime, with a tendency to weightiness; he is prone to categorical[35] utterance, relatively pure in his idiom, and, even when he indulges in elaboration, yet preserves lucidity, with the result that he is clear and distinct in conjunction with his loftiness. In many places he exhibits both genuineness and persuasiveness, particularly in his *Proems for Public Speeches* (*Dêmêgorika Prooimia*).[36] Conscious stylist though he is, nevertheless he does not employ such adornment absolutely or, as does Antiphon, tediously and with obvious contrivance,

but in such a way as to partake even thus of genuineness.
He does not make excessive use of other types of characterization (*êthos*), such as reasonableness (*epieikeia*) or simplicity
(*apheleia*) or the like.

(Hermogenes, *On Types of Style* B401, 25 Rabe = A19)

*This very positive evaluation of Critias' style would seem to fit
well with the revival of interest in him stimulated by Herodes
Atticus, as testified to by Philostratus (*Lives of the Sophists,
564 = A21), but Hermogenes, though younger than Herodes,
does not seem, from Philostratus' account (ibid. 577–8), to
have had any contact with him, so respect for Critias in this
period would seem to be more than just an idiosyncrasy of
Herodes. The lexicographer Phrynichus of Bithynia, writing
at around the same period (ap. Photius Bibliotheca 158),
also praises Critias as 'a model of pure and unalloyed Attic
diction' (= A20).*

*Finally, a curious mention by Aristotle, in his De Anima, of a
scientific theory of Critias, concerning the nature of the soul. It
comes at the end of a protracted doxography of the views of
pre-Socratic thinkers, ending with two, Hippon of Rhegium and
Critias, whom Aristotle lumps together, rather dismissively, as
'muddle-headed' or 'light-weight' (phortikôteroi).*

19. Others,[37] like Critias, have conceived the soul to be blood,
because they have supposed that sensation is the most proper
characteristic of the soul, and that this is due to the nature
of blood.

(Aristotle, *De Anima* I 2, 495b5–6 = B23)

*It is not necessary to suppose that this opinion occurred in a
treatise explicitly concerned with the soul, or with anything
philosophical or scientific. In fact, if the commentator Johannes
Philoponus, who discusses the passage both in the preface to
his commentary (p. 9, 19), and ad loc. (p. 89, 8), is being
accurate, Critias is doing no more than quoting Empedocles
(On Nature, B105, 3), though possibly incorporating the line in
a hexameter poem of his own.[38]*

20a. Sc. the Critias who was one of the Thirty; for he stated that the soul was blood:

'For blood flowing round the heart is what perception is for men.'
(Johannes Philoponus, *In De Anima* p. 9, 19–21)

When he has occasion to comment on the passage itself, he has more to say, showing in the process that the reference had given rise to some controversy:

20b. It makes no difference to us whether he is referring to the Critias who was one of the Thirty, and who was also a follower of Socrates, or to someone else. They do actually say that there was another Critias, a sophist, who is the author of the writings which survive under his name, as Alexander[39] asserts; he would have it that the member of the Thirty wrote nothing except some *Constitutions* in verse.[40]

(Ibid. p. 89, 8–12 = A22)

A possible solution to this problem would be to suppose that Critias is indeed making use of a doctrine and verse of Empedocles, and incorporating it into a hexameter poem of his own, possibly with no very serious intent.

FRAGMENTS OF POETIC WORKS
Hexameter and Elegiac Poems

As noted in the introduction, Critias composed both poems in hexameters and in elegiacs and a number of dramas, including the notorious Sisyphus, *though there is no record of his having competed in the festivals. These may have been intended as drawing-room dramas (possibly even composed during his sojourn in Thessaly), but we must reflect that our records are very incomplete.*

It is not clear, it must be said, that many of these poems are to be classed as specifically sophistic *productions, as opposed to avocations of an Athenian aristocrat, but since some of them arguably are, it seems best to include them.*

First, then, a poem in hexameters which included some praise
of the sixth-century love-poet Anacreon, who, as we have seen,
had been a protégé of Critias' ancestor Critias, son of Dropides.
It is transmitted to us by Athenaeus, in the context of a dis-
cussion of the power of Love (erôs). What the poem was really
about we have no idea. It seems light-hearted enough, and really
more suited to elegiac couplets than heroic hexameters.

21. He [i.e. Eros] is the god of whom the ingenious Anacreon,
who is on everyone's lips, is constantly singing. Of him the
worthy (*kratistos*)[41] Critias speaks as follows:

> That poet who once wove songs of women's limbs
> Teos introduced to Hellas, the sweet Anacreon,
> enflamer of drinking-parties, deceiver of women,
> foe of flutes,[42] lover of the lyre, delightful, healer of woe.
> Never shall love of thee grow old or die,
> so long as boy bears round the water mixed with wine
> and pours it in the cups, dispensing toasts from left to right;
> so long as female choirs perform their nightly vigils,
> and the scale-pan, daughter of bronze, sits upon the high peak
> of the *kottabos* to receive the drops of the Bromian god.[43]
> (Athenaeus, *Deipnosophistae* XIII 600D)

Critias discussed the game of kottabos *also in one of his elegies,*
again preserved for us by Athenaeus, who quotes from it in two
places. Here, however, the main topic appears to be a catalogue
of cities or countries which may be credited with one or another
useful invention – possibly culminating in a praise of Athens for
inventing pottery.

22. Since,[44] then, you are not versed in this field of study, learn
from me that the game of *kottabos*, in the first place, is a Sicilian
invention, the Sicels[45] being the first to devise it, as Critias, the son
of Callaeschrus, informs us in his *Elegies* in these words:

> The *kottabos* is a notable product of the Sicilian land,
>   which we set up as a mark, to shoot at with drops of wine.

Next comes the Sicilian cart, best in beauty and luxury,
  . . . [46]

Thessalian is the armchair,[47] a most comfortable seat for the limbs.
  But the glory of the couch whereon we sleep belongs
to Miletus and to Chios, the sea-girt city of Oenopion.
  The Etruscan cup of beaten gold is best,
as well as all bronze that adorns the house, for whatever use.
  The Phoenicians discovered letters, preservers of words.[48]
Thebes was the first to join together the chariot-box,
  and the Carians, stewards of the sea, cargo-bearing clippers.
But the potter's wheel, and the child of clay and the oven,
  noblest pottery, useful in housekeeping,
    is the invention of that city who raised the glorious trophy at
Marathon.[49]

– and indeed Attic pottery is very highly regarded.
(Ibid. I 28B and XV 666B)

*This, again, is a light-hearted piece, with some nice turns of
phrase. In particular, the terming of the humble pot 'child of clay
and the oven' is reminiscent of the description of the scale-pan of
the* kottabos *as 'daughter of bronze' in the previous poem –
both mock-heroic or mock-Aeschylean squibs. If we are to
speculate on the point of this rather random catalogue of inventions, it might be that Critias is in fact building up to a praise of
pottery, and thus of Athens.*

*A further detail that possibly may have been included in
this poem, but in any case relates to Critias' interest in 'first
begetters', is one preserved by the metrician Mallius Theodorus:*

23. Critias asserts that the dactylic hexameter was invented
originally by Orpheus, while Democritus says it was Musaeus.
  (*Mallius Theodorus*, On Metres VI 589, 220 Keil)

*This may or may not imply that Critias is entering into contro-
versy with Democritus on this question. It shows, however,
both that he had an interest in the question, and that he regarded
the Orphic poems extant in his day as genuine, and thus earlier
than Homer.*

Ode to Alcibiades

Next, an ode in elegiacs in honour of Alcibiades, presumably in connection with his recall from exile in 407, the motion for which, as we have seen, was moved in the Assembly by Critias. The relationship between Critias and Alcibiades is an odd one; they were both aristocrats and had cultural and philosophical interests in common (including companionship with Socrates), but Alcibiades was far more ready than Critias to court the favour of the common people. Nevertheless, Critias proposed his recall in 407, and when Alcibiades once again fell out of favour in 406, after one of his lieutenants suffered defeat in the sea-battle at Notion, Critias was also driven into exile. At the end of the war, however, after Aegospotami, Critias seems to have connived with the Spartan commander Lysander in Alcibiades' assassination (cf. Plutarch, Life of Alcibiades, ch. 38). This elegy, however, is, once again, a thoroughly light-hearted production, even embodying a metrical joke – which is why some lines of it are preserved by the second-century AD metrician Hephaestion.[50]

24a. [On *synizesis*, which Hephaestion terms '*synekphonêsis*'] . . . or two short syllables into one short, which is found in other metres . . . but is rarely employed in epic verse; so Critias, in his Ode to Alcibiades, considered it impossible to get Alcibiades' name into the metre, saying:

> And now I will crown the Athenian, son of Cleinias,
>   Alcibiades, hymning him in newfangled mode;
> for it was not possible to fit his name to elegiac verse;
>   so now, not unmetrically, he shall figure in an iamb.

(Hephaestion, *Handbook of Metre* 2, 3 = B4)

Some further lines of this ode are quoted by Plutarch, in his Life of Alcibiades:

24b. The vote for his recall had been ratified earlier on the proposal of Critias, son of Callaeschrus, as Critias has himself recorded in his *Elegies*, reminding Alcibiades of the favour he had done him, in the following verses:

> The decision that brought you home, 'twas I that moved it,
>> and by my own proposing did the deed;
> upon these words the seal of my tongue is set.[51]
> (Plutarch, *Alcibiades*, ch. 33 = B5)

There is also the possibility[52] that an allusion made by Plato in the Republic *(II 368A) to an ode written to his brother Glaucon by an unnamed lover is in fact a reference to Critias, who would have been his first cousin once removed, but it is hardly justifiable to include it.*

The Constitution of the Spartans [?]

It is really only the Aristotelian commentator Johannes Philoponus (above, §20) who makes mention of the composition of politeiai emmetroi[53] *by Critias, and the attribution of the following passage to a* Constitution of the Spartans *is simply an assumption (though a plausible one) on the part of Diels. In the passage – which we owe, once again, to the worthy Athenaeus – Critias is contrasting the drinking habits of the Spartans and the Athenians, to the advantage of the former. This is in a somewhat more serious vein than the extracts from his other poems, and brings out the strongly laconophile tendencies which led ultimately to his assuming leadership of the pro-Spartan quisling regime of the Thirty.*

25. This too is a custom and practice established at Sparta,
>> to drink from one and the same cup of wine,
> and not to give the cup when naming one's toasts,
>> nor to pass it round the festive circle to the right.[54]
> . . .
> 'Twas a Lydian hand, Asian-born,[55] that invented pitchers,
> and the offering of toasts in turn, and calling out
>> explicitly by name him to whom one wishes to drink;
> Then, after such draughts, they loose their tongues

into the telling of foul stories, and render the body
dimmer; over the eyes there settles a darkling mist,
    and oblivion melts the memory from the wits;
the intellect goes astray; the servants get out of hand,
    and ruinous expense falls upon the household.
But the young men of the Spartans drink only so much
    as to bring all hearts into a cheery hopefulness,
and every tongue into good fellowship and moderate laughter.
    Such drinking benefits alike the body,
the mind and the pocket; it well befits the works of love,
    and is suited to sleep, our haven from toil;
it is suited also to Health, the god most pleasing to man,
    and to Moderation, near neighbour of Piety.

and a little further on he says:

for toasting from cups beyond due measure makes for present
    delight, only to bring grief for all time afterwards;
whereas the custom of the Spartans has an even spread,
    eating and drinking in due proportion, to keep one's wits,
and retain the power to act; there's no right day
    for soaking the body with immoderate draughts.
(Athenaeus, *Deipnosophistae* X 432D = B6).

*This extract is pretty narrowly focused on drinking habits. That
may well simply reflect Athenaeus' own interests, but the fact
remains that there is nothing to suggest the broader topic of the
Spartan constitution. However that may be, to the same elegy
may belong the following lines, preserved in a scholion to Euripides, Hippolytus 264.*

26. A saying of one of the Seven Sages is 'Nothing in excess',
which, according to Critias, is to be attributed to Chilon (= B7):[56]

It was a Lacedaemonian, Chilon the sage, who said this:
    'Nothing in excess.' All good things are linked to right measure
    (*kairos*).
(Scholion, Euripides, *Hippolytus* 264 = B7)

This sentiment could well have introduced a poem such as the preceding, if it was not after all a 'Constitution'.

Another short extract, however, this time preserved by Plutarch, in his Life of Cimon, *in connection with praise of the generosity of the early fifth-century Athenian statesman Cimon, probably comes from another poem. It is a good expression of Critias' aristocratic value-system.*

27. Critias, who became one of the Thirty,[57] prays in his *Elegies* for:

> the wealth of the Scopadae, the great-heartedness of Cimon,
>   and the victories of Arcesilaus the Lacedaemonian.[58]
> (Plutarch, *Life of Cimon* ch. 10)

*And finally, a single pentameter line quoted by Stobaeus, on the subject of the value of industriousness and practice (*meletê*):*

28. From Critias:

> More men attain excellence by practice than by nature.
> (Stobaeus, *Anthology* III 29, 11)

FRAGMENTS OF DRAMATIC WORKS

Three tragedies and a satyr-play (?)[59] are generally now credited to Critias, though the attribution of the tragedies is less than certain. However, in the case of the three titles listed in the introduction, we have the testimony of the Anonymous Life of Euripides *(p. 135, 33) that they are considered spurious, and that of Athenaeus (below, §38) that at least the* Pirithous *was attributed to Critias as well as to Euripides, while Sextus Empiricus attributes to him the passage from the* Sisyphus.

That these plays should have been attributed to Euripides does, we think, attest to a certain similarity of both style and outlook between the two men. Euripides was notoriously sympathetic with, and well-informed on, the doctrines of the major sophists (as well as on those of a number of contemporary philosophers, such as Anaxagoras, Diogenes of Apollonia and Archelaus), and Critias on his part was doubtless an admirer of his somewhat older contemporary. How far the two men were personal friends we have no idea, but it is interesting that in 408, about two years before Critias retired in exile to Thessaly, Euripides left Athens (so far as we know of his own accord), and went to the court of King Archelaus of Macedon, where he died in 406.

The surviving fragments of the tragedies do not reveal a great deal of philosophical interest, but it is tempting to speculate on Critias' choice of heroes. Tennes and Rhadamanthys are generally positive figures, but they are both driven into exile, the former by a jealous father (at the instigation of an amorous stepmother), the latter by his brother Minos, who denied him the honour and position due to him; while Pirithous is pretty much of a delinquent, who effectively exiles himself, by embarking on a mad escapade to abduct Persephone from Hades, and being in consequence confined there, involving his friend Theseus in his punishment (until Theseus is rescued by Heracles). Can Critias have identified to any extent with any of these? Perhaps most readily with Rhadamanthys, but to some extent, we would suggest, with all of them. At any rate, let us look at the plays in turn.

Tennes

Tennes, the eponymous founder of Tenedos, an island just off the Troad, was, like the more famous Bellerephon and Hippolytus, the victim of his amorous stepmother, Phylonomê, whose approaches he had rejected. She slandered him to his father, Cycnus, king of Colonê in the Troad, who put him (and his sister) afloat in a chest (like Perseus). He was kept safe by Poseidon, and washed up on Tenedos, where he became king. His father later discovered the truth, buried the wicked stepmother alive and sought a reconciliation, but this appears to have been aborted by Tennes cutting the cable of his father's ship, when he had sailed over to apologize to his son. We have only one rather banal line of this drama, quoted by Stobaeus, who plainly found it edifying. It sounds as though it may come from an attempt by Tennes to defend himself before his enraged father (in the same way as did Hippolytus); but it could conceivably be uttered by his father!

29. Alas! There is no justice in the present generation.
   (Ibid. III 2, 15)

Rhadamanthys

Of this play we have rather more traces, but not much indication as to what the plot was about. Rhadamanthys, as has been remarked above, was driven out of Crete by his brother Minos, who was jealous of his reputation for justice, and ended up wandering around the Greek islands, helping people out. We have, in a papyrus, the end of a summary of the plot of the play, but this does little to dissipate the mystery. What seems to be the case is that Rhadamanthys has become involved in the fight between the Dioscuri, Castor and Polydeuces, and another pair of twins, Idas and Lynceus, over the abduction by the Dioscuri of the two daughters of their uncle, Leucippus, in which both Castor and the other pair are killed.

30. . . . . fighting alone, he[60] was killed by Polydeuces. While Rhadamanthys rejoiced at the victory, yet was grieving over the daughters,[61] Artemis appeared and commanded Helen to establish honours for both the dead brothers,[62] and announced that his [i.e. Leucippus'] daughters would become goddesses.
   (Papyrus *ap.* C. Gallavotti, *Rivista di Filologia e di Instruzióne Classica* XI (1933), p. 179)

Artemis, it must be said, is behaving here very like a Euripidean deus ex machina, but that does not preclude Critian authorship, since Critias may be presumed to be a warm admirer of Euripidean dramaturgy. What remains unclear is what role Rhadamanthys had in the action. The first extract is a single line, preserved by a lexicographer, which may possibly relate to the refusal of the Dioscuri to hand over the maidens.

31. Remove (*exairein*), in place of 'take away' (*aphairein*). Euripides, in the *Rhadamanthys*:

'For there is no one who will remove (them)[63] from us.'
(*Antiattista Bekkeri* p. 94, 1)

The next extract makes a mysterious reference to the island of Euboea, as being a polis which is 'neighbouring' (proskhôros), presumably across the strait from the Boeotian mainland to which the speaker is referring. We know that Rhadamanthys had something to do with Euboea, since in the Odyssey *(7, 321–2) Alcinous, king of the Phaeacians, mentions giving him a lift there, to visit Tityus, son of Gaia. However, the action of this play should have taken place in Messenia, in the Peloponnesus, so this does not seem to fit. Perhaps Rhadamanthys (if it is he) is simply reminiscing, or making a point.*

32. Euripides . . . in the *Rhadamanthys:*

'Those who hold Euboea, the neighbouring state (polis) . . .'
(Strabo, *Geography*, VIII, p. 356)

The third passage (from Stobaeus)[64] is more substantial, but still rather banal. It may be the exordium of a moralizing speech by Rhadamanthys, leading up to a criticism of the behaviour of the Dioscuri.

33. 'In life all sorts of desires assail us;
      This one yearns to gain nobility;
      that one has no concern for such, but in his home
      longs to be called lord of many possessions.
      It pleases another, speaking nothing healthy from his wits,
      to persuade his neighbours to embark on evil daring.
      Still others among mortals seek out base gains
      before the good; thus does the life of men wander astray.
      But none of these ends do I desire to gain;
      rather I should like to have a reputation of good fame.'
      (Stobaeus, *Anthology* II 8, 12 and *Florilegium* IV 20 ii, 61)

Pirithous

The story of Pirithous is much less edifying than those of the first two. He was a Lapith, son by Zeus of Ixion's wife, Dia. He is generally associated in his adventures with the Athenian hero Theseus, whom he led astray on a number of occasions. Together they abducted Helen, fought the Amazons and finally headed down to Hades in an attempt to kidnap Persephone. It is this last exploit that is the subject of the present play (the only known tragedy, therefore, to have its scene set in Hades). In the event, Pirithous is overpowered and shackled to a rock, while Theseus, who could have departed, feels in honour bound to stay with him. Ultimately, Theseus is rescued by Heracles, who has come down to capture Cerberus.

Critias can hardly have identified himself with Pirithous, but he may have seen himself as Theseus, involved in the downfall of Alcibiades/Pirithous. We may note that the Lapiths were traditionally situated in Thessaly, and it is possible that Critias composed this play when in exile there.

In the case of this play too papyrus finds have been of some help. Bits of fully eighty-five lines have been found in Oxyrhyncus Papyri XVII 2078, which comprises five fragments. Of Fr. 1 some sense can be made of ll. 7–20. This passage probably comes from the prologue, spoken by Pirithous himself; he is recounting the follies of his putative father, Ixion – perhaps in an attempt to excuse his own behaviour.

34.'The god straight away sent upon him a folly
   born of madness; <assaulting> a cloud <in the shape> of a
      woman,
   he spread among the Thessalians <a most impious tale.>
   He said that he had copulated <with Kronos'> daughter[65]
   <in the procreative bed>; and for such boasts
   <he later paid fitting> penalties to the gods . . .
   Around the cycle of madness . . .[66]
   Zeus drove him on gadfly-driven <wanderings?>,
   and then hid him, out of sight of men, <in the depths
   of the aether>; there my father, for his sins, was

dragged along[67] on the blasts of the North Wind
in a <punishment commensurate to his boasts> against the gods.
I, bearing on myself <the image of his woes,
by name Pirithous, have garnered equal fortunes.>[68]
(*Oxyrhynchus Papyri* XVII 2078, Fr. 1)

*At this point we can insert a passage preserved by the Byzantine
commentator Gregory of Corinth, on the rhetorician Hermogenes, with useful introductory comment. This presumably concerns the opening episode of the play (following on Pirithous'
prologue – and a chorus?), where Heracles appears on the scene,
in search of Cerberus. He is met by Aeacus, acting as the janitor
of Hades (much as in Aristophanes' Frogs).*

35. And in the case of Euripides, 'Zeus, as it is told us' – which
serves as an attribution (*anaphora*), 'by a true account' – which
is the confirmation (*bebaiosis*).[69] This verse is found in two plays
of Euripides, both in the so-called *Pirithous* and in *Melanippe
the Wise*.[70] It would not be inapposite to set out the plots and
the scenarios of these two plays for lovers of learning. The plot
of the *Pirithous* is as follows: Pirithous, having descended into
Hades along with Theseus in order to woo[71] Persephone, was
visited with appropriate punishment. Shackled to an immovable
seat of rock, he was guarded by the gaping jaws of dragons,
while Theseus, deeming it disgraceful to abandon his friend,
chose existence in Hades over life [on earth]. When, however,
Heracles was sent by Eurystheus to fetch Cerberus, he prevailed
over the beast by force, and, by the favour of the subterranean
deities, freed Theseus and his entourage[72] from the constraint
which bound them – in a single action both overcoming his
opponent and gaining favour from the gods and taking pity on
his friends in misfortune.[73] At any rate, Aeacus is introduced,
addressing himself to Heracles, as follows:

AEACUS: Ho! What have we here? I perceive someone approaching
    in haste and with a very bold demeanour.
    Stranger, it is right that you tell me who you are
    who approach this place, and what your errand is.

CRITIAS OF ATHENS

HERACLES: I have no problem in telling you the whole tale.
My fatherland is Argos, Heracles my name.
I spring from Zeus, father of all the gods;
for Zeus came to my mother's noble bed,
as it is told us by a true account.
Hither I have come under compulsion, obeying
the dictates of Eurystheus, who sent me with orders
to bring back alive the hound of Hades to the gates
of Mycenae – not that he wished to see the beast,
but thinking to set me this as an unfulfillable task.
In pursuit of such a task, I have tramped all over Europe
and into the nooks and crannies of all Asia.

(Gregory of Corinth, *In Hermogenem* B 445, 7 Rabe = B 16)

Aeacus must have retired to report this news to Hades, because we next find Heracles in conversation with Theseus – these lines from Frs. 2–3 of Oxyrhynchus Papyri are all that yield a continuous sense.

36. THESEUS: I will not blame you for that, Heracles;[74]
        but I must say, for the man was a trusty friend to me.
        It is base to betray one who is trapped in hostile hands.
    HERACLES: Theseus, these sentiments are fitting to you
        and to the Athenian state; for always you are an ally to those
        in trouble. It is unseemly[75] to return to one's fatherland
        having to plead excuses. For take Eurystheus –
        how pleased do you imagine he would be
        if he heard that I had achieved this task with your help?[76]
        He would declare the labour had not been performed to its
        completion.
    T: But at any rate, for what you desire, you have
        my full good will, not rashly given, but like a free
        to enemies hostile, but benign to friends . . .

(*Oxyrhynchus Papyri* XVII 2078, *Frs.* 2–3, ll. 2)

The papyrus tails off again at this point; but following unattached fragment (from Stobaeus, Anthol. 14, 2, attributed specifically to Critias) may belong to it:

37. From Critias:

'He who in dealing with his friends does everything
to please them, in exchange for the pleasure of the moment
sets up a cause of enmity for a future time.'
(Stobaeus, *Anthology* III 14, 2 = B27)

*Next, a fragment of chorus – the chorus, as we have suggested,
being composed of followers of Theseus. This fragment from
Athenaeus adds little to our understanding of the plot, but is
valuable as containing the only (albeit half-hearted) attribution
of the play to Critias. Since it is in anapaests, it may well come
from the parodos of the Chorus.*

38. Plēmochoê is a ceramic dish shaped like a top which some
call a kotyliskos, as we are told by Pamphilus, hey use it at
Eleusis on the last day of the Mysteries, a day which they
derive from it the name *Plēmochoai*; on that they fill two
plēmochoai, which they then turn upside do, standing up
and facing the east in one ase, the west in the er, and reciting
a mystical formula over them. They are made ation of by the
author of the *Pithous*, whether that be Cria the tyrant or
Euripides, as follows:

at these *mochoai* into earth's chn
holy sille we may pour forth.'
(Athena *Deipnophistae* XI 496A = B1expanded)

*The Chosen heto be making a sacrifor offering to
chthonic – which is old, if they are alre in Hades!
Another ent, ossibly, again, from th rodos (also in
anapaests served by Clement of Alexand.*

39. In coin with this, what has been recled about the
holy Ark aspects of the intelligible world hich is hidden
away and off from the multitude. Indeed, even those
golden or s, six-winged, each of them, w ether they sym-
bolize the ears, as some would wish, or, preferably, the

two hemispheres, at any rate the name 'Cherubim' seems to indicate great insight. But the two together have twelve wings and indicate the perceptible universe through the circle of the zodiac and the time sequence connected with it. And I think that tragedy,[77] speculating on nature, says:

> 'Unwearied time journeys around
> The everflowing stream;
> Full, it gives birth to itself, and the twin Bears
> Borne on swift-flapping wings
> Keep watch over Atlas' celestial pole.'
>   (Clement of Alexandria, *Stromateis* V 35 = B 18)

This does seem to exhibit a certain interest in physical philosophy, though it is probably only an elaborate way of lamenting the seemingly endless passage of time, as the Chorus wait in hope for release.

Clement preserves also another passage from what is still probably the parodos, *since it is also in anapaests. This is of somewhat more interest philosophically, since it appears to invoke a kind of Anaxagorean Mind of the World (such as Euripides himself is well able to invoke, indeed; cf. e.g.* Trojan Women *884ff.). The Chorus are appealing, or complaining, to the supreme deity.*

40. In his play *Pirithous*, the same author [i.e. Euripides] presents also the following:

> 'You, the self-begotten, who in the whirl[78]
> of aether have woven all things together,
> around whom light, and spangled murky night,
> and the numberless horde of stars
> continuously dance.'

Here he has called 'self-begotten' the creative mind (*dêmiourgos nous*). What follows refers to the cosmos, a feature of which is the opposition between light and darkness.
   (Ibid. V 115 = B 19)

A passage from Plutarch drives home the point that Critias
is plainly concerned to make, that Theseus is being dragged
down by his loyalty to a reckless and immoral companion.[79]
The line, in iambics, is spoken by some third party about
Theseus.

41. For even as the gold [i.e. headband] and the robe of Creon's
daughter were of no benefit to Creon, but, as he impulsively ran
to her and embraced her, the fire, fastening upon him, burned
him up and destroyed him along with his daughter,[80] so some
persons, without deriving any benefit from their friends' good
fortunes, perish with them in their misfortunes. This is an experience suffered predominantly by philosophers and men of
culture, as Theseus, for example,[81] shared with Pirithous his
punishment and imprisonment.

> 'Yoked fast in duty's bonds not forged of bronze.'[82]
> (Plutarch, *On Having Many Friends* 96c = B20, expanded)

There is a further passage (Euripides Fragmentum 964 Nauck),
also quoted by Plutarch, not positively identified as coming
from the Pirithous, but in our view very probably from that
source,[83] *which reinforces this characterization of Theseus as*
philosophos. We would see this as forming part of his conver-
sation with Heracles.

42. 'But I can't,' he says, 'for I never expected or looked to suffer
such an experience.'[84] But you ought to have looked for it, and
to have previously exercised your judgement on the uncertainty
and insignificance of human affairs, and then you would not
now have been left unprepared as if at the sudden onset of
enemies. For it is fine how Theseus in Euripides is seen to have
prepared himself for such crises, for he says:

> 'But I have learned this from a certain sage,
> and on these cares and troubles fixed my mind,
> and to myself applied exile from my land,
> untimely deaths, and other forms of ill,

> that if I suffered aught my mind imagined,
> it should not, being unexpected, bite the more.'
>
> (Plutarch, *Consolation to Apollonius* 112D)

Then a passage preserved by Stobaeus, in a section concerned with 'what is in our power'. It is not easy to determine who is speaking. It could be Pirithous, Theseus or Heracles.

43. Euripides, in the *Pirithous*:

> 'Not unskilled in mind was that first speaker
> who uttered the thought, coining a new phrase,
> that chance becomes ally to men of prudent wit.'
>
> (Stobaeus, *Anthology* II 8, 4)

Another fragment from Stobaeus, this time from a section concerned with 'goodness' (khrêstotês). Once again, it is impossible to discern who is speaking; perhaps Heracles, commending Theseus? In any event, coming from Critias' pen, the passage can be seen as a gibe at Athenian democratic politicians.

44. 'An honest (*khrêstos*) character is more steadfast than law.
   The former no orator[85] could ever twist or turn;
   the other, distorting it this way and that
   with arguments, he frequently corrupts.'
   (Ibid. III 37, 15 = B 22)

A further extract from Stobaeus, under the rubric 'Comparison of Life and Death', could, again, be a statement of Theseus', justifying his remaining in Hades.

45. 'Is it not better, then, not to live at all than to live badly?'
   (Ibid. IV 53, 23 = B 23)

One further line (Euripides, Fragmentum incertum 936 Nauck) has reasonably been proposed as deriving from this play. It could have been uttered by Theseus (possibly even by Pirithous), but more probably by Heracles. The line survives because it was parodied by Lucian in his Menippus, *or* The Descent into Hades, *where Menippus makes use of suitable lines from various Euripidean plays.*

46. 'No, but while still living Hades took me in.'

In conclusion, there is much that is odd about this play. How did it end? We know from other sources that Heracles brought back Cerberus to exhibit to Eurystheus, and that he managed to rescue Theseus; but equally the sources tell us that Pirithous stayed where he was. What tragic development or denouement there can have been for Pirithous, who is after all the titular 'hero' of the play, it is not easy to see. And why was Critias inspired to compose it? We have made a suggestion above, but it is quite conjectural, and advanced with due hesitation.

Sisyphus

The last play attested for Critias is perhaps the most interesting in terms of the content of what survives. It is normally described as a satyr-play, that is, the 'after-piece' to a tragic trilogy, in which a playwright poked fun at, or presented an irreverent view of, some mythical theme, and in which there was properly a chorus of satyrs, who provided an element of slapstick or knock-about fun. However, there is a problem of identification here. We know (from the gossip-writer Aelian, Varia Historia II 8) *that Euripides composed a* Sisyphus *as the satyr-play of a trilogy which he presented in 415. This cannot, therefore, be the play which Critias composed (unless we are to suppose that Critias composed it, and Euripides presented it!).*[86] *In that case, there is no particular reason for Critias' play to have been a satyr-play; nor is there anything in the surviving fragment to indicate this.*

Why should Critias have been attracted to Sisyphus? He was an even worse character than Pirithous, one of the traditional 'great sinners' in Hades, whose punishment was endlessly to push a great rock up a hill without ever getting it to the top. A legendary king of Corinth, who was famous as a rogue and a trickster, he qualified for this by outwitting Death, who had

come to collect him, and thus annoying Zeus. His character
does indeed make him a suitable subject for a satyr-drama, but,
as it seems, not a necessary one.

In the surviving fragment (which runs for forty lines, with
two further lines following), Critias chooses to make him the
mouthpiece for a cynical account of the origins of religion,
in what context we know not. Since, however, Sisyphus was
famously punished by Zeus, this inevitably undercuts any
remarks he might make on the subject of gods.

The passage is preserved by Sextus Empiricus in the context
of a survey of well-known 'atheists', or those who try to explain
away belief in gods, such as Diagoras of Melos, Prodicus (cf.
ch. 3, §§20–21), Theodorus and Euhemerus. Sisyphus is
brought on – possibly introducing himself, in a prologue, but
perhaps as part of a conversation, or agon, with another charac-
ter – expounding his views on the origins of religion.

47. And Critias, one of those who ruled as tyrants in Athens,
seems to gain admission to the camp of the atheists when he
declares that the legislators of old fabricated God as a kind of
overseer of the right actions and sins of men, in order to make
sure that nobody injured his neighbour secretly, through fear
of vengeance at the hands of the gods. The passage goes as
follows:[87]

> 'There was a time when anarchy did grip
> the life of men, which then was bestial,
> enslaved to force; nor was there then reward
> for good men, nor for the wicked punishment.
> Next, as I see it, did men establish laws
> for punishment, that justice might be lord
> of all mankind, and hold insolence enslaved;
> and anyone who sinned was penalized.
> Next, as the laws inhibited men from acts
> of open violence, but still such acts
> were done in secret – then, I would maintain,
> some clever fellow first, a man in counsel wise,
> discovered unto men the fear of gods,

that sinners might be frightened should they sin
e'en secretly in deed, or word, or thought.
Hence it was he introduced the Deity,
telling of a God who enjoys unfailing life,
hears with his mind, sees and perpends,
taking note, with a nature that is divine,
so that he is aware of man's every word
and is capable of seeing man's every act.[88]
And so, if you plot in silence some foul deed,
This will not evade the gods; for in them
wisdom resides. So, with reasonings like these,
a most clever doctrine did he introduce,
hiding the truth beneath a speech untrue.
    The place he declared the dwelling-place of gods
was that which would strike most alarm in men –
the source from which, he knew, both terrors came
and benefits to the wearisome life of men –
that is to say, the heavenly vault, wherein do dwell
the lightnings, he beheld, and awesome claps
of thunder, and the starry face of heaven,
the adornment of that cunning craftsman, Time[89] –
whence, too, the meteor's glowing mass doth speed
and liquid rain descends upon the earth.
    Such were the fears wherewith he enveloped men,
and so to God he gave a noble home,
by this his speech, and in a fitting place,
and thus extinguished lawlessness by laws.'

And, a little further along, he concludes:

'Thus first did some man, as I think, persuade
men to repose belief in a race of gods.'
(Sextus Empiricus, *Against the Mathematicians* IX 54 = B25)

What is Critias up to here? A difficulty is that all the known myths about Sisyphus involve his interaction with Zeus and other gods, so that it is hard to see how he can deny their existence without dire consequences – such as in fact befell him. Critias would seem to be getting his point across (as does Euripides on occasion), while undercutting the sentiments expressed effectively enough to defuse the indignation of the audience – if there was an audience![90]

Apart from these identifiable fragments, we have a few lines, all in Stobaeus, and all attributed to Critias, from unknown works in iambics, presumably dramas, but only one passage seems worth quoting. It does not immediately appear to fit the plot of any of the known plays, but could conceivably be an utterance of either Rhadamanthys or Sisyphus.

48. 'Wise poverty or rich ineptitude –
   which is the better companion in one's house?'
   (Stobaeus, *Anthology* IV 33, 10 = B29)

FRAGMENTS OF PROSE WORKS

Of prose works, we have evidence of treatises on the constitutions of the Lacedaemonians (Spartans), whom Critias plainly admired, and the Thessalians, about whom he was more ambivalent; there is also some evidence for a work about Athens, whether from a constitutional or historical perspective. These works seem not to have confined themselves to strictly 'constitutional' subjects, but to have concerned the ways of life of the nations concerned in all their aspects.

*He also seems to have composed a book of aphorisms, and one of lectures (*homiliai*), and a treatise* On the Nature of Love.[91] *There are also a number of fragments not certainly attached to any of these titles. Critias obviously left behind sufficient material of a rhetorical nature to attract the admiration of such a connoisseur as Herodes Atticus, but we have little to go on, unless we are to accept the surviving speech of Herodes,* On the Constitution *(of Larisa), as actually a work of Critias (on which see above, ch. 6, pp. 212–13). For reasons stated previously, we do not believe that it is, though it may well represent Herodes' idea of a 'Critian' style.*

The Constitution of the Lacedaemonians

First, a passage from Athenaeus, once again on drinking habits, a topic on which, as we have seen (cf. §25 above), Critias had strong views.

49. In answer to those persons it should be said that there are distinctive modes of drinking peculiar to different cities, as Critias explains in his *Constitution of the Lacedaemonians*:

'Your Chian and your Thasian will drink their toasts out of large cups from left to right, while an Athenian will drink from small cups, again from left to right, but a Thessalian pledges in large cups to whomsoever he wishes. The Lacedaemonians, on the other hand, drink each his own cup separately, and the slave who acts as wine-pourer fills it up again with as much as he has drunk down.'

(Athenaeus, *Deipnosophistae* XI 463E = B33)

This was only one aspect, however, of Critias' commendation of the Spartan way of life. Another passage of Athenaeus concerns the distinctive Spartan drinking-cup, the kôthôn:

50. *Kôthôn:* a Laconian cup, of which Xenophon makes mention in the first book of *The Education of Cyrus* (2.8); and Critias, in the *Constitution of the Lacedaemonians* writes as follows:

'Apart from these, the smallest details of their daily life (are admirable). Laconian shoes are the best; their cloaks are the pleasantest and most convenient to wear; the Laconian *kôthôn* is a drinking-vessel most suitable for taking on campaign and most easily carried in a knapsack. The reason why it is so well adapted to military use is that it is often necessary to drink water that is not pure. It is first of all useful because the liquid to be drunk cannot be seen with any clarity; and secondly, since the *kôthôn* has inward-turning edges, it catches a residue of the impurities inside the lip.'[92]

(Ibid. XI 483B = B34)

There is a further short notice by Athenaeus at XI 486E, where he is discussing terms for objects made in various places, but its content is somewhat baffling. We have no idea in what context Critias can have been discussing these objects, though one presumes that they are among the luxuries which Spartans would spurn.

51. Also Critias in his *Constitution of the Lacedaemonians*:
   'A couch of Milesian work, and a stool of Milesian work; a couch of Chian work, and a table of Rhenaean[93] work.'
   (Ibid. XI 486E = B35)

Next, a passage from the Byzantine commentator on Homer, Eustathius of Thessalonica, where the Phaeacians are showing off their dancing skills. Eustathius does not specify from which work of Critias he is quoting, but since it concerns the Spartans, we may assume the Constitution.

52. It was an old custom to play such games, and, they say, a traditional context among the Lacedaemonians was the 'ball-match' (*sphairomakhia*) . . . It is to be noted that such a game played with a ball was also a kind of dance, as he makes clear likewise who wrote thus: 'The *thermaustris* ("tong-dance") is a dance involving vigorous leg movements.'[94] At any rate, Critias writes as follows:
   'Leaping up high off the ground before dropping back to earth, they executed many crossings-over with their feet, and this they called "doing the tong-dance".'
   (Eustathius of Thessalonica, *Commentary on the Odyssey* 8, 376 = B36)

The fourth-century AD rhetorician Libanius, in an extended passage in Orations, *shows an interesting degree of acquaintance with Critias' work.*

53. What, then, [are we to say] of the Lacedaemonians, who reserve a licence to kill in respect of the Helots, and concerning whom Critias says that 'in Lacedaemon there are to the greatest

degree both slaves and freemen'. And how better to put the situation than Critias himself, when he says:[95]

'Owing to his mistrust of these Helots, the Spartiate, when at home, strips off the sling from the Helot's shield. Not being in a position to do this on campaign because of the frequent necessity to employ speed,[96] he always goes about with a spear in hand in order to have the advantage of the Helot in this respect, in case the latter should try to jump him, relying on his shield alone. And they have devised locks as well,[97] which they consider to be stronger than any conspiracy that could arise from that quarter.'

But this is the situation of people living in fear, and not being allowed to breathe freely by reason of the fearful expectations that they entertain. Thus, when they sit down to breakfast, or lie down to sleep, or go about any other aspect of their business, fear of their own servants keeps them constantly armed. How would these people then, son of Callaeschrus, be enjoying freedom in its purity, seeing that their slaves actually set upon them when encouraged by Poseidon,[98] and thereby laid down a marker that, in similar circumstances, they would do the same again? Just as their kings, then, were not particularly free, inasmuch as it was in the power of the ephors to put a king in chains and even to kill him, even so the Spartiates as a body were deprived of freedom, by reason of the hatred directed at them by their servants.

(Libanius, *Orations* 25, 63)

Lastly, a quotation from Clement of Alexandria concerning the breeding of good progeny. Diels includes this as a fragment of the Constitution of the Lacedaemonians *(indeed, as the first one, B32), but it is not obvious why. Clement gives no attribution, and Critias' mode of address, speaking in his own person, seems much more suitable to one of his* homiliai *than to such a work as a 'constitution'. Nevertheless, we leave it here, with due caution.*

54. Again, Euripides having said:[99]

'From a father and a mother who observe
a strict regime, the offspring are superior',

Critias writes:

'I take my start, you see, from a man's birth. How might he become most excellent and strong in body? If his progenitor would exercise and eat vigorously and take steps to toughen his body, and if the mother of the future child would strengthen her body and take exercise.'

(Clement of Alexandria, *Stromateis* VI 9)

It is possible, we suppose, that such a speech could have been put into the mouth of some Spartan lawgiver, such as Lycurgus, but, other than that, the passage does not seem to fit well into the format of a constitutional treatise.

The Constitution of the Thessalians

Of this treatise only one fragment remains, very much along the same lines as most of the surviving fragments of the other 'constitution', though rather less complimentary. Critias' relationship with his Thessalian hosts during his exile would seem to have been rather fraught, if we are to attach any credence to the allegations of Theramenes, as relayed by Xenophon (cf. above, §9). From Philostratus (cf. above, §1) we derive the opposite impression of his political activity, but still a sense of his adversative quality. This fragment derives, once again, from Athenaeus.

55. The Thessalians are generally agreed to have been the most luxurious of all the Greeks in the matter both of clothing and of food; this, in fact, was the cause of their bringing the Persians into Greece, that they admired Persian luxury and extravagance. Critias tells of their luxuriousness in his work on their constitution.

It is not quite clear whether the allegation about the reason for the Thessalians bringing the Persians into Greece is to be credited to Critias or not, but it probably is. It would appear to be a slander without foundation: certainly the Thessalians submitted readily to the Persians when they invaded in 480 (cf. Herodotus, Histories VII 130–2), but there is no evidence that they invited them in.

*There is one further reference to a 'constitution' not definitely
attributed to either of the above (in the Lexicon of Pollux), but
not incompatible with either of them, though perhaps more
appropriate to the Thessalians (the word for 'trousers' occurs
nowhere else).*

56. They call trousers (*anaxyrides*) also *skeleai*; the word occurs
in Critias, in his *Constitutions*.[100]
   (Pollux, *Lexicon* VII 59)

The Constitution of the Athenians *postulated by Diels would
appear to be a mirage. Diels wished to relate to this 'constitution'
a series of distinctive words used by Critias listed in Pollux's
Lexicon (B53–73), but there is nothing to relate them to such a
work, as opposed to some forensic or other oration.[101] There
is mention, as we have seen (above, §20b), in Alexander of
Aphrodisias (ap. Philoponus) of a number of 'constitutions in
verse', but no trace of any other survives.*

Aphorisms

We have evidence from Galen, in his Commentary on Hippocrates, 'The Doctor's Workshop', *of a work by Critias, entitled*
Aphorismoi, *in more than one book, the content of which
seems to relate, to some extent at least, to philosophy. Galen is
discussing the topic of sense-perception, and the various terms
used to denote it. He is here quoting a certain Aeficianus.*

57. And he recalls, in discussing the term 'thought' (*gnômê*), that,
among the ancients, it was used as an equivalent of 'intellect'
(*nous*) or 'intelligence' (*dianoia*) and even of 'reflection' (*ennoêsis*).
From many possible examples to illustrate this, I will cite just a
few. Critias, for instance, in Book I of his *Aphorisms*, writes as
follows: '... neither what one perceives (*aisthanetai*) through
one's body in general nor what one cognizes (*gignôskei*) through
thought (*gnômê*)';
   and again: 'Men come to knowledge (*gignôskousin*) if they
are accustomed to being healthy in their thought.'

> (Galen, *Commentary on Hippocrates, 'The Doctor's Workshop'* XVIII B 656, 2ff.)

This latter statement, at least, does appear to bear some philosophical weight. It could be interpreted in a 'Socratic' sense (and Critias was, after all, for much of his life, to some extent, a follower of Socrates), to the effect that knowledge only comes to men if they practise virtue and pursue rational inquiry. But in truth we do not have much to go on here.

Lectures

In the same passage (directly following the last quotation), Galen also presents us with two references to Critias' Lectures (Homiliai).[102]

58. And also in Book I of the *Lectures*: 'But if you yourself were to undergo practice, in order that you might be competent in thought (*gnômê*), you would in this way be least wronged by them.'[103]

And often elsewhere in the same book, and in Book II of the *Lectures*, in making a distinction between thought and sense-perception, he often speaks in the same terms as does Antiphon in the first book of his *On Truth* . . . [cf. above, ch. 5, §14].

(Ibid. XVIII B 656, 2ff. = B39)

One cannot be sure here whether Galen is conducting researches for himself into the works of Critias and Antiphon, or whether he is using the findings of some previous Atticist lexicographer, but in either case he attests to knowledge of, and interest in, these works in the later period.

One further attestation, this time from the early second-century AD grammarian Herodian, is of some slight interest, as giving evidence of attention to Critias' works in the generation before Herodes Atticus.

59. The substitution by Critias, in his *Lectures*, of *orsotês* for *hormê* ('impulse') is eccentric (*parasêmos*).[104]

(Herodian, *On Anomalous Words* p. 40, 14)

One further curious item may relate to the Lectures. *In Plato's*
Charmides *(161B), young Charmides is made to produce a
definition of* sôphrosynê *('moderation' or 'self-control'), and* ta
heautou prattein *('minding one's own business' or 'doing what
is appropriate to one'). Socrates accuses him of borrowing it
from 'Critias here, or some other of our wise men* (sophoi)*'.
Critias denies authorship (161C), but a little later (162B), when
Socrates has ironically picked it to pieces, Charmides, when
admitting that not even its author may have known what he
meant by it, 'gives a sly laugh and glances at Critias', which
rather gives the game away. Diels, correctly in our view, concludes that this is indeed a definition offered by Critias, and
probably in his* Homiliai, *and includes it as B41a.*

On the Nature of Love, or of Loves

*We also have one snippet preserved, again by Galen, from a
rather curious work entitled* On the Nature of Love, or of
Loves,[105] *which, however, gives little clue as to its contents.*

60. *Dysaniês* ('hard to please, cranky'): Critias, in his treatise
On the Nature of Love, or of Loves, explains the word in the
following way:

'A cranky (*dysanios*) person is one who gets into a fuss (*ania-
tai*) about small things, and over major things to a greater degree
or for a longer time than other people.'

(Galen, *Glossary of Hippocratic Terminology*, XIX 94 Kühn)

Unidentified Prose Works

Of the Dêmêgorika Prooimia *mentioned by Hermogenes
(above, §18) no identifiable trace remains, but there are a
number of interesting passages preserved from unidentified
prose works, which are worth including.*

*First, an interesting criticism of the poet Archilochus, pre-
served by Aelian – which may, indeed, come from the* Lectures.
*It indicates something of Critias' aristocratic ethos, which was
offended by Archilochus' revelation of his own dirty linen. It
probably formed part of some more general disquisition on how
best to present oneself in writing, or something such.*

61. Critias blames Archilochus for speaking very ill of himself.

'For if', he says, 'he had not spread about this kind of opinion of himself among the Greeks,[106] we should not have found out that he was the son of the slave-woman Enipo, or that because of poverty and need he left Paros and went to Thasos; that, on his arrival, he fell into enmity with the residents of that island; and that he poured abuse on friends and enemies alike. In addition,' he declares, 'we should not have known that he was an adulterer if we had not learned of it from him, nor of his lechery and outrageous behaviour, and – what is much more disgraceful – that he threw away his shield. So Archilochus was not a good witness in his own case, in spite of the fact that he left behind him such renown and reputation.'

These criticisms of Archilochus are not mine; they come from Critias.

(Aelian, *Varia Historia* X 13 = B44)

Aelian returns to Critias a little further down in his jottings. He may conceivably have had a single work of Critias' in front of him at the time, in which he was browsing – in which case, probably the Lectures. *Critias is presumably here engaged on a criticism of the venality of democratic politicians.*

62. Critias says that before embarking on his political career Themistocles, son of Neocles, possessed family property to the value of three talents. However, after he had become prominent in public life, and then suffered exile and had his property confiscated, he was discovered to own property worth more than 100 talents. Similarly, Cleon, before entering public life, possessed nothing of his own that was free of debt; but subsequently he left a household worth fifty talents.[107]

(Ibid. X 17 = B45)

Next, a reference in Plutarch's Life of Cimon, *also on the subject of Athenian politics. This may, again, come from the* Lectures, *but also possibly from the* Constitution of the Lacedaemonians. *The situation referred to is the aftermath of the Spartan earthquake of 464, when the Spartans appealed to Athens for help in*

*quelling an uprising of the Helots (referred to above, §53), and
Cimon, in 462, led out an expedition to help them (which was
later snubbed by the Spartans).*

63. Critias tells us that, whereas Ephialtes[108] made difficulties
and protested against aiding or helping to raise up a city which
was a rival to Athens, but advised, rather, that the pride of
Sparta should be allowed to fall and be trampled in the dust,
Cimon,[109] ranking the aggrandizement of his fatherland lower
than the advantage of the Lacedaemonians, and having convinced the people of the correctness of this, went out to assist
them with a large force of hoplites.

   (Plutarch, *Life of Cimon*, ch. 16)

*We turn now to some more literary judgements. The rhetorician
Aelius Aristides (AD 129–189), in commenting on the beginning
of Xenophon's Symposium (where Xenophon begins with the
phrase, 'But to me, at any rate, it seems . . .'), says the following:*

64. For since what was said in the *Symposium* seemed undignified, to wit, that one should relate what people did in moments
of relaxation,[110] and that no public man would have done this,
since it was undignified, he begins on this apologetic note ('But
to me, at any rate, it seems . . .'). But if he had begun with a
positive word,[111] e.g. 'But it seems to me . . .', his expression
would have come out stronger, and rather more like that of
Critias or some author of that sort.

   (Aelius Aristides, *Art of Rhetoric* II 15 Schmid = B 46)

*The basis of this criticism is somewhat obscure (as, indeed, is
the following one), but it does attest to the revived popularity
of Critias in the second century AD.*

   *Here is Aristides again, commenting this time on a passage
just below in the Symposium (I 4), where Callias, the host, is
welcoming Socrates and his friends with the remark (which
Socrates takes as bantering) that 'I'm sure that my establishment
would seem much more stately if my dining-room were graced
by persons of purity of mind, like yourselves, than if my guests*

were generals or cavalry commanders or ambitious politicians.'
*Aristides criticizes this too – quite ineptly, it must be said (*Art
of Rhetoric *II 50 Schmid), but interestingly, since it seems to
concord to some extent with the analysis of Critias' style given
by Aristides' contemporary Hermogenes (cf. above, §18).*

65. But if, turning the expression around, you had said, for
example, 'All who choose such men, whom they see excelling
others in office or honour or some such power, do not seem to me
to act correctly,' this manner of expression would have seemed
much more proper to Critias or some other of the ancient sophists.
   (Ibid. II 50)

*A further small stylistic snippet, preserved by the Byzantine
polymath Maximos Planudes (c. AD 1255–1305), in his commentary on Hermogenes'* On Types of Style, *while banal enough
in itself, seems to attest to continued access to, and interest in,
the works of Critias at this late era.*

66. As for instance 'in the contest of the Pythian (Games)' (*tôi
agôni tôn Pythiôn*) – this is the everyday and straightforward
way of saying it, but Critias, employing inversion, said *tôi tôn
Pythiôn agôni.*
   (Maximos Planudes, *Commentary on Hermogenes* V 484
   Walz)

*Planudes misses the point here, surely. If Critias puts the genitive
between the article and its noun, it merely means that he is
treating it as possessive rather than descriptive. More interesting, though, is the unanswerable puzzle as to where Planudes
got his information from.*
   *Next, some dicta of Critias, preserved in later writers. First,
Dio Chrysostomus (c. AD 40–115), in one of his orations. Dio
is discussing the apparent deficiency of male beauty in his own
day, and is being ironic.*

67. Or are you not aware that Critias, the member of the
Thirty, said the following: 'The fairest form among males is the

feminine, and among females the opposite.' On the basis of this, then, the Athenians quite properly chose him as lawgiver (*nomothetês*) in order to revise the old laws,[112] and he left none of them in place.

(Dio Chrysostomus, *Orations* 21, 3 = B48)

Presumably Dio's point is that a man who could make such an outrageous statement about male beauty could be relied upon to wipe out a whole legal system.

Another epigrammatic saying of Critias is preserved by Pseudo-Dionysius – a fairly conventional piece of Greek folk-wisdom, along the lines that the only certainties in this life are death and taxes.

68. For a man, once born, according to the son of Callaeschrus, the member of the Thirty, 'nothing is sure, except dying once one has been born, and the impossibility, while living, of stepping outside one's fate'.[113]

(Pseudo-Dionysius, *Art of Rhetoric* 6 = B49).

Then a passage from Philostratus' dedicatory preface to his Lives of the Sophists *(p. 480), where he is excusing himself to the future emperor Gordian for not mentioning the names of the fathers of all of his subjects.*

69. Their fathers' names I have not added in all cases, no indeed, but only for those who were the sons of distinguished men. For one thing, I am aware that the sophist Critias did not begin with the father's name as a rule, but only in the case of Homer mentioned his father, because the thing he had to relate was a marvel, namely that Homer's father was a river.[114]

(Philostratus, *Lives of the Sophists*, Preface p. 480 = B50)

To what work of Critias Philostratus is referring we have no idea.

Apart from these testimonies, we have quite a collection of individual words, all from Pollux's Lexicon *(B53–73), which, though of some philological interest, do not seem worth listing individually. We will simply call attention to two curiosities.*

The first (B70) is an extraordinary list of vulgar professions (e.g. vegetable-dealers, cheese-dealers, cabbage-dealers), mostly ending in the suffix -pôlai, which may possibly have formed part of a satirical survey of the multiplicity of trades plied in and around the Athenian agora.

The second (B71) is an odd little lexicographical note (VIII 25) which may in fact contain a clue of some significance. It runs as follows:

70. Critias used *apodikasai* ('acquit') as meaning to dissolve a trial or to deny it a victory, as we would say *apopsêphisasthai.* The same author uses *diadikazein* to mean 'to give judgement throughout the year'.

(Pollux, *Lexicon* VIII 25 = B71)

The first part of this note is unremarkable: apodikazein *is used in this sense also by Antiphon (6, 47); but the second is most interesting. As was noted long ago by August Boeckh, the verb* diadikazein *is used repeatedly in a remarkable work attributed falsely to Xenophon (the author is customarily known, affectionately, as the 'Old Oligarch'), The Constitution of Athens – a sustained, and at times shrewd, assault on fifth-century Athenian democracy. In ch. 3, 4–6 of this work, the author repeatedly uses* diadikazein, *which properly has the technical meaning in Athenian law 'give judgement in a* diadikasia, *or suit between rival claimants', in contexts which could lead Pollux to suppose that he means 'judging throughout the year'. If Pollux in fact has this passage in mind, the conclusions are momentous. It would mean that, as Boeckh proposed, the 'Old Oligarch' is none other than Critias. The question is too complex to be pronounced upon in a work of this sort. We simply present this snippet as constituting some evidence in favour of the identification, which needs to be countered by evidence which would preclude it, such as we have not seen. The work is certainly rather roughly constructed, but the style is not incompatible with the style of Critias as described by Hermogenes in §18 above.*

8 EUTHYDEMUS AND DIONYSODORUS OF CHIOS

We follow the lead of Rosamund Kent Sprague[1] in including
Euthydemus in the company of the older sophists, though we
thought it fair, as she did not, that he should share this privilege
with his brother Dionysodorus. As she very reasonably remarks,
there is sufficient evidence (specifically from Aristotle) that he
and his brother are not simply fictions of Plato in his dialogue
Euthydemus. If Diels omitted him from his collection, it was
doubtless because he was acting on the assumption, current
among German scholars at the time of his edition, that Plato's
Euthydemus was simply a mask for his own rival, Socrates'
senior follower, Antisthenes. Even if it be granted that Plato is
indirectly taking a dig at Antisthenes (who does seem to have
borrowed some of the 'doctrines' and devices of the earlier man,
such as, in particular, the argument for the impossibility of
contradiction), few, if any, nowadays would take this as a reason
to deny the existence of Euthydemus. So he must be included,
even though virtually all that we have of him is what we can
derive from Plato's highly satirical portrayal in the dialogue
called after him. Despite Plato's satirical purposes, there is no
reason to doubt the essential accuracy either of the biographical
details given, or of the form of the sophists' arguments.

The dramatic date of the dialogue may be fixed at some time
in the period 420 to 405, and probably nearer to the latter date,
since Socrates lays some emphasis on his own advanced age.
This would seem to give Euthydemus and his brother, as his
slightly older contemporaries, a birthdate in the mid to late
470s. We know that they originated from the island of Chios,
but went as colonists to the 'pan-Hellenic' colony of Thurii in

southern Italy (see below, §1), presumably at or near the date of its foundation by Pericles in 444, from where, however, they were exiled some time afterwards (probably in a political upheaval – Thurii was a rather volatile place), and later plied their trade (it would seem originally as physical training instructors) in Athens and other parts of the Greek mainland. Only subsequently, Socrates tells us, did they turn their talents to the art of verbal combat.

The portrayal of the brothers is important, since it constitutes an introduction to what was plainly a significant part of the instruction offered by many sophists: the eristic art, or argumentation, that plays on ambiguities of language or thought. Plato, of course, regards this as pernicious, distinguishing it from Socrates' own procedure of dialectic (which often resembles it rather closely) by the fact that Socrates is actuated by a higher purpose, the search for accurate definitions of ethical and aesthetic terms. Nevertheless, rather than simply rejecting the eristic practice of sophists as some form of specious verbal trickery, we might see it as performing the perfectly valid role of a mental gymnastic, alerting the pupil to linguistic and conceptual ambiguities, which he can then learn to manipulate.

LIFE AND WORKS

We may begin with the introduction to the dialogue Euthydemus, where Socrates is explaining to his old friend Crito with whom he was conversing the previous day.

1. CRITO: Who was that fellow that you were talking to yesterday in the Lyceum,[2] Socrates? There was such a crowd around you that, although I wanted to listen, I couldn't get close enough to hear distinctly. But I craned my neck over the crowd and got the impression that you were talking to some foreigner. Who was it?

SOCRATES: Which one did you mean, Crito? There were actually two of them, not just one.

C: I mean the one who was sitting next but one to you, on

your right, on the other side of Axiochus' boy[3] – who struck me as having grown up a good deal, Socrates, and indeed to be little different in age to my son Critobulus. But Critobulus is rather puny, whereas this lad is mature and good-looking.

s: It is Euthydemus that you're asking about, Crito, and the other one, who sat next to me on my left, was his brother Dionysodorus, who also joined in the discussions.

c: I don't know either of them, Socrates – I suppose they are more new sophists. Where are they from? And what expertise do they profess?

s: In origin, I think, they are from this part of the world, that is to say, from Chios, but they went as colonists to Thurii;[4] they have been exiled from there, however, and for a good many years now they've been spending time in these parts. As to your inquiry about their field of expertise, Crito, it is quite wonderful: they are absolutely omniscient – I hadn't realized before what it was to be a true all-rounder.[5] These two are absolutely all-round fighters, not like the pair of pancratiast brothers from Acarnania.[6] They were only able to fight with their bodies, after all. This pair are most formidable not only at the bodily level, and in the sort of fighting which can overpower anyone – they are expert fighters in armour, and can make others the same, for a fee – but also, they excel both at contesting legal battles and at teaching others to compose and deliver speeches suitable for the law-courts. These attainments *used* to be the limits of their ability, but now they have put the finishing touches to their pancratiastic skills.[7] They have now mastered the only form of fighting they had neglected, so that no one at all can stand against them, so formidable have they become at verbal battle – specifically, the refutation (*exelenkhein*) of any statement, no matter whether it be true or false. At any rate, Crito, I propose to put myself in their hands, since they claim that in only a short while they can make anyone else equally skilled.

c: What, Socrates? Are you not worried, at your time of life, that you might already be too old?

s: Not a bit, Crito. I have sufficient indication to encourage me not to worry. You see, these two themselves were already old men (*geronte*) when they embarked on what *I* am anxious to acquire – the art of disputation (*eristikê*). A year or two ago they had not yet acquired this wisdom.

(Plato, *Euthydemus* 271A–272B)

That there was indeed a time when the brothers professed the teaching of purely military skills is attested by the following passage from Xenophon's Memoirs of Socrates:

2. I shall now tell how Socrates used to assist people with honourable purposes by making them apply themselves to the objects that they strove for.

Hearing on one occasion that Dionysodorus had come to town and was offering to teach the art of generalship (*stratêg-ein*),[8] he said to one of his companions, who he knew was eager to attain this position in the state,[9] 'You know, young man, it's a bit of a disgrace for one who aspires to the position of general in the state to neglect the opportunity of instruction when one has the chance ... So how would a man who strove to get himself elected to this position without bothering to learn the relevant skill not deserve to be penalized?'

(Xenophon, *Memoirs of Socrates* III 1, 1–3)

The concept of expert knowledge as the only valid basis for administrative office (for the generalship was an elective, political appointment) is very much in accord with Socrates' views as we know them from Plato. So also is his criticism of Dionyso-dorus just below (1, 6ff.) for only teaching tactics, and not paying attention to the higher purposes of warfare, or 'what is good and bad'.

DOCTRINES/TECHNIQUES OF

INSTRUCTION

In fact, much of the dialogue could be adduced to illustrate the eristic techniques of the brothers, but we may confine ourselves to the selection of passages already picked out by Sprague.

First, a passage a little further on in the dialogue Euthydemus, *where the brothers introduce themselves, asserting how they have moved on from the teaching of military tactics to the teaching of human excellence (*aretê*) in general.*

3. SOCRATES: It was by some divine dispensation that I found myself sitting on my own in the changing-room, where you saw me, and I was just about to get up and go; but when I got up to go, my regular daemonic sign occurred,[10] so I sat down again, and just a little while later these two, Euthydemus and Dionysodorus, entered, accompanied by lots of other people – pupils, as I assumed. Once inside, the two of them began to walk around the covered walk.[11] Hardly had they completed two or three circuits, when in comes Cleinias, who, as you rightly point out, has grown up a lot. In his train was a crowd of admirers, including Ctesippus, of the deme of Paeania, a young man of very good breeding – except for exhibiting a certain insolence, by reason of his youth.

When Cleinias caught sight of me from the doorway sitting by myself, he came directly over and sat on my right, just as you say; and when Dionysodorus and Euthydemus saw him, they first stopped and began to collogue with each other, while glancing repeatedly in our direction – I was keeping my eye on them.[12] Then they came and sat down, Euthydemus by the boy, Dionysodorus next to me on my left; and the rest found places as best they could.

I had not seen them for some time, so I greeted them, and then I said to Cleinias: 'Cleinias, these two men here are skilled, not in trivial things, but in great ones. Both of them know all about warfare, that is, what someone who proposes to be a general (*stratêgos*) should know – they know about tactics and about military leadership, and everything that needs to be taught about fighting in armour – and they are also capable of making anyone able to get redress in the law-courts, if he is wronged.'

When I said this, I received a contemptuous response from them. At any rate, they exchanged glances and laughed, and Euthydemus said: 'We no longer bother with those matters, Socrates. We regard them as marginal.'

I expressed astonishment. 'If you treat such important matters as marginal,' I said, 'then your main occupation must be a fine one indeed! Do please tell me what this fine occupation might be.'

'It is human excellence (*aretê*), Socrates,' he said. 'We consider that we are the finest and speediest teachers of human excellence in the world.'

(Plato, *Euthydemus* 272E–273D)

Under further ironic prodding from Socrates, the brothers reveal that they are in Athens to give an exhibition (epideixis) of their expertise, and this leads Socrates to express a desire to enrol under them as a student, and also to enrol the young men Cleinias and Ctesippus. This in turn leads to a series of exhibition-arguments that make up the body of the dialogue, from which we will select just the most significant. Despite the satirical tone of the narrative, it probably gives a reasonably accurate idea of the circumstances in which these events took place.

Who are the Learners?

The first involves a puzzle which Plato also makes use of in the Meno (80DE): how can one seek to know about something, if one does not know what it is one is seeking to know about (because one would not recognize it if one were confronted with it)?

4. So Euthydemus started from more or less this position, as I recall.

'Tell me, Cleinias, which sort of men is it who learn, the wise (*sophoi*) or the ignorant (*amatheis*)?'[13]

Sensing the seriousness of the question, the young man blushed and looked to me helplessly. I saw that he was confused, and said: 'Don't worry, Cleinias. Just answer boldly, whichever way you think is right; for you are having the greatest benefit conferred on you.'

In the midst of this, Dionysodorus leaned over to me, grinning broadly, and whispered in my ear. 'Let me tell you, Socrates,' he said, 'that whatever answer the lad gives, he will be proved wrong.'

As it happened, Cleinias gave his reply at the same time as Dionysodorus was telling me this, so I was unable to warn him to watch out; [276] he replied that it was the wise who were the learners.

Euthydemus now intervened.

'Do you recognize that there are such people as teachers, or do you not?'

Cleinias agreed that he did.

'And teachers are teachers of learners – in the same way as you and your school-mates had a music teacher and a writing teacher, from whom you used to learn?'

He agreed.

'So wasn't it the case that when you were learners, you didn't yet know what you were learning?'

He agreed that they did not.

'And were you wise when you did not know this?'

'Of course not,' he said.

'Then, if you weren't wise, you were ignorant, weren't you?'

'Yes.'

'So, while learning what you did not know, you were learning because you were ignorant.'

The lad nodded.

'It is ignorant people, then, who learn, Cleinias, not the wise, as you thought.'

At these words of his, the followers of Dionysodorus and Euthydemus broke out into cheers and laughter, like a chorus at a sign from their director. And now before the young man could recover his breath, Dionysodorus took over and said: 'Now, Cleinias, when the writing teacher was reciting a piece, which of the boys learned it, the wise or the ignorant?'

'The wise,' said Cleinias.

'So it is wise people who learn, not ignorant ones: you gave the wrong answer to Euthydemus just now.'

At this point there arose much laughter and applause from the pair's admirers, delighted as they were with their heroes' cleverness, while the rest of us were depressed into silence. Then

Euthydemus, recognizing the effect he had produced, in order to astound us even more, did not give up in his questioning of the lad, but, like an expert dancer, began to turn his questions back around the same spot.

'Do those who learn learn what they know,' he asked, 'or what they do not know?'

Dionysodorus whispered again to me softly: 'Here comes another one just like the first, Socrates!'

'Heavens!' I exclaimed. 'Your first question was certainly impressive enough!'

'All our lines of questioning of this sort are designed to leave no avenue of escape, Socrates,' he said.

'That, I think,' said I, 'is why you are held in such high regard by your pupils.'

Meanwhile Cleinias had replied that those who learn learn what they do not know, and Euthydemus used the same line of questioning as before.

[277] 'But surely you know your letters, don't you?'

'Yes,' said Cleinias.

'All the way through?'

He agreed.

'Now, if you learn something for recitation, are you not reciting letters of the alphabet?'[14]

He agreed.

'So, if you know all your letters, then a recitation consists of what you know, doesn't it?'

He agreed to this as well.

'Well then,' he said, 'do you *learn* what is dictated to you, or is it just someone who does not know their alphabet who would be learning?'

'No,' he replied, 'I learn.'

'Then you learn what you know,' he said, 'if you know the whole alphabet.'

He agreed.

'So your earlier answer was not correct,' he said.

The last word was hardly out of Euthydemus' mouth when Dionysodorus took up the argument, like a ball to catch and throw at the lad.

'Euthydemus is fooling with you, Cleinias,' he said. 'Tell me, isn't learning the acquisition of knowledge of that which is being learned?'

Cleinias agreed.

'And is it not the case that knowing is just the possession of knowledge at any given time?'

He agreed.

'Not knowing, then, is not yet possessing knowledge.'

He agreed with him.

'Well, are those who acquire something those who have it already or those who do not have it?'

'Those who do not have it.'

'And you agree that those who do not know are of the class of those who do not have something?'

He nodded.

'And those who learn are of the class of those who acquire something, not of those who have it already?'

He agreed.

'Then, Cleinias,' he said, 'it is those who do not know who learn, not those who know.'

(Ibid. 275D–277C)

Despite the satirical nature of this portrayal of an eristic pattern of argument, it can be seen that such a procedure could serve a relatively worthy purpose, the sensitizing of the neophyte to the ambiguities of language. Such is also the case with the other major pattern of argument which we select from the dialogue, this time concerning such major questions as the nature of being and not-being, the impossibility of making a false statement and the impossibility of contradiction.

Change as Destruction/The Impossibility of Contradiction

5. *[283]* So, Crito, that is what I had to say,[15] and I then gave the closest attention to what would happen next, observing how they would take up the argument, and how they would set about encouraging the lad to practise wisdom and moral excellence.

Dionysodorus, the older of them, spoke first, and we all turned our attention to him, expecting to hear straight away some remarkable arguments. And that indeed was our experience; for marvellous indeed, Crito, was the argument that he launched upon, and well worth your hearing, as a notable exhortation to moral excellence.

'Tell me, Socrates,' he said, 'and all you others who say you want this young man to become wise, are you joking when you say this, or do you really mean it?'

Now I supposed that they had previously taken us to be joking, when we had asked them to converse with the young man, and that this was the explanation for their fooling about and not being serious now; and this made me insist emphatically that we were indeed remarkably serious.

'Be careful, then, Socrates,' rejoined Dionysodorus, 'that you do not end up repudiating what you say now.'

'I am being careful,' I said; 'and I am quite clear that I shall never repudiate that.'

'All right, then,' he said; 'you say that you want him to become wise?'

'Yes.'

'And at present, is Cleinias wise or not?'

'Well, he says he isn't, as yet; and he is not an idle babbler.'

'And you want him to become wise, and not to be ignorant?'

We agreed.

'So you want him to become what he is not now, and what he is now, you wish him no longer to be?'[16]

When I heard this, I was thrown into confusion; and while I was still confused, he interjected: 'In other words, since you want to stop him being the person he now is, you apparently want him to perish. And yet, what great friends and lovers are they who make it their highest priority to see that their loved one perishes!'[17]

Ctesippus, on hearing this, was indignant on his beloved's account, and said: 'Visitor from Thurii, if it were not rather rude, I would say "May that recoil on your own head!" What could possess you to suggest such a lying slander – something that I would regard as unholy even to utter – as that I and these others should wish this lad to perish?'

'Well now, Ctesippus!' said Euthydemus. 'You think it's possible to lie, do you?'

'Certainly I do,' he said. 'I should be mad to think anything else.'

'Does a lie come about when someone utters (*legei*) the thing (*pragma*) about which the utterance is, or when he does not?'[18]

[284] 'When he utters it,' he said.

'So if he utters that, then, out of all possible facts, he is uttering precisely the one which he is uttering, is he not?'

'Of course,' said Ctesippus.

'So at least this thing which he utters is one out of all facts, distinct from all other facts, isn't it?'

'Yes.'

'So in uttering this, he is stating (*legei*) that which is (*to on*)?'

'Yes.'

'But surely he who states what is, and things that are, is stating the truth. So if Dionysodorus states things that are, he is stating the truth, and not telling lies about you at all.'

'Yes,' said Ctesippus; 'but anyone who says what *he* says, Euthydemus, is not saying what is the case (*ta onta*).'

To this Euthydemus replied: 'But things that are not the case, surely, simply are not?'

'No, they are not.'

'And things that are not the case have no sort of existence?'[19]

'No sort, no.'

'Now, is it possible for things that do not exist to be the object of any sort of action, in the sense that things which have no sort of existence can have anything done to them?'

'I don't think so,' said Ctesippus.

'Well then, when politicians speak before the people, do they do nothing?'

'No, they do something.'

'So, if they are doing something, they are also making something?'[20]

'Yes.'

'Now, is speaking both doing something and making something?'

He agreed.

'So no one,' he said, 'speaks what is not; for he would thereby be making something, and you have agreed that it is impossible for non-existent things (*ta mê onta*) to have anything made of them by anybody. So, by your account, no one speaks what is false, but if Dionysodorus speaks, he speaks what is true and is the case (*ta onta*).'

'Yes indeed, Euthydemus,' said Ctesippus, 'but he speaks things that are the case only in a certain sense – not, however, as they are.'

'What do you mean, Ctesippus?' said Dionysodorus. 'Are there people who speak things as they are?'

'There are indeed,' he said, 'gentlemen (*kaloi kagathoi*) – people who speak the truth.'

'Now, aren't good things in a good state and bad things in a bad state?'

He assented to this.

'And you agree that gentlemen tell things in the way they are?'
'Yes.'

'So these good people of yours speak badly of bad things,[21] if they tell things the way they are.'

(Ibid. 283A–284D)

The discussion now degenerates for a while, amusingly, into mudslinging (284D–285D), since Ctesippus is incensed by the suggestion that gentlemen would indulge in 'ill-talk', until Socrates steps in to rescue it. Ctesippus then backs off, claiming that he was not abusing Dionysodorus, merely contradicting him; but this in turn leads him into further knots, concerning the impossibility of contradiction. The passage has, however, already been quoted, in ch. 1, §14 above, since the argument for the impossibility of contradiction is there attributed by Socrates also to Protagoras, and we therefore direct the reader to that section.

A third and final[22] sequence of argument occurs at 293B–297C, developing the position that everyone always knows everything, if they know anything. The whole sequence is too long to quote in full, but the most significant portion can be presented (293B–294A). The puzzle about the nature of *knowledge (*epistêmê*) surfaces in the* Double Arguments *(below, ch. 10, §8), and it continued to bother Plato and Aristotle, though not in the absurd form in which it is presented here.*

Socrates has just been telling Crito of his frustration in the search for a type of knowledge which will lead to the acquisition of moral excellence, which he was hoping that the brothers would impart to him.

The Nature of Knowing

6. *[293B]* [Euthydemus is speaking] 'Socrates, in respect of this knowledge which you've been puzzling over for some time now – would you like me to instruct you in it, or would you rather that I proved to you that you already have it?'

'You remarkable fellow,' I said. 'Can you do that, then?'

'Indeed I can,' he said.

'Then do please demonstrate that I have it,' I said. 'For someone of my age, it's far easier than learning it.'

'All right, then,' he said. 'Just answer me this; do you know anything?'

'Yes,' I said, 'lots of things – trivial ones, though.'[23]

'That'll do,' he said. 'Now, do you think that it is possible for any of those things not to be what they are?'

'Of course I don't!'

'Now,' he said, 'you do know something?'

'I do.'

'Then, if indeed you know, you are in possession of knowledge (*epistêmôn*)'.[24]

'Certainly – in respect of that thing that I know.'[25]

'That makes no odds. Aren't you bound to know everything, if you are in possession of knowledge?'

'Good heavens, no!' I said. 'There are lots of other things that I don't know.'

'Well, if you don't know something, then you are not in possession of knowledge.'

'Not *of that thing*, my dear sir,' I replied.

'But are you then,' he said, 'any the less not in possession of knowledge? And yet just now you said that you were in possession of knowledge. So you both are what you are, and again are not what you are, in the same respect and at the same time.'

'All right, Euthydemus,' I said; 'as they say, "All you have said is well said." But how, then, do I know that knowledge which we were in search of – since it is impossible, after all, for the same thing to be and not to be? If I know any one thing, then, I know everything – for I cannot at the same time be both in possession of knowledge and not in possession of knowledge – and since I know everything, I have that knowledge as well. Is that what you're saying, and is this that wisdom of yours?'

'Yes, Socrates,' he said. 'You see, you are refuting yourself by your own words.'

'But come now, Euthydemus,' I said, 'are you not yourself in the same boat? I assure you, as long as I have yourself and dear old Dionysodorus to share my fate, I don't feel too badly about this. Tell me, is it not the case that you both know some things, while there are other things you do not know?'

'Not at all, Socrates,' said Dionysodorus.

'What do you mean?' I said. 'Are you saying that you don't know anything?'

'Oh yes, indeed we do,' he said.

[294] 'So you know everything, then,' I said, 'once you know anything at all.'

'Yes, everything,' he said; 'and what's more, so do you know everything, if you know any one thing.'

'Good gracious!' I said, 'what a wonderful piece of news, and what a great blessing has been revealed to me. And how about the rest of mankind? Do they know everything, or nothing?'

'Well certainly,' he said, 'they cannot know some things, and not know other things, and so be both in possession and not in possession of knowledge.'

'But what, then, is their situation?'

'All men', he replied, 'know all things, if they know anything at all.'

(Ibid. 293B–294A)

This argument goes on for quite some while longer, getting progressively more and more absurd, but we have the essential core of it here. The grain of serious philosophy that lurks in it is surely, as has been noted above, the puzzle about the nature of knowledge that continued to intrigue Plato and later philosophers.

Apart from the Euthydemus, *there are some further scraps of evidence about the sophistical brothers. First of all, a mention of Euthydemus in the* Cratylus, *at the end of a passage (385E–386C) in which Hermogenes' view of naming as conventional is assimilated by Socrates to Protagoras' principle 'Man is the measure of all things'.*

7. SOCRATES: But surely you don't agree with the view of Euthydemus that all things are possessed by all men simultaneously and forever (*hama kai aei*)? For in this case too it could not be that some people are good and others bad, if virtue and vice were the property of all equally and for ever.

(Plato, *Cratylus* 386D)

This seems to refer to a generalizing of the argument portrayed above in the Euthydemus *about the possession of knowledge, but it is not clear how it worked. Euthydemus may in fact only have intended it to apply to moral and intellectual qualities, in which case it would not be dissimilar to those put forward in* Double Arguments *1–5, based as they are on the suppression of qualifying expressions (see below, ch. 10).*

*Aristotle, at two points in his works (*Rhetoric II 24, 1401a25–29), *and* Sophistical Refutations 20, 177b12ff.), *makes reference to an argument of Euthydemus which does not figure in Plato's dialogue, but which is of very much the same type.[26] First, the* Rhetoric *passage, which is fuller, though still elliptical. Here Euthydemus is brought in to illustrate a type of fallacy which involves the illegitimate combination or disjunction of concepts or propositions.*

8. Another [fallacy] is to pronounce in combination what is properly to be kept separate, or, conversely, what is properly to be combined as separate; for since it often *seems* to be the same, whereas it really is not, one can avail oneself of whichever of

the two alternatives best suits your purpose. This is the type of argument employed by Euthydemus: for instance, one knows that there is a trireme in the Piraeus, because one knows each of the two things [separately].[27]

(Aristotle, *Rhetoric* II 24, 1401a 25–29)

Then the reference in Sophistical Refutations *where the same subject is being dealt with. This, while being extremely elliptical, adds another wrinkle – the person's presence in Sicily. It is followed by a series of further puzzles, which may or may not be intended to be credited to Euthydemus, though the method of introducing them suggests that they are. In any case, they are thoroughly sophistical, so they may reasonably be included.*

9. Then there is Euthydemus' argument: 'Do you, being presently in Sicily, know that there are triremes in the Piraeus?'[28]

And again, 'Can someone who is good be a bad cobbler?' ('Yes.') 'Well then, one would be, while being good, a bad cobbler.' ('Yes.') 'So a bad cobbler would be good.'

'Is it not so that, in the case of things of which the knowledge (*epistêmê*) is good, the learning (*mathêma*) of them is also good?' ('Yes.') 'But the process of learning about evil is good.' ('Yes.') 'So evil is a good object of learning.' ('Yes.') 'But then again, evil is both evil and an object of learning, so that evil is an evil object of learning.' ('Yes.') 'But we have already agreed that knowledge of evil is good.'[29]

'Is it true to say at the present moment (*nun*) you are born?' ('Yes.') 'Then you are born at the present moment.'[30]

'When you perform some action in a given way, do you not perform it in virtue of a specific capacity?' ('Yes.')[31] 'Is it not the case that when you are playing the *kithara*,[32] you have the capacity to play the *kithara*?' ('Yes.') 'Then you would be playing the *kithara* even when you are not playing the *kithara*.'

(Aristotle, *Sophistical Refutations* 20, 177b12–26)

Sextus Empiricus, in the late second century AD, also makes mention of the brothers in a number of places in Book VII of Against the Mathematicians, *but, as in the case of Aristotle, this*

*does not necessarily betoken any acquaintance with a written
work of either of the brothers. The first links the brothers with
a number of later eristic philosophers as being concerned only
with the logical part of philosophy.*

10. Logic, on the other hand, was the only part (of philosophy)
which was practised by Panthoides and Alexinus, and Eubulides
and Bryson,[33] and Dionysodorus and Euthydemus.

(Sextus Empiricus, *Against the Mathematicians* VII 13)

*The second (rather oddly) lists Dionysodorus, without Euthyd-
emus, among those who reject the 'criterion'.*

11. On the other hand, [the criterion] has been rejected by
Xenophanes of Colophon and Xeniades of Corinth and Anach-
arsis the Scythian and Protagoras and Dionysodorus.

(Ibid. VII 48)

*And the third, with the brothers reunited, comes at the end of a
protracted reference to Protagoras' rejection of the 'criterion'
(quoted in ch. 1, §9b, above).*

12. Euthydemus and Dionysodorus are also said to have shared
these views;[34] for they too regarded both the existent and the
true as relative things (*pros ti*).

(Ibid. VII 64)

9 ALCIDAMAS OF ELAEA

Alcidamas is included here as a representative of the younger generation of sophists.[1] *He was born, son of a certain Diocles, in Elaea, a town of the Aeolid, on the coast of Asia Minor opposite Lesbos. He became a pupil of Gorgias, and a rival of Isocrates, Gorgias' most distinguished follower. The* Suda *speaks of him as taking over Gorgias' school (§2 below), which would imply that he was Gorgias' favourite pupil. He taught mainly in Athens, and sought to develop further the techniques of his master as he interpreted them. This brought him into conflict with Isocrates, who was also teaching in Athens – one monument to this conflict being the surviving treatise* On the Sophists *(below, pp. 294–302). His most distinguished pupil (if we can trust the* Suda *on this – §3 below) was Demosthenes' great rival, the orator Aeschines.*

Alcidamas' dating is quite uncertain, but it would seem reasonable to postulate a life-span stretching from about 420 to 360 BC. His most important work would seem to have been that entitled Mouseion,[2] *which may possibly have been identical with a general* Handbook of Rhetoric *such as he is known to have composed,*[3] *but he is also attested to have composed an* Oration for the Messenians, *datable to 366/5 (see §§ 19–20 below), an* Encomium on Death *(see §§6 and 21 below) and a eulogy of the famous courtesan Nais, who flourished in the first half of the fourth century (see §5 below) as well as a number of other epideictic orations of which we have extracts. However, his surviving works comprise a defiant treatise, directed against his rival Isocrates, entitled* On Those who Compose Written Speeches, *or on Sophists, which presents a ringing defence of*

orality and improvisation; and a model forensic oration,
Odysseus: Indictment of Palamedes for Treason, *a rather witty
effort, which plays fast and loose with established Greek mythology, and constitutes a sort of answer to the oration of his
master Gorgias on Palamedes' behalf.*

LIFE AND WORKS

*All we have are a number of short biographical entries, from
the* Suda *and elsewhere.*

1. Alcidamas, the Elaeite: from Elaea in Asia, a philosopher,[4]
son of Diocles, who wrote on music (*mousika*);[5] a pupil of
Gorgias of Leontini.

   (*Suda* I 117 Adler)

2. Gorgias ... teacher of Polus of Acragas and Pericles and
Isocrates and Alcidamas of Elaea, who succeeded him as head
of his school.

   (*Suda* I 535 Adler)

3. Aeschines: ... pupil in rhetoric of Alcidamas of Elaea ... He
[i.e. Aeschines] was the first of all men to acquire the reputation
of speaking divinely because of his ability to improvise (*skhedi-
azein*),[6] as though inspired.

   (*Suda* II 184 Adler)

4. Demosthenes: ... studied with Isaeus, the pupil of Isocrates,
and made use of the speeches of Zoilus of Amphipolis, who
practised as a sophist at Athens, and of Polycrates and Alcidamas, the pupil of Gorgias, and indeed of Isocrates himself.

   (*Suda* II 45 Adler)

5. Alcidamas of Elaea, the pupil of Gorgias, himself composed
an *Encomium* of Nais the courtesan.

   (Athenaeus, *Deipnosophistae* XIII 61, 592C)

6. One must specify that, of encomia, some are of things of high esteem (*endoxa*), others of things of low esteem (*adoxa*), and yet others are frankly paradoxical (*paradoxa*) ... Among the paradoxical may be included the encomium of Alcidamas *On Death*, or that *On Poverty*, or that on *Proteus the Cynic*.[7]

(Menander Rhetor *On Epideictic Orations* III 346.9–18 Spengel)

STYLE AND RHETORICAL TECHNIQUE

We have a number of evaluations of Alcidamas' style, mostly uncomplimentary. We may begin with that of Aristotle in the Rhetoric, *in the course of a discussion of 'frigidity' or 'tastelessness' in style* (psychrotês), *of which he regards Alcidamas as a prime instance.*[8] *We need not agree with Aristotle here: most, if not all, of the examples he gives actually seem reasonably legitimate embellishments of language, suitable to epideictic oratory; but we must be grateful to him for sharing them with us.*

7. Tastelessness in style (*lexis*) may take any of four forms:

(1) *in the use of compound words.* Lycophron, for instance, talks of the '*many-visaged* heaven' above the '*vasty-peaked* earth', and again, of the '*strait-pathed* shore'; and Gorgias of the '*beggar-witted* flatterer', and of those who 'oath-break and *over-oath-keep*'.[9] And Alcidamas uses such expressions as 'his soul filling with rage, and his face becoming *flame-flushed*';[10] and '*end-fulfilling* (*telesphoron*) deemed he would be their zeal', and '*end-fulfilling* established he the persuasion of his words';[11] and '*sombre-hued* (*kyanokhrôn*)[12] is the floor of the sea'.

This, then, is one form of tastelessness; another is

(2) *the employment of rare words* (*glôssai*). For instance, Lycophron talks of 'the *prodigious* (*pelôros*) Xerxes' and 'Skiron, that *plunderous* (*sinnis*) man'; and Alcidamas of 'a *toy* (*athyrma*) for poetry,'[13] and 'the *witlessness* (*atasthalia*)[14] of nature', and '*whetted* (*tethêgmenon*) with the *unadulterated* (*akratôi*) wrath of his wit'.[15]

A third form consists in

(3) *the use of long, inept or excessively frequent epithets*. For instance, in poetry it is quite appropriate to talk of 'white milk', but in prose such epithets are sometimes lacking in appropriateness, or when laid on too thickly, convict the author plainly of turning his prose into poetry. Certainly, one must make use of poetic elements – for they raise our style above the level of the ordinary, and give it an air of distinctiveness – but we must aim at the due mean (*to metrion*), or the result will be worse than if we took no trouble at all; for the latter situation may betoken a lack of excellence, but the former is positively bad.

That is why the epithets of Alcidamas seem so wanting in taste; he does not use them as the seasoning of the food, but as the food itself[16] – so frequent, and unduly long and conspicuous are they. For instance, he does not say 'sweat', but 'the *moist* sweat'; not 'to the Isthmian Games', but 'to the *public gathering* (*panêgyris*) of the Isthmian Games'; not just 'laws', but 'laws *the kings of cities*';[17] not just 'at a run', but 'his soul impelling him to speed of foot'; not merely 'a school of the Muses (*mouseion*)', but 'Nature's school of the Muses (had he inherited)'[18]; and so '*frowning* care of heart',[19] and 'contriver', not of 'popularity (*kharis*)', but of '*universal* (*pandêmos*) popularity',[20] and '*dispenser* (*oikonomos*) of pleasure to his audience', and 'he concealed it' not 'with boughs', but 'with the boughs *of the wild-wood* (*tês hylês*)', and 'he clothed' not 'his body', but '*his body's nakedness*',[21] and 'his soul's desire was *counter-imitative* (*antimimos*)'[22] – this is at the same time both a compound and an epithet, so that the result comes out thoroughly poetical; and 'so *inordinate* (*exedros*)[23] the extent of his wickedness'. We thus see how this poetical language, by its inappropriateness, introduces absurdity and tastelessness into speeches, as well as the obscurity consequent on this empty verbosity[24] – for when you pile more words upon someone who already grasps the sense, you only obscure and spoil the clarity of the utterance.

. . .

(4) There remains a fourth area in which bad taste can be exhibited, and that is in *the use of metaphor*. Metaphors, like other things, may be inappropriate – some because they are

ridiculous (for metaphors are employed also by comic poets), others from the exaggeration of the stately and tragic style: if they are too far-fetched, the result is obscurity. For instance, Gorgias talks of 'events that are green and full of sap', and says 'foul was the deed you sowed, and evil the harvest you reaped': these expressions smack too much of poetry.[25] Alcidamas, again, called philosophy 'a bulwark (*epiteikhisma*) of the laws';[26] and the *Odyssey* 'a fine mirror (*katoptron*) of human life'; and 'introducing no such plaything (*athyrma*) into his poetry':[27] all these expressions fail, for the reasons given, to carry the reader with them.

(Aristotle, *Rhetoric* III 3, 1405b35–1406b19)

Then, a testimony from Dionysius of Halicarnassus, in the course of his essay on the orator Isaeus (§19), which largely confirms the judgement of Aristotle. He is just telling why he has neglected to discuss certain orators of the Classical age:

8. I was certainly not ignorant of orators who are known to everyone; nor should I have refrained from writing about them, if anything useful would result from such writing. But it was because I considered that none of them emerged as superior to Isocrates[28] at the elaborate, elevated and 'ceremonial' (*pompikos*) style that I deliberately passed them over, since I knew that they were less successful than he was in these forms of oratory – seeing, for instance, that Gorgias of Leontini exceeds the bounds of moderation and frequently lapses into puerility, whereas the diction (*lexis*) of his pupil Alcidamas is at once rather turgid (*pakhyteron*) and lacking in content (*kenoteron*) . . .[29]

FRAGMENTS OF KNOWN WORKS

The Mouseion

A work of Alcidamas called the Mouseion *is attested to by an entry in the* Anthology *of Johannes Stobaeus, which, however, carries with it its own problems. It comes in the form of a*

quotation of two lines of hexameter verse, which seem to be
borrowed from the elegiacs of the sixth-century poet Theognis
(425–8), but with the omission of the intervening pentameters.
The lines also occurred, attributed to Homer, in that curious
work The Contest of Homer and Hesiod, which is, however, in
its present form, much later than Alcidamas.[30] Stobaeus includes
it under the rubric of 'Praise of Death', which, interestingly, is
a topic on which Alcidamas is known to have composed an
encomium. Possibly this was included in his Mouseion.

A larger question, however, is raised by this reference, and by
a fragmentary papyrus (Inventory of Michigan Papyri 2754)
containing parts of a version of the Contest, at the end which
is to be found the tantalizing title]DAMANTOS PERI
HOMEROU, which might plausibly be restored as [The Book
of Alci]damas, On Homer.[31] In addition to this, there occurs in
the course of the Contest a passing reference to 'Alcidamas, in
the Mouseion' (§9 below), of a sort which seems to betray a
much wider dependence upon him. On the basis of this evidence,
M. L. West[32] has advanced the reasonable suggestion that the
existing document is based on a similar literary effusion
composed by Alcidamas. It is further suggested[33] that the fact
that the trick[34] poem quoted by Socrates in the Phaedrus (264D)
as having been carved on the tomb of Midas the Phrygian
appears as a composition of Homer in the Contest (ll. 265–70)
indicates the priority of Alcidamas' work to Plato's dialogue,
but that, though interesting, is not an entirely safe conclusion.
At any rate, there does seem sufficient evidence available to
suggest that it was another of Alcidamas' historical/mytho-
logical conceits to concoct, as part of his Mouseion, a literary
contest between Homer and Hesiod, which survives, in somewhat altered form, in the document which we have. We do not
feel quite justified, however, as does Avezzú (1982), in printing
large swathes of the Contest as broadly belonging to Alcidamas,
probable though this seems to us.

9. From the *Mouseion* of Alcidamas:

'Best of all for mortal man is never to have been born at all;
but once born, to pass as quickly as one may through the gates of
  Hades.'[35]
(Stobaeus, *Anthology* IV 52, 22)

10. When the corpse [i.e. of Hesiod][36] was conveyed to land two
days later by dolphins, at a time when there was a local festival
of the inhabitants devoted to Ariadne, they all ran to the shore,
recognized the body and, after mourning it, gave it burial. They
then went in search of the murderers. They, however, fearing
the wrath of the citizens, commandeered a fishing boat and
sailed off for Crete. But Zeus smote them with a thunderbolt in
the midst of their voyage and drowned them, as Alcidamas tells
us in his *Mouseion*.
  (*The Contest of Homer and Hesiod* (anonymous), ll.
  232–40)

The Mouseion *(or Shrine of the Muses), then, is probably a
work which, whatever else it contained, could also be described
as 'On Homer'. It presumably constituted a show-case for various aspects of Alcidamas' art.*

Treatise on Nature (Physikos)

*The only certain reference to this work (in Diogenes Laertius,
§11 below) would seem to indicate that it contained biographical gossip about physical philosophers rather than reflections
on Nature as such, but we cannot be sure. Apart from the
reference in Diogenes, Diels wished to refer to this work an
anecdote handed down by Simplicius (Commentary on the
Physics 1108, 18–28 Diels), commenting on Aristotle, Physics
VII 5, 250a19) involving Zeno quizzing Protagoras about
whether a single grain of millet made a sound when it fell, but
there is really no adequate reason to include it as a fragment, as
is done by Avezzú. As for the reference by Aristotle in the
Rhetoric to an inductive argument (epagōgē) used by Alcidamas,*

*the evidence is slim enough also, but at least it is a reference to
Alcidamas, so we include it here, with due caution, as §12.*

11. Alcidamas tells us in his *Treatise on Nature* that Zeno and
Empedocles were pupils of Parmenides about the same time,
that afterwards they left him, and that, while Zeno framed his
own system, Empedocles became the pupil of Anaxagoras and
Pythagoras,[37] emulating the latter in dignity of life and bearing,
and the former in his physical investigations.

(Diogenes Laertius, *Lives of the Philosophers*, VIII 56)

12. A further instance [sc. of induction] is the argument of
Alcidamas, in support of the claim that all men honour those
with expertise (*sophoi*): 'Thus the Parians have honoured Archilochus, in spite of his savage tongue; the Chians Homer, though
he was not a fellow citizen of theirs;[38] the Mitylenaeans Sappho,
though she was a woman; the Lacedaemonians actually made
Chilon a member of their senate, though they are the least
literary of men; the Italian Greeks honoured Pythagoras; the
inhabitants of Lampsacus gave public burial to Anaxagoras,
though he was an alien, and honour him even to this day.'

(Aristotle, *Rhetoric* II 23, 1398b10–16)

*This argument, however, as was suggested by Sauppe, might
just as well come from the* Mouseion, *for all we know of its
contents. At any rate, there follows immediately on this in the
text another argument, which Aristotle may have intended as
another of Alcidamas', or the author's name may have fallen
out. We may perhaps give Alcidamas the benefit of the doubt.
If we may claim it for Alcidamas, it shows his sympathy for the
Theban regime led by Epaminondas and Pelopidas, who were
thought to have been influenced by Pythagoreanism.*

13. And: 'The Athenians prospered under Solon's laws, and the
Lacedaemonians under those of Lycurgus, while at Thebes no
sooner did the leaders become philosophers than the country
began to enjoy prosperity.'

(Ibid.)

Handbook of Rhetoric (Tekhnê Rhetorikê)

*There is adequate evidence of the existence of such a work,
together with some slight suggestions of what it contained. First,
a reference to it by Dionysius of Halicarnassus, in his* Letter to
Ammaeus, *in the course of an argument to prove that
Demosthenes cannot have learned his craft from a study of
Aristotle's* Rhetoric, *as a certain patriotic contemporary Aristotelian has been claiming.*[39]

14. 'I should not want them [sc. those setting out to study
rhetoric] to suppose that all the rules of rhetoric have been
developed by Peripatetic philosophers, and that nothing of significance has been discovered by Theodorus, Thrasymachus,
Antiphon and their associates; nor by Isocrates, Anaximenes,
Alcidamas or those of their contemporaries who composed
rhetorical handbooks (*parangelmata tekhnika*) and engaged in
oratorical contests.'

(Dionysius of Halicarnassus, *Letter to Ammaeus*, I 2)

Then, a report from Plutarch, in his Life of Demosthenes,
derived from the third-century BC *Peripatetic biographer Hermippus of Smyrna, concerning Demosthenes' instructors in
rhetoric.*

15. But Hermippus says that he once discovered some anonymous memoirs in which it was recorded that he [sc. De-
mosthenes] was a pupil of Plato and gained a great deal from
him in his rhetorical studies. He also quotes Ctesibius as saying
that from Callias the Syracusan and certain others Demosthenes
secretly obtained the rhetorical handbooks (*tekhnê*) of Isocrates
and Alcidamas and mastered them.

(Plutarch, *Life of Demosthenes* 5, 7)

*Apropos reporting that Protagoras was the first to mark off the
parts of discourse into four (cf. ch. 1, §1, 53–4), Diogenes
Laertius gives also Alcidamas' division.*

16. Alcidamas says that there are four divisions of discourse: affirmation, negation, question, address (*phasis, apophasis, erôtêsis, prosagoreusis*).[40]

In his Scholia on Hermogenes *(Diogenes Laertius,* Lives of the Philosophers *IX 54), John Tzetzes provides evidence that Alcidamas discussed the placing of narrative in forensic speeches (a topic that one would certainly expect him to have covered).*

17. One should not provide narrative (*diêgêsis*) in the case of a situation that is well known, and when the facts are incredible. Some say that one should not always place the narrative immediately after the prologue, but after the proofs, and on the other hand these same people who tell us to put it after the proofs say that one should not have it in the epilogue. And in the epilogue we tell you, following Alcidamas, that one can place a supplementary narrative (*paradiêgêsis*), which may be either a repetition (*epanalêpsis*) of the narrative itself, or a summation or reprise (*deuterologia*).[41]

(Tzetzes, *Scholia in Hermogenem*, Anecdota)

The same Tzetzes, in his Chiliades, *provides a further snippet. We may note, in passing, how often, in the sources, Alcidamas is linked with his rival Isocrates.*

18. We are told by Isocrates the rhetorician and by Alcidamas that there are four excellences of discourse: clarity, nobility, brevity and credibility – with, of course, the adornment of the figures of rhetoric.

(Tzetzes, *Chiliades* XII 561–7 Leone)

The Messenian Oration

This speech can be fairly accurately dated to 366/5 BC, being a response by Alcidamas to the re-establishment of an independent Messene, after centuries of domination by the Spartans, a process which had begun in 369, with the help of the Theban leader Epaminondas, and which had been confirmed by a peace treaty in 366. It is also more particularly a response to a pro-

Spartan oration, the Archidamus, *which had recently been composed by his arch-rival Isocrates. Only two short fragments of it survive, but one of them is probably Alcidamas' most famous utterance, and one which is worthy of the best traditions of the sophistic movement. It is not clear in what circumstances such a speech as this would have been delivered. It may have been simply published as a pamphlet, but this would not preclude the possibility of Alcidamas declaiming it as an epideictic oration.*

The first fragment is preserved only by an anonymous commentator on Aristotle's Rhetoric, *explicating a passage (*Rhetoric I 13, 1373b18), *where Aristotle actually sets out to quote Alcidamas, to illustrate a point he is making about the contrast between universal and particular law, or the law of nature and the law of man, but the quotation from Alcidamas has fallen out of the text. The commentator supplies it.*

19. On the occasion of the Messenians revolting from the Spartans, and no longer consenting to be enslaved by them, Alcidamas, in delivering a speech on their behalf, uttered the following sentiment:

'God left all men free; Nature has made no man a slave.'

(Anonymous, in *Rhetorica Aristotelis*, CAG XXI: 2, p. 74 Rabe)

This, remarkably, is the only surviving testimony to what must have been a fairly widespread sophistic thesis, that slavery is contrary to nature (referred to disapprovingly by Aristotle at Politics *1253b20ff.).*

A second extract is preserved by Aristotle himself, once again in the Rhetoric. *He is giving examples of 'argument from opposites'.*

20. One variety of positive proof is based upon taking the opposite of the thing in question. Observe whether that opposite has the opposite quality. If it has not, you refute the original proposition; if it has, you establish it; as for instance the proposition 'Moderation is good; for licentiousness is harmful.' Or, in the *Messenian Oration,*

'If war is the cause of our present troubles, it is with peace
that we should remedy our situation.'

(Aristotle, *Rhetoric* II 23, 1397a 7–12)

The Encomium of Death

*Apart from the report of the bare fact that Alcidamas composed
such a treatise (cf. above, §6), the only testimony to its contents
comes from Cicero, in* Tusculan Disputations, *but this does
indicate that the treatise enjoyed something of a succès d'estime.*

21. Alcidamas, for instance, an ancient rhetorician of the greatest distinction, actually composed an encomium on death, which
consists of a list of the evils to which mankind is exposed. He
has failed to give those deeper arguments which the philosophers
assemble, but he has not failed in wealth of eloquence.

(Cicero, *Tusculan Disputations* I 116)

SURVIVING WORKS

On Those who Compose Written Works, or
On the Sophists

*This is a most remarkable piece of polemic, aimed, it would
seem, primarily at Alcidamas' chief rival on the Athenian sophistic scene, Gorgias' other distinguished pupil, Isocrates, who
was not an effective impromptu orator, but a noted composer
of written orations, most of which survive. This ringing assertion
of the superiority of speaking over writing, dating as it probably
does from somewhere in the first decades of the fourth century,
seems to mark a kind of watershed in the changeover from a
predominantly oral to a predominantly literate society, such as
has been widely conjectured to have taken place at about this
time in Athens – though that is perhaps to dignify this production with somewhat more significance than it deserves. It
provides an interesting counterpoint to the denunciation of
writing which Plato makes Socrates put into the mouth of
the Egyptian god-king Thamous at* Phaedrus *274Cff., a work
composed at about the same time as this speech.*

22. *[1]* It has come to my notice that some of those who are termed 'sophists' have neglected research and culture,[42] and exhibit an incompetence in speaking equal to that of a layman, but, having taken up the art of writing, and choosing to exhibit their expertise through that precarious medium, have now acquired a high opinion of themselves, and having mastered an insignificant part of rhetoric, now lay claim to mastery of the whole art. It is for this reason that I have resolved to embark on a critique of written discourses, *[2]* not because I consider such a competence to be beyond me, but rather since I pride myself more on other accomplishments and consider that writing should be practised only as a sideline. I also feel that those who have frittered away their careers in such pursuits fall far short of the ideals of rhetoric and philosophy,[43] and would much more aptly be considered poets than sophists.

[3] The first reason for having a low opinion of writing arises from its ready accessibility, straightforwardness and suitability to the most mediocre natures. For the ability to speak extempore, with reasonable fluency, on any subject that comes up, to make ready use of plausible arguments[44] and suitable words, and to adapt oneself felicitously both to the opportunities of the occasion and the feelings of the audience, is not something attainable by every level of natural ability or training; *[4]* while, on the other hand, to put pen to paper over an extended period and then make corrections at one's leisure, drawing upon the collective productions of previous sophists, lining up their arguments and borrowing their well-turned phrases, taking the opportunity both to emend the wisdom of the general public and to polish up and forge anew reiterated insights of one's own – that is a practice easily within the grasp even of the uneducated.

[5] All things fine and noble are rare and difficult of attainment, and come about only as the result of protracted labour, while low-grade and trivial things are easily acquired; and thus, since writing comes more readily to us than speaking, it is reasonable that we should consider it an achievement of lesser worth. *[6]* Then, in the case of skilled speakers, no one in his right wits would doubt that, with a minimum of mental adjustment, they will be able to compose a passable written

treatise, whereas in the case of those who have schooled themselves in writing, on the other hand, no one would believe that, on the basis of this same skill, they will attain the capacity to speak. For it is to be expected that those who have mastered difficult skills, when they turn their attention to easy ones, will have no problem in dealing with the procedures involved; while those, on the other hand, who are practised in easy skills will find it a tough, uphill battle to master more difficult ones.

The following examples will serve to clarify what I mean. *[7]* A man who can raise a heavy burden, when he turns his attention to lighter ones, will easily be able to deal with them; while someone whose strength is adequate for light burdens would not be able to handle any of the heavier ones. And again, the swift runner will easily be able to keep up with the slower ones, but the slow runner would not be capable of keeping pace with the faster. And further to this, one who is able accurately to strike a farther target with javelin or bow will easily hit a nearer one; whereas it is not yet clear that one who can strike a nearer target will also be able to strike a further one. *[8]* In the same way also, in the case of literary activity,[45] he who has the ability to make a fine presentation on the spur of the moment will obviously, with the help of time and practice, turn out to be an outstanding composer of written speeches, while on the other hand one who devotes his efforts to writing will plainly, when he switches over to extempore discourses, be filled in his wits with bafflement, wandering and confusion.

[9] Furthermore, I consider that, in the life of men, speaking is always and in every circumstance a useful thing, while the faculty of writing is relevant only occasionally. For who does not know that the ability to speak on the spur of the moment is a necessity for both those involved in public affairs and in law-cases, and those organizing private discussions, and that often critical situations arise unexpectedly, in which those who remain silent come across as contemptible, while we see those who are able to speak being honoured by their peers as possessing a wisdom well-nigh divine. *[10]* For when one needs either to chastise transgressors or to console the unfortunate or to calm the angry or to defuse accusations which may suddenly

be directed at one, then it is the power of speaking that is able to come to men's aid; writing, by contrast, needs leisure, and involves stretches of time that are too protracted for the crisis at hand; for crises demand a rapid source of assistance for the contest at hand, whereas writing brings its arguments to completion in a leisurely and tardy manner. So who in his right mind would admire the possession of such a skill, which is found so gravely wanting in a crisis? [11] And how would it not be a matter for mirth if, when the herald calls out[46] 'Who of the citizens wishes to speak?', or in a court of law, when the water in the water-clock is already flowing, a speaker were to go off to his desk,[47] in order to compose and then learn off his speech? For really, if we were *tyrants* of our cities, it would be at our discretion that the law-courts would be summoned, or a council be called to deliberate on public affairs, so that, whenever we had a speech written, we could then call together the rest of the citizens to hear it. But since discretion in these matters is in the hands of others, is it not foolish for us to employ any other strategy for making a speech[48] <than extemporaneous composition?> . . .

. . . their situation is precisely the opposite. [12] For if those who put a fine finish on their words, producing an effect more akin to poetry than to reasoned prose,[49] and abandoning a procedure that is spontaneous and more akin to truth, but rather giving the appearance of moulding and composing their thoughts with careful preparation, fill the minds of their hearers with distrust and begrudgery[50] . . . [13] And the greatest proof of that is this: those who write speeches for the law-courts seek to avoid a high degree of finish, and imitate rather the mode of delivery of those who are improvising, and indeed are generally thought to be writing most excellently when they contrive speeches which least resemble written ones. But if this is regarded as the limit of excellence for speech-writers, when they succeed in imitating spontaneity, surely it follows that we should accord most honour to that branch of learning which most conduces to mastery of this type of speech?

[14] It seems to me that this is also a reason for dismissing written speeches, that they cause an unevenness in the style of

those that employ them. For to have the expertise to construct speeches on all subjects is something which one must take to be quite impossible; so necessarily, when one improvises one part, and gives a literary polish to another, the unevenness of the resulting speech will attract criticism to the speaker, some aspects giving an impression of bombast and floweriness,[51] while others appear feeble and rough, by comparison with the polish of the former passages.

[15][52] It is a poor look-out if someone who lays claim to be able to say something about philosophy and to educate others in it, provided he has to hand a writing-tablet or a book, can demonstrate something of his wisdom, but if he happens to be lacking these tools, shows himself to be no better than one of the uneducated; and if, when given time, he can crank out a speech, but on the spur of the moment, when set a topic, he is left more tongue-tied than a layman; and if he is prepared to advertise courses in rhetoric (*logôn tekhnai*), but is able to exhibit in his own case not even the slightest capacity to speak.[53] Indeed, the practice of writing produces a grave deficiency in speaking. [16] For when one is accustomed to working up speeches step by step, and putting together one's words with careful attention to rhythm, and perfecting one's style by the leisurely employment of one's intellectual faculty, necessarily then, when such a person is faced with making an improvised speech, since he is doing the opposite of what he is used to, he will have his mind full of bafflement and confusion, will be uncomfortable from every point of view, and indeed will in no way differ from the feeble-voiced,[54] and will never be able to put language to smooth and public-spirited use, by rousing his spirit to fluency and wit; [17] but just as those who have been freed from chains after a long period are not able to walk like other people, but are distorted into those attitudes and that gait in which they were compelled to proceed when they were in chains, so in the same way writing, by accustoming the mind to making slow transitions and creating in it the opposite habits to speaking, renders the soul resourceless and hide-bound[55] and gets in the way of achieving any fluency at all in impromptu speaking.

[18] I think also that the learning of written speeches is difficult, and the memorizing of them tedious, while the forgetting of them, in the midst of a contest,[56] is humiliating. Everyone would agree, after all, that it is more difficult to learn and to memorize small things than big ones, and many things rather than few. In impromptu performances, one only has to concentrate on the concepts (*enthymêmata*), while the words come of themselves; in the case of written compositions, on the other hand, one has to be concerned with an accurate learning and memorizing of both concepts and words and even syllables. [19] For the concepts present in speeches are few but weighty, while the nouns and verbs are many and insignificant and differ little from one another; and of the concepts each one manifests itself once, while in the case of words we are obliged to make use of the same ones many times. For this reason the memory is easily able to handle the former, while the learning of the latter is both difficult to achieve and difficult to retain. [20] And further, the embarrassment attendant on losses of memory is concealed in extempore oratory. For, since the mode of expression is flexible and the word-order is not finely polished, even if some of the concepts escape one's memory, it is not difficult for the orator to skip over them, and, by picking up on the next thought, to avoid casting shame on one's speech; indeed, one can easily insert what one has forgotten, if one happens to remember it later. [21] But those who are delivering written speeches, on the other hand, if, in the stress of the moment, they omit or alter even a little of their text, are necessarily plunged into confusion and rambling and are at a loss for words, and hesitate for long periods, and often even interrupt their speech by silence, and get into a fix that is awkward and derisory and difficult to rescue themselves from.

[22] It is my view also that those who improvise are better able to respond to the mood of the audience than those who speak from written texts. For those who have put a great deal of work into their compositions prior to the occasion sometimes find themselves falling short at the critical moment; for they either annoy their hearers by going on longer than they have any desire for, or alternatively they leave off their discourse too

soon, when people are in the mood for listening to something. *[23]* For it is difficult, if not impossible, for human forethought to hit on how things are going to work out, so as to foresee accurately what way the minds of the audience will be disposed to the length of a discourse. In the case of impromptu speaking, on the other hand, it is in the power of the speaker to tailor his speech with an eye to the stamina of the audience, in such a way as to both cut short undue length and expound more copiously ideas which were initially compressed.

[24] Apart altogether from this, we do not observe one or the other set of people making like use of the ideas (*enthymêmata*) that come up in actual contests. For in the case of those who deliver unwritten speeches, if they pick up any idea from their opponents, or, through quickness of wit, think of one for themselves, they find it easy to fit it into the framework of their speech; for since they are composing their whole discourse on the spur of the moment, not even when they utter more than they had planned do they render their speech unbalanced or disorderly. *[25]* In the case of those who enter upon contests with written speeches, on the other hand, if any idea is presented to them over and above what they have prepared, it is difficult for them to fit it in and make proper use of it; for exactness in the construction of sentences does not admit of improvisation, but necessarily one must either make no use of ideas which are given to one by chance or else, by alternating prepared discourse with casual speech, render one's presentation disorderly and dissonant. *[26]* And yet who in his right mind would be satisfied with a form of expertise (*meletê*) which actually precludes itself from utilizing advantages that occur spontaneously, and offers to those engaged in contests even less help, on occasion, than could be derived from chance, and which, while other arts normally lead the life of men towards betterment, actually manages to stand as an obstacle to advantages accruing unexpectedly?

[27] I actually consider that it is incorrect to describe written speeches as speeches at all; they are, instead, like shadows and sketches and imitations of speeches, and we might reasonably view them in the same light as busts of bronze or statues of stone

or paintings of living things. For even as these are imitations of
real bodies, and, while they give pleasure to the eye, contribute
nothing useful to human life, *[28]* by the same token the written
speech, utilizing as it does one single form and structure, when
viewed in a book may make a certain impression, but when
faced with a real live moment of decision, being inflexible as it
is, can bestow no advantage on those that make use of it; but
even as real bodies, while perhaps enjoying a much lower degree
of beauty than fine statues, yet prove many times more useful in
the vicissitudes of life, so a speech which is delivered straight
from the heart in the heat of the moment is inspired with soul,
and lives, and is able to adjust to circumstances, and is analogous
to real bodies, while the written one, since it has a nature which
is like the mere image of a speech, proves itself devoid of all
effectiveness.

[29] Now one might perhaps object that it is illogical to
depreciate the art of writing, while manifestly making use of it
to publicize one's views, and to stir up prejudice in advance
against the practice by means of which one is striving to enhance
one's reputation among the Greeks; and furthermore, for someone who is engaged in the practice of philosophy[57] to commend
impromptu discourses, and consider chance to be of more consequence than forethought, and those who speak off the top of
their heads to be wiser than those who compose with adequate
preparation. *[30]* In reply to that, I want to say first of all that I
do not absolutely condemn the art of writing; I merely consider
it to be inferior to that of extempore speaking, and I have set
down these remarks because I feel that one should take most
care about developing a facility in speaking. Then again, I do
not resort to the use of writing out of any high regard for it, but
simply in order to demonstrate to those who pride themselves
on this accomplishment that we, by putting forth some minimal
effort, can overshadow and neutralize their treatises. *[31]* And
in addition to this, it is for the sake of getting the general public
acquainted with my work that I am taking to writing. For in the
case of those who frequent our company, we can encourage
them to make trial of us in the former mode,[58] when we are able
to speak aptly and artistically on any subject proposed to us; in

the case of those, however, who are only occasional visitors to lectures, and may never previously have come across us, we start off by showing them something of what we have written; for since they are accustomed to listening to written speeches from others, they might perhaps derive a lesser opinion of our competence if they simply hear us improvising. And apart from that, it is in written discourses that one may most clearly observe signs of the progress that is likely to take place in one's intellectual prowess. For it is not easy to discern whether one is improvising better now than formerly, for it is difficult to hold previous speeches in one's memory; but if one looks to written speeches, it is easy to discern the progress of someone's mind, as in a mirror. And further, if we aspire to leave to posterity memorials of ourselves, and grant indulgence to our ambition, we will essay written speeches.

[33] In any case, one should not assume that, just because we accord greater honour to the power of improvisation, we therefore encourage students to speak off the top of their heads. We consider, after all, that orators should make use of the premeditated ordering of ideas, while employing improvisation in the actual choice of words. For the precision of detail characteristic of written speeches does not confer sufficient advantage to balance the appositeness (*eukairia*) associated with the mastery of improvisation. [34] Therefore,[59] whoever desires to become a first-class orator, and not just a competent composer of speeches, and wants to make the best use of opportunity rather than simply to develop precision in the use of words, and who aspires to have the good will of the audience as his ally rather than their distrust as his antagonist, and, further, who wishes to have his intellect flexible and his memory ready, and forgetfulness nowhere to be seen, and is keen to acquire a facility in speaking adequate to the necessities of life – is it not reasonable that such a one should dedicate himself primarily, always and in all circumstances, to the practice of improvisation, and, by concerning himself with writing merely as a recreation and sideline, be adjudged wise by those who are themselves wise?

Odysseus: Indictment of Palamedes for Treason

This work has been widely rejected by scholars as spurious, but it also has had its defenders, including such heavyweights as Ernest Maass and Ulrich von Wilamowitz-Möllendorf. Avezzú, the most recent editor of Alcidamas, accepts it, and we can see no reasons of language or content against that, though one can never, it must be said, prove that it could not have been put together by a clever rhetorician of the Second Sophistic. It seems, in fact, to fit well as a sort of friendly riposte to the Defence of Palamedes of Alcidamas' master, Gorgias. It also serves as a useful exemplum *of a forensic speech for the prosecution, making use, as it does, of all the main divisions of such a speech, and employing various commonplaces (even though it is hard to imagine that Alcidamas intended it to be taken entirely seriously). The style is certainly quite different from that of the previous treatise, but that is to be expected. It also further undermines Alcidamas' claim to be a champion of orality over writing, but the same could be said of various other orations of his of which we have evidence. In any case, as we have seen, his objection to writing was by no means absolute.*

The structure of the speech, modelled as it is on that of a forensic oration, is as follows: 1–4: introduction (prooimion); 5–28: narration (diêgêsis); and 29: peroration (epilogos). The narration is divided into a number of sections, interspersed with summaries, casting abuse on the opponent. Alcidamas makes use of much mythological material, employing it in interestingly ironic ways, as we shall see, to represent the calculated distortions which an orator might introduce into his narration of the background 'facts of the case'.

23. *[1]* I have often, men of Greece, when I think about it, wondered about the intentions of those who address you, with what purpose in mind they come forward so readily to give you advice, from which no advantage accrues to the commonwealth, but cause torrents of mutual abuse to pour forth, while they waste words at random on whatever topic occurs to them.[60] *[2]* For each of them delivers his opinion in the hope of some gain,

while some even extract a fee before they speak, from whomever
they think they can get the most out of. And so, if anyone in the
camp[61] indulges in crooked practice or does injury to the body
politic while acquiring profit for himself, we see nobody giving
a thought to that, but if one of us, by bringing in a prisoner,
manages to gain from the enemy some prize greater than the
general run, this becomes an occasion for the kindling of great
disputes amongst us, through the zeal of these persons. [3] As
for me, I consider that the good and just man should not nurture
private enmities[62] nor, through joining exclusive cliques, give
the greatest attention to accumulating personal wealth to the
exclusion of what is going to be for the benefit of the multitude.
However,[63] setting aside ancient troubles and arguments, I will
attempt to bring Palamedes here to trial before you in due
accordance with justice.

[4] The charge, that you may know it, is treason, a crime that
attracts to itself penalties ten times those of all others. I bring
this case, as you all know, despite the fact that there has never
existed between myself and the defendant any enmity or quarrel
on any subject,[64] not even on the wrestling-ground or in a
drinking session, which is where most quarrels and brawls
habitually arise. This fellow, however, on whose indictment I
am embarking, is a clever, intellectual type (*philosophos te kai
deinos*), so that you must keep your wits about you, and not
disregard what I am now telling you.

[5] You yourselves know perfectly well, after all, in what
danger we found ourselves at that time when some of us had
taken refuge in the ships, others in the trenches, the enemy was
falling upon the tents, and there was the greatest uncertainty as
to where the disaster would end. To put you in the picture,
the situation was as follows: Diomedes and I happened to be
stationed in the same place, near the gates, and near us were
Palamedes and Polypoetes.[65] [6] As we came to close quarters
with the enemy, a bowman ran forward from their ranks and
took aim at this fellow, but his arrow missed and landed near
me. This fellow launched a spear at him, and the other took
himself out of there, and retreated to the enemy camp. I pulled
the arrow out of the ground, and gave it to Eurybates to give to

Teucer, for him to make use of it.[66] When there was a brief
pause in the battle, some time later, he brought me the arrow
and showed me that it had writing on it under its feathers. [7] I
was astonished at this, and, summoning Sthenelus and Diomedes, showed them what was on it. The writing ran as follows:
'Alexander[67] to Palamedes. Everything that I agreed with
Telephus will be yours, and my father will give to you Cassandra
for wife, as you demanded; but perform your side of the bargain
without delay.' That was what was written on it. And I now
call upon those who received the arrow to come forward as
witnesses.

<Witnesses:>[68]

[8] I would have produced the actual arrow for you, to demonstrate the truth of this, but in fact, in the general confusion,
Teucer by mistake fired it back.[69] However, I must relate to you
the rest of the affair, so that you may not be in the position of
condemning to death with undue haste one who is a member of
our alliance, fastening a most shameful charge on one who had
previously a high reputation amongst you. [9] Now, before we
set sail hither, we spent quite some time together,[70] and none of
us ever saw this fellow with an emblem on his shield; but when
we disembarked here, he had inscribed a trident on it. Now,
why did he do that? In order to make himself conspicuous by
the inscription of the emblem, so that his opposite number could
direct an arrow at him according to the compact he had made,
and he could fire a spear back at him. [10] From this we can
also draw a probable conclusion about the throwing of the
spear. For I maintain that there was writing on it as well,
detailing at what precise time and in what circumstances he
would perform his treasonous act; for they had worked out
for themselves such a trusty communication system as this, he
sending messages to them and they to him by such a method,
dispensing with messengers. [11] And let us bear in mind this
point also. We passed a resolution that whoever recovered a
weapon from the enemy should bring it to the leadership, by
reason of the scarcity of weapons from which we suffered. Every-

one else obeyed this resolution, but this fellow, out of five arrows
that were fired at him, conspicuously returned not one of them to
our communal store; so that even on this ground it seems to me
that he would justly be condemned to death. *[12]* Do you really
think, men of Greece, that these matters <would have slipped>[71]
the mind and wit of this clever fellow (*sophistês*), who has been
directing his cleverness (*philosophôn*)[72] against those he should
least of all have picked on? I shall now proceed to demonstrate
that the situation in which we find ourselves and this whole
expedition are the fault of this man's father and of himself. To
do that, however, I must fill in the background at some length.[73]

[13] This man's father was a poor man, Nauplius by name,
by occupation a fisherman. This man caused the destruction of
very many Greeks, and robbed much wealth from their ships,
and committed very many outrages upon the crews, and, in a
word, neglected no variety of villainy. You will learn the details
of this as my narrative proceeds, revealing to your ears the
whole truth about these events. *[14]* You see, Aleus, the king of
Tegea, when on a visit to Delphi, received an oracle from the
god to the effect that, if a son was born to his daughter, that son
would bring about the death of his sons.[74] When he heard this,
Aleus returned home with all haste, and appointed his daughter
priestess of Athena, telling her that, if she ever had intercourse
with a man, he would put her to death. As it happened, Heracles
came to visit, on his expedition to Elis against Augeas, and Aleus
put him up in the precinct of Athena. *[15]* Heracles caught sight
of the girl in the temple and, under the influence of drink, lay
with her. When her father Aleus realized that she was pregnant,
he sent for the father of this fellow, having learned that he was
a skilled boatman. When Nauplius arrived, he gave him his
daughter, with orders to drown her at sea. *[16]* Nauplius took
the girl away, and when they reached Mount Parthenius,[75] she
gave birth to Telephus. Disregarding his orders from Aleus, he
took her and her son to Mysia,[76] and sold them to Teuthras, the
king of that country. Teuthras, being childless, made Auge his
wife, and adopted her son as his own, naming him Telephus,
and he gave him to Priam to be educated in Troy.

[17] In the course of time, Alexander conceived a desire to

visit Greece, wishing to visit the temple at Delphi, and at the same time, as you know, hearing of the beauty of Helen, and having heard also about the origins of Telephus, where he had come from, and under what circumstances and by whom he had been sold.[77] So Alexander embarked on his visit to Greece for the aforementioned reasons. Now it happened at this juncture that the sons of Molus[78] arrived from Crete to ask Menelaus to arbitrate between them and make a division of their goods, because, in consequence of their father's death, they were at odds with each other about their ancestral property. [18] Well, what happens? Menelaus decided to sail, and gave instructions to his wife and her brothers to look after the guests, that they should want for nothing, until he got back from Crete. And so he departed. Alexander, however, seduced his wife, removed from his house as much wealth as he could carry, and sailed away, showing no respect for the Zeus of strangers or any other of the gods, but perpetrating lawless and barbarous deeds, such as would challenge the credulousness of all, whether contemporaries or later generations.

[19] When he got back to Asia, with his booty and his woman, did you do anything to help the cause, or raise the alarm among your neighbours, or get together a relief expedition? You cannot claim to have done anything of the sort, but you allowed Greeks to suffer outrage at the hands of barbarians without lifting a finger.[79] [20] However, when the Greeks learned of the robbery and Menelaus was apprised of it, he gathered an army and sent around to each of us in our various states to ask for support. And he sent this fellow to Oenopion in Chios and to Cinyras in Cyprus.[80] He . . .[81] and Cinyras he persuaded not to join our expedition, and, having received many gifts from him, sailed off home. [21] He gave to Agamemnon a bronze breastplate, of virtually no value, while holding on to all the rest of the things himself. And he announced that Cinyras would be sending a hundred ships; but you see yourselves that not a single ship has come from him. So for this reason also it seems to me that he would justly be punished with death – if indeed it is thought proper to punish a clever-dick (sophistês) like this, who has been exposed as contriving the vilest plots against his friends.

[22] It is also proper that you should learn of the fruits of his ingenuity,[82] which he brought to bear for the deception and seduction of the youth, claiming that he discovered the principles of strategy, writing, numbers, measures, weights, draughts, dice, music, coinage, fire-signals.[83] And he shows no sign of shame, when he is clearly proved among you to be lying about this. *[23]* For Nestor here, the oldest of us all, himself, at the wedding of Pirithous, did battle with the Centaurs in due military order; and Menestheus[84] is said to have been the first to marshal ranks of men and to set up companies and battle-lines (*phalanges*), when Eumolpus, the son of Poseidon, led an army of Thracians against the Athenians; so this is not an invention of Palamedes, but of others before him. *[24]* And it was Orpheus who first produced writing, having learned this from the Muses, as is indicated by the epitaph on his tomb:

> Orpheus, pupil of the Muses, the Thracians laid here,
>> Whom Zeus who rules on high slew with smoking thunderbolt,
> The dear son of Oeagrus, who taught Heracles,
>> And revealed to men writing and wisdom in general.

As for music, that was invented by Linus, son of Calliope, whom Heracles slew. And numbers were invented by the Athenian Musaeus the Eumolpid, as is indicated by his own poems:

> A six-part hymn in twenty-four measures . . .
> A hundred men to live to the tenth generation.[85]

[26] And was not money the invention of the Phoenicians, those most numerate and clever of barbarians? For they made an equal division of a solid metal bar,[86] and were the first to stamp a mark on it, indicating greater and lesser weights. But this fellow comes along in their wake, speciously claiming to have made the same invention. So all these things, of which this fellow is claiming to be the inventor, are thus shown to be older than him. *[27]* Weights and measures he *did* invent – to be a source of trickery and perjury for traders and denizens of the

market-place, and draughts – to be an occasion of quarrelling and mutual abuse for idle men! And dice, in turn, he produced as the greatest of evils, a source of grief and expense for the losers, and for the winners an occasion of mockery and reproach; for gains from dicing lead to no good, most of them being squandered away again on the spot. *[28]* And he did also devise fire-signals, but he intended to create them to our disadvantage, and to be of use to the enemy. To sum up, it is the proper virtue of a man[87] to give heed to his commanders and to do what he is ordered and to be pleasing in all respects to the general public, and to see to it that he is in all respects a decent man, doing good to his friends and harm to his enemies. This fellow, however, has schooled himself to do exactly the opposite of this, benefiting his enemies and harming his friends.

[29] As for me, I expect you now, after considering his case together, to come to a decision about him, and not to let him go free, after having got him into your power. But if you take pity on him, by reason of the cleverness of his speech, an astonishing degree of lawlessness will ensue in the camp; for each and every individual, knowing that Palamedes, despite being manifestly guilty of crime, suffered no penalty, will himself try out some act of lawlessness. So if you are sensible, you will vote as is best for yourselves, and in taking vengeance on this fellow will set a headline for all others.

10 THE ANONYMUS IAMBLICHI AND THE DOUBLE ARGUMENTS

The Anonymus Iamblichi

This rather unwieldy title is conferred on the work of an unknown, but fairly certainly fifth-century BC, sophist which is preserved in the twentieth chapter of the Protrepticus, *or Exhortation to Philosophy, of the late third-century Neoplatonist philosopher Iamblichus. There are seven passages in all, amounting to a total of 2,500 words in English, and offering a more or less continuous argument. The topic appears to be, broadly speaking, 'How to Succeed in Life' – a subject central to the projects of all of the figures (at least the professional ones) dealt with in this volume, though the last section focuses more particularly on the political topic of obedience to law.*

Various conjectures have naturally been made over the years as to the identity of this writer, but none has found general acceptance. The problem continues to intrigue, however, as it seems on the whole improbable that the person concerned should be a complete nonentity; he is far more likely to be one of the main figures of the sophistic movement with whom we have been dealing (though the possibility remains that he might have been a faithful follower of one or other of them). As will be seen from what follows, our tentative choice for authorship would fall upon Protagoras, and specifically on his so-called Great Discourse (Megas Logos), but it seems on the whole more prudent to leave the work in its state of anonymity. One major problem, it must be said, in the way of Protagorean authorship is that the only fragment that we have of Protagoras' prose (ch. 1, §6 above) is in the Ionic dialect. One would have to suppose

*either that Protagoras was capable of composing in Attic as
well, or that his treatise was 'atticized' at some later stage –
neither of which supposition, however, is impossible.*[1]

The first passage seems to come from the beginning of the
work, being suitably programmatic. It sets out the basic conditions necessary for success in life, and they are very much
those attributed to Protagoras in what would seem to have been
a major statement of his doctrine, the Great Discourse *(cf.
above, ch. 1, §19), to wit, natural ability (*physis*), willingness
to learn (*mathêsis*) and willingness to practise (*askêsis*).*[2] *The
precise phraseology attributed to Protagoras in that passage
does not, admittedly, occur here, but it is very doubtful, despite
Diels' mode of presenting it, that that is a verbatim quotation.*

1. *[1]* In whatever field of endeavour one wishes to achieve the
very best results, whether it be wisdom, courage, eloquence
(*euglôssia*)[3] or excellence (*aretê*),[4] either as a whole or any part
of it – he will be able to achieve this on the following conditions.
[2] First, one must possess natural ability (*phynai*), and this is a
matter of good luck (*tykhê*);[5] the other elements, however, are
in one's own hands: he must be eager for noble things (*kala kai
agatha*) and willing to work hard, beginning his studies very
early in life and seeing them through to completion over a long
period of time.[6] *[3]* If even one of these factors is absent, it is
impossible to reach the highest goal in the end; but if any human
being has all these things, he will be unsurpassed in whatever he
takes on.

   (p. 95, 13–23 Pistelli)

*After a short bridge-passage by Iamblichus, the text continues,
possibly without a break from what precedes. In this section the
author dwells on the importance of the gradual attainment of a
reputation for excellence, in order to minimize the envy and
begrudgery (*phthonos*) that normally attends exhibitions of
excellence. This has some relation, perhaps, to the remarks
attributed to Protagoras by Plato at *Protagoras* 316D about the
phthonos *which naturally attaches itself to those professing
wisdom.*

2. [1] If one wishes to acquire good repute among men, and to give a proper impression of his capacities, he must start straight away at a young age, and must apply himself to his task consistently and unvaryingly. [2] When he has possessed each of these qualities of his for a long time, tended to from the very beginning and brought to perfection, it will procure him a firm reputation and fame, for this reason, that he has now the unqualified confidence of others; and envy (*phthonos*) does not attach to him, such as causes men not to praise or give proper credit to some things and to falsify and unjustly criticize others. [3] People do not enjoy honouring someone else (for they think that they themselves are being in some way diminished by this); but when they are overcome gradually over a period of time by the force of necessity, they concede praise, though even then unwillingly. [4] However, when once they have reached this stage, they no longer question whether the person concerned is the sort of man he seems, or is setting a trap, hunting reputation by deceit and leading on others to give excessive credit to his achievements. If excellence is worked at in the way I have set forth, it gains trust for itself, and fair fame. [5] For once people become convinced by main force, they can no longer give in to envy, nor do they conceive that they are being duped. [6] Furthermore, whenever any action or piece of business[7] takes a long time, that lends strength to one's achievement, whereas a short time cannot have the same effect. [7] For instance, if someone were to learn and master the art (*tekhnê*) of argument (*logoi*), he could become no worse than his teacher in quite a short time, but the excellence that accrues from many achievements cannot possibly be brought to fruition in any short time by a late beginner; one must be nurtured and grow up along with one's art, steering clear of bad arguments and habits, while practising and exercising oneself in the opposite kind over a long time and with much care. [8] At the same time, a favourable reputation gained over a short period has the following disadvantage, that those who suddenly, in a brief while, become either rich or wise or good or brave are not in general well received by their fellow men.

(pp. 96, 1–97, 8 Pistelli)

Again, a short bridge-passage by Iamblichus, and the text continues:

3. *[1]* When someone has set his heart on one of these objectives, whether it be eloquence or wisdom or strength, and has carried it through to complete and full mastery, he should employ it for good and lawful purposes.[8] But if he employs the good which he possesses for unjust and lawless purposes, this is the worst of all, and it would be better that his excellence be absent from him than present to him. *[2]* And even as a person who has one of these excellences and uses it for good ends is perfectly good, so in turn he who uses it for evil purposes is entirely evil.[9] *[3]* We must also consider, in the case of someone striving after excellence in general, on the basis of what word or deed he might become as good as possible; and he would attain this state by becoming useful to the greatest number of people.[10]

[4] If someone engages in expenditure of money for the benefit of his neighbours,[11] he will also be compelled in turn to be dishonest, by collecting the money in the first place. Then again, he could not collect it in such abundance that he would not, in consequence of his grants and donations, run short; and then this second evil is added, after that involved in the gathering of the money, if he becomes poor after being rich, and goes from having money to having none.

[5] How, then, might one become a benefactor[12] of men, not by distributing money, but in some other way, and achieve this not with the accompaniment of evil but of excellence? And further, how, in giving gifts, can he ensure that his capacity to give will be inexhaustible? *[6]* This will come about in the following way, if he acts in support of the laws and of justice; for it is this that both establishes and holds together men and cities.[13]

(pp. 97, 16–98, 11 Pistelli)

Again, a small bridge-passage, after which we find our author turning to a praise of self-control (enkrateia). Here there would seem to be something of a gap in the text.

4. [1] Furthermore, every man should be concerned to be exceptionally self-controlled. One would best achieve this, if he should rise above the love of money, which is something which brings all men to ruin, and if he should be unsparing of his life (*psykhê*)[14] in the pursuit of justice and the striving for moral excellence; for most people lack self-control in these two matters. [2] They suffer this for the following reason: they love their soul, because the soul is the principle of life, and therefore they cherish it and seek to preserve it through love of life and the familiarity which they have developed with it. And they love money, because of the following things, which cause them fear. [3] What are these? Diseases, old age, sudden losses – not losses resulting from law-suits (for these can be avoided and guarded against), but losses resulting from such things as fire, deaths of household members or of animals and other misfortunes, of which some relate to the body, some to the soul, some to one's external possessions. [4] Because of all these, in order that he may be able to use his money to meet such contingencies, every man strives after wealth. [5] But there are some other factors which no less than the above-mentioned drive men on to money-making – to wit, ambitious rivalry with one another, jealousy and the struggle for political power – situations in which they consider money of great importance, because it contributes to such purposes. [6] But the man who is really good does not hunt for a reputation decked out in borrowed finery, but in his own virtue.

(pp. 98, 17–99, 14 Pistelli)

Again a few lines of summary by Iamblichus, after which the treatise seems to continue more or less directly from what precedes.

5. [1] As for love of one's own life (*philopsykhia*), one might persuade people by the following reasoning: if it were a feature of the human condition that, if one did not die at the hands of another, one would live to be unaging and immortal for all future time, then one might readily excuse someone for being sparing of his own life. But since in fact it is man's lot, if his life

is extended, to suffer old age, which is a greater evil for men, and not to be immortal, then it is a mark of great ignorance and of falling under the influence of base arguments and desires, to seek to preserve one's life with dishonour, and not leave in its place something immortal, an eternal and ever-living good name.

(pp. 99, 18–100, 1 Pistelli)

Once again a few lines from Iamblichus, specifying that it is only philosophy which enables us to do this, after which he turns to a rather different topic.

6. *[1]* Again, one should not seek to maximize one's own advantage (*pleonexia*), nor consider that power which is based on such maximization is virtue (*aretê*), or that to obey the laws is cowardice;[15] for this attitude of mind is most wicked, and from it arises everything that is opposite to what is good, to wit, evil and harm. For if in fact men are by nature unsuited to living in isolation, and have formed associations with one another under pressure of necessity, and if the whole of life and its technical skills (*tekhnêmata*) have been developed by them for this end, and if they cannot associate with one another without the observance of law (for this would be a greater source of suffering to them than living in isolation), because of all these necessities law and justice hold the kingship among men,[16] and can in no way be displaced; for they are firmly fixed in us by nature. *[2]* If there should be anyone born with such a nature as the following: invulnerable, not subject to disease, free from emotions, of supernatural power, with body and soul of adamant, perhaps one might suppose that power based on aggrandizement would serve for such a one (for such a one, one might argue, would be unscathed even if he did not submit to the law); but one would not be correct in such a supposition. *[3]* For even if one admitted the possibility of such a man, as in fact there cannot be, he would only survive if he allied himself with the laws and with justice, supporting these and lending his strength to backing up these and what conduces to them. Only thus would he ensure his safety; otherwise he could not survive. *[4]* For I think that

all men would stand opposed to a person of such a nature because of their own devotion to legality (*eunomia*), and in virtue of their numbers they would overcome such a man by craft or by force and get the better of him. *[5]* Accordingly it becomes apparent that power – true power, that is – is preserved by law and through justice.

(pp. 100, 5–101, 6 Pistelli)

The last, and longest, passage from the work seems to flow on pretty well directly from this, after another Iamblichean bridge-passage. The author turns to an encomium of law-abidingness (eunomia) *and a condemnation of lawlessness* (ano-mia). *The overall tone here is not unlike that of Thrasymachus in ch. 6, §12 above, but it is not clear that the author is speaking from a conservative or anti-democratic perspective; rather he appears to be criticizing a Calliclean 'might is right' stance.*

7. *[1]* The first consequence of law-abidingness is a climate of trust (*pistis*). This benefits all men greatly, and is to be classed among the great goods. The common use of money is a result of this, and accordingly, even if there is only a little money about, it suffices, by reason of the fact that it circulates; but without mutual trust even a great deal of money would not be sufficient.[17] *[2]* Also, the changes of fortune which affect both wealth and the quality of life, whether for better or for worse, are most effectively managed by men as a result of the observance of law-abidingness. Those who have good fortune can enjoy it in safety, without fear of being plotted against; and those who suffer bad fortune can receive aid from those who enjoy good fortune by virtue of their commingling and mutual trust, since these have their basis in law-abidingness. *[3]* Further, by reason of law-abidingness men need not spend their time on public affairs (*ta pragmata*), but can turn their attention to the personal concerns (*ta erga*) of life.[18] *[4]* In a state of law-abidingness, men are freed from the most unpleasant of concerns, and can engage in the pleasantest: for a concern about public affairs is the most unpleasant, while concern for one's own affairs is the most pleasant.

[5] When they turn to sleep, which is a rest from troubles for men, they go to it without fear and without painful anxieties, and when they rise from it, they enjoy the same state of mind; they do not leap out of bed in sudden terror, nor, after a pleasant period of release, face the day to come with apprehension [?][19] but rather, free from fear,[20] they direct untroubled attention to the tasks of life, and lighten their toils with credible and well-founded hopes of obtaining benefits in return. For all this we are indebted to law-abidingness.

[6] Also, that which provides the worst of evils to men, war, which leads people to ruin and slavery, this too is more a threat to the lawless, and less to the law-abiding.

[7] Many other goods inhere in law-abidingness, such as to provide assistance in life and consolation for the hardships which arise from it; but the evils which result from lawlessness are the following. *[8]* First of all, men have no leisure for private concerns (*erga*), and are preoccupied with what is most unpleasant, public affairs (*pragmata*), rather than private concerns; they hoard money, because of their mutual distrust and lack of social intercourse, and do not spread it around, and thus money becomes scarce, even if there is lots of it.

[9] Also, good and ill fortune have opposite consequences [sc. to what they would be in conditions of law-abidingness]; for good fortune is not safe in conditions of lawlessness, but is the target of plots,[21] while ill fortune is not thrust away but reinforced as a result of lack of trust and social intercourse.

[10] External war is provoked all the more by the same cause, and internal strife (*stasis*) as well, and even if it was not endemic previously, it arises then. It comes about since men are constantly involved in public concerns because of plots being hatched by each other, by reason of which they have to be constantly on their guard, and to initiate counter-plots against each other.

[11] And neither when they are awake are their thoughts pleasant ones, nor when they have gone to sleep do they find a pleasant refuge but one full of terror, and an awakening full of fear and anxiety leads the man to a sudden recollection of his troubles. And all this, and all the other evils aforementioned, are the result of lawlessness.

[12] And also tyranny, an evil of such magnitude and nature, arises from no other cause than lawlessness.[22] Some men think – but their reckoning is wrong – that a tyrant arises from some other cause, and that men who are deprived of their freedom are not themselves to blame, but they are overborne by the tyrant who manages to establish himself. But they do not reason correctly; *[13]* for whoever thinks that a king or a tyrant comes into power from any other cause than lawlessness and aggrandizement (*pleonexia*) is a fool. It is whenever everyone turns to evil that this happens; for it is not possible for men to live without laws and justice. *[14]* So whenever these two, law and justice, depart from the mass of people, then the administration and supervision of these pass into the hands of one person. For in what other way would authority pass into the hands of one person, if not through the banishment of law, which is in the interest of the multitude? *[15]* For that man who will dismantle justice and eliminate law, which is to the common advantage of all, must be made of adamant, if he is going to rob the mass of men of this, being one against many. If, however, he be made of flesh like the rest of men, he would not be able to achieve this, but, on the contrary,[23] only by reconstituting them [sc. law and justice] when they have perished could he attain monarchy; and that is the reason why this comes about without some people noticing.[24]

(pp. 101, 11–104, 14 Pistelli)

Here Iamblichus ceases his quotation of his source, rounding off the chapter with a summary of his own. How much of the original document he has transmitted to us it is impossible to say, but what we have is a reasonably well-rounded essay, in the archaic mode, which constitutes a valuable supplement to our meagre total of sophistic prose.

The Double Arguments

The so-called Double Arguments (*Dissoi Logoi*) are a rather simple-minded collection of arguments for and against a series of propositions (or, in the case of the last few, for or against), composed in 'literary' Doric dialect, shortly after the end of the

Peloponnesian War,[25] *probably in the 390s or 380s. Unlike the* Anonymus Iamblichi, *which is a document worthy of being attributed to one or another of the major sophists, these arguments read much more like the compilation of an enthusiastic student than of any master. Nevertheless, they are not without interest, as they deal with many of the issues, moral, political and epistemological, which exercised the minds of thinkers, professional and amateur alike, during this period.*

The form of the treatise – in so far as it can be credited with a form – is distinctly odd. The author launches initially into a series of four 'double arguments' for and against the identity or distinctness of a set of moral qualities ('good' and 'bad'; 'fine' and 'shameful'; 'just' and 'unjust'; 'true' and 'false'), followed by a somewhat fragmentary one on the question whether madness and sanity are the same or not. But he then turns rather to the discussion of a series of four controversial 'issues of the day' ('Is Human Excellence Teachable?'; 'Should Public Offices be Assigned by Lot?'; 'The Advantages of the Study of Rhetoric'; and 'A Praise of Mnemonics'), all of which might certainly have formed the basis for epideictic orations on these topics, but which are no longer presented in the form of 'double arguments'. This leaves it somewhat unclear what the author's overall plan really was.

One mode of argument of which the author makes much use is one which systematically confuses the absolute and relative uses of terms, in order to set up a contradiction. This device, characteristic as it is of the infancy of logical theory, is reminiscent of a number of the moves made by the brothers Euthydemus and Dionysodorus, as portrayed by Plato in the Euthydemus (*cf. ch. 8 above*).

The fact that the document is composed in Doric might be taken as an argument in favour of its having emanated from the 'school' of Hippias of Elis, since Doric would have been his native dialect, and this has in fact been proposed by Max Pohlenz,[26] *who draws attention also to the commendation of memorization in the final passage of the work (section ix), since that was a particular enthusiasm of Hippias', as we know. On the other hand, it is Protagoras who is chiefly known for*

*propounding arguments on both sides of a question (in his
Antilogies), so that one might think of a Doric-speaking follower
of his. But the document is not likely to have emanated from
anyone of substance. In translating, we have tried to preserve
the naive and disjointed quality of the original.*

8. (i) Concerning Good and Bad

[1] Double arguments are put forward in Greece by those who
profess philosophy concerning the good and the bad. Some say
that good is one thing and bad another; others, that they are the
same, and that a thing might be good for some people, and bad
for others, or even for the same person at one time good and at
another time bad.[27] [2] I myself side with the latter opinion,[28]
and I shall examine it, taking as an example human life, and its
concern for food, drink and sex; for these things are bad for
someone if he is sick, but good for someone who is healthy, and
has need of them. [3] And further, lack of self-control in respect
of these things is bad for those who lack control, but good for
those who are selling the relevant commodities and making
money out of them. And again, illness is bad for the sick, but
good for the doctors. And death is bad for those who die,
but good for undertakers and gravediggers.

[4] Farming, again, when it produces good crops, is good for
the farmers, but bad for the merchants. And when merchant
ships are wrecked and broken up, it is bad for the ship-owner,
but good for the ship-builders. [5] And again, if an iron tool is
corroded by rust or blunted or broken, it is bad for everyone
else concerned, but good for the blacksmith; and certainly, if a
pot is broken, that is bad for everyone else, but good for the
potters; and if shoes are worn out or break apart, that is bad for
the users, but good for the shoemaker.

[6] Again, take the case of various types of contest, athletic,
musical or military – a foot race, for example: victory is good
for the winner, but bad for the losers; [7] and the same is true
for wrestlers and boxers, and for all those as well who compete
in musical contests – victory, for instance, in lyre-playing is
good for the victor, but bad for the losers.

[8] In the case of war, again (to mention most recent events

first),[29] the victory of the Spartans, which they won over the Athenians and their allies, was good for the Spartans, but bad for the Athenians and their allies; and the victory which the Greeks won over the Persians was good for the Greeks, but bad for the foreigners. *[9]* And again, the capture of Troy was good for the Achaeans, but bad for the Trojans; and the same is true for the experiences of the Thebans and of the Argives.[30] *[10]* And the battle between the Centaurs and the Lapiths was good for the Lapiths but bad for the Centaurs;[31] and further, the battle which is said to have taken place between the Gods and the Giants (and the victory which resulted) was good for the Gods, but bad for the Giants.

[11] But on the other hand there is another argument to the effect that the good is one thing, and the bad another, and that even as the name differs, so too does the reality. And I too would make this distinction; I consider that it would not be clear what sort of thing was good and what was bad, if they were the same and each was not different from the other – and indeed it would be remarkable if that were the case.[32] *[12]* And I think that one who makes this argument would have nothing to say if anyone should put to him the following question:

'Just tell me, did your parents ever do you any good?'

He would say, 'Yes, a good deal.'

'You then owe them a great deal of bad in return, if good is really the same as bad.'

[13] 'And again, did you ever do your relations any good?'

<'Indeed, a good deal!'>[33]

'Well then, you were doing your relations harm.'

'Come now, did you ever do your enemies any harm?'

'A good deal, indeed!'

'Well then, you did them the greatest good.'

[14] 'Come now and answer me the following: is it not the case that you are pitying beggars, because they are beset by many evils, and at the same time counting them lucky, because they enjoy many goods, if good and bad are really the same thing?'

[15] And indeed there is nothing preventing the Great King himself from being in the same state as the beggars; for his many

great goods are many great evils, if good and bad are the same.

And the same goes for every situation. *[16]* I shall go through individual cases, beginning with eating, drinking and sex. For the sick, these things are <bad to do, and again>[34] they are good for them to do, if good and bad are the same. And for the sick it is bad to be ill, and again good, if good is the same as bad. *[17]* And the same goes for all the other cases mentioned in the previous argument. Mind you, I am not saying here what the good is; I am simply trying to show that the bad and the good are not the same, but that each is distinct from the other.

(ii) *Concerning Fine and Shameful*[35]

[1] Double arguments are also put forward about the fine and the shameful. For some say the fine is one thing, and the shameful another, and that, as the name differs, so does the thing named; others that the fine and the shameful are the same. *[2]* I shall approach this question also, making my exposition on the following lines.[36]

For example, it is fine for a boy in the bloom of youth to gratify a lover, but it is shameful to gratify a non-lover. *[3]* And for women to wash themselves indoors is fine, but for them to do so in the palaestra would be disgraceful[37] (but for men to do so in the palaestra or the gymnasium is fine). *[4]* And to have sexual intercourse with one's husband in private is fine, where one will be concealed by walls; but outside it is shameful, where one will be seen. *[5]* And to have intercourse with one's own husband is fine, but with another man it is shameful. And for a man to have intercourse with his own wife is fine, but with another woman it is shameful.[38] *[6]* And to adorn oneself and put on make-up and wear gold ornaments for a man is shameful, but fine for a woman.

[7] And to do good to one's friends is fine, but to do so to one's enemies is shameful. And it is shameful to run away from the enemy in battle, but fine to run away from one's opponents in the athletic stadium.[39] *[8]* To slaughter one's friends and one's fellow citizens is shameful, but to slaughter the enemy is fine. And the same argument can be made on every topic.

[9] I pass on now to what the various states and nations

consider to be shameful.[40] For example, among the Spartans it is fine for young girls to practise athletics and to go around with bare arms and no tunics; whereas for the Ionians it is shameful. [10] And among the former it is fine for their children not to learn music and letters, while for the Ionians it is shameful not to have mastered all these things. [11] Among the Thessalians it is fine for a man to select horses and mules from a herd himself and break them, and also to take an ox and slaughter, skin and cut it up himself,[41] but in Sicily these activities are thought shameful, and the work of slaves. [12] To the Macedonians it appears to be fine for girls, before they are married, to have love affairs and sleep with men, but when they are married, it is shameful; but for Greeks[42] it is shameful in either case. [13] Among the Thracians, it is regarded as an ornament for girls to be tattooed, but for other people tattooing is a punishment for wrongdoers. And the Scythians think it fine for anyone who has killed a man to scalp him and to carry the scalp on the front of his horse,[43] and, having covered the skull with gold or silver, to drink from it and pour libations to the gods; whereas in Greece no one would be willing to enter the same house as a man who had done such things.

[14] The Massagetae cut up their parents and eat them, and they consider that to find burial in their children is the finest of tombs;[44] but among the Greeks, if anyone did such a thing, he would be driven out of the country and would die a wretched death, as having committed shameful and lawless deeds. [15] The Persians think it fine that men should adorn themselves like women, and that they should have intercourse with their daughters, mothers and sisters; but the Greeks regard these things as shameful and lawless. [16] And again, it seems fine to the Lydians that girls should prostitute themselves and earn money and so get married;[45] but among the Greeks no one would be willing to marry such a girl.

[17] And the Egyptians do not think the same things fine that other peoples do; for here it is thought fine that women should weave and do housework, but there they think it fine that the men do so, and that the women do what the men do here.[46] It also seems fine to them to moisten clay with the hands and

dough with the feet, but it is just the opposite with us. *[18]* I think, indeed, that if someone should order all men to bring into one heap everything that each of them regards as shameful, and then to take from the collection what each of them considered to be fine, not a thing would be left, but they would all divide up everything, because all men do not hold the same views.[47]

[19] I shall offer some verses on this subject:[48]

> 'For you will see this other law for mortals
>   if you distinguish well: nothing is fine or shameful
>   in every way, but occasion (*kairos*) takes the same things
>   and makes them shameful or changes them to fine.'[49]

[20] To sum up, everything done on the right occasion is fine and everything done on a wrong occasion is shameful.[50]

What have I, then, achieved? I said that I would show that the same things are both shameful and fine, and I have done so in all these cases. *[21]* But it is also said about the fine and shameful that each is distinct.[51] For if one should ask those who say that the same thing is both fine and shameful whether, in case they have ever performed any fine action, they would admit that they have also performed a shameful one; *[22]* and if they know a man who is handsome,[52] whether they would know the same man to be ugly; and if they know a man to be fair, whether they also know him to be dark. And it is fine to worship the gods, and also shameful to worship the gods, if fine and shameful are the same.

[23] And we may assume that I have made the same points in all cases. I will now turn to the argument which they present. *[24]* If it is fine for a woman to adorn herself, then it is also shameful for a woman to adorn herself, if shameful and fine are really the same; and in all other cases it is the same. *[25]* In Sparta it is fine for girls to practise athletics; in Sparta it is shameful for girls to practise athletics – and so forth. *[26]* And they say that if someone were to collect shameful practices from all the nations of the world, and then should call people together and ask them to pick out what each considered fine, everything

would be taken away as being fine. But I would be astonished if what were shameful when gathered together turned out to be fine (when selected), and not such as they were when they came in.[53] [27] At least if people had brought horses or oxen or sheep or men, they would not have taken away anything else; nor again, if they had brought gold, would they have taken away bronze, nor if they had brought silver, would they have taken away lead. [28] Do they then take away fine things in place of shameful ones? Come now, if anyone brought in an ugly man, would they take him away as handsome? They adduce the poets as witnesses, but they compose with an eye to pleasure, not to truth.[54]

(iii) *Concerning Just and Unjust*

[1] Double arguments are also put forward about the just and the unjust; of which the one says that the just is one thing and the unjust another, while the other in turn says that they are the same. And I shall try to support this latter position.

[2] In the first place, I shall argue that it is just to tell lies and to deceive. The other side might assert that it is <fine and just>[55] to do this to one's enemies, but shameful and wicked to do it <to one's friends>. <But how is it just to do this to one's enemies,> and not to one's nearest and dearest? Take first the case of one's parents: suppose one's father or mother ought to eat or drink a remedial drug, and is unwilling to do so, is it not just to give the drug in a dish of porridge or a drink, and deny that it is in it? [3] So then it follows that it is just to lie to and to deceive one's parents.[56]

And, in fact, it is just to steal the property of one's friends and to use force against one's nearest and dearest. [4] For instance, if a member of the household should be in a state of grief or upset about something, and proposes to destroy himself with a sword or a rope or some other such thing, it is surely right to steal[57] these things, if one can, and, if one comes upon the scene too late and catches the person in the act, to take the instrument away by force.

[5] And how is it not just to enslave one's enemies, and to sell a whole city into slavery if one is able to capture it?[58] But it also

seems just to break into the public buildings of one's own citizens. For, after all, if one's father has been imprisoned by his enemies with a view to execution as a result of civic strife (*stasis*), how is it not just to dig your way through the wall, and steal away and rescue your father? *[6]* And what about oath-breaking? Suppose that someone is captured by the enemy and takes an oath that if he is set free he will betray his city, would such a man be acting justly if he kept his oath? *[7]* I certainly don't think so; but rather if he should save his city and his friends and his ancestral temples by breaking it. So then, breaking one's oath is just. And what about temple-robbing? *[8]* I am not talking here about the temples of one's own city, but about those common to the whole of Greece, such as those at Delphi and Olympia. When the barbarian[59] was about to capture Greece, and salvation lay in the temple funds, was it not just to take these and use them for the war? *[9]* And it is just to kill one's nearest and dearest; since both Orestes and Alcmaeon did this, and the god declared in an oracle that they were right to do so.[60]

[10] I will turn now to the arts, and to the writings of the poets. In the writing of tragedies and in painting, whoever is most deceptive in creating things similar to the true, he is the best.[61] *[11]* I want also to present the testimony of older poetry – of Cleobulina, for instance:

> I saw a man stealing and deceiving by force,
> And to accomplish this by force was entirely just.[62]

[12] These lines were written a long time ago. But these are by Aeschylus:

> God does not shrink from deceit if it is just.

and

> Time is when God respects the moment for a lie.[63]

[13] But to this too an opposite argument is put forward, to the effect that the just and the unjust are different things, and as

the name differs, so does the thing. For instance,[64] if anyone should ask those who say that unjust and just are the same whether they have ever done anything just for their parents, they will say that they have. But then they have done something unjust, because they maintain that just and unjust are the same. *[14]* And take another case: if you know that some man is just, then you know the same man to be also unjust; and again, by the same reasoning, if large, also small. And if it is said: 'Let so-and-so die, as having committed many unjust acts!', he must also die for having performed <many just acts>.[65]

[15] But enough about this. I shall turn to what is said by those who claim to prove that just and unjust are the same. *[16]* To say that stealing the enemy's property is just would show the same action to be unjust, if their argument is true, and it is the same in all other cases. *[17]* And they bring in the arts, to which justice and injustice are irrelevant. As for the poets, they do not write their poems with truth in mind, but to pander to the pleasures of men.

(iv) *Concerning True and False*

[1] Double arguments are also uttered about the false and the true, about which one person says that a false statement is one thing and a true another; while others say that, on the contrary, they are the same. *[2]* And I support the latter view: firstly, because they are both expressed in the same words; and then, because whenever a statement is made, if things should turn out to be as stated, then the statement is true, while if they should not turn out to be as stated, the same statement is false.[66] *[3]* Let us first of all suppose that a given statement accuses a certain man of temple-robbery: if the act took place, the statement is true; if it did not take place, the same statement is false. And the same argument is used by the defendant. And the courts judge the same statement to be true and false.[67] *[4]* And again, suppose we are all sitting in a row, and each of us says, 'I am an initiate';[68] we all utter the same words, but I would be the only person making a true statement, since I am the only person who is one. *[5]* It is clear, then, from these examples, that the same statement, whenever falsehood is present to it, is false, and

whenever truth is present, is true – just as a man is the same person when he is a child and a young man and an adult and an old man.[69]

[6] But it is also claimed that a false statement is one thing and a true statement another, and that, as the name differs, <so does the thing named>.[70] For if anyone should ask those who say that the same statement is both false and true which of these their own statement is, if they answer 'false', then it is clear that the false and the true are two different things; whereas if they answer 'true', then this same statement is also false. And if anyone ever says or testifies that certain things are true, then, on that argument, these same things are also false; and if one knows some man to be truthful, one knows him also to be a liar.

[7] On the basis of this reasoning, they say this: if a thing comes about, the statement they make about it is true, but if it doesn't come about, then it is false. If this is so, it is not <the linguistic component (*onoma*)[71] that differs, but rather the state of affairs referred to (*pragma*). [8] And> again, <it is improper to ask?>[72] jurymen what their judgement is, for they were not present at the events. [9] And they themselves[73] agree that that in which falsehood is mixed (*anamemeiktai*)[74] is false, while anything in which truth is mixed is true. But this constitutes a total difference . . .[75]

(v) <*Concerning Madness and Sanity?*>
[1] . . . The mad and the sane, and the wise and the foolish, both say and do the same things. [2] For a start, they use the same words for things, 'earth' and 'man' and 'horse' and 'fire' and so on for everything else. And they do the same things: they sit and eat and drink and lie down, and similarly with other activities. [3] And indeed the same thing is (for them)[76] larger and smaller and more and less and heavier and lighter; for in this sense all things are the same. [4] A talent is heavier than a mina, and lighter than two talents;[77] so the same thing is both lighter and heavier. [5] And the same man both lives and does not live, and the same things both are and are not; for the things that are here are not in Libya, nor are the things in Libya in Cyprus. And

the same line of argument applies to the rest of things. Therefore things both are and are not.[78]

[6][79] Those who maintain this – that the mad and the sane, and the wise and the foolish, do and say the same things – and the other consequences of the argument do not argue correctly. [7] For if you ask them whether madness differs from sanity, and wisdom from foolishness, they say 'yes'. [8] For either group distinguishes itself clearly by its actions, as they will agree. So it is not the case that,[80] even if they do the same things, both the wise are mad, and the mad wise, and that all is in confusion. [9] And again, we ought to raise the question about *appropriateness* – whether it is the sane or the mad who speak appropriately (*en deonti*). But of course they say, whenever they are asked, that the two groups make the same utterances, but that the wise speak at the appropriate time, while the mad do so when they should not. [10] And in saying this, they appear to be making a small addition, in adding 'appropriately' or 'inappropriately', so as for the situation not to be the same. [11] But I do not think that the situation is altered so much by the addition of an element,[81] as by an alteration, as it were, of tone (*harmonia*);[82] as for instance *Glàûkos* (the proper name) and *glaukós* ('grey'), or *Xánthos* (the proper name) and *xanthós* ('fair-haired'), or *Xòûthos* (the proper name) and *xouthós* ('nimble'). [12] These examples differ from one another by a change in the pitch-accent, while certain other words differ according as their vowel is long or short: for example, *Turos* (the city-name) and *tûros* ('cheese'); *sakos* ('shield') and *sâkos* ('enclosure');[83] and others again by reason of a change in the order of letters: *kartos* and *kratos*,[84] *onos* ('donkey') and *noos* ('mind').

[13] Since, then, there is such a difference when nothing is taken away, what do you think is the case when something is added or taken away? [14] If one takes one away from ten, for example, the result is no longer ten or one, and similarly in all cases.[85]

[15] As for the same man being and not being, I would ask the following: 'Do we mean in some respect or in all respects?' Then if someone denies that a man 'is',[86] he is in error, if he is treating <the particular and> the general as the same.[87] Everything, after all, exists *in some way*.

(vi) *About Wisdom and Excellence:*[88] *Are they Teachable?*

[1] A certain proposition is put about that is neither true nor new, to the effect that wisdom and excellence can neither be taught nor learned. And those who say this have recourse to the following arguments: *[2]* that it is not possible, if you bestow something on someone else, for you still to retain that thing; this is one argument. *[3]* Another one is: if they had been teachable, there would have been designated teachers of them, as in the case of music.[89] *[4]* A third argument is that the men in Greece who achieved expertise would have taught their art to their nearest and dearest.[90] *[5]* A fourth argument is that, before now, some have gone to study with sophists and have derived no benefit from them. *[6]* A fifth is that many who have not associated with sophists have gone on to become distinguished.

[7] But I consider this line of argument to be extremely naive; for I know that schoolmasters teach letters, which is something that the master knows, and lyre-players teach lyre-playing.[91] In answer to the second argument, that there are no designated teachers, what on earth else do the sophists teach except wisdom and excellence? *[8]* And what about the followers of Anaxagoras and Pythagoras?[92] As to the third argument, Polycleitus in fact taught his son to be a sculptor.[93] *[9]* And even if a particular individual did *not* manage to teach, this would not be an indication of anything; but if even one *did* succeed in teaching, this would be a proof that it is possible to teach. *[10]* In response to the fourth point, that some do not acquire expertise in spite of associating with sophists, we may note that many do not become proficient at their letters in spite of studying them.

[11] And there is also the element of natural ability (*physis*),[94] by virtue of which one who does not study with sophists may become competent, if he has natural ability, to pick up a good deal with ease, after learning a few elements from those from whom we learn the words of our language; and these, to a greater or lesser extent, we learn from our father or our mother. *[12]* And if someone is not persuaded that we learn our words, but thinks that we are born knowing them, let him come to a conclusion on the basis of the following consideration: if someone should send a child away to the Persians as soon as he was

born and should bring him up there, without ever hearing any Greek, he would grow up speaking Persian; and if one were to bring a Persian child over here, he would speak Greek. So we learn our words in this way, and we do not know who our teachers are.

[*13*] So that is my argument, and you have the beginning and the middle and the end of it. I don't say that wisdom and excellence are teachable; it is just that the arguments (against this proposition) do not convince me.[95]

(vii) <*Whether Public Offices should be Assigned by Lot*>

[*1*] Some of the politicians assert that public offices should be assigned by lot, but their opinion is not the best.[96] [*2*] For suppose that one were to ask someone who maintains this view, 'Why, then, don't you assign your slaves their tasks by lot, so that if the wagon-driver, for example, drew the lot of cook, he would do the cooking, and the cook would drive the wagon, and so with all the others? [*3*] And why do we not gather together the smiths and the cobblers, and the carpenters and the goldsmiths, and draw lots, and compel each one to engage in whatever trade he happened to draw, and not the one in which he is skilled? [*4*] The same procedure could also be followed in musical contests: one could have the contestants draw lots, and each could compete in the contest that he drew; so the flute-player, for example, would play the lyre if that fell to his lot, and the lyre-player the flute. And in war, archers and infantrymen will ride in the cavalry, and the cavalryman will take to the bow, so that each will be doing the job that he does not understand and is incapable of doing.

[*5*] Now they say that this procedure is good and extremely democratic, but I consider that it is very far from democratic. For there are in all states those who are hostile to the common people (*misodêmoi*), and if the lot falls to them, they will destroy the people. [*6*] But the common people themselves should keep their eyes open and elect solely those who are well disposed towards them, and choose suitable people to be generals, and others such to be guardians of the law (*nomophylakes*), and so on.

(viii) <*The Importance of Rhetorical Training*>

[1] I think that it is proper to the same man and to the same art both to be able to conduct short question-and-answer discussions,[97] and to comprehend the truth of things,[98] and to know how to plead a case correctly in court, and to be capable of making public speeches, and to understand the art of rhetoric, and to teach about the nature of things, how things are and how they came to be.[99]

[2] And first of all, how will it be possible for a man who knows about the nature of all things not to do the right thing also in every case?[100] *[3]* Again, the man who has mastered the art of rhetoric will also know how to speak correctly on every subject *[4]* (for necessarily, one who is going to speak correctly must speak on those subjects which he knows about); therefore it follows that he will know everything.[101] *[5]* The reason is that he knows the techniques of all kinds of speech, and the sum-total of kinds of speech have as their subject-matter all existent things. *[6]* The person who is going to speak correctly, after all, must have a knowledge of whatever things he proposes to discuss, and thus give the city correct instruction in doing good things, and so prevent it from doing bad ones. *[7]* And if he knows these things, he will also know what is other than these, because he will know everything. For the same things are the elements of everything, and he will do the needful in relation to everything, if the necessity arises [?][102] *[8]* After all, if someone knows how to play the flute, he will always be able to play, if the necessity for this arises.

[9] A man who knows how to conduct a law-case must have a correct knowledge of what is just; because it is with this that law-cases are concerned. And if he knows this, he will know what is opposite to it, and the things that differ from both of these. *[10]* And he must also know all the laws. However, if he does not have knowledge of the subject-matter (*ta pragmata*), he will not understand the laws. *[11]* For it is the same man who understands the 'law'[103] in music who understands music, and he who does not understand music, does not understand its law either.

[12] In the case of someone who knows the truth of things,

the argument follows readily that he knows everything; [13] and so he is able <also to engage in> brief <question-and-answer discussion> on any subject, <if ever>[104] he is required to answer questions; so he necessarily knows everything.[105]

(ix) <*In Praise of Memory*>[106]

[1] The greatest and finest discovery that has been developed, and the most useful for all purposes, both for technical expertise (*sophia*) and for life in general, is memory (*mnâmâ*). [2] The first step is this: if you focus your mind, advancing by this means, your consciousness (*gnômâ*) will perceive more acutely. [3] The second thing is that you must say over [a name] whenever you hear it; for it is by many times hearing and saying the same things that what you have learned generally commits itself to the memory. [4] Thirdly, whatever[107] you hear, make sure to connect it up with something you know: for example, you have to remember the name Chrysippus – connect it in your mind with *khrysos* ('gold') and *hippos* ('horse')[108]; [5] or again: Pyrilampes – connect it in your mind with *pyr* ('fire') and *lampein* ('shining'). These examples for names;[109] [6] for things (*pragmata*), you may proceed as follows: if you want to remember courage, connect it with Ares and Achilles; if metal-working, Hephaestus; if cowardice, Epeius . . .[110]

Appendix: A Conspectus of Sources

It may be useful, over and above what has been said about the main sources for the sophists, to append brief notes about the chief later sources drawn on in this volume. We give here only brief biographical notes. More detail will be available in any Classical dictionary.

Aelianus, Claudius (Aelian), c. AD 170–235. Taught rhetoric at Rome, but later turned to writing. Author of a miscellany of 'facts' and anecdotes about animals, *De Natura Animalium (On the Nature of Animals)*, and another on human life and history, *Varia Historia (Historical Miscellany)*.

Aetius, a doxographer of the first or second century AD, whose work is preserved in Stobaeus.

Athenaeus of Naucratis (in Egypt), fl.* c. AD 200. Composed a vast miscellany of information on every conceivable subject, in fifteen books, in the form of an interminable dinner-party conversation, entitled *Deipnosophistae* (or *Doctors at Dinner*) including various anecdotes about the leading sophists.

Cicero, Marcus Tullius, 106–43 BC, distinguished Roman orator and statesman, whose works on rhetoric contain much information on the early sophists, in particular Gorgias.

Clement of Alexandria (Titus Flavius Clemens) c. AD 150–215, a convert to Christianity, who became the first real Christian philosopher. He preserves details about the sophists in particular in the eight books of his *Stromateis* (or *Miscellanies*) in which he compares Greek to Christian thought, to the disadvantage of the former.

Diogenes Laertius, fl. early third century AD, author of *Lives of the Philosophers*, a compendium on the lives and doctrines of the ancient philosophers from Thales to Epicurus. The only sophist he includes in

---

* The abbreviation 'fl.' stands for 'floruit', a rather vague estimate characteristic of ancient biographical notices, indicating that the subject was 'flourishing', or at the peak of their powers, at that time.

the collection is Protagoras, since he regards him as a philosopher, but he provides many incidental details about others.

Dionysius of Halicarnassus, fl. *c.*30 BC, rhetorician and historian, who taught at Rome for many years. In various rhetorical works he includes many reflections on the style of various of the sophists.

Galen of Pergamum, AD 129–*c.*200, doctor and philosopher. In his numerous writings on medicine and philosophy he makes various references to the sophists.

Harpocration, Valerius, late first century AD, lexicographer. Preserves details of rare or interesting words used by various sophists.

Hermogenes of Tarsus, second century AD, writer on rhetoric. Gives an account of Antiphon of Rhamnus.

Pausanias, fl. *c.* AD 150, Greek geographer and travel writer, who wrote a *Guide to Greece*, and mentions various sophists in the course of describing the sites that he visits.

Philodemus of Gadara, first century BC, Epicurean philosopher, many of whose works have been recovered from the ruins of Herculaneum, where he was 'house philosopher' to a Roman nobleman. He mentions various of the sophists in his works on rhetoric.

Philostratus, Flavius, fl. *c.* AD 200, historian of the so-called 'Second Sophistic' movement. In his *Lives of the Sophists* he includes biographies also of the older sophists.

Phrynichus of Bithynia, late second century AD, Atticist rhetorician and lexicographer. Compiled a lexicon of 'Attic' words in thirty-seven books (only surviving in abridged form), which includes many references to sophistic usages.

Plutarch of Chaeroneia, *c.* AD 45–120, historian, philosopher and man of letters. Makes frequent mention of various of the sophists both in his *Parallel Lives* and in his *Moral Essays*.

Proclus of Lycia, 412–485 BC, Neoplatonic philosopher, who makes occasional mention of one or other of the sophists in the course of his commentaries on Plato.

Scholia are ancient notes preserved in the manuscripts of many Classical authors, often relaying valuable information, usually deriving from lost commentaries by Hellenistic scholars.

Sextus Empiricus, fl. late second century AD, physician and Sceptical philosopher. In his *Outlines of Pyrrhonism* and *Against the Mathematicians*, he preserves much information about the sophists – most notably, perhaps, a version of Gorgias' treatise *On Not-Being* (also preserved in the pseudo-Aristotelian treatise *On Melissus, Xenophanes, Gorgias*).

Stobaeus, Johannes, fl. early fifth century AD, author of an *Anthology* of poets and prose-writers, arranged by subject-matter, which includes notices concerning various sophists. He includes material from earlier doxographic collections, notably that of Aetius (valuable in particular for details of Antiphon's *On Truth*).

Suda, The (Suidas) is the name of a Byzantine lexicon, composed probably late in the tenth century AD, which contains many biographical notices of sophists.

Notes

INTRODUCTION

1. 100 drachmae to the mina. The reckoning of £10/$16 to a drachma is actually very conservative, a drachma being a good day's pay for a skilled workman in fifth-century BC Athens, but the cost of basic commodities was low, while that of luxuries (such as sophistic lecture courses) was very high, which makes realistic calculations difficult.

2. The way in which the sophists charged their clients for providing them with 'wisdom' is one aspect of their profession which Socrates finds particularly objectionable. Socrates, of course, never charged a fee for his philosophical discussions and he often draws attention to this distinction between himself and the sophists: see e.g. *Apology* 19D.

3. Thucydides was of course much influenced in his style by Gorgias, especially in the speeches, and may have studied also with Antiphon.

4. Quoted by Plato, at *Gorgias* 484B.

5. An alternative view of Antiphon would be that he is taking up a neutral, 'objective' position, merely observing the contradictions between *physis* and *nomos*. In that case, he would constitute a third point of view, between the two others.

6. These topics arise, in surviving sources, mainly in the context of speculations about the origins of human society, as in Protagoras, ch. 1, §18, but also in such a work as the *Truth* of Antiphon, ch. 5, §22.

7. The issue of whether the 'virtues', or proper excellences (*aretē*), of men and women are distinct or the same is raised, not in a sophistic source, but rather in Plato's *Republic*, where, however, it may reflect a real line of argument by the historical Socrates. But the fact that the whole issue, along with the notion of

communism with regard to property (including women), is satirized by Aristophanes in the *Women in Assembly*, which certainly antedates the *Republic*, being a product of the late 390s, indicates that it was an established sophistic topic.

8. The unnaturalness of slavery is actually only raised, in surviving sources, by the younger sophist Alcidamas, in a speech delivered around 366 BC (ch. 9, §19), but certain disapproving remarks from Aristotle in the *Politics* (I, 1253b20ff.) indicate that it was a recognized topic: 'There are others, however, who regard the control of slaves by a master as contrary to nature. In their view, the distinction of master and slave is due to law or convention; there is no natural difference between them.'

9. This issue is raised by Antiphon in *Truth* (ch. 5, §22), as an example of situations where convention is at variance with nature.

10. Such as H. Gomperz, *Sophistik und Rhetorik*, Leipzig and Berlin, 1912.

11. C. C. W. Taylor, *Protagoras*, Oxford: Oxford University Press, 1976; Terence Irwin, *Gorgias*, Oxford: Oxford University Press, 1979; Robin Waterfield, *Plato: Early Socratic Dialogues*, Harmondsworth: Penguin, 1987.

12. B. Jowett, *The Dialogues of Plato*, 4th edn, Oxford: Oxford University Press, 1953; W. K. C. Guthrie, *Protagoras and Meno*, Harmondsworth: Penguin, 1956; W. D. Woodhead, *Gorgias*, Edinburgh: Nelson, 1953; W. H. D. Rouse, *Euthydemus*, Princeton: Princeton Univeristy Press, 1961; R. Waterfield, *Xenophon: Conversations with Socrates*, Harmondsworth: Penguin, 1990.

1 PROTAGORAS OF ABDERA

1. We omit some irrelevant material, indicated by ellipses.

2. This Artemon is reported elsewhere (by the lexicographer Hesychius) as having been a porter by trade, and this is pretty certainly a malicious falsehood, perhaps emanating from a comic poet (see the story about Protagoras as a porter below). The more reliable sources give his father as Maeandrius.

3. This would be the chronographer Apollodorus of Athens (fl. *c.*140 BC). He composed, among many other works, *Chronika*, in iambic trimeters, covering the history of the world from the fall of Troy (1184 BC) to his own time (144 BC).

4. Dinon of Colophon, a historian of the fourth century BC. His work is now lost.

5. His name is of interest, as being formed from the name of the

Maeander River, which flows into the sea on the coast of Asia Minor a little south of Teos, the city from which Abdera was colonized around the middle of the sixth century, probably not long before Maeandrius' birth.

6. The verb used by Diogenes here, *synerôtaô*, means 'propound arguments in question form'. The precise significance of this is not clear.

7. We must assume that Diogenes means this. He says only 'he began in this manner'. The book in question will be that entitled *Truth*, or *The Overthrowing Arguments* (*Kataballontes*).

8. This is a reference to *Theaetetus* 152Aff, where Plato is drawing somewhat tendentious conclusions from the dictum of Protagoras just quoted. It is not impossible that Protagoras held this view of the soul, but it is not a necessary inference from the above dictum. Similarly, that 'everything is true', or 'all opinions are true', could be regarded as following from Protagoras' stated position, but Protagoras himself may not have drawn this inference.

9. This could also mean (and probably does mean): 'He was the first to charge a fee: one hundred minae' – a vast sum, about £100,000 or $160,000 at 2003 prices, if we reckon the real value of a drachma at roughly £10 (100 dr. = 1 mina). But this sum, for a full course, is attested also for other sophists (cf. Plato *Alcibiades* I 119A; *Hippias Major*, 282E), so it probably should be accepted. There were quite a number in Athens, such as Callias, son of Hipponicus, who could afford such sums. This would have been a maximum charge, however. One could have shorter courses for a mina.

10. Diogenes says 'the parts of time', which could mean various things; the broad consensus of scholars, however, is that this is what is meant, and it serves to identify Protagoras as substantially the father of Greek grammar.

11. Presumably in the context of forensic oratory. Cf. the report of Philostratus about Gorgias, in ch. 2, §2 below.

12. This is presumably the sense of the distinction made here between *dianoia* and *onoma*. It would seem to prefigure the sort of eristic rhetoric practised by the sophists Euthydemus and Dionysodorus in Plato's *Euthydemus*. See ch. 8 below.

13. An interesting aside. Is Diogenes speaking of his own time (*c.* AD 200), or is he repeating this complaint from some source?

14. Fr. 47 Diels.

15. The sense of *epimeiktos* here is less than clear, but it is unlikely to be complimentary. It can also mean 'mixed' (as of salads, or

metres), or 'all-purpose'. It might also mean 'ready to mix it up' (i.e. in a fight).

16. Again, what the sense of *Sokratikon eidos* may be here is obscure. Precisely the distinction between Socrates and the sophists, or 'eristics', is presented to us by Plato as lying in his concentration on the *dianoia* rather than the *onoma* (see above, n. 8). Is this an anti-Platonic remark, or is the point simply that Protagoras indulged in question and answer? But that has already been said, surely.

17. 286C. See below, §13.

18. This report sits uneasily with the very next remark and with the tradition that Protagoras maintained that he could present two opposed *logoi* on any subject (he actually composed a work called *Antilogiai*, or *Opposed Arguments*). See below, §14.

19. This must be the sense of *epicheireseis pros tas theseis*, and it inevitably implies the possibility of contradiction.

20. Not otherwise known.

21. Fr. 63 Rose. Not much else is known about this treatise. The story of Protagoras' origins as a porter would be easier to dismiss if it were not apparently attested to by Aristotle. As for Epicurus, his remarks on his predecessors are uniformly malicious, but even he must have had some pretext for his allegations. All one can say is that there is nothing inherently impossible about the story, though its improbability is increased by the circumstance that Democritus is generally taken to be at least twenty years younger than Protagoras. Hermann Diels, however, in a note on this passage in *Die Fragmente der Vorsokratiker* (II, p. 254), makes the attractive suggestion that this story may derive from an example adduced by Protagoras himself in some work, showing how good argumentation is like the efficient tying-together of bundles of sticks by a porter. This would indeed be characteristic of the way such stories find their way into ancient biographies.

22. In a letter *On Occupations*, referred to more extensively by Athenaeus in his *Doctors at Dinner*, 354b-c (Fr. 172 Usener). Epicurus also alleged in that letter that Democritus took on Protagoras as his secretary (*grapheus*), and that he went on from that to become a village schoolteacher, before taking up the profession of sophist. See below, §19.

23. The extra three categories, narration, report and invitation, may come from a rhetorical, rather than a purely grammatical, context.

24. This seems to amount to a claim that Protagoras was the first to identify the moods of the verb: optative, indicative (covering question and answer – unless 'question' conceals a reference to

the subjunctive) and imperative. It certainly indicates an interest in grammatical theory.

25. This report may contain some element of fact. Apart from Euripides, the persons concerned are unknown, which actually lends likelihood to the story.

26. This would be for impiety, in connection with the public reading of the book *On the Gods*. It is possible, however, that Pythodorus simply denounced him in the Assembly. This detail at least lends credence to the idea that *something* untoward happened to Protagoras in consequence of his irreverent views on the gods.

27. This is no doubt a confusion, since Euathlus figures in the other law-suit mentioned below. It is to that trial to which Aristotle will have referred, possibly in his lost dialogue, *The Sophist*.

28. This list is certainly incomplete. We have evidence from elsewhere (Porphyry, *ap.* Eusebius, *Praeparatio Evangelica* X 3, 25 = 80B2) of a work *On Being*, in which Protagoras seems to have brought various arguments against Parmenides' doctrine that Being is one. And then there is the so-called *Great Speech* (*Megas Logos*), mentioned in the *Anecdota Parisiensia* (= 80B3), which may bear some relation to the 'great speech' of Protagoras presented by Plato in the *Protagoras* (below, §18).

29. This title sounds odd, but it seems to be referred to in a passage of Plato's *Sophist*, 232DE = §26 below.

30. This may well have contained his views on the origins of human society, of which, as we shall see, we may possibly see reflections in such a work as Book I of Diodorus of Sicily's *Universal History*, as well as in Plato's presentation of his political philosophy in the *Protagoras* (see below, §18).

31. *Prostaktikos* – this should mean something like *protreptikos*, i.e. an exhortation to live correctly, but we cannot be sure.

32. This may relate to the anecdote told just below, about his dispute with his pupil Euathlus (whom Aristotle is reported just above to have identified as his 'accuser').

33. Mario Untersteiner, in *I Sofisti* (ch. 3), puts forward the rather speculative hypothesis that all or most of the preceding titles are no more than section-headings of the *Antilogiai*, but there is no real evidence for this.

34. Plainly this list, apart from its other oddities, is incomplete, since it fails to mention his most famous work, *On the Gods*. Nor is there any mention of the treatise called *Truth*, which began, 'Man is the measure of all things . . .'

35. This is, of course, the *Protagoras*, of which extracts are printed

below (§§11, 18, 24, 25). Protagoras also features, to his disadvantage, in the *Theaetetus* (see below, §§7, 8).

36. The Atthidographer (c.345–260 BC). Presumably he listed this under the relevant year, but it seems odd that he quoted Euripides as evidence.

37. *Kata tên hodon* may imply a *land* journey, which would differentiate this from Philochorus' account.

38. Apollodorus of Athens. See n. 3 above.

39. I.e. 444–441 BC. 'Flourishing' is often a matter of having attained the age of forty, though this may be connected with his being invited by Pericles to make laws for Thurii. In fact, on the best calculations of his birth, he would have been in his early to mid-forties.

40. Of this anecdote we have a possible reflection in Plato, *Protagoras* 328B. See below, §18c. It is told in a fuller and clearer form in Aulus Gellius, *Attic Nights*, V 10.

41. Philostratus seems to be confused here. This story is told by Diogenes Laertius (*Lives of the Philosophers* IX 34), and by others, not of Protagoras' father, but of that of Democritus. He cannot, then, presumably, have derived this from his source, if that source was Dinon.

42. Philostratus says *pasês gês*, which could mean 'from every land', or 'from the whole earth', but what he presumably means is 'from all territory controlled by them'. Again, this is a hyperbolic version of the story reported in Diogenes Laertius.

43. This seems to be a rhetorical amplification of the not improbable report that he was drowned on a voyage to Sicily.

44. A shrewd comment by Philostratus, himself a professional sophist.

45. This seems to be the meaning of *mythos* here, this being a reference to the dialogue *Protagoras*.

46. *Logoi eristikoi.*

47. I.e. 'argument', or 'speech'. A parallel version of this dictionary entry in the late Byzantine encyclopedia, the *Suda*, gives this nickname as *logos emmisthos*, 'Argument for Sale', which makes rather better sense.

48. Isocrates (436–338 BC) is elsewhere attested to have been a pupil rather of Gorgias and of Prodicus, which is more probable chronologically; as for Prodicus, he was about twenty-five years younger than Protagoras, and could have learned from him, but he is not elsewhere attested as having been his pupil (except by the *Suda*, which is not independent of Hesychius).

49. This is almost certainly wrong, being probably a confused reflection of Apollodorus' calculation that he died at the age of *seventy*, having been a sophist for forty years. See above, §1. The Greek numerals for seventy and ninety are not very different.

50. The Greek term *aretê* denotes either 'virtue' (i.e. moral excellence) or 'excellence' in general. In this particular context, the general term is needed, although, as the passage continues, *aretê* will be translated with its specific moral sense, 'virtue'.

51. Sc. the young Thessalian aristocrat Meno, who is visiting Athens. Socrates is pretending to consult the politician Anytus as to whom Meno should apply to in order to be trained to excel in household management, and in social and political graces.

52. On the question of Protagoras' fees, see above, §1, and below, §18c.

53. This would seem to give the lie to stories of his being prosecuted and banished. Even if Plato allowed Socrates to gloss over such an unpalatable fact, one would expect him to make Anytus allude to it. See also Plato, *Hippias Major*, 282B–E, quoted below (pp. 122–3) in connection with Hippias, for evidence of Protagoras in Sicily.

54. This is a puzzling remark, since Protagoras is generally regarded as the first of the sophists, in so far as charging fees for teaching excellence is concerned.

55. This topic of debate is not by any means as silly as it might seem at first sight. The issue is that of causality and responsibility, and a prelude to much subsequent philosophical discussion. We may also note that in Athenian law an inanimate object that had caused an accident could be prosecuted for murder, as being liable to pollution. The fifth-century orator Antiphon actually makes a similar case the subject of his second Tetralogy (below, ch. 5, pp. 183–92).

56. They both died of the plague, in 429 (cf. Plutarch, *Life of Pericles* ch. 36).

57. The quotation appears to end here, but what follows may be a paraphrase of what Protagoras said.

58. An adaptation of Homer, *Iliad* 2, 273.

59. That is, 'the overthrowing arguments' (*hoi kataballontes [logoi]*) – a metaphor from wrestling. It would seem from this alternative title that the treatise had a fairly practical, rather than abstractly metaphysical, purpose, the general principle enunciated at the beginning being just a prelude to a series of demonstrations of contradictory arguments.

60. The Greek is ambiguous, as between 'any given man' and the human race as a whole, but Protagoras no doubt intends the former, since the example of the wind, which is presumably Protagoras' own, requires that each individual be an independent 'measure' of the temperature, or 'quality', of the wind.

61. Protagoras would not have felt that his argument was affected by the reading on a thermometer (which in any case the Greeks did not have); your or my personal sensation of cold or heat cannot be measured by a thermometer.

62. It was Theaetetus' earlier suggestion that 'perception is knowledge' (151d) which allowed Socrates to introduce Protagoras' thesis about appearance and reality. Thus, his identification of 'appearance' with 'perception' here is necessary if he is to claim that Theaetetus' suggestion and Protagoras' theory are essentially the same.

63. An ironic reference to the title of Protagoras' book *Alêtheia* (*Truth*).

64. We include here Socrates' ironic account of Protagoras' secret doctrine, though it is probably an extrapolation of Plato's, since it imputes to Protagoras an 'Heraclitean' physical doctrine which is then regularly attributed to him by later authorities. It is not necessary that he advanced any such doctrine, though it is certainly compatible with his position, and Plato doubtless felt that Protagoras was committed by his position to some such theory.

65. More naturally here we might expect such a sentence to read that 'things are and appear to be *in a certain way* . . .', rather than having simply 'certain things are and appear to be' stated by itself. However, the strangeness of the language, both here and in the sentences which follow, might be seen to emphasize what is, for Plato, the strangeness of Protagoras' view that something just *is* exactly how it appears to each individual.

66. Plato's Protagoras, both here and below, uses simply one or other of the comparatives of the basic positive value word *agathos*, 'good' (*ameinô*, *beltiô*), though without any objectivist implications. For him, the term can only mean something like 'more advantageous', 'more socially acceptable'.

67. Sextus also quotes the famous opening line of the treatise, to which he gives the title of *The Overthrowers* (*Hoi Kataballontes*), in *Against the Mathematicians* VII 60 (= 80B1), claiming Protagoras as 'one of those philosophers who abolish the criterion (of truth)'.

68. *Kritêrion* was the technical term, in Hellenistic philosophy, for

the instrument, organ or faculty which judged the truth-value of
objects or states of affairs.

69. The distinction between *khrêmata*, 'things', and *pragmata* is not
very clear, but *ta pragmata* can also mean 'reality', including
states of affairs, and so is a rather broader term. Also, *khrêmata*,
in the sense of 'things' (as opposed to 'money', its more specialized
meaning), would be somewhat archaic by Sextus' time.

70. This is a technical term of later Greek philosophy, both Stoic and
Platonist, denoting the formal principles of things as they appear
in matter. It is, to say the least, highly unlikely that Protagoras
expressed himself in these terms. For one thing, he cannot have
employed the term 'matter', since that was only developed first in
its technical sense by Aristotle.

71. That is, adherents of Scepticism such as Sextus.

72. This is not quite adequate, however, as a rebuttal of the *peritropê*
argument (see next passage), since the opponent by definition does
not accept Protagoras' position that this *is* only 'what appears to
him'; but Protagoras may have thought that it did. The question
still excites controversy.

73. We cannot be sure that Protagoras himself adduced these
examples, but he may well have done. Certainly, the example of
the impressions of madmen figures in §5 of the *Double Arguments*, a document which in other respects seems to owe much to
Protagoras (see below, ch. 10).

74. This is an intriguing figure, known only to us from various
references in Sextus' works (from *Against the Mathematicians*
VII 53 we learn that he was criticized by the Atomist philosopher
Democritus, so he is probably Sextus' source). He will have been
a contemporary of Protagoras; whether he should be regarded as
a sophist or a philosopher is not quite clear, but Diels included
him among the latter (81 Diels-Kranz).

75. Democritus wrote treatises *On Intellect* and *On the Senses* (Diogenes Laertius *Lives of the Philosophers* IX 47), in either of which
he may have criticized Protagoras (and Xeniades).

76. E.g. *Theaetetus* 170E–171A: 'And what is the consequence for
Protagoras himself? Is it not this: supposing that not even he
believed in man being the measure and the world in general did
not believe it either – as in fact it doesn't – then this Truth which
he wrote would not be true for anyone? If, on the other hand, he
did believe it, but the mass of mankind did not agree with him,
then, you see, it is more false than true by just so much as the
unbelievers outnumber the believers.'

77. It bears an interesting resemblance also to various utterances of Heraclitus, e.g. Fr. 9 Diels-Kranz: 'Donkeys would choose rubbish rather than gold'; or Fr. 61: 'the sea is both the purest and most disgusting of water, for fish drinkable and preservative, for men undrinkable and destructive'. But if it comes to that, Protagoras could well have been acquainted with the sayings of Heraclitus.

78. Sc. that the same thing can both be and not be, or be judged both to be and not to be – the denial of the law of contradiction – which he has been engaged in refuting.

79. Or 'that contradiction is possible'.

80. Or 'state of affairs' (*pragma*).

81. The definite article here implies that there is only one *logos* proper to each *pragma*, an assumption essential to the argument.

82. The reference here is mysterious. It cannot refer to Antisthenes (see below), since he was younger than Protagoras.

83. I.e. once again, the denial of the law of contradiction.

84. The first sentence of it is also quoted by Eusebius, *Praeparatio Evangelica* XIV 3, 7 (= 80B4).

85. See e.g. the comments of Philostratus, §2 above.

86. Sc. demonstrate that virtue can be taught, which is a proposition on which Socrates has just expressed his doubt.

87. One topic which runs both explicitly and implicitly through the *Protagoras* is the question of what constitutes proper philosophical discussion and argument. In view of this it is interesting that Protagoras explicitly draws a distinction between argument (*logos*) and myth (*mythos*), and then chooses the latter because it is 'more agreeable'. His distinction may lead us to wonder what constitutes the difference between these two methods (before we jump to the conclusion that Plato necessarily sees 'argument' (*logos*) as more worthwhile, we should remember that it is Plato who has chosen to devote a large section of a *philosophical* dialogue to the mythical account given in Protagoras' speech). Furthermore, the fact that Protagoras' decision is based not on what will provide the clearest, truest or most philosophically legitimate account, but on 'agreeableness', could also be seen to imply that for the sophists all other factors are secondary to their desire to please their audience.

88. This mention of gods has been thought to be an un-Protagorean feature, in view of his well-known scepticism as to their existence; but such critics need to remind themselves that this is a myth. If he had opted for argument (*logos*), rather than myth (*mythos*),

he may well have made his points without mentioning either the gods or mythical characters such as Prometheus and Epimetheus. In fact, in a later section of the speech (324eff.), after he claims to have switched from myth to argument, there is no further mention of the divine or mythical.

89. The pair of Prometheus and Epimetheus, that is to say, personified 'Forethought' and his improvident brother 'Afterthought', are borrowed from Hesiod's *Works and Days*, 69–89, where they figure in the story of Pandora. For Prometheus as bestower of characteristics and benefits on the human race, however, the closest analogy is the (probably pseudo-) Aeschylean *Prometheus Bound* (cf. esp. 11, 436–506), which is widely recognized to exhibit sophistic influence.

90. The reference here is obscure, in particular the mention of Epimetheus, which may be a later insertion in the text.

91. This is a rather curious remark, and might be thought less 'Protagorean' than the rest of the text, but it may only be a reference to Prometheus' stealing for man of the 'technical expertise' (*entekhnos sophia*) of Hephaestus and Athena, which would confer a certain kinship with divinity. Certainly there is no suggestion elsewhere in the myth of kinship between god and man.

92. *Politikê tekhnê*: one could say, 'the art of administering city-states' (*poleis*).

93. The *polis*, or 'city-state', was the highest form of political unit recognized by the Greeks; it is not simply a city in our sense.

94. The term *aidôs* is difficult to render. It can mean, generically, 'shame', but more specifically, reverence towards the gods, and mutual respect between men (insofar as this early Greek conception of shame refers far more to the idea of being shamed before one's fellows than to the more internal emotion which we now associate with shame). It is a more archaic term for what was later termed, not least by Plato himself, *sôphrosynê*, 'sound-mindedness', and may well have been the word used by Protagoras himself.

95. This is the core of Protagoras' political doctrine, and it constitutes a defence of the Athenian democratic ideology, with which Plato himself had little sympathy.

96. Socrates has raised this problem just previously, at 319B–C.

97. Now we have the later, more properly Platonic term, *sôphrosynê*.

98. Up to this point, we have been translating *aretê* as 'excellence', since it has referred to aptitude in all types of technical skill. From this point on, however, it makes sense to take it in its more

restricted moral sense as 'virtue', since it is these kinds of moral excellence on which the discussion now focuses.

99. There might appear to be some degree of conceptual confusion behind this rhetorical point. Is the man concerned admitting to being totally lacking in a sense of justice, or just to being deficient in that regard? If the former, then how does this square with Protagoras' claim that a sense of justice has been bestowed by Zeus on all men? In reply, one may point out (a) that Protagoras does allow for a small number of moral defectives (who must be excluded from participation in civic life), and this does not compromise his general position; and (b) that even to admit that one is deficient in justice, one must have some concept of what justice is, so that probably only a *comparative* deficiency in justice is what is envisaged as being admitted to here.

100. As Protagoras moves from the mythical to the actual, his language displays more and more characteristic features of sophistic rhetoric, such as carefully balanced lists and pairs, or rhetorical questions.

101. This sequence of characteristics (*epimeleia, askêsis, didakhê*) bears some resemblance, which may be significant, to the factors which Protagoras is said to have declared in his *Great Speech* (*Megas Logos*) to be necessary for teaching to be successful (80B3 = § 19 below).

102. This is rather oddly phrased, as he would appear to have abandoned myth back at 322D. Perhaps, though, 322D–324C is to be seen as a sort of exegesis of the myth.

103. *Khrêsimoi*, literally 'useful', a key Protagorean term. All this praise of the virtues of musical education, as in the case of that of gymnastics below, is very much in accord with Plato's own prescriptions in the *Republic* (Book III) and the *Laws* (Books II and VII), but applying it to actual Athenian practice is quite un-Platonic.

104. *Euthynai*, the technical term for the public examination, or audit, which every official in Athens had to undergo at the end of his term of office.

105. *Paideia* is education in the broadest sense, including moral and social conditioning, such as Protagoras has been describing.

106. This play, *The Savages*, was produced at the Lenaea of 420, so this is a glaring anachronism, and perhaps a deliberate one, since the dramatic date of the dialogue is around 433 BC. It is not impossible, of course, that Protagoras himself used this example in some essay or oration composed in 419 – though that would be very near the date of his probable death.

107. Two real-life bad hats, of whom we know nothing further.

108. This presumably reflects a real 'money back guarantee' that Protagoras offered. It may be related to the notorious tale of his court case with his pupil Euathlus, cf. §1 and n. 38 above.

109. The sons of Pericles.

110. In his letter *On Occupations* Fr. 172 Usener. Cf. n. 22 above.

111. In fact, Diels-Kranz have chosen to include it among the testimonia to Protagoras, as 80A26.

112. For Thrasymachus, see ch. 6 below.

113. That is to say, fees. Socrates is being highly ironic.

114. Literally, 'depositions of witnesses'.

115. *Fl. c.*430 BC. A younger contemporary of Thrasymachus – with whom, and the Sicilian Teisias, Aristotle couples him (*Sophistici Elenchi* 183b32) as one of the most important contributors to the development of rhetoric. Cf. also Aristotle *Rhetoric* III 1414b7ff., where others of his devices are mentioned.

116. A sophist and poet of the late fifth century, mentioned also by Plato in the *Apology* (20B), and the *Phaedo* (60D). In the former passage he is asserted to charge five minae for his course in rhetoric; in the latter we hear of him inquiring after Socrates' efforts at composing poetry in prison – plainly as a fellow-practitioner.

117. A pupil of Corax, generally regarded as the founder of 'scientific' rhetorical theory, and teacher of Gorgias of Leontini.

118. These balanced and antithetical short clauses, which verge on paradox, are typical of Gorgianic style, and a good example of the way in which Plato engages in stylistic parody of his predecessors.

119. A pupil of Gorgias, also a Sicilian, who figures prominently in Plato's *Gorgias*.

120. Licymnius of Chios was a rhetorician and dithyrambic poet of the late fifth century. He is mentioned by Aristotle in the *Rhetoric* (1413b14; 1414b17), in the latter passage as indulging in futile distinctions.

121. If this is really the title of a work by Protagoras, it does not figure in the list provided by Diogenes Laertius, but it could be the work in which he did such things as distinguish the tenses of the verb, and the parts of speech, as mentioned in §1 above.

122. It is not quite clear how far the reference back is intended to go, but presumably at least to the *gnōmologia* and *eikonologia*.

123. Thrasymachus again.

124. Aristotle, and presumably Protagoras, use, as a term for 'neuter', *skeuē* – 'objects', 'things'.

125. Feminine participles.

126. Both these nouns are grammatically feminine, so what Protagoras must be claiming is that they are somehow *naturally* masculine, by virtue of their subject matter. A comic reflection of this concern for correctness of gender may be discerned in Aristophanes' *Clouds*, ll. 658ff., where Socrates is teaching the ignorant Strepsiades that the feminine of 'cock' (*alektryôn*) should really be 'cockess' (*alektryaina*), and that 'kneading-trough' (*kardopos*) is *naturally* masculine (it is *grammatically* feminine).

127. As, of course, does Homer at the beginning of the *Iliad* (1, 2).

128. The normal meaning of this phrase in later authors is 'figures of speech', but Aristotle is using it here more in the sense of 'manner of speaking'.

129. The translation 'excellence' rather than 'virtue' is better suited to the present context.

130. Lived *c*.650–570 BC; statesman and sage; ruler of Mytilene on Lesbos around the beginning of the sixth century; counted as one of the Seven Sages of Greece.

131. Hippias of Elis (see ch. 4, below), who was also present at this gathering of sophists, and who laid great stress, as we shall see, on mastery of the 'arts'.

132. This seems to be the meaning of *genesis te kai phthora* in the context.

133. This is presumably the source of Diogenes Laertius' assertion that he wrote a treatise *On Wrestling*; see above, §1.

134. *Kanôn*, i.e. a physical straight line.

135. This is not in the Greek, but implied by the sense.

136. In his Commentary on the Psalms, published in M. Gronewald (ed.), *Didymos der Blinde, Psalmenkommentar* (Tura-Papyrus), Teil III: Komm. zu Ps., 29–34, Bonn, 1969, p. 380.

137. The fact, for example, that *adêlon* ('unclear') is a technical term of Stoic and Epicurean philosophy certainly does not preclude Protagoras from having used it in a rather less technical sense two centuries earlier. It is a perfectly normal Greek word.

2 GORGIAS OF LEONTINI

1. We take this work to be essentially a philosophical spoof, which is not to say that some serious points cannot be derived from it. There are some, however, it must be said, who take it more seriously.

2. Or alternatively, according to Pausanias and Pliny (see below, §§9–10), he dedicated it to himself. This rather curious gesture

was presumably a form of self-advertisement, but it also betokens a considerable degree of prior success. Gorgias, like Protagoras, is reported to have charged as much as 100 minae for a course, an enormous sum (see below, §§3 and 5).

3. If we may emend the impossible LXX (Olympiad 70) of Pliny, *Natural History* 33.83 (cf. §10 below) to LXXXX (Olympiad 90).

4. A reference back to p. 482 (below, §2), where Philostratus gives it as his opinion that Gorgias was the founder of extempore oratory (*skhedios logos*).

5. Initially in 427 BC.

6. Quoted from Aristophanes, *Thesmophoriazusae*, 49.

7. I.e. of Apollo at Delphi.

8. This is a theme taken up in the next century by his pupil Isocrates, e.g. in his *Panegyricus*, and it may possibly find an echo in certain remarks Plato grants to Socrates in *Republic* V 469Bff. regarding the war of Greek against Greek as a kind of 'civil war', which should be pursued differently from war against barbarians. The speech at Olympia was presumably delivered at some games during the Peloponnesian War (probably 420 BC), which would add to its point.

9. Philostratus thus presents him as establishing his tradition of rhetoric, in mainland Greece at least, only in his old age, when he moved to Thessaly. In this he may be influenced by Plato's remarks at the beginning of the *Meno* (70B), quoted below, §16.

10. This was in 330, after the crushing defeat of his attempt to indict Ctesiphon for voting a gold crown to Demosthenes for his services to the state.

11. The *kairos* is literally 'the right moment', but it is used here in a rhetorical context as the term for improvisation.

12. This story will be dealt with again below, under Prodicus (pp. 111–16), but it is worth bringing in here, as giving some indication of the relations between the great sophists.

13. It is not clear that Philostratus is right about this. At the beginning of Plato's *Gorgias* (cf. below, §17), Socrates' follower Chaerephon is represented as claiming to be a friend of Gorgias. It is quite possible, in fact, to see the present anecdote as good-humoured banter, rather than evidence of begrudgery; so we need not, in all probability, postulate more than one Chaerephon.

14. He is playing upon two senses of the Greek verb *physaô*, which can mean 'inflate' or 'blow'.

15. Again, there is play on two meanings of the word *narthêx*, 'fennel stalk', which can be used either as a receptacle in which to carry

fire, and presumably also to blow through, as a kind of bellows, or as a schoolmaster's rod, to beat erring schoolboys. Also, the last phrase, *epi tous toioutous*, is deliberately ambiguous, as between 'for such purposes' and 'to deal with such people (as you)'. 'Presumably this anecdote is intended to illustrate Gorgias' readiness at repartee, which would be an aspect of *autoskhediazein*, or improvisation.

16. The oldest known one being the third-century BC Peripatetic biographer Satyrus (*ap.* Diogenes Laertius, cf. §4 below), who reports Gorgias as claiming to have been present when Empedocles performed an act of magic – reasonably conclusive proof, if reliable.

17. On Alcidamas, see ch. 9 below. He stoutly upholds the Gorgianic tradition of improvisation in his polemical discourse *Against the Sophists, or Those who Compose Written Speeches*, aimed primarily at Isocrates.

18. This is certainly correct if we suppose that Porphyry was intending to give the date of his birth, rather than of his 'flourishing'; if the latter, however, it is rather too early.

19. This seems a great deal of money, over twenty-five times the yearly salary of a skilled worker (about a drachma a day), but it is attested also for Protagoras (see above, p. 3), so it must be taken seriously. This, however, was presumably for a whole course, which could have lasted a year or more.

20. At least as being fellow Ionians.

21. A quotation from Plato, *Phaedrus* (238D), describing Socrates' ironic reference to his inspired state.

22. Licymnius of Chios (fl. *c.*410 BC), lyric poet and rhetorician, linked with Polus by Socrates in the *Phaedrus* (267C) in such a way as to make it seem that Polus learned some techniques from him: 'And what shall we say of Polus and his "shrines of learned speech" (*mouseia logôn*), such as duplication (*diplasiologia*) and the use of maxims (*gnômologia*) and of figures (*eikonologia*), and what of the names which Licymnius donated to him for the creation of beautiful diction (*euepeia*)?'

23. That is to say, in the composition of prose (cf. §28 below).

24. This is a sage remark on the part of Dionysius. It may well be that too much has been made of the seminal influence of Gorgias' visit on the growth of rhetoric in Athens, though it was doubtless a great boost to it.

25. Not a real district of Athens, but comic invention: 'Phanae' would have the connotation 'Informerville', or 'The Informeries', and

the waterclock (*klepsydra*) was the instrument by which speeches in court were measured (though there was a spring of that name on the north-west spur of the Acropolis).

26. This comic word (*englôttogastôr*) is a play on the words *kheirogastôr*, 'one who feeds his stomach (= earns his living) by his hands', and *engastrimythos*, 'ventriloquist' (literally 'in-stomach-talker'), and has the sense of something like 'one who earns his next meal by his tongue', with the connotation of deceiving to do it.

27. Again, a pun: *sykazô*, 'harvest figs', gives an echo of *sykophanteô*, 'be a sycophant, or vexatious prosecutor'.

28. This is a parodic reference to a feature of Greek ritual, according to which the tongue of the victim was cut out and offered to the god as a special item.

29. *En dikêi* can also mean 'justly'.

30. *Philippon ton Gorgiou* would normally mean 'Philip, son of Gorgias', but this cannot be literally true, since Gorgias was unmarried (cf. §15 below).

31. This is very curiously put. Who, one wonders, does Pausanias think of as the earlier masters of language? Homeric heroes such as Nestor and Odysseus, perhaps.

32. It seems highly unlikely that he came *with* Teisias, since Teisias was a Syracusan, and the point of the embassy was to ask for Athens' aid against Syracuse. But Teisias may conceivably have chosen to visit Athens at more or less the same time.

33. Polycrates was a fairly distinguished rhetorician, of whom we know the names of various speeches, but his most famous effort was an attack on Socrates, put into the mouth of his accuser at his trial in 399, Anytus. It is chiefly in response to this that Xenophon composed his *Memoirs of Socrates*.

34. This is the date of Socrates' birth, rather than of his 'flourishing' (approximate age forty), which is the date one would have expected in this context.

35. This, as it stands, is rubbish. Empedocles and Socrates had no connection whatever. Either there is a lacuna in the text (e.g. 'the teacher of Gorgias, <was younger than Parmenides, and> studied with him'), or Olympiodorus is profoundly confused. Victor Cousin proposed to read 'Parmenides' instead of 'him', which is reasonable, but does not entirely solve the textual problem.

36. This, again, is rubbish, the result of juxtaposing a birth-date for Socrates with a 'flourishing' date for Gorgias. In fact, Gorgias was the older by about ten years. Whether he really published the treatise *On Nature* in this year is debatable; it is suspiciously close

to the conventional date of 'flourishing' (i.e. forty). But at least it indicates that the work was considered to be a major achievement of his, from a philosophical perspective.

37. The figure 109, as opposed to 105 or 108, is supported by the chronographer Apollodorus (*Fragments of the Greek Historians* 244 F 33), and the *Suda* (above, §3).

38. Clearchus of Soli (*c.*340–250 BC), historian. He has been quoted by Athenaeus just above.

39. The mss. give the Greek figures for 80, but this is almost certainly a scribal error for the figures for 110, which are not dissimilar. Gorgias' (approximate) age was too well known for Clearchus to be so mistaken about it.

40. A Peripatetic philosopher of the first century BC, a friend of Cato the Younger.

41. Once again, a textual problem. The mss. have *heterou*, giving the meaning 'for the sake of another', which would be a recommendation of absolute selfishness, something in no way concordant with the tendency of the passage as a whole, which concerns the evils of living for pleasure. A reasonable conjecture is *enterou*, meaning 'of the intestine'.

42. We must bear in mind here that Isocrates is speaking as one who might himself be included among this number, and so his verdict must be taken with a grain of salt.

43. The equivalence of this in Athenian money is disputed, but a rate of 30 drachmae to the stater is a reasonable estimate, which would give Gorgias a fortune on his death of 30,000 dr., or 5 talents, which is respectable, but not princely.

44. In fact, Menon has just asked Socrates a question (such as he might, indeed, have asked Gorgias), whether or not excellence (*aretê*) can be taught; but Socrates is encouraging him to answer equally fearlessly.

45. Indeed, on the head of this, some scholars have disputed as to whether Gorgias should be called a 'sophist' at all, rather than simply a rhetorician. One takes their point, but this is really to accord too strict a meaning to the rather fuzzy term 'sophist'. Plato does actually refer once to Gorgias as 'the sophist from Leontini' (*Hippias Major* 282b5).

46. Callicles, with whom Gorgias is staying, has just invited Socrates to come round and hear Gorgias giving a 'display' (*epideixis*), which is the technical term for a sophistic display-speech.

47. I.e. Chaerephon, who had made the suggestion, rather than Callicles.

48. Polus has just offered a rather well-turned Gorgianic linguistic pirouette in lieu of a definition.

49. We are doubtless meant to conclude that Polus is somewhat embarrassed to own up to practising the craft of rhetoric.

50. This claim recalls that attributed to Protagoras by Socrates at *Protagoras* 334E: 'Well, I've heard that you can speak at such length, when you choose to, that your speech never comes to an end, and then again you can be so brief on the same topic that no one could be briefer, and as well as doing it yourself you can teach someone else how to do it.' Also, at *Phaedrus* 267AB, we are told that Teisias and Gorgias 'invented both conciseness of speech and immeasurable length on all subjects'. This seems to have been a widespread claim of rhetoricians.

51. Specifically the two words *kheirourgêma*, 'manual work', and *kyrôsis*, 'effectiveness', which were certainly not in common use.

52. Aristotle may well be borrowing from the *Meno* passage here, but that does not preclude his having independent knowledge that this is an accurate portrayal of Gorgias' position. In what context Gorgias may have expounded his views on *aretê* it is hardly profitable to speculate, but it is more likely to have been in the course of an epideictic discourse than in a special treatise on the subject, of which we have no evidence.

53. This is not to be taken to imply that the following doctrine is not that of Gorgias; it is just that Socrates prefers to argue with people who will stand up for their own views.

54. This seems somewhat compressed. The excellence of a slave, of whatever age, would be of quite a different nature to that of a free man. But that is what the Greek says.

55. Sophocles, *Ajax* 293.

56. His brother Herodicus was a distinguished physician back in Sicily.

57. The notion of comparing the rhetorician with the doctor does seem to be characteristic of the historical Gorgias, no doubt stimulated partly by the fact of his brother's profession. In the *Helen* (14), as we shall see below, he says that oratory is to the mind as drugs are to the body. Plato, of course, would compare the rhetorician, not to the doctor, but to the pastry-cook (cf. *Gorgias* 464Bff.).

58. *Loci communes*, translating the Greek *topoi*.

59. This plainly relates to the (tendentious) testimony of Plato in the *Phaedrus* passage quoted just above, §24.

60. This represents Cicero's attempt to describe the devices of *antithesis, parison* and *homoioteleuton*.

61. A reference to 266E, quoted at Protagoras, §20. Socrates there applies the epithet specifically to Theodorus.

62. This is an interesting remark. The Greeks (and Romans) do not seem to have striven for rhyme in either verse or prose as an end in itself, but rather it occurs as a by-product of other types of symmetry. There is nonetheless a good deal of rhyme involved in the balanced clausulae of Gorgias' epideictic speeches, such as the *Helen* and the *Funeral Speech* (see below).

63. In that case, one might ask, what is it exactly of which Thrasymachus is the inventor? We have the problem of possessing only one extract from the works of Thrasymachus, but he is elsewhere attested (see below, ch. 6, p. 203) as having first defined the period (*periodos*) and the clause (*kôlon*), presumably in his *Tekhnê Rhetorikê*, so he may have formalized innovations of Gorgias.

64. Cicero's term *festivitates* renders Gorgias' original term *poikiliai*, cf. Isocrates, *Philippus* 27.

65. This is presumably the meaning of *balbis* here. The temple would be that of Olympian Zeus.

66. I.e. Empress Julia Domna.

67. *To mê on* may be translated 'not-being', or 'the non-existent', or 'what is not', and any of these versions may be used in the text.

68. This slightly curious double title may owe something to the fact that Melissus appears to have called his treatise *On Nature, or On Being* (Simplicius, *Commentary on the Gorgias*, Preface, p. 557, 10).

69. Isocrates, indeed, links Gorgias with Zeno and Melissus, who certainly seem to have been his primary targets, as follows: 'For how could one surpass Gorgias, who dared to assert that nothing exists of the things that are, or Zeno, who ventured to prove the same things as possible and again as impossible, or Melissus who, although things in nature are infinite in number, made it his task to find proofs that the whole is one!'

70. See on this the useful discussion of Kerferd (1981), 93–100.

71. Such as Guthrie (1969), 197.

72. The treatment of Gorgias is part of Sextus' discussion of the 'criterion of truth'. Just preceding this he has treated of Protagoras (§§60–64).

73. It is interesting that, already at this stage, Gorgias is introducing epistemological factors into his proofs. This is not the case in the first stage of the *MXG* version.

74. It becomes clear here that Gorgias is making no hard and fast distinction between the existential and predicative senses of 'to

be'. On this see Kerferd (see n.70). One might then argue that many points in the argument are simply exploiting a linguistic ambiguity. However, the point can also be seen to go deeper than this, in terms of questions such as the extent to which a thing's identity is determined by its properties, etc.

75. This is a more than usually sophistical move: temporal infinity does not involve spatial infinity. To be fair, however, Melissus had asserted both the temporal and the spatial infinity of 'what is' (30B3), and it seems to be Melissus whom Gorgias has primarily in his sights.

76. Here, at least, he is at one with the Eleatic philosophers.

77. This seems to be an ingenious extrapolation of an argument of Melissus' against what is being many (30B8), that 'if there exist many things, they must be such as the one is'. Zeno, of course, also argues against a multiplicity of beings (cf. 29B3).

78. An immaterial reality is, of course, not envisaged.

79. This could be taken, broadly, as referring to the Eleatics and either Anaxagoras or the Atomist school respectively – the former maintaining that being is one, and ungenerated, the latter that it is many (the homoeomeries, the atoms), and that at least the ordered world came into being.

80. Again the systematic confusion of the existential and predicative senses of 'is'.

81. This is referred to by Aristotle in the *Physics* (210b22–5): 'if places exist, they will be in something; for everything that exists is in something. But what is in something is in a place. Therefore places are in places, and so on *ad infinitum*. Therefore places do not exist.'

82. That is, change *essentially*.

83. What Alexander of Aphrodisias describes as the second argument of Zeno's treatise maintains that 'if what exists has magnitude and is divided, then it will be many and no longer one' (29B2).

84. The reason for this is, as we learn from the parallel passage of Sextus, is that 'the many is a sum of ones'. *MXG* is elliptical here.

85. This argument is not to be found in Sextus. To be coherent with the main theme, the argument should run: 'if anything exists, it could not be mobile'. 'Mobility' covers all forms of change. The ban on motion or change comes in Fr. 8, 26–33 of Parmenides' Poem.

86. The ban on divisibility is to be found in Parmenides, Fr. 8, 22–5.

87. This is a most interesting remark, linking up as it does the Atomist concept of void, as that which exists to make atoms distinct

(which Leucippus characterized as 'non-existent'), with the idea of divisibility, which is banned in Eleatic philosophy.

88. This follows if we take 'the things thought' (*ta phronoumena*) as implying '*all* objects of thought'. In that case, if anything were to exist, it could not be an object of thought.

89. Again, the force of this depends on taking 'things thought' to mean '*all* objects of thought'.

90. This is a fair representation, we think, of what the Greek of this very vexed passage says, but we can make no sense of it. For a reasonable sense, we must turn to the passage of Sextus above.

91. Lacuna filled thus, very plausibly, by Diels.

92. The reference here is quite unclear, but it seems to be an empty rhetorical flourish.

93. Added, plausibly, by Diels on the basis of §15 below.

94. Here Gorgias turns to what is the central point of this display-speech, a celebration of the power of rhetoric, presented as a quasi-magical force.

95. What follows here makes possible sense, but sounds a little abrupt. There may well be a lacuna in the text, as suggested by Max Pohlenz, *Aus Platos Werdezeit*, Berlin, 1913, p. 40, who fills it plausibly, as follows: '<of which the one with drugs produces changes, which are illnesses of the body and diseases of the flesh, while the other with words engenders new ideas>, which are ...' Cf. [14] below.

96. *ennoian* supplied here reasonably by Blass, to balance *pronoian* in the next column. Note that Gorgias, in speaking of mental capacities, speaks always of 'opinion' (*doxa*), never of 'knowledge' (*epistêmê*). Plato would agree with him that rhetoric may hold sway over *doxa*.

97. The text here is unfortunately seriously corrupt. We adopt a blend of the conjectures of Blass (1887–98) and Radermacher (1951), as giving an acceptable sense and balance.

98. A very significant final remark!

99. Arguing purely from probability was plainly regarded as a special rhetorical skill. There is a speech of Isocrates called the *Amartyros* (*The Speech without Witnesses*), which was regarded as a particular achievement of his.

100. Eliminating the *holou* of the manuscripts as meaningless.

101. It is less than clear to us what Gorgias means here; it sounds as if truth and necessity are the teachers in question, but why should they produce danger?

102. Accepting a probable supplement.

103. This would be his brother Oiax, who survived him.

104. A contemporary touch here! Slaves in Athens (and no doubt elsewhere) could win their freedom by informing on their masters in cases of high treason or sacrilege; and they were also subject to having to testify under torture.

105. Supplied, with great probability, by Diels.

106. Accepting the filling of a lacuna by Diels.

107. Palamedes came from Nauplia in Argos; presumably he is referring to Argos as a whole as his fatherland.

108. Reading *adikēsasi* (active) with Diels for *adikētheisi* (passive) of mss. But there may be something worse wrong here.

109. Accepting the filling of a lacuna by Keil.

110. On the mythical level, Palamedes is addressing Odysseus, whose reputation for roguery far surpassed his own, but Gorgias is also demonstrating the value of attacking the credentials of your opponent in all circumstances.

111. Lacuna filled plausibly by Diels.

112. Gorgias here illustrates a device much favoured by Greek forensic orators (the Latin term for which is *praeteritio*), which involves alluding to misdeeds of one's opponent which one does not care to specify for one reason or another.

113. Employing the word *euthynai*, the technical term for the scrutiny which an Athenian official had to undergo after his year in office. At this point in a speech a defendant would normally enumerate his past benefactions to the state, and those of his ancestors.

114. Palamedes is indeed attested in various sources to have been the inventor of all of these things (cf. Alcidamas, *Odysseus*, below, p. 308, where these claims are amusingly attacked or refuted). Draughts, in fact, he was credited with inventing in order to pass the time during the siege of Troy, which rather cuts across the story of his being framed by Odysseus at the beginning of it.

115. As would indeed normally be the case in an Athenian court, at least. However, such a point as this would be suitable to a trial before the Areopagus, for example.

116. The Greeks did, of course, condemn and execute Palamedes, despite his proverbial wisdom and eloquence. Gorgias' point in composing this, presumably, is to suggest that with the help of *his* technical expertise Palamedes would have got off.

117. Adopting a probable supplement.

118. Again, a necessary supplement.

119. Once again, a supplement. The scribe seems to have had some difficulty with the word *rhōmē*, which must surely be what has fallen out.

120. Note the little *variatio* in the last member of this sequence of cola.
121. Or possibly, if *anaima* is read for *enaima*, 'pale and bloodless' –
     either way, a strong image.
122. Nicely balanced: *aiskhrôs men espeiras, kakôs de etherisas*. This
     imagery of sowing and reaping has, of course, enjoyed wide
     currency in later European literature.
123. We take this to mean that a noble deed, for instance (this might
     come from his *Funeral Oration*), will languish in obscurity if no
     one knows about it, while the false impression of nobility will
     not survive hard facts. But it is possible, I suppose, that we are
     faced here with a serious epistemological observation.

3 PRODICUS OF CEOS

1. He is portrayed by Plato, in the *Protagoras*, as being in Athens,
   and an already well-known figure, with a patron and followers,
   in the late 430s, just before the outbreak of the Peloponnesian
   War, which is the dramatic date of the dialogue – but unfortunately, as we know, Plato is by no means free of anachronisms in
   these matters. In the *Hippias Major*, on the other hand (cf. §4
   below), he is portrayed as giving his most notable address to the
   Council some time later than Gorgias, and near to the dramatic
   date of the dialogue (c.420 BC).
2. Prodicus was probably around twenty years younger than Protagoras, and could conceivably have been his pupil at some stage,
   but he is not portrayed as such by Plato, or any other authority.
3. A sophistic circumlocution for Xenophon. This is a peculiar
   story. That Xenophon was a prisoner in Boeotia is not otherwise
   attested, but this may have occurred following the Boeotian seiz-
   ure of the border-town of Oropus in the spring of 412, where
   they captured the Athenian garrison by treachery. This would
   imply that Prodicus was teaching in Thebes at the time. Xenophon
   himself would only have been in his late teens (he is generally
   agreed to have been born in around 430). He must, however,
   have been ransomed not long afterwards, as he plainly consorted
   with Socrates for a number of years before departing on the
   'March Up-Country' in 401.
4. This is attested to by Plato also, in the *Protagoras* 316A (cf. §3
   below) – unless this report is taken from that source! The embassy,
   if this is his initial appearance on the Athenian scene, must have
   taken place much earlier, perhaps in the late 430s.
5. In his *Memoirs of Socrates* II 1. 21.

6. It is not absolutely clear what Philostratus means here. At the end of his version of Prodicus' fable, Xenophon makes Socrates say: 'That is roughly how Prodicus describes the education of Heracles by Virtue, except that he actually dressed up the sentiments in language still more splendid than I have used now.' Philostratus must be commending him, at any rate, for giving an adequate imitation of Prodicus' style, since that is all that Xenophon says about it.

7. A satirical reference to Odysseus' account of his visit to the Underworld in *Odyssey* XI, where, after meeting his companions, he is now viewing the great sinners. This is a quotation of l. 582. He has just viewed Orion and Tityus, and Tantalus is third. There is no need, it seems, to see any other significance than this to the identification of Prodicus with Tantalus.

8. Callias' devotion to sophists is widely attested. He spent a good deal of his inherited fortune on taking their courses. Xenophon, for example, in his *Symposium* (I 5), portrays him as having taken instruction from Protagoras, Hippias and Prodicus, and there is no reason to believe that he is dependent on Plato for this information (cf. also §§ 7–8 below).

9. This is the future avant-garde tragic poet, at whose victory celebration in 416 Plato's *Symposium* is set. (Pausanias is still there, as his lover, nearly twenty years later!) Plato portrays Agathon there as being very much influenced by the style of Gorgias.

10. This may after all be the sole source of Philostratus' information above, §2 – combined with the information about his deep voice culled from the *Protagoras* (§3, above).

11. An attempt to render *meteōrosophistai*, literally 'experts on high-flown, or celestial, things', a favourite abusive epithet of sophists and philosophers (cf. 'sky-pilots').

12. I.e. over Callias' enthusiasm for spending money on sophists.

13. Athenian politician, a moderate oligarch, who was derided for his political changes of direction (for which he was nicknamed *kothornos*, 'the Buskin', that being an actor's boot which could be worn on either foot). He initially joined the Thirty Tyrants at the end of the Peloponnesian War, but fell out with their leader Critias and was executed in 403. Cf. below, p. 227.

14. A well-known glutton of the late fifth century.

15. Possibly in the dialogue Hipponicus was allowed to make these gibes, in an effort to dissuade his son, but there are chronological difficulties in that.

16. This does seem expensive – the equivalent of more than a month's

salary of a skilled craftsman – but it may perhaps be envisaged as something like a whole-day seminar, such as are even now given at considerable expense to businessmen.

17. He is addressing Hermogenes, one of his interlocutors in the dialogue. Note Plato's emphasis on Socrates' willingness to impart instruction free.

18. Another late rhetorician, of unknown date (but plainly older than Marcellinus!).

19. Prodicus did not actually make this distinction in the passage quoted above.

20. A paraphrase of *Works and Days*, 289 and 291–2.

21. This is deeply ironic. Simonides was only a generation older than Prodicus.

22. Prodicus may indeed have composed a work with this title, *Peri onomatôn orthotêtos*, or *Peri orthoepeias*, but we have no clear information on the subject.

23. A noted musician and theorist of music (fl. *c*.435 BC), to whom Plato makes Socrates acknowledge indebtedness at various points in the dialogues. The dramatic date of this dialogue is *c*.420 BC.

24. This is presented as a verbatim quotation, but it is probably more of a summary of his views.

25. Also worth considering is the view of Böttiger, reported by Diels (*Die Fragmente der Vorsokratiker*), that the title may allude to the fact that it contained three *logoi*, one for each of the three Hours, Eunomia, Dikê and Eirênê, on the model e.g. of Herodotus' *Histories*, which he named 'The Muses' (as having nine books).

26. That is, Zeus (or possibly Amphitryon) and Alcmene.

27. The immediately following passage, in particular, rises to almost Gorgianic heights of *antithesis* and *parisôsis* of clausulae (showing that Prodicus was quite capable of this if he chose), so it seems appropriate to set it out in 'poetic format'.

28. Plato, we may note, in the *Timaeus* (83Cff.), uses *phlegma* in the broader sense which Prodicus is 'correcting' here, identifying only one form of phlegm, 'acid phlegm', which is produced by excessive heat; 'white phlegm', on the other hand (which Prodicus wants here to rename) is connected with cold wetness. The Pythagorean Philolaus, on the other hand, it would seem (cf. Fr. A27) asserted that phlegm was hot (and laid emphasis on the derivation from *phlegein*), so that Prodicus has some warrant for his position.

29. Cf. §§14–18 above.

4 HIPPIAS OF ELIS

1. Unfortunately, we know nothing more about Hegesidamus, presumably an Elean philosopher. The *telos* is the Hellenistic philosophical term for the overall purpose or focus of human activity, and the ideal of self-sufficiency would make Hegesidamus a kind of primitive Cynic. Hippias' famous propensity for making everything that he wore or used (cf. below, §11) could be seen as a sophistic adaptation of this philosophical ideal.

2. Once again we may note the use of mythological material to drive home a message.

3. That is to say, he was awarded the privileges of citizenship.

4. *Hippias Major* 282E (= §7 below).

5. We can deduce from this at least that Hippias was married, and (perhaps) that his daughter, who was widowed, lived in Athens. Unless she was a citizen, however, Isocrates could not have contracted a valid marriage with her, so perhaps we may also conclude that Hippias himself had been granted Athenian citizenship. Aphareus, it seems, went on to compose both orations and tragedies, presenting the latter between 369/8 and 342/1 (ibid., *839CD*).

6. The learned philosophical doctor who figures in Plato's *Symposium* (as does Phaedrus of Myrrhinus).

7. This is an interesting anticipation of the later Stoic doctrine of the kinship of all wise men, and their common citizenship of the world (cf. *Stoicorum Veterum Fragmenta* III 333–9). The contrast between nature (*physis*) and convention (*nomos*) was of course a very widespread one at this time. Hippias himself is represented by Xenophon, at *Memoirs of Socrates* IV 4, 14–25, in conversation with Socrates, as accepting that certain moral rules are 'unwritten laws' laid down by the gods, and thus natural rather than conventional (not included; see below, p. 127).

8. The use of *prytaneion*, literally 'town hall', in this metaphorical sense is unexampled before this passage – and virtually so after it – and may well have been a turn of phrase employed by Hippias. It would seem, however, from a reference in Athenaeus' *Deipnosophistae* V 187D, that the Pythian oracle had hailed Athens on some occasion as 'the hearth and *prytaneion* of the Greeks', so this would in that case not be an original image by Hippias.

9. Conveniently available in the excellent Penguin translation of Robin Waterfield, in *Plato: Early Socratic Dialogues*, Harmondsworth, 1987.

10. The salutation *Hippias ho kalos te kai sophos*, while ironic, is not overtly rude, and Hippias certainly takes no offence at it.

11. It was indeed natural that Elis, which is situated in the western Peloponnese just north of Sparta, should be most concerned about relations with its powerful neighbour.

12. The dramatic date of the dialogue is generally agreed to be around 420 BC, a period of temporary peace between Athens and Sparta.

13. The last part of this sentence is carefully balanced, in sophistic style.

14. In 427 BC. Cf. ch. 2, §5.

15. = Ch. 3, §4.

16. It is not possible to date this visit. Protagoras had been invited by Pericles to draft laws for Thurii in 444 BC, but this must refer to a later time than that.

17. This is an enormous sum, when one considers that the yearly salary for a skilled workman at Athens at this time would be less than four minae (i.e. about a drachma a day). There is no reason, however, to doubt the essential accuracy of this account.

18. It is reasonable, I think, to assume that these two references are to the same event, and are thus a cross-reference linking the two dialogues.

19. He would still be on home ground, since Olympia was a district of Elis.

20. This boast is reminiscent of that of Gorgias (*Meno* 70AB; *Gorgias* 447Cff. = ch. 2, §§16–17). It was doubtless a standard ploy of sophists.

21. It is not clear in what sense Hippias felt himself to be competing. There were contests for poets and musicians at the ancient Olympics, but it is not known that there were any for sophists. More probably Hippias simply means that he never found anyone who could get the better of him in argument.

22. Sc. in Sparta. See §10 below, which comprises the immediately preceding passage of this dialogue.

23. It is not quite clear whether this refers to musical theory or metrics (as an aid to rhetoric), but probably the latter – in which case *harmonia* here probably means rather 'intonation', in the sense of modulation of high and low pitch. It also seems to show an overlap with some of Prodicus' concerns, though Prodicus is more concerned with the meanings of words.

24. Socrates has just been pursuing a tendentious argument to the effect that expertise in a given area confers a greater ability to lie about it than does ignorance in that area.

25. What the point of this *tour de force* might have been is not easy to see, apart from simply attracting attention. There seems no reason, however, to doubt the accuracy of the report.

26. Even Hippias' assertion of belief in 'unwritten laws' transcending all positive law (IV 4, 19ff.), though doubtless representing his true position, is presented simply as a foil to Socrates' own exposition of his view that what is right (*dikaion*) is what is lawful (*nomimon*).

27. Presumably the meaning of *opse* here, rather than 'late in Hippias' career'.

28. Thargelia is also given an entry in Hesychius' *Lexicon*, perhaps from the same source, but Hesychius adds the information that 'she controlled cities and rulers'.

29. Clement is detailing instances of plagiarizing, or at least derivativeness, in the Hellenic tradition. Here, however, Hippias is actually acknowledging his sources, at least vaguely. What the subject-matter was is not clear – possibly mythological or genealogical.

30. Aristotle mentions this doctrine of Thales at *De Anima* I 2, 405a19, without any reference to Hippias, but he may well have dwelt on it more fully in some lost work, such as his *On Philosophy*.

31. A third-century BC mathematician of whom little else is known.

32. The quadratrix (*tetragonizousa*) is a curve, originally devised to trisect any rectilineal angle, but then used in a effort to square the circle. See T. L. Heath, *A Manual of Greek Mathematics* (Oxford, 1931), pp. 142–4.

33. That is to say, the Etruscans. How far the latter part of this report owes anything to Hippias is not clear, but it may well do, as Hippias would have had to explain his statement somehow.

34. Normally, in fact, the wicked stepmother in question is given as Ino. It was Phrixus who brought the ram with the Golden Fleece to Colchis. Gorgopis is otherwise only known as the name of a part of the Corinthian Gulf.

35. Presumably Hippias' approximate contemporary Ion of Chios. In fact, Herodotus also uses this term for 'deposit'. It could be seen as Ionic, therefore, rather than Attic.

5 ANTIPHON

1. For Antiphon, we have a particularly good treatment by J. S. Morrison, in *The Older Sophists* (ed. Rosamund Kent Sprague).

He, however, includes the forensic speeches and the *Tetralogies*, while we include only the latter.

2. It is very possibly this man, and not our Antiphon, who is to be credited with 'being a successful general, being victorious in many engagements, and adding sixty triremes to the navy', as is attributed to the composite Antiphon in the biographical tradition, but we cannot be sure.

3. Even as between the *Tetralogies* and the other speeches doubts have been raised, some quite substantial (linguistic differences, apparent instances of ignorance of Athenian law in the *Tetralogies*), but it still seems that we may accept the identity, albeit with reservations.

4. There is the particular problem with the psychiatrist that he set up his consulting rooms in Corinth, which would be a very odd thing for an Athenian gentleman to do, and unthinkable after the beginning of the Peloponnesian War in 432 – so this would have to be a relatively early enterprise of Antiphon's; but it is in fact presented as such in the *Life* (below, §3 and n. 25)

5. A *teratoskopos* is someone who examines ominous signs and pronounces on the significance of remarkable events.

6. In fact, we are told in the Life of him by Pseudo-Plutarch (§3 below) that he was taught by his father, who was a schoolmaster.

7. This is Didymus of Alexandria (*c*.80–10 BC), nicknamed 'Brassguts', a contemporary of Caecilius (who could therefore have been reacting to him), a man of prodigious industry, who is said to have written 3,500 or even 4,000 books.

8. That is to say, *Against the Stepmother, On the Murder of Herodes* and *On the Chorus-Boy*, which will not be included in this edition, as being practical forensic productions.

9. We have reports of speeches to the Assembly *On the Tribute of the Lindians* and *On the Tribute of the Samothracians*, as well as of a speech *On the Revolution*, which he made in his own defence at his trial for treason in 411.

10. This may have included some remarks on the ideal form of state, or it may simply have been an attack on the Athenian democracy, but we can tell little of significance from the surviving fragments of it, cf. below §§57–61.

11. *Menexenus* 236A (= §6 below), where 'Antiphon of Rhamnus' is mentioned as a teacher of rhetoric.

12. That is to say, either between the two styles or the two authors.

13. Cf. ch. 7, §18 below.

14. *Memoirs of Socrates* 16 (= §9 below). This seems a rather benign

interpretation of the encounter, as presented by Xenophon; it comes across as distinctly eristical.

15. Archinus was a prominent democratic politician of the last decades of the fifth century. He assisted Thrasybulus in the restoration of the democracy in 403, and was instrumental in introducing the Ionic alphabet to Athens in 403/2. The other three are well enough known.

16. The manuscripts here have *mathêtên*, 'pupil', but Wyttenbach reasonably substitutes *kathêgêtên*, 'teacher', in accord with the evidence of Hermogenes above (and all probability). It is possible, however, that this is an error on Caecilius' part, based on Thucydides, *History of the Peloponnesian War* VIII 68 (= §11 below), since it is repeated in Photius' *Bibliotheca* (see below), which seems to be derived from Caecilius directly.

17. This is unsatisfactorily vague, but seems to place Antiphon's birth, as we have said above, somewhere in the mid-470s.

18. In 411, when for about four months (May to September) an oligarchic clique took over Athens. They were overthrown in the autumn by democrats in the fleet at Samos, and Antiphon and his associates were put on trial and condemned to death.

19. This was the mole which formed the northern side of the Great Harbour of the Piraeus, which was fortified by the Four Hundred in order to control the entrance and defend against an attack by the fleet at Samos. The account of Antiphon's military exploits, however, may be an error, applied to him through confusion with Antiphon, son of Lysonides, whose achievements would have been praised by Lysias in his speech in defence of his daughter. There is not much evidence of military successes scored by the Four Hundred in their few months of power.

20. At this point Pseudo-Plutarch descends into complete inconsequentiality, bringing in Lysias' Antiphon (see previous note), and even the tragic poet who was executed by Dionysius of Syracuse – probably in the 390s or 380s, since Dionysius' rule is stated to have been then 'at its height'.

21. That is, Plato the comic poet. The Peisander of the title will be Antiphon's fellow oligarch and prominent member of the Four Hundred, who managed to escape to the Spartans in Decelea after the overthrow of the regime.

22. At this point, Pseudo-Plutarch wanders off again, back to the tragic poet, whom this time he credits with setting up the psychiatric clinic in Corinth. This is almost certainly wrong. We need not suppose that 'our' Antiphon composed tragedies.

23. There is a section of Aristophanes' *The Clouds* (produced in 423 BC), II 694–793, which bears an uncanny resemblance to this procedure. It seems very much as if Aristophanes was aware that this was a procedure that sophists might employ.

24. This is probably Hippocrates, son of Ariphron, and nephew of Pericles, general in 426/5 and 424/3, when he died in the battle of Delium. It is likely, in that case, that it was during his earlier period of office that Antiphon prosecuted him, possibly as part of a conservative political strategy. Some manuscripts, however, read 'doctor' for 'general', making the reference to the famous doctor and medical writer Hippocrates of Cos. This is possible, but much less likely – though it is strange that the general allowed a case to go against him by default.

Our author ends his account with the decree recording the trial and condemnation of Antiphon (borrowed from Caecilius). This is historically interesting, but not strictly relevant to our purpose; we therefore omit it.

25. Indeed, Photius purports to be reading Caecilius directly, and even quotes him verbatim. The only item of interest contributed by the Life prefixed to his works is the information that he set up his psychiatric clinic in Corinth *as a young man*, which, if it is not just a deduction by the author, is valuable, as contributing to the credibility of the story.

26. As remarked above (nn. 2 and 19), this may really refer to the career of the democrat Antiphon, son of Lysonides.

27. That is to say, Alcibiades.

28. This is an elaboration and rationalization of the story about the psychiatric clinic in Corinth, as can be seen from a comparison with the accounts of Pseudo-Plutarch (§3 above), Photius and the Life – all dependent on Caecilius. On the likelihood of this being an enterprise of 'our' Antiphon, see above, n. 4. The epithet *nêpenthês* may actually be a reference to the drug employed by Helen for this purpose in Book 4, 221 of the *Odyssey*.

29. This seems to us to be the probable meaning of *autois malista tois kinduneuousin*, but we are by no means certain. Most of the surviving titles of speeches seem in fact to be prosecutions, but that does not exclude the possibility of Antiphon's coming to the aid of people who were under attack e.g. from *sykophantai*.

30. Philostratus, himself a rhetorician, feels sensitive on this point. In fact, since Antiphon seems to have been the first man to compose speeches for a fee, this new-fangled practice, with its connotations

of dishonesty, naturally attracted the suspicion of the public and the attention of the comic poets.

31. It is interesting that Philostratus, rhetorician though he is, is not disturbed, as was Hermogenes, by the palpable differences in style between the forensic and the sophistic works.

32. Presumably the tragic poet. He is portrayed by Plato in the *Symposium* as being a great admirer of Gorgias, and presumably he admired Antiphon also.

33. This will be his lost dialogue *Gryllus*, or *On Rhetoric*, not his surviving *Rhetoric*.

34. That is to say, his speech in his own defence in 411.

35. This would seem to attest to the fact that Antiphon ran a school of some sort.

36. One may presumably deduce from this that Antiphon, according to Xenophon, would define the purpose of the study of 'philosophy' (which is a description that he would accept for what he was teaching himself) as happiness (*eudaimonia*), and that he conceived this to reside (in part, at least) in the acquisition of material goods.

37. We omit a number of further sections, which develop the same theme.

38. This expression, *par' hēmin*, is somewhat troublesome. This is the most natural meaning, it seems, but that would appear to imply that Antiphon is a *foreigner*, and that would rather undermine his identification with the orator and politician. One might render it, alternatively, 'my theory is this', but that would more naturally translate *kata tēn emēn (gnōmēn)*, or something such. It is possible, however, to see Socrates as here simply 'putting down' Antiphon by reminding him of normal Athenian moral attitudes.

39. This question at least comes more appropriately from Antiphon the Athenian politician than from a foreign sophist.

40. Diogenes describes this as the treatise *On Poetry (peri poiētikēs)*, but he is probably referring to this work, which is attested as having been in three books.

41. The executive council of the 'Five Thousand' (this latter being never more than notional).

42. The text here is somewhat confused, but this is substantially the sense.

43. The text is unfortunately rather corrupt; we follow the restoration of Diels, which gives a reasonable sense.

44. Cf. below, ch. 7, §58.

45. Presumably the fact that there is no objective reality out there.

46. Diels, in appending to this quotation a passage from the Hippocratic treatise *On Art (Peri Tekhnês)* – or better, *On the Concept of an Art* – wishes to suggest that that document (which seems to be composed by a fifth-century sophist or rhetorician), since it stoutly maintains the objective existence of the subject-matter of the arts and sciences, is to some degree a response to Antiphon's position, and that may well be so. Indeed, in ch. 2, the author seems directly to respond to the terminology employed by Antiphon in this fragment.

47. This seems strange, since *apathê* would normally be an adjective, not a noun; perhaps Antiphon actually talked of *apathê pathê*.

48. He alludes to it also at *Sophistical Refutations* 11, 172a7, in a similar context. It is not made clear in what work Antiphon produced this 'proof', but it is generally agreed that it must have been in the *On Truth*.

49. This was the solution of the mathematician Hippocrates of Chios, which at least had the virtue, from Aristotle's perspective, of proceeding according to geometrical principles – although it too fails to solve the problem.

50. Since the edition of Diels-Kranz some more papyrus text has been discovered, and edited by Fernanda Decleva Caizzi, 1989, and we have followed her order of the fragments. What had been Fr. B in Diels-Kranz is now somewhat amplified, and placed before the larger fragment.

51. Col. 1 consists of mere scraps. The subject is now the question of conventional distinctions between classes and races.

52. Or possibly 'gods'. The papyrus begins in mid-sentence.

53. The connotation of this remarkable verb is presumably that of ignorance and alienation. The following remark about there being no natural distinction between barbarian and Greek is echoed, interestingly, in Plato, *Statesman* 262D, where the distinction is condemned as an example of false division.

54. The minimal remains of col. 4 suggest that it concerned the early history of the human race. It is reckoned that there was a gap of about three columns between this and the beginning of Fragment B.

55. This is a straight statement of the conventionalist view of justice, of which Thrasymachus is made to give a much more offensive version in Book I of Plato's *Republic*, see below, ch. 6, §8.

56. Here Antiphon, like Callicles in the *Gorgias* (482Cff.), and unlike Polus earlier in the same dialogue, denies that there is any shame in committing injustice.

57. This is, of course, more than a little tendentious, but contains enough validity to make Antiphon's point; i.e. it is a matter of total indifference to 'nature', it will not injure our eyes, if we spy on respectable women at their toilette.

58. This is very much the point made by Callicles in the *Gorgias* (see n.56).

59. There follows a patch of seven lines where too little remains to make sense, but Antiphon must have made the point that what is advantageous by nature must maximize pleasure and minimize pain, which many conventional 'advantages' do not. The papyrus resumes with a series of examples of people who observe conventional justice.

60. The point of this example is that, if one gives a dishonest opponent in a law-case the chance to swear an oath, he may take it unscrupulously, and thus strengthen his case before the jury.

61. This is curiously put, but the point seems to be that conventional law, unlike the law of nature, does not bring down an automatic penalty on those who transgress it.

62. Once again, the point presumably is that, if a law of nature has been breached, there can be no question of dispute, or of appeal against it: the doer will inevitably suffer.

63. Antiphon here is making rather sophistical use of the ambiguity of the verb *adikein*, which can mean either 'do wrong' or just 'do harm'. We have chosen to render it by the latter verb, as being the lesser of two distortions. The truthful witness may certainly 'harm' the opponent of his friend, though he will not 'wrong' him conventionally. This whole convoluted argument is designed to show how conventional justice militates against the 'justice' of the natural order.

64. That is to say, giving evidence in the normal way.

65. We accept here Kranz's suggestion of reading *mêden auton adikoumenon* (cf. col. 1 above, p. 150, 226) for the senseless *mêde auton adikeisthai*, which can reasonably be seen as a scribal error.

66. I.e. by having a verdict go against them.

67. This seems to be the peculiar force of the compound verbal form *hyponotizomenou*.

68. The unique word *idiophengês*, 'shining by one's own light', is probably not a coinage of Antiphon, but of the doxographic tradition.

69. Or planets; *astra* may denote both or either.

70. Addition by Diels, filling a lacuna in the text on the basis of a similar phrase in a previous entry.

71. Presumably in the course of a discussion of the formation of the human species. It was probably the verbal form that Antiphon used, rather than the noun.

72. Presumably also in the context of the formation of humans, or at least of animals.

73. It seems more properly to be neuter (*epiploon*), as in the Hippocratic corpus and Aristotle.

74. Composed by Xenophon perhaps fifty years later than Antiphon, but given a dramatic date approximately contemporary with him. Xenophon would, of course, be of conservative sympathies.

75. Xenophon, significantly, here uses (in the plural) the term for the Spartan senate, *gerousia*.

76. By John Morrison, *ap.* Sprague, 1972, p. 226.

77. We may note that the Neoplatonic philosopher Iamblichus (*c.* AD 245–325) devotes one of his letters to the subject of *On Concord*.

78. 1995, 248–52.

79. There is a contrast set up here by the particle *men*, which demands an answering *de*, 'on the other hand'; the 'other hand' would presumably have been some falling short of the ideal of divinity by the human race.

80. *O makarie*, a form of address much favoured by Plato's Socrates. This would seem to indicate that *On Concord* was either a dialogue or at least contained addresses to an interlocutor.

81. It looks here as if Antiphon is engaged on a survey of man's life as a whole, from cradle to grave, presumably to point out the advantages of *homonoia* at each stage.

82. The text is slightly suspect here, but the balance of clausulae is distinctly Gorgianic: *isa phronountes isa pneontes, axiôsanta kai axiôthenta*. And this is true of many sections of the passage.

83. All this covered by the word *sophiai*.

84. A notable turn of phrase here: *to neotêsion skirtêma*.

85. That is, than one who is not so deterred.

86. Reading *emphrassôn* for *emphrassei*.

87. With *politikos* we are presumably to understand *logos*, which would imply that it was in the form of a speech, viz. 'A Discourse on Politics', or 'on the State'. It could have been delivered to members of a political club, and then published as a pamphlet.

88. This word has other meanings, 'easy to deal with', 'easy to understand', but only Antiphon is attested as using it in this sense.

89. A remarkable noun, formed from *hêmiolios*, 'one and a half times'.

90. That is to say, possibly, leaving recklessly large tips.

91. The genitive is in fact far more usual, though another example of the accusative is attested for Xenophon (*History of Greece* 6.2.39).

92. Antiphon as a dream-interpreter was famous enough to be included by Lucian, as the archetypal dream-interpreter, in his fantasy *The True History* (II 33), when he comes to the Island of Dreams: 'There they have a sanctuary and prophetic seat where Antiphon the interpreter of dreams stands forth to give prophecy, receiving his commission from Sleep.' (= A7).

93. And presumably consulted Antiphon – though normally in such circumstances one consulted the *exêgêtai*. It is possible, of course, that Antiphon was an official *exêgêtês*.

94. This may, indeed, serve to answer the objection of E. R. Dodds, in *The Greeks and the Irrational* (Berkeley and Los Angeles, 1951), pp. 132–3, against the identification with the sophist, since the sophist is alleged by Origen (cf. §13 above) to have argued against the existence of divine providence. This dictum would be in accord with such a position.

95. Antipater of Tarsus, a successor of Chrysippus as head of the Stoic school; fl. *c.*140 BC.

96. Presumably Chrysippus, rather than Antiphon.

97. Diels-Kranz, it must be noted, only give the first few lines (down to 'commentators') as pertaining to Antiphon, but the whole passage seems to go together. We would claim it for Antiphon, though recognizing the probability of Ciceronian embellishments.

98. Presumably one of the regular *exêgêtai*.

99. One might conjecture that in his own work Antiphon told this and the following story in his own favour.

100. This was the name of the first Pythian priestess, and also of the Sibyl of Samos, but any treatise attributed to either of them on the subject of eyelid-twitches would doubtless be spurious.

101. It is possible, indeed, that what Antiphon has done here is to select real cases in which he was involved, and abstract from their particularity sufficiently to make them into *exempla*. This would explain the peculiarity of some of the details remaining.

102. Added in by the editor of the Aldine edition, to fill a probable lacuna.

103. That is to say, a quarrel not brought on by drink.

104. All the previous motives, apart from the first (robbery), would be free from premeditation, and thus attract a lesser penalty (though still involving pollution).

105. Pursuing one another through the law-courts was a favourite

occupation of enemies in Classical Athens, as the surviving corpus of forensic speeches bears witness.

106. A *graphē hierôn klopês*. This would have concerned embezzlement of public funds deposited in one temple or another while one was filling some public office; it attracted a ten-fold penalty of repayment.

107. Antiphon has here cleverly piled up a whole sequence of probabilities, or *eikota*, such as we can observe being done in many real trials, including his own *Prosecution for Poisoning: Against the Stepmother* and *On the Murder of Herodes*.

108. In a real trial there would here be inserted *martyriai*, affidavits from witnesses.

109. The argument from the fear of pollution, like the argument from the necessity of being true to one's juror's oath, is a common feature of perorations.

110. This is the nub of the argument, being the only part of the case that approaches direct evidence. Presumably Antiphon introduces this feature in order to address the problem of the evidence of deceased persons, and in particular slaves (who could normally not give evidence except under torture). The evidence of a now deceased slave is troublesome, but challengeable.

111. It is not asserted elsewhere that the victim was discovered by members of his household, but even if they were only his friends, they would fill the role of 'masters' (*kyrioi*) for the slave. At any rate, it appears from the beginning of the second speech for the prosecution that they were not the same as the prosecutors.

112. The technical term for this sort of interest-free loan was *eranos*. Bailing out friends down on their luck for one reason or another was quite a feature of Athenian civic life.

113. This was nearly always a *de facto* option in capital cases.

114. The word-play here, *eikotôs men, ontôs de mê*, is not easy to render.

115. This sentiment is convoluted almost to the point of incoherence. His point is, however, that he deserves sympathy for the wrongs he has received at the deceased's hands.

116. A reference back to the allusion to pollution at the end of the prosecution speech.

117. The defendant now embarks on a standard feature of perorations, a catalogue of his (and, if relevant, his ancestors') previous benefactions to the city. Here, it must be said, the logic by which they are introduced leaves something to be desired: the performance of *leitourgiai* does not, after all, preclude the possibility that one

would plot against one's personal or political enemies; but this would hardly be noticed by the jury.

118. This would be the same sort of *eranos* which he earlier envisages having to receive himself.

119. A nice piece of word-play: *ou dikazomenon, all' ergazomenon.*

120. We have here another standard feature of a peroration: abuse of one's opponent, and blackening of his character. Since the defendant's opponent is dead, however, he feels it indecent to attack his character directly, and contents himself with what in Roman rhetoric was known as a *praeteritio*, a 'passing allusion' to what he might have said – which can be almost as effective.

121. In Athenian law, a prosecutor received a percentage of the property confiscated from the person convicted by his efforts.

122. The prosecution here picks up directly on the defendant's closing remarks.

123. The phrase *to thymoumenon tês gnômês* is an interesting one. This seems to be what is meant by it. These two paragraphs answer the arguments made by the defence in ii [5–6] above.

124. This is the other side of the well-worn argument on the value of slave-evidence aired in ii [7] above. The argument made here is somewhat specious: since the slave was supporting his master, he would have been freed as a reward, and then would be exempt from torture. But this, of course, anticipates a certain outcome; meanwhile, he is still a slave, and his evidence would only be admissible under torture.

125. This reasoning is somewhat convoluted, but probably valid: the lesser enemies would still, on this reckoning, have more to fear from suspicion of murder than from their various law-cases.

126. A reference back to his closing remark at the end of his first speech, and his opponents' criticism of that.

127. The defendant really appears by this stage to be running out of steam. The arguments that follow are remarkably tortuous and implausible. The only substantial thing he does is to offer his slaves for torture to provide an alibi for him ([8] below); but one wonders why he did not do this at the outset!

128. He refers to his pending charge of embezzlement. Cf. iii [6].

129. This is assuming, convolutedly, that the true murderers were a gang of robbers who were disturbed at their work, as he has suggested in his first speech (ii [5–6]), to which suggestion the prosecution have effectively replied (iii [2]).

130. This argument from *to eikos* is quite absurd, because in fact the passers-by *did* interrogate the slave, and report the murder.

131. Again, a reference to a point made by the prosecution in iii [2]: if, as he suggested, the murder was committed to cover up another crime, then that crime should have been reported.

132. But no free men have given evidence (other than himself). The defendant is rambling.

133. This too is quite illogical, if it was random passers-by, and not the victim's friends, who interviewed the slave, as appears to have been the case.

134. This is perfectly normal procedure – an offer repeatedly made and frequently refused – in actual law-cases; but the offer should have been made long before this.

135. A festival in honour of Zeus, which took place at the beginning of June.

136. The word used is *neôterizein*, which usually connotes stirring up revolution, but here has no such portentous meaning.

137. This conventionally conservative sentiment takes on a certain irony in Antiphon's case, since the two revolutions that took place in Athens in his time were engineered from the right, in the former of which he had a considerable part to play; but then, under Athenian democracy, it was the well-to-do who may have felt that they were 'doing badly'.

138. For the rhetorical contrast *ouk eikotôs all' ontôs*, cf. n. 114 above.

139. He uses *tekmêria* here, which normally means 'evidence'; but there is really no evidence, other than the testimony of the dying slave.

140. This opening speech is extremely brief – apparently as a rhetorical ploy, to indicate that there is really nothing to be said, the case being an open-and-shut one (cf. the beginning of the second speech for the prosecution).

141. The gymnasium could, of course, be an open-air arena; the word simply means 'exercise area'.

142. The word used here is *âkôn*, the negative of *hekôn*, 'willingly'; it can denote both unwilling and involuntary action.

143. This attempts to translate *enthymios*, a curious term which means 'burdensome to the conscience' or 'preying on the mind'.

144. This is a variation of the conventional disclaimer made by many litigants in real cases, that they are quite unaccustomed to going to law, and have no desire to do so.

145. An interesting contrast is set up here between *doxa*, 'opinion' or 'appearance', and *alêtheia*, 'truth', 'reality' – one that in the hands of Plato would take on a metaphysical significance that it does not have here (though Antiphon, of course, wearing another hat, has written a treatise on Truth).

146. This is an odd way of putting the situation, perhaps, but an interesting one – especially if one bears in mind the sense that 'truth' (*alêtheia*) has in Antiphon's treatise of that name.

147. Added, necessarily, by Reiske.

148. The notion of *hamartia* becomes crucial for the rest of the argument. Since the word can mean either 'error' or 'fault' (cf. the ambiguity surrounding Aristotle's concept of tragic *hamartia*), the speaker can propound the notion that, since the death is the victim's own *fault*, he is essentially guilty of his own death. Thus the defendant can be cleared of being an agent even of involuntary manslaughter.

149. Athenian law did certainly distinguish between voluntary and involuntary manslaughter, but even the latter was deemed to incur pollution, which normally necessitated withdrawal from the state for at least a year and a process of ritual cleansing.

150. The defendant now turns to his peroration, appealing to the jury's recognition of his uprightness of life and to their pity for his grey hairs.

151. He is making rather too much of this, for rhetorical purposes. The lad would only be liable to exile for a year, so far as we can see.

152. A striking image, picked up by the prosecution in iii [12].

153. This can only refer, rather convolutedly, to the contention that he was in fact his own killer, so that demands for vengeance must be directed against himself and have been satisfied with his own death.

154. An interesting use of the poetical adjective *aôros*, 'untimely'.

155. Rendering the Greek expression *ergôi kai ou logôi*, 'in deed and not in word', which he employs again just below, [3].

156. He chooses to regard his opening speech as merely a bald statement of the case, and so not properly a speech (see n. 140).

157. This reasoning is so convoluted as to be virtually incoherent, and that is reflected in the Greek text. What accusations is the prosecution referring to? Presumably the suggestion that the dead boy, through his own carelessness, is in fact his own killer. But there is an opportunity to answer that point now, and it is taken up.

158. Accepting Reiske's emendation *eumenôs* for *sykhnôs* of the manuscripts. That would have to mean 'frequently' or 'urgently', which makes little sense, even if it is taken with 'beg'.

159. *Ergôi kai ou logôi* again.

160. This whole paragraph is highly wrought rhetorically, employing

antitheses and balanced clausulae, hard to render comfortably in English.

161. This, of course, is a distortion of what the defendant is claiming, but it would not suit the prosecution to recognize the subtleties of the defence's argument about causation.

162. This is a new fact, not adduced in the opening speech, which actually tends to cast the blame for the accident on the trainer, rather than the defendant.

163. He now appears to associate the father with the act of his son, since he is defending it – that is, if we accept Blass's reasonable emendation of an ungrammatical genitive absolute into a nominative plural.

164. Some very convoluted reasoning! The 'death penalty' referred to here is simply getting in the way of the javelin.

165. A crafty move here! By conceding some measure of wrongdoing on the part of his son, he feels that he can involve the defendant in wrongdoing too.

166. That is from the market-place and from all temple precincts of Attica; this was, in fact, a way of forcing people into exile.

167. This passage is corrupt, but its broad sense seems to be this.

168. That is to say, to pollution from the curse of the dead lad. This may seem far-fetched, but it was in fact not an uncommon motif in perorations in real cases to suggest that a wrongful verdict would incur divine displeasure, or a curse from beyond the grave.

169. Recalling the striking image used at the end of the previous speech (ii [10]).

170. That is, by implication, give a fair hearing to me as well as to my opponent.

171. A reference to his rather exotic theory of responsibility, to which he now gives a further twist.

172. That is, which of the two lads; the trainer, having been introduced, is now – rather unexpectedly – set aside.

173. This, it must be said, seems a distinction without a difference.

174. There is an interesting parallel to this situation from real life, mentioned by Demosthenes in his speech *Against Meidias* (XXI 71–5). In that case, the defendant was condemned, but only by a single vote.

175. Cf. i [7], iv [3] and [8].

176. Like the opening speech of the *Second Tetralogy* this is remarkably short – presumably as a rhetorical ploy.

177. This is a most interesting line of argument. The creation of man by God, or the gods, actually forms no part of the canon of Greek

myth, as propounded by Homer and Hesiod, but it must have been part of popular belief. In the myth told by 'Protagoras' in Plato's *Protagoras* (cf. above, ch. 1, §18a), the creation of man is the work of Prometheus and Epimetheus, under orders from Zeus. It is always problematical what a Greek means by 'God' (*ho theos*), but in this context it seems virtually interchangeable with Zeus.

178. Once again the motif of pollution and the vengeance of the dead, which pervades these speeches. The *alitêrioi* are more or less the Furies of Greek tragedy.

179. Of course, the witnesses themselves will not be produced. However, in the second speech for the defence, it is stated that they (or at least some witnesses) testified that the old man had in fact started the brawl (iv [3]).

180. Here a complication in the chain of causation is introduced, as with the trainer in the previous case.

181. This is somewhat tendentious: Athenian law does make premeditation a condition of a murder charge in a case of assault (cf. Lysias, *Against Simon*), but all that is at issue here is who started the brawl, not what the brawler's intention might have been.

182. A necessary supplement by Reiske.

183. Accepting Thalheim's conjecture of *anatropês* for the corrupt *phonês* of the manuscripts.

184. Antiphon now introduces a form of argument from probability first recommended, we learn, in Plato's *Phaedrus* (273BC), by Teisias, the father of scientific rhetoric. It is very probable that Antiphon was familiar with this.

185. This answers (rather tendentiously) the defence made in ii [2] that the defendant used only the same weapons with which he was attacked.

186. The prosecution here uses an adverb of considerable ambiguity, *thanasimôs*, which can mean 'with deadly intent', or just 'with deadly result', in order to generate a thoroughly tendentious argument.

187. A reference to ii [6] above, though the defendant there imputed *atykhia* to the dead man.

188. So it is admitted, after all, that the defendant is not guilty of *wilful* murder.

189. As was done in ii [4].

190. It is not clear whether this refers to a definite clause in the law on premeditated killing absolving doctors from the consequences of unsuccessful treatments, or is just a general claim.

191. They have, of course, *not* done this in the speeches before us. We must assume, in this case, a proper array of witnesses, such as are suggested at various points in both the prosecution and defence speeches. In this, this case differs somewhat from the first two, where witnesses were unavailable or hardly relevant.

192. There is at this point a rather dramatic development: the defendant decamps into exile, effectively giving up on the case. This was provided for in trials for murder, but it normally meant that one accepted conviction. Here, however, the friends or relations weigh in with a spirited defence (the longest speech of the four), maintaining the defendant's innocence at least of intentional killing, and asserting that he left solely because of intimidation. It is not quite clear what Antiphon is up to. Perhaps such a speech would induce the jury not to impose further penalties, such as confiscation of property.

193. A reference back to iii [2].

194. An interesting echo here of the point made in *On Truth*, §22a, col. 3.

195. Once again, unseen witnesses adduced, this time for the defence.

196. That is to say, the doctor, as claimed previously by the defence.

197. This takes up the very tendentious claim made by the prosecution in iii [4], and is an important point. The defendant acted *intentionally*, certainly (he meant to strike), but he did not intend to *kill*; therefore this is not a case of wilful murder.

198. Reading *phoreus* for *phoneus*; otherwise, one must postulate a lacuna.

199. This is a response to iii [3] above.

200. There has been a good deal of systematic ambiguity in the position of the prosecution on this question. All killing, even if involuntary, involved some degree of pollution, which had to be expiated, but not liability to a charge of murder. The defence's point is that even this degree of pollution attaches to the doctor, not the defendant.

201. Two remarkable and unique adjectives are used here, *apolysimos* ('acquittable') and *katalêpsimos* ('condemnable').

202. The defence here introduce the concept of 'reasonable doubt'.

203. Reading *alitêrios* for *apokteinas* of the manuscripts, which makes no sense.

6 THRASYMACHUS OF CHALCEDON

1. Also spelled Calchedon in some sources.
2. To what period of history this refers is quite unclear; possibly the second century AD, the period of the so-called Second Sophistic – though this entry is not borrowed from Philostratus, our chief authority for that period. The *Suda* itself is Byzantine.
3. This is a preposterous statement, both as concerns Plato and Isocrates. Some scholars have suggested emending the 'pupil' (*mathêtês*) to 'teacher' (*kathêgêtês*), but that is almost equally preposterous – though it could be seen as a simple-minded conclusion drawn from a statement of Dionysius of Halicarnassus (cf. §13 below). A more sensible suggestion is that there is a lacuna, and that Thrasymachus is stated to be the pupil of someone else, possibly the Sicilian Teisias (cf. §2), and a rival, or enemy, of Plato and Isocrates.
4. An intriguing title. We may note that Gorgias, at the end of the *Helen*, describes it as a *paignion*.
5. Quoted, in part, above, pp. 33–5.
6. The only figure that we know of prior to Teisias was his fellow-Sicilian Corax; and his more immediate follower will have been Gorgias.
7. This does not necessarily assert that Thrasymachus was a *pupil* of Teisias (though it does not exclude it), even as it does not guarantee that Theodorus of Byzantium was a pupil of Thrasymachus.
8. In his lost treatise *On Style*, Fr. 695 FHSG
9. Lysias is generally reckoned to have been born in the early 450s, therefore probably slightly younger than Thrasymachus.
10. The reference is presumably to the word in brackets, which occurs nowhere else in surviving literature, but must have had a technical meaning, possibly given to it by Thrasymachus.
11. Niceratus, son of the famous Athenian general Nicias, is made to tell in Xenophon's *Symposium* (3, 5) that his father made him learn all of the *Iliad* and *Odyssey* off by heart. It seems that he once challenged a professional rhapsode called Pratys to a contest in recitation and lost. The Greek hero Philoctetes was bitten by a snake in the foot, causing an incurable wound. It is indeed an ingenious and witty comparison, though the precise point of it escapes us.
12. From his lost *Tyro* (Fr. 658 Radt). Sidêro ('Steel') was the name of Tyro's wicked stepmother.

13. Two prominent Athenian politicians of the 390s.
14. The follower of Gorgias, featured in Plato's *Gorgias* – where Plato also plays on his name (463E).
15. The earliest Greek lawgiver (late seventh century). In his code, nearly every offence was punishable by death.
16. Or so we presume; otherwise it would have been worth quoting in full.
17. Socrates has just dismissed the definition of justice as 'helping friends and harming enemies', and has called for an alternative one.
18. A humorous reference to the old Greek superstition that, if a wolf looked at you before you looked at it, you would be stricken with paralysis. This furthers the wild animal imagery with which Plato is characterizing Thrasymachus.
19. That is, a long syllable followed by three shorts, or three short syllables followed by one long (the long being equivalent to two shorts).
20. A fourth-century rhetorician, follower of Gorgias; author of the attack on Socrates to which Xenophon is responding in the *Memorabilia*.
21. A pupil of Polycrates, most famous for his attacks on Homer (now lost).
22. Dionysius presumably means that Antiphon did not compose speeches on his own behalf. But what about his famous 'speech from the dock' at his own trial in 411? And a number of the titles of his lost speeches sound political enough, though we cannot be sure that he composed them for delivery by himself.
23. A poet and antiquarian of the Alexandrian age (early third century BC). Parion is a town on the coast of the Hellespont not far from Chalcedon.
24. Spelled thus, as is occasionally the case.
25. In his treatise *On Style* (Fr. 685 FHSG):
26. We take that to be the meaning of *prohairesis* here.
27. Accepting a supplement of Stephen Usher in his Loeb edition of Dionysius of Halicarnassus, *Critical Essays*, Cambridge MA and London, 1974, I, p. 248.
28. This is a curious antithesis between 'others' and 'us'. One can only suppose that the young speaker (rather like the Knights in Aristophanes' *Knights*) is contrasting himself and his companions with demagogues like Cleon. But would he dare to address the Assembly in this vein? It is possible that the piece was not intended for delivery, but perhaps for distribution as a pamphlet.
29. Note the introduction of this significant catch-word of conserva-

tism, familiar to us from the title of the treatise of Antiphon. The opposite to it is demagogue-provoked civil strife (*stasis*) and unrest.

30. The contrast is perhaps between the time of Pericles' domination and the present – though Pericles himself was regarded as a dangerous radical by true conservatives. A little further on, the speaker seems to look back to the era of the Persian Wars, and the 'ancestral constitution' (*patrios politeia*) of Cleisthenes.

31. This would seem to imply that the speaker is looking back to the generation of the Persian Wars and their immediate aftermath, who would still be alive, as old men, in the 420s.

32. Though there is one reference which is troubling (section 19), since it seems to refer to events in the Archidamian War (*c.*424 BC), long before Archelaus came to power: 'Archelaus did not join in the Athenian attack on the Peloponnesus, and he neither stopped those who wanted to pass through his territory [i.e. Brasidas?] nor provided them with money.' Unless such a reference can be attached to some event in the period 413–399, which, on the basis of our knowledge, it cannot, we must assume authorship by Herodes himself.

There is also the problem that the one verbatim extract which we are given of Thrasymachus' speech does not occur in this one, though the general sentiment does. This, however, might indicate that Herodes is playing variations on an existing speech in his possession, presumably that by Thrasymachus.

33. A useful translation of the document may be found in *Early Greek Political Thought from Homer to the Sophists*, ed. M. Gagarin and P. Woodruff, Cambridge: Cambridge University Press, 1995, pp. 267–74.

34. Fr. 719 Nauck. The *Telephus* was produced in 438 BC.

35. The fourth-century BC historian (Fr. 104 Jacoby). Theopompus is adduced as evidence that the Chians were included in the Athenian official prayer at the beginning of the Peloponnesian War. He came from Chios, which gives him an interest in the matter.

36. I.e. of Persia. This will be Xerxes, who ruled till 465 BC. Timocreon had been exiled after the Persian defeat in 479 for his pro-Persian sympathies, but seems to have returned to Rhodes at some later stage.

37. He was officially a pentathlete, which involved wrestling, though not boxing; here, however, boxing seems to be in question.

38. It is not quite clear whether this is meant to represent a verbatim quotation, but it is possible.

7 CRITIAS OF ATHENS

1. Andocides, *On the Mysteries* 47–8. He includes Critias among a list of eight persons, all of whom were relations of his. Critias, he tells us, was a cousin of his father Leogoras. This links Critias to another prominent family of conservative tendencies.

2. These were also in antiquity attributed to Euripides, no doubt because of certain similarities in style, but are generally agreed now to be the work of Critias. As to when – or indeed whether – they were produced, however, we have no idea. On the status of the *Sisyphus*, see below, p. 250.

3. For the problem of the speech *For the People of Larisa*, credited in the manuscript tradition to Herodes Atticus, but assigned by some modern scholars to Critias, see above, pp. 212–13. We judge it to be a sophistic exercise by Herodes, in the style of Critias, but modelled on the speech of that title by Thrasymachus – and, as such, not without interest.

4. This may be an allusion to an apologia for Critias from the hand of Herodes Atticus, who was quite a partisan of his. Critias spent the period 406–404 in Thessaly, and the Thessalians were notorious for aristocratic licentiousness.

5. I.e. in 593/2 BC, at which period the eponymous archon wielded considerable power.

6. I.e. in the summer of 403.

7. This is an oddly anachronistic remark on the part of Philostratus, but it nonetheless, no doubt, conveys a valid point about Critias' style.

8. This figure of speech, a kind of asyndeton, which Philostratus calls *prosbolê*, he attributes as an invention to Gorgias (cf. ch. 2, §29 above), from whom Critias will have picked it up.

9. Potone was in fact Plato's sister, the mother of Speusippus.

10. Dropides, as we can gather from Plato's *Timaeus* (20E), was not a brother of Solon, but a more remote relation (possibly first cousin). The Critias who figures in the *Timaeus*, by the way, is not our Critias, but his grandfather (who describes the original Dropides as his great-grandfather).

11. This too Diogenes has got wrong, as we can deduce from Plato's *Charmides* (below, §3). Glaucon was in fact a brother of Callaeschrus, and Critias and Charmides (and Plato's mother Perictione) were first cousins.

12. Plato is here, of course, also incidentally praising his own ancestry on his mother's side.

13. The poet Anacreon (c.570–500 BC), as we learn from a scholion on Aeschylus' *Prometheus* 130, stayed in the household of Critias, son of Dropides, when he came to Athens, originally in the 540s.

14. Pyrilampes was actually Plato's stepfather, having married Plato's mother, Perictione – his own niece – after the death of Plato's father Ariston. A son of this union, Antiphon, Plato's half-brother, appears in the *Parmenides*.

15. This is probably the passage to which Philostratus is responding in §1 above.

16. Not the sophist of that name, but a youth of good family who was a follower of Socrates.

17. This incident hardly bears the weight laid upon it, and it is most unlikely that it constituted the sole cause of Critias' alleged 'enmity' against Socrates. Far more plausible, as we shall see, is the story (relayed in the *Apology* 32C, and alluded to here, just below, §§31–2) that the Thirty (no doubt at the instigation of Critias) tried to involve Socrates in their activities, and failed.

18. Presumably, the gibe that they made the worse argument appear the better – a gibe more properly directed against the sophists.

19. One of the leaders of the regime of the Four Hundred.

20. Two prominent democrats, the latter of whom later, in 403, led the uprising which overthrew the regime of the Thirty presided over by Critias.

21. Presumably of slaves; it was most unusual to torture free men.

22. He had just returned from negotiating with the Spartans.

23. Fr. 18 Diehl. This refers, of course, to the Critias who was son of Solon's friend and relation Dropides. It is generally agreed that Solon was intending here, not a criticism of the life-style of Critias, but simply a compliment to Dropides, so that Cleophon would be shamelessly misusing the verse.

24. There is a textual problem here, but this must be the sense. Critias has just been criticizing Theramenes' role in the condemnation of the generals after the battle of Arginusae in 406.

25. This seems a most extraordinary allegation to make against a man like Critias, but there must presumably be some basis to it, however distorted. Perhaps, indeed, Critias did take a hand in Thessalian politics – of which Herodes Atticus' speech in support of the Larisaeans may after all be a reflection, instead of just being a pastiche of the speech of Thrasymachus. As for Prometheus, we have no idea who he was. It is a rather peculiar name.

26. I.e. members of conservative political clubs, or *hetaireiai*.

27. A Peripatetic writer of about 300 BC.

28. This title usually denotes an exhortation to philosophy, but, given the topic, it may here denote an exhortation to *mousikê*.

29. It could be argued, presumably, that Aristotle is not necessarily advocating that one *should* praise Critias; he is only saying that, if one *did* choose to, one would have to remind one's audience of his achievements. But why select Critias as an example?

30. It is interesting that Archinus is mentioned here; he was a democratic politician who was one of the leaders, along with Thrasybulus, of the move to overthrow the Thirty in 403.

31. We, at least, certainly have no remains of either Pericles or Alcibiades independent of speeches ascribed to them, composed by Thucydides, so that is possibly all that Cicero is referring to.

32. Again, it is interesting that these three are mentioned together, since, of the other two, Critias, as we have seen, murdered the former and did his best to murder the latter.

33. Literally, 'eyebrow' (*ophrys*), but used in this sense in rhetorical contexts.

34. It is unfortunately not quite clear which is which, though if *ho men* and *ho de* have their normal reference, fluency of speech (*euglottia*) would be attributed to Thucydides, and force of expression (*rhôme*) to Critias; but we suspect it is the other way round.

35. The word used by Hermogenes, *apophatikôs*, would normally mean 'negatively', which makes little sense, but it can be used as the equivalent of *apophantikôs*, which is the meaning suitable here.

36. These were presumably specimen introductions to speeches before the assembly – though it is not clear whom Critias was purporting to instruct.

37. Hippon has just been reported to have declared it to be water.

38. A difficulty is that Aristotle himself attributes to Empedocles, not this doctrine, but one that declares the soul to be composed of all the elements (404b10), for which he quotes relevant verses (Fr. B109), and Philoponus certainly seems to think that he is quoting Critias.

39. That is, Alexander of Aphrodisias (late second century AD), greatest of the commentators on Aristotle. His commentary on the *De Anima* is unfortunately lost. Alexander seems to be the only ancient authority who proposed to split up the Critiases, as opposed to the many who were prepared to split up the Antiphons.

40. Of these, we have some verses from his *Constitution of the Spartans* (below, §§25–6).

41. The precise force of this adjective is not clear, but it is at any rate highly complimentary.

42. Critias himself, we may recall, liked to play the flute – if Chamaeleon of Heraclea may be trusted (cf. above, §12).

43. An elaborate, mock-heroic reference to the popular drinkers' game of *kottabos*, which involved tossing the dregs of one's wine-cup into a bowl set up in the middle of the room.

44. We take the introductory text from *Deipnosophistae* XV 666B, but the bulk of the text, after the first two lines, must be taken from I 28B.

45. The original inhabitants of Sicily; and indeed *kottabos* is not a Greek word.

46. A pentameter is omitted here.

47. Probably the best rendering of *thronos*, often translated 'throne'.

48. *Alexiloga*, a notable coinage. It rates a mention from Photius in his *Lexicon* (A 73, 3).

49. That is, Athens.

50. The joke consists in inserting an iambic line, in place of a dactylic pentameter, into elegiac couplets – on the ground that Alcibiades' name will not scan in dactyls, having too many short syllables in succession. The line in question is the second one above. It is beyond our capacities to render the strangeness of this properly in English.

51. This line probably embodies a reference to a programmatic line of the sixth-century poet Theognis (19), whose verses would be well known to both Critias and Alcibiades. This would have the ironic effect of putting Alcibiades into the position of Cyrnus, Theognis' beloved, and addressee in his poems.

52. The suggestion goes back to Friedrich Schleiermacher. It is certainly not susceptible of proof one way or the other.

53. This probably, but not certainly, means simply 'constitutions in verse form', but *emmetros* can also have the meaning 'well-balanced', 'well-proportioned', 'fitting', and this has attracted some editors into giving the title 'Well-balanced Constitutions'. In fact, as we can observe, Critias is praising the balanced and moderate way of life of the Spartans, but it is most unlikely that Philoponus is intending to give Critias' original title of his work, rather than a simple description of its form.

54. This is a criticism of the Athenian custom of drinking toasts (*proposeis*) to one or another of the company, identified by name, which seems to have involved toaster and toastee each draining a glass – which is what Critias is objecting to. There is a line or more omitted after this.

55. The references to 'Lydian' and 'Asian-born' are derogatory; Asiatic Greeks were despised, in pro-Spartan circles, for softness and luxury, and for being unduly influenced by contiguous Asiatic peoples such as the Lydians.

56. Chilon was the Spartan member of the traditional grouping of 'Seven Sages'. He was ephor (one of the senior Spartan magistrates) in 546/5, and is credited with significant developments in Sparta's foreign policy.

57. There is a small problem in the text here. If one sticks to the manuscript reading, Plutarch would be saying 'having become one of the Thirty', or 'after he had become one of the Thirty', implying that Critias composed this elegy while in office, which seems improbable. Rather than accept that, we thought it better to adopt Wilamowitz's insertion of a *ho* before *tôn triakonta*, and translate that.

58. The Scopadae were a famously wealthy noble Thessalian family who ruled in Pharsalus in the sixth and fifth centuries. Simonides and Pindar composed odes in their honour. As for Arcesilaus, we learn from Pausanias (*Description of Greece* VI 2, 1) that he was a noted Spartan horse-breeder, and won the chariot-race at Olympia twice in the earlier part of the fifth century.

59. On this question, see below, introduction to *Sisyphus* passage. We have our doubts on this, for reasons given there.

60. Presumably either Idas or Lynceus.

61. It sounds from this as if the daughters of Leucippus were also killed in the affray.

62. This would appear to refer to Idas and Lynceus, not her own brothers (which is odd), since Polydeuces was still alive (though he did offer to share death with his brother); so perhaps after all it does refer to the Dioscuri.

63. We take this to be the meaning, although there is only one accusative, *hêmas*, 'us', in what survives; but *aphaireô* can take two accusatives, and this makes better sense.

64. Stobaeus actually quotes it under two headings, first in a section on 'What is in our power', and secondly, in one 'On Love'.

65. I.e. Hera, wife of Zeus.

66. Traditionally, Ixion was punished by being bound eternally to a fiery wheel (cf. Pindar, *Pythian Odes* 2, 21–48), but this punishment here seems to be allegorized, and wanderings pursued by a gadfly substituted. The text, however, is very fragmentary here.

67. The verb used is *diasparattô*, which properly means 'tear apart', but can hardly mean that here, since Ixion's punishment was eternal.

68. These last few lines are highly conjectural, but they seem broadly the lines on which Pirithous is introducing himself.

69. These are both technical terms of rhetoric, which Hermogenes (and therefore Gregory) has been discussing.

70. Therefore, if our assumptions are correct, Critias will have borrowed this verse from Euripides, where it appears to have stood at the beginning of Melanippe's prologue-speech (Fr. 481, 1 Nauck).

71. *Epi mnêsteiâi* – a rather polite version of what his intentions were!

72. A slightly mysterious phrase. Perhaps this includes the chorus; it does not include Pirithous.

73. Heracles had reason to be grateful to Theseus for supporting him after his killing of his wife and children in a fit of madness; see Euripides, *The Madness of Heracles*.

74. Presumably Heracles has been exhorting him to save himself if he can.

75. Reading <*de toi*> after *skêpsin*, rather than <*d' emoi*>. We are still not sure of having grasped the meaning, however. Heracles' reasoning remains somewhat opaque.

76. This may be an allusion to the story that Eurystheus had disallowed the killing of the Lernaean Hydra as a Labour, because Heracles had received help from his nephew Iolaus.

77. A scholion on Aristophanes, *Birds* (179), quotes the last line of this and identifies it as coming from 'Euripides' *Pirithous*' (= A18, part).

78. Critias uses here the word *rhumbos*, which may betoken Orphic influence.

79. Plutarch likes this line, which he quotes on three other occasions (*Moralia* 482A, 533A and 763F).

80. A reference to Euripides' *Medea* (1136ff.).

81. It is intriguing that Plutarch should characterize Theseus as a *philosophos* here. This must reflect the quality of the sentiments which Critias has put into his mouth; in which connection, see the next fragment.

82. The adjective *akhalkeutos*, like many words occurring in these fragments, is not found in Euripides, but rather in Aeschylus (*Choephoroe* 493). Critias, despite his intellectual affinity with Euripides, does seem to appreciate Aeschylean orotundity of expression.

83. One has to ask oneself in what other known circumstance of Theseus' life would he have had occasion to utter such sentiments as these. Only, we think, in his old age on the island of Scyros,

after having been exiled from Athens. Euripides did compose a *Skyrioi*, but that concerned not Theseus' sojourn on Scyros, but that of Achilles. Euripides' play *Theseus* concerned his expedition to Crete to overcome the Minotaur, and Nauck in his first edition of the fragments attributed the fragment to that play, but thought better of it in his second edition. We think that he was right. It seems an odd speech for a young man to make. It suits the sojourn in Hades much better.

84. That is to say, bereavement.

85. The word used here, *rhêtor*, normally connotes a politician.

86. This, bizarre as it may seem, is not absolutely impossible. It was widely alleged, by comic poets such as Aristophanes, that Euripides was helped by *Socrates* in composing his plays. This is doubtless false, but it is interesting that the allegation could be made, even in jest. There is, on the other hand, no improbability about two playwrights composing plays with the same title; this was often done – indeed, more or less inevitably so.

87. Sextus does not identify the play, only the author. We can attach it to the *Sisyphus* only through the authority of the doxographer Aetius (I 7, 2, p. 298 Diels), who is also listing atheists, and produces much the same list as Sextus (Diagoras, Theodorus, Euhemerus), but credits the *Sisyphus* extract to Euripides.

88. This account of the divinity seems to owe rather more to such a thinker as Xenophanes than to traditional religion, but no matter.

89. What is Critias implying here? He is presumably not seeking to personify Time, despite his language, but rather to assert that in time all things come to pass, by an automatic process.

90. One might compare, and contrast, the modern use of Sisyphus by Albert Camus in *Le Mythe de Sisyphe* (Paris, 1942).

91. This, in the manuscripts (of Galen), has a curious double title, *Of the Nature of Love, or of Virtues*. This seems most suspicious. We would prefer to read *erôtôn*, 'loves', rather than *aretôn*, 'virtues'. We doubt, in any case, that its subject-matter was very edifying or philosophical.

92. Plutarch, in his *Life of Lycurgus* (ch. 9, 7) also describes the *kôthôn* in these terms, and quotes Critias as an authority.

93. Rhenaea is a small island adjacent to Delos.

94. Apparently resembling the movements of a smith's tongs; hence the name. We may imagine, in all probability, as with certain modern Greek and Russian dances, the dancers leaping into the air and crossing their legs a number of times before landing.

95. Presumably in a different part of the work to that in which he has

made the previous claim. Libanius is trying to make Critias sound sillier than he was.

96. That is to say, because the Helot has to be ready to fight at short notice.

97. Presumably on their front doors – Critias is being somewhat elliptical here. A *kleis* was properly a bolt fastening a door.

98. An allusive reference to the great Helot Revolt of 464 BC, which was provoked by an earthquake – Poseidon being the god of earthquakes.

99. It is not quite clear what Clement is meaning to imply with this genitive absolute construction; it should normally mean that Critias is somehow reacting to this dictum of Euripides – and that is, after all, by no means impossible. The quotation is from Euripides' *Meleager* (Fr. 525 Nauck, also preserved by Stobaeus).

100. The plural is slightly curious; perhaps the *Constitutions* were available in one volume in later antiquity.

101. There is a remarkable collection of terms for types of trader at VII 196–7 (= B70), but on the whole these words do not seem worth presenting here, as having no discernible 'sophistic' or other intellectual content. They do at least testify to the availability of works by Critias in the second century AD and beyond, but we know that from the evidence of Philostratus.

102. It is not in fact quite clear what *homilia* can properly mean in the Classical period. In later times, it certainly could mean a philosophical lecture, or 'homily', but in Classical times it seems to have meant rather a conversation or chat. In Xenophon, *Memoirs of Socrates* I2, 6 and 15, for instance – the latter passage referring explicitly to Critias and Alcibiades – it refers to consorting or conversing with Socrates. So the meaning here rather depends on whether this is really Critias' own title, or a later one.

103. Probably, as Diels suggests, the reference is to the senses; in which case the purport of the remark is very much the same as that of the previous quotation.

104. Or possibly even 'incorrect', from an Atticist point of view. It is certainly an odd formation.

105. As we would prefer (cf. n. 91 above). The manuscripts read 'of Virtues'.

106. That is to say, in his poems, which contain much that is autobiographical.

107. The prominent demagogue Cleon, the most powerful figure in democratic politics in the years after Pericles' death in 429, died in battle at Amphipolis in 422. Critias will have had personal

acquaintance with him, as he would not have had of Themistocles. However, the valuation of Creon's property does seem improbably large.

108. One of the leaders of the democratic faction in Athens.

109. Cimon, as an aristocrat and leader of the more conservative faction in Athens in the 460s, is someone of whom Critias would naturally approve.

110. Which is Xenophon's introductory point in this work.

111. *Onoma apophantikon*; normally *onoma* means a noun, rather than verb (*rhêma*), but Aristides seems to be using it in a more general sense here. How *dokei d' emoi* appears 'stronger' than *all' emoige dokei*, however, remains something of a mystery.

112. That is, when the Thirty were appointed in 404, since they were officially appointed as a commission to revise the laws (cf. Xenophon in §8 above).

113. This might be a loose quotation of some lines of iambic verse – in which case we have to deal with an extract from one of Critias' tragedies. The phrase 'stepping outside one's fate' (*ektos atês bainein*) certainly has a poetical ring to it.

114. That is, the river Meles, near Smyrna – for which reason Homer in some sources is given the name Melesigenes.

8 EUTHYDEMUS AND DIONYSODORUS
OF CHIOS

1. In *The Older Sophists*, pp. 294ff.

2. One of the chief parks and gymnasia of Athens, which (like the Academy) was at this time a favourite place for sophists to teach and give exhibitions.

3. This is the young aristocrat Cleinias, son of Axiochus, and a cousin of Alcibiades.

4. Pericles had, in fact, invited colonists from all parts of the Greek world to take part in this enterprise. It will be recalled that Protagoras was invited to give laws to the new colony.

5. Literally, *pankratiastes*, a practitioner of the ferocious sport of all-in wrestling-cum-boxing.

6. Nothing further is known of these, but they were plainly successful at a number of panhellenic games. Acarnania is a district of western Greece.

7. This suggests an intermediate period, in which the brothers professed rhetoric, but had not yet developed their eristic skills.

8. This would seem to imply that the brothers also operated on their own. There are also, as we shall see, a number of references in the sources to Euthydemus without Dionysodorus.

9. This could conceivably refer to Xenophon himself, but in that case the incident would have to date from the last decade of the fifth century.

10. This is one of Socrates' best-known ironic conceits, that he is gifted with a supernatural voice or premonition, which usually tells him, however, *not* to do something, rather than to do it.

11. This is a good portrayal of how sophists operated. Cf. the scene in Callias' house at the beginning of the *Protagoras*.

12. The implication, of course, is that they have spotted a likely customer, and their sophistic rapacity is aroused.

13. The conundrum, as we shall see, is based on the double senses of *sophos* and *amathês* – 'proficient in a skill' and 'clever', and 'ignorant' (in the sense of not yet having learned something) and 'stupid'.

14. This refers to a common feature of Greek education, learning by heart from dictation by the master, and then reciting, passages from the poets. This argument is known to Aristotle (cf. *Rhetoric* II 24, 1401a29ff., and *Sophistici Elenchi* 4, 166a31ff.), in a slightly different form, and so probably not derived from this passage.

15. Socrates has just been giving his idea of what a hortatory, or protreptic, discourse should be like (277D–282E), and he now challenges the brothers to give their version of how to teach a young man to become 'wise and good'.

16. There may here be a suggestion of philosophical problems about change, such as were addressed earlier in the century by Anaxagoras, for example.

17. Dionysodorus is here indulging in the sort of play with the existential and predicative senses of the verb 'to be' that appears to have been rather popular in the period of the infancy of logic, as exemplified also by section 5, 15 of the *Double Arguments* (below, ch. 10). The final dig is aimed particularly at Cleinias' lover Ctesippus, who promptly responds.

18. There is here lurking something like a correspondence theory of truth, according to which there is a definite object or state of affairs (*pragma*) corresponding to each meaningful utterance (*logos*). Therefore, two contradictory or inconsistent utterances cannot concern the same object or state of affairs.

19. This seems the best rendering of *oudamou estin* (literally 'are nowhere').

20. Euthydemus is trying to get some mileage out of the distinction, but also the connection, between *prattein*, 'to do something, to perform an activity', and *poiein*, 'to make something, to create a product'.

21. There is some degree of word-play involved here: *kakôs legein* normally means 'speak badly' in the sense of 'abuse' or 'slander'. The suggestion that *kaloi kagathoi* would do this infuriates Ctesippus.

22. There are various other amusing arguments presented in the course of the dialogue (e.g. that Ctesippus' dog is also his father – since the dog is *his*, and is also a *father*), but the three arguments selected here are those of chief philosophical significance.

23. It is important for Socrates to maintain his official position of ignorance.

24. This is a rather clumsy way of rendering the adjective *epistêmôn*, but 'knowing' or 'knowledgeable' do not seem quite to fill the bill.

25. Note that Socrates is careful to introduce the qualifier here – which is just what Euthydemus is determined to ignore.

26. From the way in which these examples are presented, it sounds as if Aristotle is drawing on oral reminiscence of Euthydemus, rather than on any written work of his.

27. I.e. 'trireme' and 'Piraeus'.

28. The answer presumably is: 'Yes, you do; because you know "trireme", and you know the Piraeus.'

29. This does sound rather like a characteristic double-whammy by the sophistical brothers.

30. The force of this depends on the manipulation of Greek word-order, in a way rather difficult to convey in English.

31. This puzzle plays on the double sense of *dynamis*: (1) the capacity to do something when you are doing it; and (2) the potentiality to do it when you are not doing it.

32. A stringed instrument resembling the modern harp.

33. Later (third- and second-century BC) philosophers of the Megarian School founded by Eucleides.

34. Sc. that there is nothing either real or false in itself.

9 ALCIDAMAS OF ELAEA

1. See Introduction, p. xiv. We have omitted other figures, such as Lycophron and Anaximenes of Lampsacus, as too little is known about them, and no works of theirs survive (unless the latter be the author of the *Rhetorica ad Alexandrum* – but that is in any

case easily accessible); and Isocrates, on the contrary, because too much of him survives.

2. Quoted as such by Stobaeus (*Florilegium* IV 52, 22), though rather mysteriously (cf. §9 below).

3. Cf. Plutarch, *Life of Demosthenes* 5, where Demosthenes is reported (on the authority of the Hellenistic biographer Hermippus) to have studied the *tekhnai* of Isocrates and Alcidamas (§15 below).

4. This is significant, since this would seem to be how Alcidamas would have described himself, to judge from *On the Sophists*, §2 below.

5. This must be wrong, whether the error is that of the compiler himself or of a later scribe. The reference should not be to a work of Alcidamas' father (as the participle in the genitive implies), but rather to one of Alcidamas himself, and no doubt his *Mouseion*, which seems to have been his best-known work.

6. This, as we shall see from the treatise *On Sophists* below, was something on which Alcidamas particularly prided himself.

7. It is not clear whether these last two are still by Alcidamas, and in the case of the latter of the two, whether the object of a praise is a Cynic or a real dog (*kyôn*).

8. We base ourselves here on the Oxford translation of Aristotle's *Rhetoric* by W. Rhys Roberts, with some emendments.

9. The objection here seems to be to the intensive prefix *kata*, in *kateuorkêsantas*.

10. Aristotle objects to the compound *pyrikhrôs*, but in fact the phrase is a good example of Gorgianic *parisôsis*, or balancing of equal cola. This is presumably taken from an epideictic oration.

11. Aristotle presents these as two different passages, but it is possible that they could be taken together, and that Alcidamas is indulging in *anaphora*, with the repetition of *telesphoron*. Apart from this usage, the word is exclusively poetical in the Classical era.

12. Before Alcidamas, this compound occurs only in Euripides.

13. Quoted with fuller context below, under (4).

14. Once again, the complaint is that this word is poetic (though Herodotus uses it at *Histories* II 111).

15. *Tethêgmenos* is distinctly Homeric (of a boar whetting his tusks); it is not quite clear whether Aristotle is also objecting to *akratos*, which is common enough in prose in its literal sense (of unmixed wine); but he may not approve of the bold metaphorical usage.

16. Aristotle himself here resorts to word-play between *hêdysmati* (seasoning) and *edesmati* (food).

17. Perhaps here an echo of Pindar's notable phrase (Fr. 152 Bowra), quoted by Plato (*Gorgias* 584B), 'Law the king of all, mortals and immortals'.

18. The participle *paralabôn* here is presumably intended to go with both phrases. What exactly the phrase refers to is not clear: perhaps Alcidamas is referring to someone of great *natural* ability.

19. The complaint here is, presumably, that *skythrôpos*, 'frowning', as agreeing with *phrontis*, 'care', is a 'transferred' epithet.

20. Again, the complaint is that the adjective is poetical.

21. These last two phrases could conceivably refer to Odysseus' meeting with Nausicaa in *Odyssey* 6, 127ff., but in what context is obscure; perhaps in an epideictic oration on Odysseus, or on Homer (cf. the characterization of the *Odyssey* quoted below).

22. Presumably the meaning is that his desire concorded with that of someone else. The adjective is only attested, before Alcidamas, in Aristophanes (*Thesmophoriazusae* 18), where Aristophanes is being mock-tragic – imitating Euripides, in particular.

23. A thoroughly poetical usage, meaning literally 'out of its proper seat, or place'.

24. Aristotle here uses a word, *adoleskhia*, 'idle prating', much used of the sophists, including Socrates, by the comic poets in the previous century.

25. Cf. ch. 2, p. 96 above.

26. This is a troublesome expression, since Alcidamas could mean by *epiteikhisma* also 'a bulwark *against* the laws' – and one does not expect to find Alcidamas speaking in defence of philosophy; but the only other metaphorical use of this word with a dependent genitive (by Sextus Empiricus, *Against the Mathematicians* I 198) has a positive meaning, so we may take it, it seems, that (like Isocrates, after all) Alcidamas is appropriating the title of 'philosophy' for what he himself is doing – or at least speaking kindly of it.

27. Again, an expression of some obscurity, but if it is taken as referring to Homer, it can be given a plausible sense. *Athyrma* is a thoroughly poetic word; we find Bacchylides referring to songs as *athyrmata Mousôn*, 'playthings of the Muses' (Fr. 33). As for the image of the mirror, Alcidamas makes use of it again, in the form of a simile, in his speech *Against the Sophists*, §32.

28. To whom he has devoted an essay.

29. He goes on to dismiss also Theodorus of Byzantium, Anaximenes of Lampsacus and a number of Isocrates' own pupils.

30. It is indeed generally considered to date from the second century AD.

31. A version of the *Contest* is also to be found in a Flinders Petrie papyrus (XXV 1 = *Papyri Literarii Londinenses* 191), but without the subscription attributing it to Alcidamas.

32. 'The Contest of Homer and Hesiod', *Classical Quarterly*, n.s. 18 (1967), 433–50.

33. Originally by Marjorie Milne, *A Study of Alcidamas and his Relation to Contemporary Sophistic*, Dissertation, Bryn Mawr, 1924, but approved by West.

34. Trick, because any line of the poem could be written in any order. However, this is only true of the four-line version in the *Phaedrus*, not of the six-line version published in the *Contest*.

35. These lines were much quoted in later antiquity. Sophocles, however, famously employed the sentiment expressed in them at *Oedipus at Colonus* 1224–7.

36. The tale has just been told of how Hesiod was murdered at Oenoe in Locris, opposite the island of Euboea, by some young men who thought that he had seduced their sister. They had then thrown his body into the sea between Locris and Euboea. Alcidamas had necessarily told this story, as an epilogue to the contest itself.

37. Neither of these assertions, it must be said, has much probability. Pythagoras would have been long since dead, and Empedocles hardly had much opportunity to meet Anaxagoras. If anything, this shows Alcidamas' propensity towards a reckless disregard of chronology, as in the case of his confrontation of Homer and Hesiod.

38. The *Contest of Homer and Hesiod*, in a part which may reasonably be traced back to Alcidamas (ll. 59ff.), implies that his homeland was Ios.

39. Quoted already, in part, under Antiphon, ch. 5, §8.

40. These categories seem, if anything, rather more sensible than those of Protagoras (see above). The last one must refer to the imperative mood.

41. All these technical terms are attested from later rhetoricians, but they very much resemble the technicalities that are ridiculed by Socrates in the *Phaedrus* (266C–267D, cf. ch. 1, §20).

42. Alcidamas here identifies 'research' (*historia*) and 'culture', or 'training' (*paideia*) as two essential elements in the education of a sophist or rhetorician.

43. It is interesting here that Alcidamas lays claim to the title of philosopher, a fact that has some bearing on the translation of the controversial phrase quoted by Aristotle in §7 above. His rival Isocrates, we may note, also laid claim to the title of 'philosopher',

while branding the associates of Plato as 'sophists', because of the 'uselessness' of their pursuits, as in his speech *Against the Sophists*.

44. This seems to be the meaning of *enthymēma* here.

45. We give this translation for *logoi*, with some hesitation. We need a term that will cover both oral and written discourses.

46. As he would do at the opening of a meeting of the Assembly.

47. This is presumably the meaning of *grammateion* here (normally a writing-tablet).

48. There is a lacuna in the manuscript at this point, and what follows appears to be corrupt. Our supplement seems to represent the point that Alcidamas is making.

49. This seems to be the contrast between *poiēmata* and *logoi* here. Alcidamas' low opinion of poetry is notable (cf. §2 above).

50. *Phthonos* is not really 'envy' here, but rather hostility based on a perception of excessive cleverness, such as orators strove to avoid. There follows here another lacuna.

51. *Hypokrisis* here is not 'hypocrisy', but the bombastic style proper to tragic actors; while *rhapsōidia* denotes the elaboration proper to poetic composition – again, the attack on poetry.

52. The style now takes on something of a Gorgianic structure, with careful balancing of clausulae, something of which, we hope, survives in the translation. Presumably Alcidamas is just showing us that he can do this sort of thing if he wants to.

53. A pointed dig at Isocrates in particular, whose speaking voice was poor.

54. Interestingly, precisely this epithet, *iskhnophōnos*, is applied to Isocrates in Pseudo-Plutarch's *Life of Isocrates*, 837A. Alcidamas is its earliest attested user.

55. *Desmōtis* – a striking image, not used again of the soul in extant literature before Philo of Alexandria.

56. That is to say, primarily a law-case, but also a political dispute in the assembly.

57. Once again, note Alcidamas' characterization of his own activity as 'philosophy'.

58. I.e. the improvisatory. The remainder of the discourse, it must be said, has an air of disarming frankness about the need for self-advertisement.

59. Once again here, in his peroration, Alcidamas rises to Gorgianic balancing of clausulae.

60. This exordium is plainly geared to almost any speech to a public gathering, forensic or political.

61. This relates the general point to the particular situation; the speech is being delivered, of course, in the Greek camp before Troy.

62. The irony here is that pursuing a private enmity is just what Odysseus is doing in indicting Palamedes, as the audience would well know.

63. There may be a lacuna here, as Blass suggests. The transition is rather abrupt.

64. Again, Alcidamas is having fun, in view of Odysseus' well-known grudge against Palamedes, who had exposed his fraudulent attempt to get out of joining the Trojan expedition. In a real forensic situation, of course, the prosecutor would attempt to establish his impartiality and public-spiritedness.

65. A nice piece of antiquarian detail here, the first of many. Polypoetes, son of Pirithous, was a second-ranking hero, leader of the Lapiths, mentioned occasionally in the *Iliad* (2. 740; 6. 29; 12. 129, 182; 23. 836–48).

66. Teucer, half-brother of Ajax, was a noted bowman. Eurybates was Odysseus' herald.

67. That is, Paris, son of Priam, cause of the whole war.

68. At this point in a real law-case there would have been testimony from witnesses.

69. A likely story! Alcidamas is presumably suggesting to us that this was a frame-up.

70. Sc. in Aulis, waiting for a favourable wind.

71. Accepting the suggestion of Avezzù (1982) for filling a small lacuna here.

72. We may note with what irony Alcidamas allows Odysseus, himself the supreme sophist, to use both the terms *sophistês* and *philosophos* to stir up prejudice against his opponent, exactly as would be done in an Athenian court of law.

73. Alcidamas now makes Odysseus embark on a fairly spectacular rewriting of history – or at least of accepted Greek mythology. According to the normal account (recognized by Sophocles, for example, in his lost plays on the subject), Nauplius was a perfectly respectable local king, eponymous founder of the town of Nauplia, near Argos, and participant in the Argonautic expedition, who only took to piracy and other mayhem in revenge for what the Greek army did to his son, as a result of the machinations of Odysseus. Alcidamas is presumably parodying the sort of distortions in which a forensic orator might indulge in the course of his *narratio*. It is traditional, certainly, that Nauplius was

instrumental in rescuing Auge, the mother of Telephus, whom her father Aleus had asked him to drown.

74. This is a variant of the better-known Acrisius–Danae–Perseus story.

75. A mountain ridge between Tegea and Nauplia.

76. A region of northern Asia Minor, adjacent to Troy.

77. This motive for Alexander's visit seems rather dragged in. Why should hearing Telephus' story provoke in him a desire to visit Greece? Odysseus is trying to implicate Nauplius in these events by any means he can.

78. I.e. in Sparta. Alcidamas is being elliptical here. Molus was a son of Deucalion, and half-brother of Idomeneus. We must also suppose that Alexander has by now arrived on a visit to Menelaus.

79. This is, of course, an outrageous piece of rhetoric. Why on earth should Palamedes in particular have taken any steps – except on the preposterous assumption that his father had (in some minimal way) contributed to the situation?

80. Here, of course, Odysseus is being disingenuous, in glossing over the fact that Palamedes actually came to *him* to enlist his support, and when Odysseus tried to get out of the expedition by feigning madness, Palamedes called his bluff; which is the cause of this trumped-up charge. Oenopion, son of Dionysus by Ariadne, was the founding father of Chios, and introducer of viniculture to the island; Cinyras of Cyprus is recorded in the *Iliad* (XI 20ff.) as having sent Agamemnon the present of a fine breastplate, but there is no suggestion that he had been asked for support.

81. A lacuna here, concealing whatever dealings Palamedes may have allegedly had with Oenopion.

82. A rendering of *ha kai philosophein epikekheirêken*; once again we may note the juxtaposition of *sophistês* and *philosophein*. Could there here be some reminiscence of the condemnation of Socrates for 'corrupting the youth'?

83. Palamedes is indeed credited in various sources with all of these inventions.

84. The leader of the Athenian contingent at Troy. He is in fact praised by Homer in *Iliad* II 553–4 as being 'superior to all men on earth for marshalling horses and shield-bearing warriors'. And Homer continues: 'only Nestor could vie with him, for he was the elder'.

85. There appears to be no connection between these two lines, nor is it clear what either of them means. There may be a lacuna in the text.

86. The word used here, *holosphyros*, is otherwise attested only in late Greek.

87. Odysseus rounds off this tirade with a ringing assertion of the basic values of Athenian democracy!

10 THE *ANONYMUS IAMBLICHI* AND THE
DOUBLE ARGUMENTS

1. Another possible candidate, supported by Theodor Gomperz, is Antiphon. This possibility Diels considers to be 'absolutely out of the question', on stylistic grounds, but we do not see any gross incompatibility between the style of the author of the *On Concord*, at least, and the present document.

2. These three stages are also to be found listed in Protagoras' 'Great Speech', in *Protagoras* 323D (above, ch. 1, §18b). Our author actually employs either verbal forms or periphrases to describe these basic conditions, but we present the nominal forms as they were given in later summaries of, or borrowings from, Protagoras' doctrine, such as Aristotle, *Eudemian Ethics* I 1, Philo, *Life of Abraham* 52–4 and the anonymous summary in ch. 1, §19 above.

3. This is a notable word, only otherwise occurring in poetic sources in the Classical period.

4. It is best to translate *aretê* here as 'excellence' rather than 'virtue'. This is precisely what Protagoras is claiming to teach in Plato's *Protagoras*. It is really a summation of the other 'goals' listed, rather than an alternative to them.

5. The conjunction of *physis* and *tykhê* is to be found in Protagoras' 'Great Speech', at *Protagoras* 323D.

6. The latter part of this sentence covers the elements of learning (*mathêsis*) and practice (*askêsis*).

7. The contrast here being made between *ergon* and *pragma* may be between private and public affairs; certainly the author intends such a contrast below between *erga* and *pragmata*, at §7, 3–4.

8. This adjuration is reminiscent of something that Gorgias is made to say by Plato in the *Gorgias* 456Cff. (cf. above, ch. 2, §21). However, it is certainly not incompatible with Protagoras' position either. It is the sort of 'warning on the label' that would be issued by any of the major sophists.

9. *Pankakos*, a poetical word. It is notable that the earliest prose use of it, apart from this, is in a passage of Plato's *Protagoras*

(334B), where Plato, I would maintain, is making more or less verbatim use of Protagoras (cf. above, ch. 1, §11).

10. Once again, 'usefulness' is a primary aim of Protagoras' course of instruction. Cf. above, ch. 1, §8. We follow Friedländer in excising *ho* before *pleistois*, as giving a better sense.

11. Here begins an interesting contrast between the possession and bestowal of material and spiritual wealth, to the advantage of the latter.

12. *Eupoiêtikos*, the first occurrence of this adjective, only otherwise found, in the Classical period, in Aristotle's *Rhetoric*.

13. For this thought, and what follows below in praise of 'law-abidingness' (*eunomia*), one may compare Protagoras' commendation of 'mutual respect and justice' (*aidôs* and *dikê*) as the foundation of civic life in the *Protagoras* (above, ch. 1, §18a).

14. *Psykhê* here has the archaic (and popular) sense of 'life-principle', but below it has more the sense of 'soul' as opposed to body, which makes translation difficult. Here it may best be rendered 'life'.

15. This is a most interesting line of argument, as it directly challenges that put forward by Callicles in Plato's *Gorgias* (482Cff.), that might is right. Even if Callicles is taken to be a fiction of Plato's, this is certainly an argument put forth by one strand in the sophistic movement. Protagoras, however (if we may accept the Great Speech of the *Protagoras* as essentially his), opposed this view, and maintained the essentially social nature of man.

16. This may well be a reference to a line of Pindar's (Fr. 169 Snell), which is quoted by Plato at *Gorgias* 484B (though, ironically, in the mouth of Callicles, in support of his own 'law of the nature'). Hippias, as we have seen (above, ch. 4, §5), is made by Plato in the *Protagoras* (337C–E) to speak of law as 'a tyrant over mankind, ordaining many things by force contrary to nature'. Here, however, law and nature are hand in glove.

17. The author here shows quite a sophisticated degree of insight into the laws of economics; it is indeed the rate of circulation of money, not the total amount of it, that generates wealth in a community.

18. This has been seen as a dig at Athenian democracy, but it is certainly not necessarily such.

19. The text of this clause is seriously corrupt, but this cannot be far from the true sense.

20. Accepting Wilamowitz's *adeôs* for the *hêdeôs* of the manuscripts. See *Hermes* 64 (1929), p. 480.

21. This could be a reference to the Athenian phenomenon of *syko-phantai*, persons who initiated law-cases against rich citizens for purposes of blackmail.

22. Here the author presents an analysis not unlike that of Plato in Books VIII and IX of the *Republic*, where he sees tyranny as the natural result of the excessive freedom from restraint (more or less amounting to *anomia*) characteristic of extreme democracy.

23. Reading *tounantion* for *tanantia*, with Vitelli – but the text becomes very obscure here; we take him to be remaking the point he has made back in 6 [3–5].

24. Wilamowitz sees here a reference to the attainment of power by Dionysius I in Syracuse in the years following 406 BC. This is not an implausible speculation – but it would effectively eliminate Protagoras as a possible author, so we do not favour it.

25. As becomes apparent from Argument 1, 8 below.

26. *Aus Platons Werdezeit* (Berlin, 1913), pp. 72ff. However, a number of Ionic or Attic forms, well-attested in the manuscript tradition, do occur, and raise the question of whether the author may not in fact be an Ionic-speaker composing for some reason in Doric.

27. This is all a rather simple-minded elaboration of a point made (rather testily) by Protagoras in the *Protagoras* (333E–334C = ch. 1, §11), which may well reflect a genuine argument of his.

28. Rather oddly, the author chooses to show his hand here, as in a number of later arguments. There is something naive about this; one would have expected a professional sophist to remain impartial.

29. This would seem to place this work effectively in the decade or so after 404 BC.

30. Presumably a reference to the story of the mythical expedition of the Seven against Thebes (in the generation before the Trojan War), led by Oedipus' younger son Polynices against his brother Eteocles, with the help of Adrastus, King of Argos. Presumably our author means that the expedition was good for the Thebans but bad for the Argives, though it is far from clear that it was good for anybody.

31. Again, though the Lapiths won, it can hardly be said that it was good for either side.

32. This argument shows a disregard for the difference between absolute and relative which is primitive, and recalls the sort of arguments portrayed by Plato as being touted by such a figure as Euthydemus.

33. Added in, reasonably, by Diels.

34. A necessary supplement.

35. The Greek terms here, *kalon* and *aiskhron*, have a range of meanings, but these seem the best translations in the present context.

36. This section is interesting for the amount of sociological and anthropological material that is introduced. The adducing of the differences in national customs to argue for the relativity of ethical norms is a feature of the sophistic movement, exemplified also by Herodotus' reflections on the subject in his *Histories*. Indeed, our author seems to be largely indebted to Herodotus for his information.

37. Since, in Athens at least, it would be shameful for them to be in the palaestra, or wrestling-school, at all in the first place.

38. The author may here mean 'with another man's wife' – the Greek is ambiguous. It is doubtful that for a Greek husband to have intercourse with a courtesan would have been generally regarded as shameful.

39. That is, to outstrip them – a rather strained use of the verb *pheugein*.

40. The author turns now to the 'comparative anthropology' part of his argument.

41. Thessalians were indeed famous as horse-breeders and trainers; as for butchering, we may recall Aegisthus' invitation to Orestes, whom he takes to be a visitor from Thessaly, in Euripides' *Electra* (ll. 815ff.).

42. Macedonians were not generally regarded as being proper Greeks.

43. Cf. Herodotus, *Histories* IV 64, where these customs of the Scythians are described. Herodotus specifies that they hang the scalp from the horse's bridle.

44. This example is cited by Herodotus at IV 38, though with the Indian Callatiae as the barbarians in question. Our author may simply be confused (Herodotus has just mentioned the Massagetae, in another connection, at IV 36).

45. This is a reference to the custom of temple prostitution which was widespread throughout the ancient Near East. Herodotus attests to this in the case of the Lydians at I 93.

46. Again, the source of this, and the next detail, would seem to be Herodotus, in his account of Egypt in Book II (35–6).

47. A point made by Herodotus in IV 38.

48. *Tragicorum Graecorum Fragmenta*, Fragment of Unknown Author 26.

49. This sounds like something that Euripides might have said, pos-

sibly in such a controversial play as the *Aeolus*, where one of
Aeolus' sons, Makareus, who has fallen in love with his sister,
utters the notorious line: 'What is shameful, if it seem not so to
the doer?' But we have really no clue.

50. This position is echoed, interestingly, in the speech of Pausanias
in Plato's *Symposium* (181A): 'Now the truth about every activity
is that in itself it is neither fine nor shameful. Take the activities
in which we are at present engaged, drinking and singing and
conversing. None of these is fine in itself; they derive their character from the way in which they are used. If it is well and rightly
used, an activity becomes fine; if wrongly, shameful.'

51. Our author now performs the same manoeuvre involving relative
and absolute uses of terms as in the previous chapter.

52. Another meaning of *kalos*, even as 'ugly' is another meaning of
aiskhros.

53. This response to the well-known Herodotean illustration of cultural relativity (cf. above, n. 23) seems rather feeble. The real point
is that there is no absolute criterion of fineness or shamefulness.
The examples following are for this reason quite inapposite.

54. It is quite obscure what he has in mind here, unless it be an
allusion to Homer's description of the exchange of gifts between
Glaucus and Diomedes in *Iliad* 6, 232–6.

55. This and the following brackets present an addition of Diels,
which seems necessary for the sense.

56. This and the following argument have an interesting resemblance
to one used by Socrates in Book I of Plato's *Republic* (331C), to
confute Cephalus' definition of justice as 'returning what one has
borrowed'. This is turn may have some relevance to a curious
allegation, relayed, among others, by Aristotle's pupil Aristox-
enus, that Plato borrowed nearly the whole of his *Republic* from
Protagoras' *Antilogies* (Diogenes Laertius, *Lives of the Philosophers* III 37). This, while doubtless preposterously exaggerated,
may contain a grain of truth, relative particularly to the arguments
of Book I.

57. The verb *kleptein* can mean simply 'conceal', which introduces a
measure of ambiguity into the argument.

58. It was axiomatic in popular (as opposed to Platonic) Greek ethics
that it was right and just to do whatever harm one could to one's
enemies, private or public.

59. That is to say, the Persians, in 480/79. We do not hear of any
'borrowing' of temple funds taking place at this time, however.

60. This is a pretty desperate example: both mythological figures killed

their mothers to avenge the mother's murder or betrayal of their father. But such action would not be sanctioned in real life; one would have to go to law (cf. Antiphon's *Against the Stepmother*).

61. This is interestingly reminiscent of Gorgias' characterization of tragedy (ch. 2, §36) as producing 'a deception in which the deceiver is more justly esteemed than the non-deceiver, and the deceived is wiser than the undeceived.'

62. Very little is known about this sixth-century poetess, except that she was a native of Lindus in Rhodes. She was, however, famous for her riddles, propounded in elegiac couplets. The answer to this one is quite uncertain: 'stealing a dagger from a madman' is one suggestion; 'a wrestling match' is another.

63. Frs. 301 and 302 Nauck. Hermann felt that one or both of these might come from the *Danaids*, which is not a bad suggestion.

64. These examples are very much along the lines of the second part of the two previous *logoi*.

65. Added by Diels, to complete the sense.

66. Our author is here touching on the knotty question of the truth-value of future statements, but not pursuing it to any great depth. Cf. the argument in the *Euthydemus* about the impossibility of contradiction, 283Aff. = ch. 8, §5 above.

67. It is not clear what our author means. Presumably that the court may, in different circumstances (or in the same circumstances, depending on the presentation of the statement) judge a given statement true or false. This example, incidentally, reminds us of the essentially *practical* purpose of this treatise.

68. That is to say (probably), of the Eleusinian Mysteries.

69. Again, our author is raising interesting issues here, but in a confused and superficial way. The truth-value of a statement does not inhere in the statement in the way that personal identity inheres in an individual over time.

70. Added by Diels, to complete the sense.

71. This slight over-translation seems necessary here.

72. The text becomes very lacunose here. Diels has filled the first part of the lacuna persuasively, but in the latter part, the surviving text seems to suggest that a point is being made against the validity of a judgement on truth or falsehood by a jury, since they were not present at a given event. If this is right, it could have an interesting connection with the so-called 'new fragment' of Protagoras (cf. above, ch. 1, §29).

73. Presumably those who claim that true and false are the same – not the jurymen.

74. It is hard to be sure what sense our author is giving to the concept of 'mixture' – hardly anything of Platonic participation of forms in particulars!

75. The text breaks off here (though there is no clear break in the manuscripts), and we are launched into a quite different topic. Perhaps a page was lost.

76. Our author does not specify this, but there seems little sense in the remark otherwise.

77. In this case, the reference is of course to weights, not to coinage. Our author seems here to ramble off on to another topic, with little relevance to madness or sanity, but evidence that in his mind all this was connected comes at the end of the chapter, when he returns to the subject.

78. The relevance of all this, again, is by no means clear, but it seems from what follows to be preliminary to an argument about the importance of qualifying specifications.

79. Here begins the second half of the 'double argument'.

80. Reading *oúkôn*, with recessive accent, meaning 'not, therefore', instead of *oukôn* of the manuscripts, meaning 'so'.

81. The author's language here becomes extremely obscure, but it seems that this must be the meaning.

82. The author is here referring to the accentuation of words, which in his day still involved a pitch-accent. He begins to ramble here somewhat, once again, but at least with slightly more relevance than earlier.

83. This only works in Doric; Ionic would give *sêkos*.

84. We should presumably read *kratos* (genitive of *kara*, 'head'), rather than the *kratos* of the manuscripts, which also means 'strength', since we are looking for a change of *meaning* here.

85. This argument presumably rests on treating the 'ten' as a unitary set, so that if one loses one element of it, one does not have *anything* left. Cf. Sextus Empiricus, *Outlines of Pyrrhonism* 3.85; *Against the Mathematicians* 4. 23–4; and Plato, *Cratylus* 432a8–b1.

86. We are here brought up against the difficulty of the various senses of the verb 'to be', where the existential is being conflated with the predicative.

87. Accepting a supplement and emendation of Diels. The text of the manuscripts could mean 'if he is saying this in the general sense', but it would be distinctly elliptical.

88. It seems best to translate *aretê* as '(human) excellence' rather than 'virtue', despite the slight awkwardness involved. As regards

sophia, 'wisdom' will do, but this must be understood to embrace also 'technical expertise'.

89. This argument is produced by Socrates in Plato's *Protagoras* 319A–D.

90. This argument, again, is employed by Socrates at *Protagoras* 319D–320E, and answered by Protagoras at 326E–327C and 328C.

91. I.e. while still retaining these skills themselves; this takes care of the first argument.

92. The point of this remark is not quite clear, but it does seem to attest to the existence of 'schools' of both Anaxagoreans and Pythagoreans at the turn of the century.

93. Protagoras in fact adduces Polycleitus' training of his sons (*sic*) at *Protagoras* 328C, though he adds that they were not very good. All this, we feel, goes to argue for a relatively authentic source for Protagoras' *Great Speech*, since Plato is hardly likely to have paid much attention to this rather wretched text. Far more probable is the postulate of a common origin for both documents in some work of Protagoras.

94. This is a point emphasized by Protagoras, in his real *Great Discourse*, cf. ch. 1, §19.

95. Accepting the emendation *oukh* for *hoti* of the manuscripts. If one leaves *hoti*, the last sentence would mean: 'but at least these arguments or "proofs" are sufficient for me.' This is possible, but the problem is that *apodeixeis* ('proofs', 'arguments') has been used above for the arguments *against* the proposition, which our author has been confuting.

96. This tirade is curiously phrased, if it is in an Athenian context, as most offices were already filled by lot, and this had long been the case by 400 BC. This view, however, was certainly challenged by Socrates and his followers, notably Plato, and may have been a live issue in other parts of Greece. The author does profess to have the interests of democracy at heart, but he is addressing an audience well supplied with slaves, so one wonders.

97. This is presumably the meaning of *kata brakhy dialegesthai* – Socratic-style discourse; though we may note that Protagoras is credited with proficiency at this (albeit ironically, by Socrates) at *Protagoras* 329B.

98. We may recall that both Protagoras and Antiphon composed treatises entitled *Truth*.

99. This amounts to a pretty apt summary of the full range of sophistic training.

100. This emphasis on the importance of mastering 'the nature of things' does seem to relate particularly to the teaching of Hippias, cf. ch. 4, esp. §§10–11.

101. This is what the Greek says, but it certainly does not follow. What would follow, perhaps, is that he would *have to* know everything, in order to speak correctly about everything. However, the argument now takes on a curious resemblance to a crazy 'proof' of the sophistical brothers in the *Euthydemus* (293A–297D = ch. 8, §6 above) that, if one knows *anything*, one must also know *everything*, so that everyone is always omniscient.

102. The text, and consequently the meaning, of this sentence is obscure to the point of incomprehensibility; this *seems* to be the meaning.

103. There is a word-play here between *nomos*, 'law', and *nomos*, a 'melody' in music – though the author may not have seen it that way. Plato also makes much of the two uses of the word in his *Laws*.

104. A necessary supplement. The manuscripts are very corrupt here.

105. This section seems profoundly confused – not helped by the dismal state of the text; but there is some inkling here of an awareness of the problematic nature of 'knowing', which seems to have exercised a number of thinkers in this period, and certainly exercised Plato somewhat later.

106. This fragmentary final section, as has been mentioned above, is an encomium of the science of mnemonics, developed in the last decades of the fifth century by Hippias of Elis; ch. 4, §§10–11.

107. Reading *ha* for *ai* with Blass.

108. It is not quite clear what our author has in mind, but probably he is suggesting that we form images of the substances gold and horse, rather than the words – or perhaps an image of a golden horse; and so on.

109. We may note that Hippias seems to have used his mnemonic system particularly for remembering strings of names, cf. ch. 4, §10. Our author now seems to begin to ramble somewhat. Why on earth would one wish or need to remember concepts like 'bravery' and 'cowardice'?

110. Epeius, the constructor of the Wooden Horse, figures in the *Iliad* only in Book XXIII (665ff.), in connection with the funeral games of Patroclus, where he triumphs in boxing, but in the process admits that he is somewhat wanting as a fighter (670). In later times, however, he became proverbial for cowardice. The manuscript now breaks off, there being a note in the manuscripts admitting that it is incomplete.

Index of Rhetorical Terms

We include here, in their Greek and English versions, all technical terms of rhetoric or sophistic philosophy which occur in the texts, with page numbers of this edition.

Allêgoria figurative language, 48

Anadiplôsis doubling of words, 48

Anaphora attribution, 249

Antilogia contradiction, contrary argument, 20, 40

Antiphasis contradictory statement, 20

Antithesis contrast, 104, 357 n.60

Apophasis negative statement, 292

Apostasis digression, 66

Aretê virtue, excellence, xxii, 7, 37, 59–61, 271, 311, 315, 339 n.7, 345 n.50

Askêsis practice, 32, 311, 350 n.101

Bebaiôsis confirmation, 244

Deinotês cleverness, or forcefulness, 136, 140

Deuterologia reprise, repetition, 292

Diêgêsis narration, 34, 229, 292, 303

Paradiêgêsis supplementary narration, 292

Displasiologia saying things twice, 34

Eikos, eikota probability, probabilities, 34, 174–6, 182, 376 n.107

Elenkhos refutation, 34

Epexelenkhos supplementary refutation, 34

Epexelenkhein 268

Epagôgê inductive argument, 289

Epanalêpsis repetition, 48, 292

Epideixis display-speech, 104, 112, 122–4, 219, 356 n.46

Epideiktikos logos 209

Epilogos peroration, 303

Erôtêsis question, interrogative, 292

Euglôssia eloquence, 311

Gnômologia use of maxims, 34

Homoioteleuton use of similar endings, 49, 64, 357 n.60

Hypodêlôsis implicit allusion, 34

Isokôla sentences or clauses with equal members, 49, 64

Kairos improvisation, critical moment, 47, 186

Eukairia appositeness, 302

Lexis diction, style, 36, 205, 287
   Skhêmata tês lexeôs modes of
      discourse, 36
Logos speech, discourse,
      argument, reason-principle,
      xxii, 4, 6, 13, 18–19
   Logos skhedios extempore
      speech, 46, 353 n.4
   Logoi eristikoi disputatious
      arguments, 344 n.46
Nomos convention, law, xv, 121,
      149, 339 n.5
Orthoepeia correctness of
      speech, 34–5, 105–9
Parapsogos indirect censure, 34
Parepainos indirect praise, 34
Parisôsis equalizing of clausulae,
      48, 104, 136, 397 n.10
   Parisa balanced clauses, 49,
      65, 357 n.60
Peritropê self-refutation, 15
Phasis affirmative statement,
      292

Physis nature, xv, 32, 121, 149,
      330, 339 n.5
Pistôsis proof, 34
   Epipistôsis counter-proof, 34
Prooimion prologue, 33, 214,
      218, 231, 303
Prosagoreusis address,
      imperative, 292
Prosbolê transition, 66
Psykhrotês frigidity (of style),
      285-7
Semnotês stateliness (of diction),
      231
Tekhnê art, craft, skill, technical
      handbook, xxii, 33, 56,
      213, 291, 397 n.3
   Rhêtorikê tekhnê handbook of
      rhetoric, 137, 213–14
   Tekhnê alypias manual for the
      cure of grief, 138
   parangelmata tekhnika
      rhetorical handbooks, 291
Topos commonplace, 41, 64

Index

Achilles 37, 123, 229–30
Aeficianus 258
Aelian 250, 260–61
Aelius Aristides 262–3
Aeschines 45, 66, 102, 136, 228, 283–4
Aeschylus 45, 326
Agathon 140
Alcibiades xii, 45, 137, 167, 205, 217–18, 222–3, 225, 230, 236, 242
Alcidamas xiv, xx–xxi, 84, 282–309
Alcmaeon 116, 155
Alexander of Aphrodisias 258
Alexinus 282
Ammaeus 142
Anacreon 234
Anaxagoras 1, 103, 155–7, 240, 247, 290, 330
Anaximander 157
Anaximenes xiv, 291
Andocides 217, 231
Andron 120
Antilochus of Lemnos 145
Antipater 169, 171
Antiphon xii, xv, xxi, 133–202, 137, 209, 230–31, 265, 291
Antisthenes 3, 20, 102, 112, 120, 266
Antyllus 104

Anytus 7, 222
Apollodorus 2, 5, 48, 225
Apollonius of Rhodes 127
Aratus 130
Archagoras 4
Archelaus of Macedon 203, 212–13, 240
Archeptolemus 138
Archesilaus 239
Archilochus 130, 260–61, 290
Archinus 137, 230
Ariphrades 103
Aristippus 55, 111
Ariston 221
Aristophanes xi, 44, 50, 101, 107, 110–11, 155, 162, 203, 205, 213
Aristotle xix, 20, 32, 35, 41, 55, 59–60, 63–4, 96, 98, 104, 108, 129, 140–41, 144, 146, 148–9, 166, 203, 208, 214–15, 225, 229–30, 232, 266, 280–81, 285, 289–91, 293
Aristides 137
Artemidorus 3, 168–9
Artemon 2
Aspasia of Miletus 66, 141
Athenaeus xx–xxi, 102, 128, 167, 210, 214, 229, 234, 237–8, 254–5, 257

Aulus Gellius 103

Bacchylides 98
Bryson 282

Caecilius of Caleacte 134–40
Callaeschrus 217, 221, 229, 234,
    236, 256, 264
Callias xi, 1, 98, 100, 102, 120,
    146, 229
Callicles xii, xv, 1, 218, 316
Cantharus of Sicyon 51
Cephalus 207
Chaemeleon 229
Chaerephon 47, 57
Charmides 221, 260
Chryssipus 169, 171
Cicero xix–xxi, 41, 44, 55, 64,
    109, 116, 141, 168–71,
    206, 209, 230, 294
Cimon 96, 239, 262
Clearchus 54
Cleinias 108, 139, 270–78
Clement of Alexandria 128, 168,
    212, 246–7, 256
Cleobulina 326
Cleon 261
Cleophon 225
Colotes of lampsacus 17
Conon 206
Corax 33, 43, 64
Critias xiii–xiv, 45, 66, 105,
    133, 136–7, 147, 209, 213,
    217–65
Crito 267–8
Critobulus 268
Ctessipus 270–78
Cylon of Croton 145
Cyrus 50, 55

Damon 108
Demetrius of Byzantium 54

Democritus 1, 3–5, 15, 17, 99,
    235
Demodice 131
Demosthenes xiv, 94, 131, 138,
    141, 146, 211, 225, 283–4,
    291
Diagoras of Melos 251
Didymus the Blind 42, 135
Diels xx, 256–7, 289, 311
Dinon 2, 5
Dio Chrysostomus 263–4
Diocles 283–4
Diodorus of Sicily 48
Diogenes Laertius 5, 21, 35, 45,
    129, 220, 289
Diogenes of Apollonia 155, 239
Dionysius of Halicarnassus
    xx–xxi, 49, 93, 103, 141,
    166, 204, 206, 208, 210,
    287, 291
Dionysius of Syracuse 33,
    139–40
Dionysodorus xii, xix, 49,
    267–82
Draco 206
Dropides 217, 219–20, 234

Echetus 130
Empedocles 43, 47–8, 53, 76,
    116, 157, 232–3, 290
Epamonidas 290, 292
Ephialtes 262
Epicurus 4, 17, 32
Epimetheus 23–4
Erasistratus 138
Eratosthenes 228–9
Eryximachus 120
Euathlus 4–5
Eubulides 282
Eudicus 123–4
Euenus of Paros 33, 204
Euhemerus 109, 251

Eumolpus 51
Eupolis 1
Euripides xiv–xv, 4, 99, 103,
    213, 238–42, 244, 247,
    249–50, 252, 256
Eustathius of Thessalonica 130,
    255
Euthydemus xii, xix–xx, 224,
    267–82

Galen 116, 147, 258–60
Glaucon 221, 237
Gordian 264
Gorgias xi–xiv, xviii–xix, xxi, 9,
    33–4, 43–97, 98–9, 101–4,
    112, 116, 122, 133–4, 137,
    141, 147, 160, 204–5, 209,
    219, 231, 282–5, 287, 294,
    303
Gorgopis 131
Gregory of Corinth 244
Grote xviii

Harpocration 147–9, 167
Hegesidamus 119
Helen 76–84
Hephaestion 236
Heracles 47, 112–16, 243–50
Heraclides of Pontus 3
Heraclitus 9, 155
Hermeias 215
Hermippus of Smyrna 291
Hermogenes 134–5, 231–2,
    244, 260, 263, 265, 280,
    292
Herodes 138
Herodes Atticus 212–13, 218,
    232, 253
Herodicus 48, 206
Herodotus 257
Hesiod 96, 106, 128, 288
Hesychius of Alexandria 6

Hippias xi–xiii, xxi, 33–4, 39,
    53, 100, 102, 118–32, 204,
    206, 319
Hippocrates 39, 138
Hippocrates of Cos xi, 147, 258
Hippon of Rhegium 232
Hipponicus 100, 102, 120, 229
Homer 36–7, 106, 128, 130,
    209, 226, 235, 255, 264,
    288–90
Hyperides 136

Iamblichus xiv, 311, 314–15,
    318
Ion 131
Isaeus 209, 231, 284
Isocrates xiv, 44, 48, 51, 65, 95,
    103, 120, 203, 211, 282,
    284, 287, 291–4

Jason 44, 52
Johanes Philoponus 232, 237
John of Stobi 159
John Tzetzes 292
Julia Domna 66

Kalon 127

Laches 108
Lamprus 141
Leocrates 225
Leucippus 72
Lucian 249
Lycophron xiv, 285
Lycurgus 130–31, 225, 257, 290
Lysander 219, 227, 236
Lysias 33, 133, 137, 204, 207,
    209, 227–8, 230–31

Maeandrius 1, 5
Malampus 171
Mallius Theodorus 235

Mamercus 129
Marcellinus 104
Maximos Planudes 263
Megacleides 4
Melissus 67, 70–71, 116
Meno 55
Musaeus 235, 308

Neoptolemus 119, 123–4,
    130
Neoptolemus of Parion 210
Nestor 119, 123–4
Nicias 108
Nicomedes 129–30
Nietzsche xv, 216

Odysseus 84–5, 123, 303–9
Origen 146
Orpheus 47, 128, 235, 308

Palamedes 76, 84, 303–9
Panthoides 282
Paralus 32
Parmenides 43, 53, 67, 116
Pausanias 51–2, 127
Pausanias of Cerames 100
Peisander 145–6
Pelopidas 290
Periander of Corinth 226
Pericles ix, xii, 1, 8–9, 27–8, 44,
    45, 48, 66, 137, 141, 183,
    230, 267, 284
Perictione 217, 221
Persaeus 110
Phaedrus 120
Pheidias 7
Pheidostratus 123–4
Phemonoe 171
Pherecrates 31
Pherecydes 130
Philochorus 4
Philodemus 110

Philoponus 158
Philostratus xx–xxi, 5, 45,
    47–8, 55, 66, 95, 99, 119,
    134, 138, 140, 218, 231–2,
    257, 264
Philoxenus 103
Photius 134, 138
Phrixus 131
Phrynicus 225
Phrynicus of Bithynia 232
Pindar xv, 130, 131
Pirithous 243–50
Pittacus 38, 106–7
Plato x–xiii, xv–xxi, 1–4, 6–7,
    11, 15, 20, 22, 26, 32–3,
    37, 53, 61–3, 76, 98, 100,
    103, 105, 118–21, 131,
    133, 135, 141, 162, 203–4,
    206–8, 211, 214–18,
    220–22, 228, 231, 236,
    260, 266–7, 269, 271, 280,
    288, 291, 294, 311
Plutarch 1, 8, 96, 128, 130–31,
    136, 215, 236–7, 239, 248,
    261, 291
Polemarchus 207, 227–8
Pollux 258, 264–5
Polus 47, 204, 206, 284
Polychares 226
Polycleitus 28, 32, 330
Polycrates 52, 209, 222
Porphyry 48
Priscianus 167
Proclus 96, 129
Prodicus xi–xiii, xvii, xix–xxi, 3,
    33–4, 47, 98–117, 118,
    120–22, 204, 206, 251
Prometheus 23–4
Protagoras xi–xiii, xv–xvii, xix,
    xxi, 1–42, 45, 60, 63–4, 67,
    99–100, 105–7, 116, 118,
    120, 123, 148, 183, 204,

206, 214, 280, 282, 289,
291, 311–12, 319
Protarchus 62
Proxenus 44, 50, 55
Pseudo-Dionysus 264
Pseudo-Plutarch 134, 138,
230
Pythagoras 135, 290, 330
Pythodorus 4

Quintilian xix

Rhadamanthys 241–2

Sappho 290
Scopas 37
Sextus Empiricus xx–xxi, 67,
70, 72, 74, 110, 239, 281
Simonides 37, 98, 105–7
Simplicius 148
Sisyphus xvii, 250–53
Socrates xi–xiv, xvii, xx–xxi, 7,
11, 27, 29–32, 39, 58, 64,
98–101, 103, 105, 108,
111, 118, 120–27, 137,
141–5, 158, 163, 208, 219,
221–5, 233, 259–60, 262,
266–80, 288, 294
Solon 125, 217, 219–21, 226,
290
Sophocles xv, 206
Sophroniscus 219
Steischorus 129
Stobaeus 162–3, 240, 242, 244,
249, 253
Syrianus 215

Teisias 33–4, 43, 51–2, 64, 103,
204
Tennes 240
Tertullian 119
Thales 129
Thamyris 47
Themistocles 137, 261
Theodorus of Byzantium xiv, 33,
64, 141–2, 204, 251, 291
Theophrastus 76, 204, 210
Theopompus 213
Theramenes 99, 103, 146, 227,
230, 257
Theseus 243–50
Thrasybulus 218, 225
Thrasymachus xv, 33, 56, 64–5,
116, 141–2, 166, 203–16,
291, 316
Thucydides xv–xvi, 45, 66, 104,
131, 134, 137, 141, 145,
159, 230–31
Timaeus of Tauromenium 48–9
Timocreon of Rhodes 214
Timon 3

Xanthippus 8, 32
Xeniades the Corinthian 282
Xenophanes 282
Xenophon xx–xxi, 44, 50, 99,
102, 111, 120, 127, 137,
142, 144, 158, 166, 222–4,
226–7, 257, 262, 265
Xerxes 1

Zeno 67, 70–72, 110, 289–90
Zoilus 209, 284

PENGUIN Ⓟ CLASSICS

The Classics Publisher

'Penguin Classics, one of the world's greatest series' JOHN KEEGAN

'I have never been disappointed with the Penguin Classics. All I have read is a model of academic seriousness and provides the essential information to fully enjoy the master works that appear in its catalogue' MARIO VARGAS LLOSA

'Penguin and Classics are words that go together like horse and carriage or Mercedes and Benz. When I was a university teacher I always prescribed Penguin editions of classic novels for my courses: they have the best introductions, the most reliable notes, and the most carefully edited texts' DAVID LODGE

'Growing up in Bombay, expensive hardback books were beyond my means, but I could indulge my passion for reading at the roadside bookstalls that were well stocked with all the Penguin paperbacks ... Sometimes I would choose a book just because I was attracted by the cover, but so reliable was the Penguin imprimatur that I was never once disappointed by the contents.

Such access certainly broadened the scope of my reading, and perhaps it's no coincidence that so many Merchant Ivory films have been adapted from great novels, or that those novels are published by Penguin' ISMAIL MERCHANT

'You can't write, read, or live fully in the present without knowing the literature of the past. Penguin Classics opens the door to a treasure house of pure pleasure, books that have never been bettered, which are read again and again with increased delight' JOHN MORTIMER

CLICK ON A CLASSIC
www.penguinclassics.com
The world's greatest literature at your fingertips

Constantly updated information on over 1600 titles, from Icelandic sagas to ancient Indian epics, Russian drama to Italian romance, American greats to African masterpieces

•

The latest news on recent additions to the list, updated editions and specially commissioned translations

•

Original scholarly essays by leading writers: Elaine Showalter on Zola, Laurie R. King on Arthur Conan Doyle, Frank Kermode on Shakespeare, Lisa Appignanesi on Tolstoy

•

A wealth of background material, including biographies of every classic author from Aristotle to Zamyatin, plot synopses, readers' and teachers' guides, useful web links

•

Online desk and examination copy assistance for academics

•

Trivia quizzes, competitions, giveaways, news on forthcoming screen adaptations ·

•

eBooks available to download

READ MORE IN PENGUIN

In every corner of the world, on every subject under the sun, Penguin represents quality and variety – the very best in publishing today.

For complete information about books available from Penguin – including Puffins and Penguin Classics – and how to order them, write to us at the appropriate address below. Please note that for copyright reasons the selection of books varies from country to country.

In the United Kingdom: *Please write to* Dept EP, Penguin Books Ltd, Bath Road, Harmondsworth, West Drayton, Middlesex UB7 0DA

In the United States: *Please write to* Consumer Services, Penguin Putnam Inc., 405 Murray Hill Parkway, East Rutherford, New Jersey 07073-2136. *VISA and MasterCard holders call 1-800-631-8571 to order Penguin titles*

In Canada: *Please write to* Penguin Books Canada Ltd, 10 Alcorn Avenue, Suite 300, Toronto, Ontario M4V 3B2

In Australia: *Please write to* Penguin Books Australia Ltd, 487 Maroondah Highway, Ringwood, Victoria 3134

In New Zealand: *Please write to* Penguin Books (NZ) Ltd, Private Bag 102902, North Shore Mail Centre, Auckland 10

In India: *Please write to* Penguin Books India Pvt Ltd, 11, Community Centre, Panchsheel Park, New Delhi 110017

In the Netherlands: *Please write to* Penguin Books Netherlands bv, Postbus 3507, NL-1001 AH Amsterdam

In Germany: *Please write to* Penguin Books Deutschland GmbH, Metzlerstrasse 26, 60594 Frankfurt am Main

In Spain: *Please write to* Penguin Books S. A., Bravo Murillo 19, 1°B, 28015 Madrid

In Italy: *Please write to* Penguin Italia s.r.l., Via Vittoria Emanuele 45ia, 20094 Corsico, Milano

In France: *Please write to* Penguin France, 12, Rue Prosper Ferradou, 31700 Blagnac

In Japan: *Please write to* Penguin Books Japan Ltd, Iidabashi KM-Bldg, 2-23-9 Koraku, Bunkyo-Ku, Tokyo 112-0004

In South Africa: *Please write to* Penguin Books South Africa (Pty) Ltd, P.O. Box 751093, Gardenview, 2047 Johannesburg

HOMER

The Iliad

'Look at me. I am the son of a great man. A goddess was my mother. Yet death and inexorable destiny are waiting for me'

One of the foremost achievements in Western literature, Homer's *Iliad* tells the story of the darkest episode in the Trojan War. At its centre is Achilles, the greatest warrior-champion of the Greeks, and his refusal to fight after being humiliated by his leader Agamemnon. But when the Trojan Hector kills Achilles' close friend Patroclus, he storms back into battle to take revenge – although he knows this will ensure his own early death. Interwoven with this tragic sequence of events are powerfully moving descriptions of the ebb and flow of battle, of the domestic world inside Troy's besieged city of Ilium and of the conflicts between the gods on Olympus as they argue over the fate of mortals.

E. V. Rieu's acclaimed translation of *The Iliad* was one of the first titles published in Penguin Classics, and now has classic status itself. For this edition, Rieu's text has been revised, and a new introduction and notes by Peter Jones complement the original introduction.

Translated by E. V. RIEU
Revised and updated by PETER JONES *with* D. C. H. RIEU
Edited with an introduction and notes by PETER JONES

HOMER

The Odyssey

'I long to reach my home and see the day of my return. It is my never-failing wish'

The epic tale of Odysseus and his ten-year journey home after the Trojan War forms one of the earliest and greatest works of Western literature. Confronted by natural and supernatural threats – shipwrecks, battles, monsters and the implacable enmity of the sea-god Poseidon – Odysseus must test his bravery and native cunning to the full if he is to reach his homeland safely and overcome the obstacles that, even there, await him.

E. V. Rieu's translation of *The Odyssey* was the very first Penguin Classic to be published, and has itself achieved classic status. For this edition, Rieu's text has been sensitively revised and a new introduction added to complement his original introduction.

'One of the world's most vital tales ... *The Odyssey* remains central to literature' MALCOLM BRADBURY

Translated by E. V. RIEU
Revised translation by D. C. H. RIEU
With an introduction by PETER JONES

Early Greek Philosophy

The Pre-Socratics, the first heroes of Western philosophy and science, paved the way for Plato, Aristotle and all their successors.

Democritus' atomic theory of matter, Zeno's dazzling 'proofs' that motion is impossible, Pythagorean insights into mathematics, Heraclitus' haunting and enigmatic epigrams – all form part of a revolution in human thought which relied on reasoning to justify its conclusions and forged the first scientific vocabulary.

Although none of their original writings have come down to us complete, patient detective work enables us to reconstruct the crucial questions they asked and their absorbing answers. Here Jonathan Barnes brings together the surviving Pre-Socratic fragments in their original contexts, allowing modern readers to get to grips with these pioneering thinkers, whose ideas remain at the centre of philosophical debate. The revised edition of the collection has been updated to take account of further research and a major new papyrus of Empedocles.

Revised edition
Translated and edited by JONATHAN BARNES

PLATO

The Republic

'We are concerned with the most important of issues, the choice between a good and an evil life'

Plato's *Republic* is widely acknowledged as the cornerstone of Western philosophy. Presented in the form of a dialogue between Socrates and three different interlocutors, it is an inquiry into the notion of a perfect community and the ideal individual within it. During the conversation other questions are raised: what is goodness; what is reality; what is knowledge? *The Republic* also addresses the purpose of education and the roles of both women and men as 'guardians' of the people. With remarkable lucidity and deft use of allegory, Plato arrives at a depiction of a state bound by harmony and ruled by 'philosopher kings'.

Desmond Lee's translation of *The Republic* has come to be regarded as a classic in its own right. His introduction discusses contextual themes such as Plato's disillusionment with Athenian politics and the trial of Socrates. This new edition also features a revised bibliography.

Translated with an introduction by DESMOND LEE

EURIPIDES

Medea and Other Plays

*'That proud, impassioned soul, so ungovernable
now that she has felt the sting of injustice'*

Medea, in which a spurned woman takes revenge upon her
lover by killing her children, is one of the most shocking of all
the Greek tragedies. Dominating the play is Medea herself, a
towering figure who demonstrates Euripides' unusual willingness to give voice to a woman's case. *Alcestis*, a tragicomedy, is
based on a magical myth in which Death is overcome, and *The
Children of Heracles* examines conflict between might and right,
while *Hippolytus* deals with self-destructive integrity and moral
dilemmas. These plays show Euripides transforming awesome
figures of Greek myths into recognizable, fallible human beings.

John Davie's accessible prose translation is accompanied by a
general introduction and individual prefaces to each play.

'One of the best prose translations of Euripides I have seen'
ROBERT FAGLES

'John Davie's translations are outstanding ... the tone throughout is refreshingly modern yet dignified' WILLIAM ALLAN,
Classical Review

Translated by JOHN DAVIE
With introductions and notes by RICHARD RUTHERFORD

ARISTOPHANES
Lysistrata and Other Plays

'We women have the salvation of Greece in our hands'

Writing at a time of political and social crisis in Athens, Aristophanes (*c.* 447–*c.* 385 BC) was an eloquent, yet bawdy, challenger to the demagogue and the sophist. In *Lysistrata* and *The Acharnians*, two pleas for an end to the long war between Athens and Sparta, a band of women and a lone peasant respectively defeat the political establishment. The darker comedy of *The Clouds* satirizes Athenian philosophers, Socrates in particular, and reflects the uncertainties of a generation in which all traditional religious and ethical beliefs were being challenged.

For this edition Alan Sommerstein has completely revised his translation of the three plays, bringing out the full nuances of Aristophanes' ribald humour and intricate word play, with a new introduction explaining the historical and cultural background to the plays.

Translated with an introduction and notes by
ALAN H. SOMMERSTEIN